Murder in Mérida, 1792

Diálogos Series

KRIS LANE, SERIES EDITOR

Understanding Latin America demands dialogue, deep exploration, and frank discussion of key topics. Founded by Lyman L. Johnson in 1992 and edited since 2013 by Kris Lane, the Diálogos Series focuses on innovative scholarship in Latin American history and related fields. The series, the most successful of its type, includes specialist works accessible to a wide readership and a variety of thematic titles, all ideally suited for classroom adoption by university and college teachers.

Also available in the Diálogos Series:

Nuns Navigating the Spanish Empire by Sarah E. Owens
Sons of the Mexican Revolution: Miguel Alemán and His Generation
by Ryan M. Alexander
The Pursuit of Ruins: Archaeology, History, and the Making of Modern Mexico
by Christina Bueno
Creating Charismatic Bonds in Argentina: Letters to Juan and Eva Perón
by Donna J. Guy
Gendered Crossings: Women and Migration in the Spanish Empire
by Allyson M. Poska
From Shipmates to Soldiers: Emerging Black Identities in the Río de la Plata
by Alex Borucki
Women Drug Traffickers: Mules, Bosses, and Organized Crime by Elaine Carey
Searching for Madre Matiana: Prophecy and Popular Culture in Modern Mexico
by Edward Wright-Rios
Africans into Creoles: Slavery, Ethnicity, and Identity in Colonial Costa Rica
by Russell Lohse
Native Brazil: Beyond the Convert and the Cannibal, 1500–1900 edited by Hal Langfur

For additional titles in the Diálogos Series, please visit unmpress.com.

Murder in Mérida, 1792

Violence, Factions, and the Law

~❧

MARK W. LENTZ

University of New Mexico Press ✧ Albuquerque

ISBN 978-0-8263-5960-5 (cloth)
ISBN 978-0-8263-5961-2 (paper)
ISBN 978-0-8263-5962-9 (electronic)

Library of Congress Cataloging-in-Publication data is on file with
the Library of Congress.

Cover illustration by Felicia Cedillos based off of artist rendering
Cover by Felicia Cedillos
Composed in Minion Pro 10.25/13.5

To Aunt Kathleen,

a constant supporter of education and good writing

Contents

❦

Illustrations

Prologue

On the night of 22 June 1792, an attacker outfitted as a vaquero (cowboy) stepped out of the shadows of Mérida's darkened plaza and hurled a make-shift spear deep into the chest of don Lucas de Gálvez, intendant and gover-nor of Yucatan, ending his carriage ride home and, soon enough, his life. Gálvez, Yucatan's highest-ranked royal official, had ridden eastward between the capital's cathedral and the governor's palace after departing at around 10:45 p.m. from a gathering hosted by a leading lady of the provincial capital. Accompanied only by his black coachman, José Antonio, and the province's treasurer, don Clemente Rodríguez Trujillo, the three had just passed by the convent of San Juan de Dios when the attacker materialized out of the dark-ness. Neither José Antonio nor don Clemente noticed the assassin. Only after Gálvez stood up suddenly and shouted that someone had just pelted him in the chest with a stone did the slave coachman rein in the horses. "What's that?" asked the startled treasurer. "That 'pícaro' [rascal] just hit me!" replied the stunned intendant. The treasurer saw no one but shouted for guards.[1]

While don Clemente waited inside the carriage for guards to arrive, the injured intendant responded with bravado, if not good sense.[2] Jumping down from the carriage, Gálvez ran, then stumbled, after his attacker. His head-strong valor did little more than speed up his death, as blood spurted from the wound in his chest. Instead of a rock, his assailant had thrust a knife bound tightly to a long stick that penetrated his torso, cutting his pulmonary artery and puncturing his lung. On foot and bleeding from the wound in his lung, Gálvez quickly lost his assailant's trail. Rapidly losing blood, but still unaware of the gravity of his injury, Gálvez barely made it back to his house before collapsing. As José Antonio and don Clemente hefted the dying inten-dant through the doorway and into his home one last time, don Clemente caught a fleeting glimpse of the murderous "vaquero" running down the street toward the church of San Juan de Dios and into the dark city. He vanished into the night, eluding discovery and capture for years.

Inside the governor's residence, attendants removed Gálvez's wig and coat, revealing the severity of his injury. The treasurer called for don Fernando Guerrero, the governor's surgeon. Within minutes, all present knew that the intendant was dying. The nearest available clergyman—Br. don José de Silveira, assistant priest of the parish of Santiago—rushed over, arriving just in time to administer extreme unction. Forty-five minutes after the attack, at about 11:30 that night, Gálvez died.[3]

By then, the guards who patrolled the city center finally arrived. Eugenio Cano, a Spanish sergeant who oversaw Mérida's Afro-Yucatecan (*pardo*) militias, arrived first, followed by the *campechano* militia lieutenant, don Francisco del Castillo, then the remaining guards of the governor's palace.[4] Scouring the darkened blocks around Mérida's plaza, they failed to find the assassin. Meanwhile, Guerrero walked outside after losing any hope of saving the intendant's life and ordered José Antonio to move the carriage to the house of don José Cano, a judge and city councilman. At the scene of the crime, José Antonio turned up the first piece of evidence. The sixteen-year-old slave noticed a knife, about one inch wide, stained with blood and tied to a stick with a dirty rag (see fig. 1). He turned in the probable murder weapon to Lt. Del Castillo and drove the empty bloodstained carriage to the Cano residence up the street.[5]

The paperwork began before dawn. Notaries recorded the death, authorities launched an investigation, and the orderly transition of control of the province to Gálvez's interim successor began before the sun rose. At 3:00 a.m. on 23 June 1792, the notary don Antonio Argaiz arrived to sign the death certificate. By then, the lieutenant governor don Fernando Gutiérrez de Piñeres had arrived and ordered don Juan José Fierros, lieutenant of the grenadiers of the Battalion of Castile in Campeche and personal assistant to the deceased intendant, to turn over the keys to the office and residence of Gálvez to Sgt. Maj. don Diego Antonio de Azevedo. Within a few hours of the intendant's death, Piñeres, having taken interim command of the city, ordered a messenger to speedily deliver news of the intendant's passing to the province's second-highest royal official, the *teniente del rey* (lieutenant of the king), don José Sabido de Vargas, paving the way for a quick transfer of power. In the province's primary port and second city, Campeche, access to the late intendant's personal effects soon passed into the hands of Sabido de Vargas.

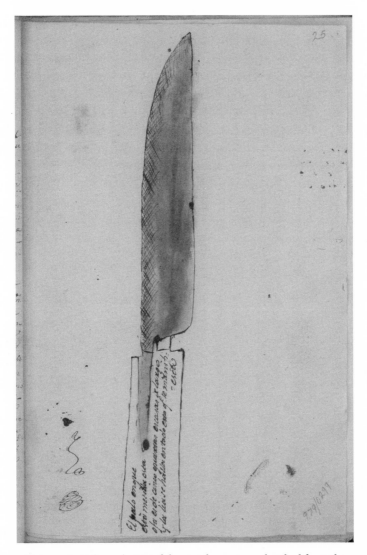

Figure 1. Artist's rendering of the murder weapon sketched from the original. Courtesy of the Archivo General de la Nación, Mexico City.

As the sun rose over the city, don Fernando Guerrero, now accompanied by a second surgeon, don Antonio Poveda, performed an autopsy to determine the exact cause of death. The improvised spear had pierced the right midsection of Gálvez's torso between the third and fourth ribs. According to the surgeon's postmortem report, a sharp, serrated blade had penetrated six inches into Gálvez's body and left a wound two inches wide, deep enough that it had punctured the right lung and severed the pulmonary artery, the most immediate cause of death.[6] At age forty-eight, and still in the prime of his life, the ambitious reformer saw his life cut short by a man who evaded prosecutors' efforts to identify him for eight more years.

Acknowledgments

Many grants and scholarships made the research and writing of this book possible—particularly recent research stays at the Max-Planck Institute for European Legal History and the John Carter Brown Library—which freed up time to put the final touches on *Murder in Mérida*. The Harvard University International Seminar on the History of the Atlantic World provided additional support.

The single-authored monograph is largely a myth. A changing cast of characters contributes ideas, editing, moral support, research assistance, translation, and, most importantly, friendship in the long process toward publishing a first book. Though this list of such supporters is undoubtedly incomplete, a few individuals deserve special recognition. First and foremost, my dissertation committee—Susan Schroeder, Colin MacLachlan, and Matthew Restall—set the groundwork for *Murder in Mérida*. Restall, in particular, offered unfailing support and encouragement at every step of the way during the work on the revisions. Other influential scholars whose input helped shape the book include Jim Boyden, Victoria Bricker, John F. Chuchiak IV, and David Dressing and Guillermo Nañez, both formerly of Tulane University's Latin American Library, as well as its current director, Hortensia Calvo, and Christine Hernández and Verónica Sánchez, the library's unit coordinator. During my research at the Archivo General de la Nación in Mexico City, a wonderful cohort of colleagues included Tulanians Jonathan Truitt, Richard Conway, Margarita Vargas-Betancourt, Brad Benton, and Erika Hosselkus, as well as Ken Ward, Tatiana Seijas, Rob Schwaller, and Martin Nesvig.

While based in Seville, I had the pleasure of meeting David Wheat, J. Michael Francis, Amara Solari, Guadalupe Pinzón, Esther Gónzalez, Carolina Giraldo Botero, Yovana Celaya, Saber Gray, Aaron Olivas, and Luis Muñoz. The family of Seila González Estrecha, David Wheat's then fiancée and now wife, made me feel more at home in Badajoz than anyone might think possible. Two sevillanas, Lola de Miguel Jiménez and Gabi Morcillo, helped a great deal with translations of arcane Spanish words and phrases. The archivists of the Archivo General de Indias—especially Clara and Antonio—made this project possible.

My coeditors of the anthology *City Indians*—Dana Velasco Murillo and Margarita Ochoa—as well as fellow yucatecologos Owen Jones and Ryan Kashanipour, also deserve credit for regular encouragement along the way. I would like to thank all of the archivists at the Archivo General de la Nación. While much of my research took place elsewhere, I was always delighted to find excuses to return to the Archivo General del Estado de Yucatán, where help from Dra. Piedad Peniche Rivero, Ernesto Aké Ciau, Cinthia Vanessa Fernández Vergara, and Karla Caballero was always readily available. Other Yucatecan scholars—including Elda Moreno Acevedo, Emiliano Canto Mayén, Laura Machuca Gallegos, and Carmen Menéndez Serralta—took a genuine interest in my research in Yucatan, welcoming me and providing useful suggestions while I was in Mérida. My time in Yucatan was also aided by the preparation provided by various Maya teachers, especially Victoria Bricker, Ema Uhu de Pech, Santiago Domínguez Couoh, and Fidencio Briceño Chel. I would like to thank my former colleagues at the University of Louisiana at Lafayette who took an interest in this project, including Tom Schoonover, Ted Maris-Wolfe, Brent Woodfill, and Tony Musacchia. Utah Valley University colleagues were very encouraging during the final stages, especially John Hunt and Lyn Bennett. Catherine Tracy Goode, Megan McDonie, Samantha Billing, and fellow Tulanian Amy George took time out of their research schedules to assist with resolving small but critical research errands before the book's publication.

Finally, as is the case with all books but especially true in this case, the editors made this book in its current form possible. Special thanks are owed to the University of New Mexico Press's Kris Lane, who brought this manuscript to press; Clark Whitehorn; and the anonymous readers for their suggestions on how to make *Murder in Mérida* worthy of printing. Most of all, I would like to thank my family, especially Tim, Jon, and Aunt Kathleen.

CHAPTER 1

Introduction

A Province at Risk

THE BRAZEN ATTACK ON THE MAN WHO REPRESENTED THE ROYAL will in Yucatan demanded a swift, exemplary, and brutal punishment. To restore authority and demonstrate their power, Bourbon-era administrators typically meted out a public and often gory execution when royal officials were killed in Spain's colonies. In this case, no one suffered such a punishment. Gálvez's murderer defied the authorities' wide-ranging efforts to find him for years. In the end, neither he nor his accomplices suffered capital punishment when their crimes came to light. Yucatan's inhabitants, far from the metropolis of Madrid, hampered the efforts to quickly deploy a show of force that characterized royal responses to insubordination elsewhere. In Yucatan, a language barrier that effectively divided *peninsulares* (European-born Spaniards) from Yucatecans of all races (including many creoles), obstructionism and passive resistance from provincial magistrates who had resented Gálvez's heavy-handed approach to administration, and the ostracism and subtle intimidation by the allies of the prime suspect postponed the case's resolution for over eight years.[1] Undermined further by complicated rules regarding the prosecution of priests and soldiers, bringing justice to the intendant's killer thwarted the efforts of some of New Spain's best-trained and experienced magistrates.

The interim authorities who replaced Gálvez before his successor arrived lacked local support and backing from Mérida's elite. Their oversight of the intensive investigation fell short. Others responsible for the inquiry had their own scores to settle with the deceased intendant and his allies. Still others

took advantage of the confusion to make allegations against political enemies unconnected to the assassination. Instead of a concerted effort to find
the attacker, a series of disjointed investigations to discover the killer's identity followed the assassination. The judges, magistrates, and law enforcement
officials charged with discovering the assassin's identity and bringing him to
justice cast a wide net that ensnared a number of suspects from Mérida and
its environs. Innocent, guilty, and suspects in unrelated crimes, they were
booked and interrogated on the off chance they might have been involved.
This phase of the inquiry sheds light on Yucatan's social networks: fictive
kinship, blood ties, marriage bonds, workplace partnerships, peregrinations,
and the interracial sociability of Mérida's urban plebe. But it did nothing to
move the case forward. Thwarted by incompetence, intransigence, and inex-
perience, Madrid decided to send in outside prosecutors to break through
the inertia.

The two outside prosecutors (*jueces comisionados*) who arrived in 1793
and 1794, respectively, embodied the ideal of Bourbon reformers.[2] Despite
the first's determination and professional reputation, he made little headway,
hindered by the collective lack of cooperation from two rival parties with
their base of power in the episcopal palace and the cabildo (city council), an
adverse situation aggravated by personal tragedies and poor health. The next
prosecutor painstakingly built a seemingly airtight case against the likeliest
suspect, a peninsular rival of the intendant. Yet he too found himself removed
from the case as a result of interference by Mexico City–based creole associates of the prominent peninsular accused of murdering don Lucas de Gálvez.
At the imperial level, Bourbon efforts to shore up control over the vast colonial holdings in America collided with the perceived privileges of local
autonomy and exemption from prosecution by royal magistrates, based on
municipal privileges, militia service, and membership in the clergy.

The strong regionalism that characterized Yucatan was abetted by factors beyond Madrid's control. Geography, demography, and resource scarcity conspired to undermine royal authority, which rested lightly on the
province. Yucatan's distance from both the viceregal capital of Mexico City
and the royal seat of power in Madrid fostered a sense of separateness and its
remote location limited oversight by faraway authorities. As Gilbert M.
Joseph noted, "There were no roads connecting Yucatán with central Mexico
until well after World War II."[3] By boat, a voyage of a week, more or less, kept
outside interference at bay.[4] Most maritime traffic between Havana and
Veracruz, the two major ports that connected Mexico to the Caribbean,

sailed past the small port of Sisal without docking. Yucatan's distance from seats of power promoted a strong regional identity. In practice, this localism led to provincial officials wielding authority with less intervention than might be expected, from the unchecked excesses of the early Franciscans of the sixteenth century to the repeated exemptions for the encomienda (a royal grant authorizing its recipient to demand tribute and labor from Indians native to a specific territory, ceded to early conquistadors and colonists and their descendants) into the final decades of the eighteenth century, long after its extinction in most of Spain's American territories.

The encomienda also owed its survival to the relative scarcity of marketable products.[5] Economically, royal and viceregal officials had little interest in curtailing the privileges of local authorities for most of the colonial period. Financially, little was at stake. Like the other two regions where the crown allowed the encomienda to persist into the eighteenth century, Chile and Paraguay, native tribute remained the primary source of income and the principal mechanism for the extraction of natural resources.[6] Two eighteenth-century *visitadores* (royally commissioned inspectors), Juan Antonio Valera and Francisco de Corres, put a positive spin on the scarcity of natural resources in the province and the longevity of the encomienda. Because Yucatan had neither mines nor large-scale commercial agriculture, its encomenderos (holders of the encomienda) "had little occasion to ignite the violent impulses of greed."[7] Thus, the king had no need to extinguish the encomienda, according to this rather tortured logic. In reality, the overworked Maya laborers of Yucatan's encomiendas produced a slight surplus of commodities such as corn (maize), cotton, honey, beeswax, and dyewood—at least in good years.[8] The end of the encomienda coincided with an upswing in economic output, as sugar, livestock, and, henequen— the green gold of the following century—began to supplement the meager exports of the province.[9]

The second half of the eighteenth century witnessed incremental economic growth as haciendas (large agricultural estates) gradually displaced the encomienda in importance, paving the way for the belated extinction of the anachronistic tributary arrangement.[10] Encomenderos, whose numbers diminished as the colonial era wore on, retained their social standing but not their status as the province's primary producers. Many encomendero families did successfully acquire large landholdings and did not fare badly when the crown abolished the encomienda.[11] Haciendas and estancias, initially dedicated to stock raising, began to flourish in the seventeenth century.[12]

Later eighteenth-century diversification saw increased production of rice and maize to meet regional demand.[13] Sugarcane estates flourished in the area around Tekax, adding an unprecedented new product to Yucatan's limited portfolio of exports.[14] Less well studied, English logging of dyewood along the coasts of eastern Yucatan and the permanent English establishment in Belize led to increased contraband trade as well.[15]

This tardy and partial prosperity coincided with royal efforts to integrate the peninsula into the Spanish Empire more fully. If Yucatan's contribution to the wealth of Spain mattered little in the late eighteenth century, in spite of tentative growth, its strategic value as a province vulnerable to competing imperial interests and exposure to rebellious elements caused consternation in Madrid. Concerns over Yucatan's vulnerability to depredations by foreign powers, from the minor threat of illicit trade by the English to the fears of revolutionary insurrections spread by the French and rebellious slaves in Saint-Domingue, led Bourbon advisers to strengthen Yucatan's defenses.[16]

England posed a persistent and predictable economic and territorial threat to Spain. Yucatan offered no lucrative prize for the British, but its capture would have served strategic interests quite well. Valera and Corres, two dismayed inspectors reporting to don Lucas's better-known distant cousin, José de Gálvez, noted that the English smugly claimed to "have taken hold of North América by its two horns," referring to its hold over Florida and Yucatan.[17] Despite bolstering Yucatan's defenses, including lookout towers (*vigias*), contraband trade undermined the crown's attempts to regulate commerce. As eighteenth-century cartographer Thomas Kitchin scornfully wrote in 1778, "the Spaniards have the town of Salamanca de Bacalar, of 120 houses, with a bad fort and a small garrison, designed to hinder the contraband trade, and the excursions of the Wood-cutters or Bay-men, but which it does not prevent."[18] Kitchin's cartographical knowledge, including a map he produced in 1779 (fig. 2), demonstrates that the British designs on undefended stretches of coastline were backed by an impressive geographical grasp of the waterways around the peninsula.

The ease with which a bribe convinced militia guards to turn a blind eye, a rare instance in which a contrabandist was apprehended, bears out this boastful claim.[19] English cartographers accurately noted the location of easily navigated waterways in maps that often bettered those of their Spanish counterparts. For one example, see figure 3, *An eye draft of Logger-head Cay near to Cape Catoche . . .* , produced around 1760.[20] The failure of repeated efforts to retake Belize and Jamaica, "an imposing presence in the heart of

Figure 2. "Map of the Bay of Honduras shewing the situation of the Spanish town and fort of St. Fernando de Omoa, taken by the Honble. John Luttrell & Wm Dalrymple Esq. Octr. 20 1779 T. Kitchin Senr. sculpt," 1779. Courtesy of the John Carter Brown Library, Providence, RI.

the Caribbean," made the English a looming threat to Spain's empire in the Americas, with Yucatan uniquely exposed.[21]

If Great Britain's intentions to strip the Spanish of as much of their empire as possible was a given, unexpected events of the 1790s struck a blow to Spain's reliable ties with its most constant eighteenth-century ally, France. The kingdom ruled by their cousins transformed into a radical republic and threatened to export revolution to the Caribbean, dangerously close to Yucatan's eastern shores. As France lurched toward its more radical phase, around the time of the intendant's death in 1792, Carlos IV, markedly less decisive and responsive to crises around him, may well have seen the demise of his cousin across the Pyrenees as a matter of more concern than the death of a distant provincial administrator.[22] In 1795, at the height of the scare, New Spain's viceroy, Marqués de Branciforte, ordered a survey of all French

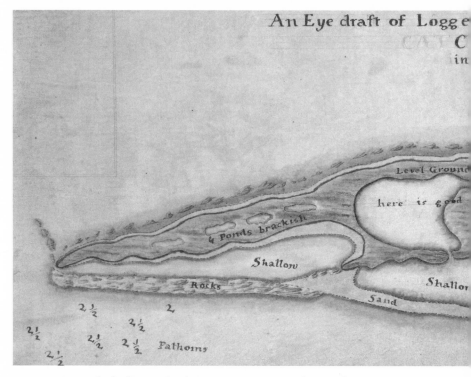

Figure 3. *An eye draft of Logger-head Cay near to Cape Catoche in 21 de: 20 mi: N: L:,*
1760. Courtesy of the John Carter Brown Library, Providence, RI.

nationals residing in the viceroyalty. Yucatan had a disproportionately high
number of French-born inhabitants. Twenty-one French residents were enu-
merated, the third highest number after Mexico City and Veracruz.[23] The
eruption of the Haitian Revolution brought even more potential insurrec-
tionaries to Yucatan. At least three sizeable boatloads of "French blacks,"
ranging from 16 to 213 in number, arrived between 1792 and 1809, fleeing the
fighting on the island in circumstances that would qualify them as refugees
today.[24] Only one boatload of refugees was allowed to disembark.

If international turmoil threatened to disrupt the calm of the Viceroyalty
of New Spain from without, internal affairs also preoccupied the king's
counselors. Too heavy a hand might incite a revolt. The Andes, where the
widespread, violent, and long Tupac Amaru Rebellion and the Comuneros
Revolt spread like wildfire through two of the three viceroyalties of South

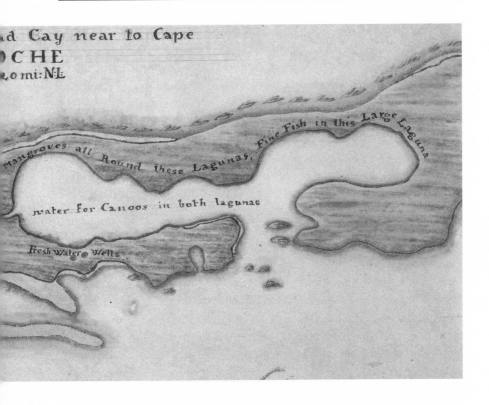

America, had erupted into violence in the 1780s.[25] In Yucatan, the 1761 Jacinto Canek uprising in Cisteil shook the province's creole elite, but its rapid suppression by local forces meant that it did little to draw attention across the ocean. Even so, in an age of revolutions beyond and within the borders of Spain's empire, royal advisers tempered their responses to disturbances, especially those led by creoles.[26]

Yucatan in the eighteenth century had changed less than central regions in colonial Latin America, but significant demographic and social changes had indeed taken place. As hacendados (landowners) emerged as the dominant social class, the rise of haciendas and estancias, with more direct administration and intensive exploitation of the land for profit, brought more non-Mayas into the countryside.[27] The peninsula remained majority Maya, though Yucatan's numbers of creoles and the so-called castas, of mixed ancestry, grew.

Economic revival led others to engage in petty commerce: both merchants dealing in licit commerce and contrabandistas engaging in forbidden trade, mostly with the English. In rural areas, Afro-Yucatecans became especially prominent.[28] Though some worked for creole hacendados, others integrated into Maya society, living as Indians.[29] Military reforms led to the stationing of ever-greater numbers of mestizos, creole, peninsular, and Afro-Yucatecans in the countryside. Efforts to eradicate the exploitative practice of the repartimiento—the forced sale of inferior goods, often on credit, at inflated prices—led to the creation of the posts of *subdelegado* and *juez español*, who answered directly to the intendant.[30] Instead of depending on the repartimiento, subdelegados were paid 5 percent of the proceeds from the native tribute.[31] The absolutism that characterized the rule of Charles III also informed this restructuring of government in the American provinces. Intendants named subdelegados. Previously, viceroys had appointed *corregidores*.[32] The Real Ordenanza de Intendentes of 1786 more clearly defined the administrative, civil, fiscal, and judicial authority of subdelegados. Employed as salaried functionaries of the crown and named by either intendants or viceroys rather than working essentially as subcontractors running a coercive scheme to extract payment from indigenous subjects, subdelegados and their assistants, the jueces españoles, resided permanently in or near the pueblos where they were assigned, judging from their ready availability during various phases of the investigation.[33] Answering to the intendants rather than distant viceroys made the office of subdelegado subject to more scrutiny than its predecessors. Other creoles moved into the countryside too, some looking to offer credit no longer available via the repartimiento. Hacendados, merchants and traders, ranch hands, militia officers and soldiers, and low-level administrators populated a countryside that had once been occupied solely by a Maya majority and a few priests and friars.

The assassination and the trial transcripts generated in its wake, summarized and reorganized for a broader audience in the following pages, offer several insights for social historians and scholars of colonial justice. For reasons of scope and clarity, this work emphasizes four main thrusts. First, it places the 1792 assassination in its rightful place as a critical yet overlooked event in the history of resistance to royal rule that marked the second half of the eighteenth and first half of the nineteenth centuries. Second, the accounts of routine life in the pursuit of suspects and the verification of alibis provide an image of Yucatecan society in microcosm, suggesting the need for revisions to current conceptions of Yucatan's population and its peoples' interactions with one another. Third, race and class divisions were more permeable than is often portrayed. Afro-Yucatecan merchants, artisans, and officers, as well as urban *batabs* (caciques) and landholders from Maya backgrounds, were at least middle class in their social standing, a status rarely recognized as attainable in much of the histories on Yucatan's colonial era.[34] Some but not all creoles also experienced unprecedented economic insecurity and little upward mobility during the late eighteenth century, in part due to royal policies and the stricter enforcement of rules. European descent did not guarantee a place in the upper echelons of society. One's place within the social hierarchy was not necessarily determined by race.[35] The colonial categories of the república de indios and the república de españoles still mattered, but other, often overlooked factors played a role in how society broke down in Yucatan. For example, rather than follow the lead of colonial authorities in grouping the Maya majority together in the broad category of "indio," this monograph examines how rural versus urban residence shaped the lives of members of the indigenous majority, differentiating between *indios hidalgos* and urban native artisans in Mérida and *principales* (elites) and *macehuales* (commoners) in the countryside. As demonstrated in the accounts of the minutiae of daily life revealed in the notes taken during the investigation, creoles, Mayas, Afro-Yucatecans, and other castas lived intertwined, entangled lives that crossed the boundaries of race and class on a regular basis.

The depth and intensity of the investigation that produced such a fine-grained portrayal of Yucatan resulted from the relative rarity of such an audacious affront to royal authority in the Americas. The killing punctuated the historical record of the Yucatan Peninsula as one of the most blatant acts of aggression against authority during the colonial era. It stands out in the overall history of the Spanish Empire in the Americas for both the high rank and prominent ancestry of the victim as well as the effrontery of the attacker who, armed and on foot, hurled a crude weapon into the chest of the province's leading administrator during a carriage ride through the heart of the provincial capital. However, such attacks were not unprecedented, though the targets typically were lower-ranked royal administrators. An uptick in aggression toward the crown administrators who represented the royal will in Spain's American empire marked the last fifty years of colonial rule in the Americas.[36] The aftermath of the assassination is striking, then, not for the attack on the province's top authority, but for the puzzling failure of authorities to quickly capture the killer and his accomplices and execute a rapid, violent, and public punishment.

Just a few examples serve to illustrate the usual response of crown administrators upon the discovery of conspiracies or the restoration of order after revolts. In English-language literature, at least, scholars have subjected eighteenth-century Andean revolts to the most scrutiny. All major leaders of Andean revolts were executed (with the exception of a few ringleaders of the Comuneros Uprising in Colombia), including the Catarí brothers and nearly all members of José Gabriel Condorcanquí's (Tupac Amaru II) family, including his wife, Micaela Bastidas.[37] The mostly indigenous leaders of the largest revolts against the colonial order—those that rocked the Andes— were executed with just one exception: Juan Santos Atahualpa, who likely died at the hands of a native rival.[38]

The Tupac Amaru revolt and the other Andean uprisings it inspired were far more large scale than other insurgencies in Spain's colonies, but Mexico did not pass the eighteenth century without turmoil. Ringleaders of smaller revolts, whether headed by indigenous caciques, castas, or creoles, also were summarily punished. In the early eighteenth century, a coalition of Tzeltal Mayas of Chiapas, joined by some nearby Tzotzil and Chol Maya pueblos, rebelled against Spanish rule, rallying to protect an apparition of the Virgin Mary condemned by Dominican authorities. After the rebel forces' early military successes in the fall of 1712, wave after wave of Spanish, allied Indian, and free black militiamen defeated the Mayas and put down the uprising. After the defeat, at least ninety-four rebels were executed, not counting those killed in battle.[39] Elsewhere in the Maya world, in Cisteil, nine leaders of the 1761 Maya revolt against Spanish rule and religion were mutilated and executed.[40] A more sanguinary reprisal took place in New Spain's northern mining territories just seven years later. In the 1767 uprisings, sparked in part by the expulsion of the Jesuits, at least sixty ringleaders were executed in ten separate municipalities at the behest of don Lucas's influential cousin, don José de Gálvez.[41] Non-indigenous instigators also faced brutal executions. Farther from New Spain, Luís Lasso de la Vega, the mestizo militia sergeant who led indigenous and mestizo rebels in the killing of Spaniards and the corregidor don Francisco García de Prado, was captured and hung along with twenty-three coconspirators within two weeks of leading Tupiza in an uprising in 1781.[42]

Creoles' European ancestry did not exempt them from the severest punishment. One of two instigators of a quickly defeated conspiracy of 1797 in Caracas, Venezuela, Manuel Gual, escaped. The other, José María de España, was sentenced, drawn, and quartered.[43] Though many of the creole instigators of the multiethnic forces of the Comuneros Revolt negotiated their way out of a harsh punishment, four prominent creoles—including José Antonio Galán, Lorenzo Alcantuz, Manuel Ortíz, and Isidro Molina—were hung, quartered, and burned.[44]

Resistance to royal rule in Yucatan fell between the extremes of the hot-beds of insurgency, such as the Andes and northern New Spain, and the zones that remained quiet in an age of revolts and revolutions. However, creole conspiracies, including the quiet collusion of those Yucatecans who knew the assassin's true identity and did not come forward, deserve more attention. Assassinations are a less studied, though integral part of this current of resistance. Defiance of royal rule ran the gamut from "everyday resistance" by commoners to major uprisings such as the Great Rebellion (1780–1782) in Peru. Scholars have covered native rebellions more thoroughly than other insurrectionary activities, with slave revolts close behind. Interest in creole discontent, one of the wellsprings of antipathy toward don Lucas de Gálvez, lags behind.[45] Criollo (Spanish for "creole"; European-descent natives of the Americas) insurgencies often rode waves of more radical indigenous and mestizo-led rebellions that overshadowed the autonomist urges of the middling classes.[46] After such revolts, creoles quickly distanced themselves from the excesses of indigenous-led movements. Yet commoners were not the only ones who resented the imposition of stricter rules and restrictions on local autonomy and corporate privileges. On one end of the spectrum, passive resistance and noncompliance with royal orders characterized low-intensity creole resistance. Violent acts justified by the abusive treatment by "bad government" fell at the other end.[47] High-level officials, including the intendant's own second-in-command and successor, dismissed Gálvez's killing as an inevitable consequence of "bad government."[48] The stalling tactics of many creoles and the evasive answers they gave when questioned, as well as the resentful murmurings against the dead intendant, demonstrate widespread circulation of "hidden transcripts of resistance."[49] Though disobedience was never overt except for the killer and his accomplices, noncompliance was pervasive.

Creoles had manifold reasons for their resentment of royal officials. Madrid's policies shook up the colonial social order, leading to a loss of status for some, such as encomenderos, friars, and priests, while elevating the standing of others, including Afro-Yucatecan militiamen and creoles who served in the newly reformed militia units. An emphasis on professionalism left many prominent subjects who felt entitled to positions based on family connections or earlier service out of a job and feeling snubbed.[50] Creole elites occupied a precarious position near the top of the local and regional hierarchy of Yucatan. Yet those of lower standing resided and worked in the same professions as their casta neighbors, especially in the cities. Descent from European ancestors never guaranteed a privileged place in society. The abolition of the encomienda, an empire-wide preference for peninsulares in many administrative and military posts, and restrictions on exploitative tribute, exchange, and labor arrangements with the indigenous majority often set middling creoles back even further.

Additional factors, such as Yucatan's extreme distance from the viceregal center and the persistence of ecclesiastical authority in spite of the anticlerical aims of the Bourbons, further blunted the force of royal rule in the region. As a result, resistance from Yucatan punctuated its colonial period—from the more drastic instances of revolt, including the Jacinto Canek uprising, to the more mundane forms of resistance, such as the political foment promoted by a coterie of liberals associated with the Church of San Juan in Mérida (1810–1811) or the widespread refusal to pay tithes in 1813 by many Maya pueblos.[51] These two minor acts of defiance marked the extent of muted impulses for independence, which arrived in Yucatan with far less violence than elsewhere in Mexico.

By the time these last two events transpired, the case had been resolved. The intellectual architect of the assassination, the killer, and their coconspirators had admitted guilt and provided contradictory versions of the intendant's death. But viceregal authorities' priorities had shifted. The momentum behind the drive to capture and kill the attacker had long since dissipated. As a result, the killer's punishment—just twenty-one years of imprisonment—also contrasts with the public and brutal decapitations and dismemberments that normally marked the swift end of those who dared to defy royal authority in the Americas. Attacks on royal authority demanded swift, retaliatory, public, and violent punishments. Gálvez's killers received none. In contrast, the four men who knew of, planned, and executed the assassination faced relatively short prison terms. None were executed, though one died in prison in 1802.

The detours and delays the prosecutors and investigators followed and experienced on the slow road to justice placed them in regular contact with Yucatecans from all walks of life, offering a close look at the province's subjects, especially its urban population. These proceedings, recorded in nearly fifty volumes of trial transcripts in archives in Mexico and Spain, offer a unique opportunity to re-create a comprehensive cross-section of Yucatecan society.[52] If the assassination itself and the array of plausible motives and suspects offer a case study of resistance to Bourbon reforms, the criminal investigation provides a granular image of Yucatan's society in microcosm.

Invasive, probing prosecutors and their assistants produced exhaustive documentation that contributes to a composite sketch of a complex society pieced together from the thousands of individuals questioned or jailed. Yucatecans identified themselves in widely varied terms, using household affiliation, professional status, military rank, guild membership, barrio, pueblo, region or nation of origin, nobility (both Spanish and indigenous), knighthood in one of the three royal orders, religious confraternity affiliation, royal and municipal administrative appointments and titles—even as encomenderos, despite the abolition of the encomienda system in 1785. Yucatecans' perceptions of themselves, their families, neighbors, and those with whom they crossed paths on a daily basis consisted of much more than the well-studied categories of race, class, and gender.[53]

If Yucatecans used a myriad of descriptors duly recorded by the notaries, a few commonalities emerge. Despite Yucatan's diversity, its inhabitants shared a few common traits that united most of the native-born population. First, almost no native-born Yucatecans had an overall positive view of the royal government.[54] Second, unlike other regions in Mesoamerica where indigenous language usage declined in the eighteenth century, Yucatec Maya became even more prevalent among both indigenous Yucatecans and many creoles and castas. Yucatecans, then, were not divided by language. Nor were marital and familial associations divided by racial background. Yucatecans of all races intermarried, worked together, worshipped side-by-side, and fought together in excursions against the English more often than historians have acknowledged. Peninsular administrators, on the other hand, were not only separated by European birth but were linguistically isolated. Some peninsulares had indeed married into local families, but the second half of the eighteenth century saw a rift open between native-born Yucatecans and outsiders charged with enacting decrees that formed key planks of the program known as the Bourbon reforms.[55]

It is entirely possible to overstate the aims and the impact of the fine-tuning of colonial administration that took place under Philip V, Ferdinand VI, and, above all, Charles III.[56] As noted in one of the most influential works on the late Bourbon era, "Reform meant calibrated adjustment, methodical incrementalism, never radical change or restructuring."[57] In the following case study of the Bourbon reforms and their reception at the local level, I argue that such adjustments, rulings, and modifications of colonial rule were not unambiguously oppressive for all subjects. Free-colored militiamen and officers benefited greatly, both in terms of improved social standing and in the salaries paid to them.[58] Some municipalities fared better from opening trade while others went into decline. In Yucatan, for example, many in Mérida resented the new administrative policies while neighboring campechanos welcomed the loosening of restrictions on trade.[59] The native population, portrayed by one historian as suffering a "second conquest," did not, in fact, experience worsening conditions across the board.[60] New administrators—jueces españoles and subdelegados—were as likely to side with caciques and indigenous cabildos as much as they were to ally with clergymen in three-sided disputes.[61] Others benefited outright, such as Mayas who found a receptive audience for their complaints against ecclesiastical burdens, repartimientos, and servicio personal among the eighteenth-century administrators. Indeed, creoles seem to have had more grievances with the changes from above than the native population in the final decades of the eighteenth century.

For Yucatan's creoles, the changes imposed from above had a more significant impact, since many of the alterations to the colonial regime eliminated vestiges of the Habsburg era that had ended elsewhere, such as the encomienda and servicio personal. Moreover, the colonial church, seen by Charles III as the most entrenched obstacle to progress, commanded more respect and fear in Yucatan than elsewhere. Bishops' terms of service often outlasted governors' and intendants' tenures and had a reputation for their ability to "ruin governors."[62] Their underlings—parish priests—echoed the assertion of political power, claiming that in the face of royally appointed jueces españoles, they "alone ruled in their pueblos."[63]

The Bourbon reforms were not passively accepted by Yucatecans, united by centuries of experience, shared bloodlines, language, and defense of the province. They and other colonial Latin Americans did not peacefully acquiesce to changes enforced from without by royal administrators. Bureaucrats holding newly created posts faced more than simple logistical issues in imposing long overdue changes in the colonies. Anger over alterations to the colonial regime ran deep, across racial and ethnic divides. Even so, scholars have focused on indigenous-headed and slave-led rebellions, ignoring the multiracial alliances that channeled resentment into actions that undermined royal rule. By ignoring all but the most dramatic and forceful forms of resistance, historians have missed the instances in which multiethnic coalitions and factions composed of diverse subjects rose up in less dramatic ways against royal authority. In Yucatan, antipathy to the king's representative in the region led to his violent death. This study of the eight years it took prosecutors to get to the bottom of his killing uncovers the deep animosity and ambivalence to authority emanating from Mexico City and Madrid that came from many sectors. The motivations behind the assassination of the intendant and the uphill battle prosecutors fought to convict the killer are examined in the following pages, demonstrating just how deeply Bourbon rule was resented.

Finally, *Murder in Mérida* tells, for the first time, the story of a real-life murder mystery, from the intendant's arrival until his killer's release.[64] The book does not omit actual plot elements that would work just as well in a telenovela: a love triangle involving a married woman, accusations of abuse of power, affairs and out-of-wedlock children, conspiracies hatched on drunken afternoon gatherings, poisonings, and killers roaming the nighttime streets in disguises. Unlike earlier works that have alluded to the assassination or have briefly summarized the event, the book does not just discuss the European-descent killers; it includes the supporting cast of casta scapegoats, Maya witnesses, and mestizo accomplices, among others. Beyond the aim to give as complete an account of the assassination and its aftermath as space permits, this comprehensive coverage better fleshes out the cross-class, interracial alliances that characterized colonial Yucatecan society. Along the way, readers will gain new insights regarding how society functioned and how different individuals fared before the law. Without wasting further space, then, let us turn now to the intendant's arrival and the long list of enemies he made during his short five-year term in Mérida.

CHAPTER 2

The Intendant's Enemies

Chronicle of an Assassination Foretold

⤜ THE FUNERAL FOLLOWED WITHIN TWENTY-FOUR HOURS OF GÁLVEZ'S passing. On the afternoon of 23 June 1792, Mérida's inhabitants turned out en masse, as much of the public and the intendant's allies honored him with the pomp and ceremony befitting a man of his rank and lineage.[1] Ringing church bells and cannon fire accompanied the final march of the province's leader. Don Fernando Antonio Gutiérrez de Piñeres, the young lieutenant governor who took the reins of government after the assassination, rode at the head of the procession.[2] Mérida's numerous clergymen and friars marched arrayed in vestments that reflected their rank and religious order, followed by cabildo members arranged according to prominence. Next came the army and militia in their dress uniforms, followed by the unorganized plebe. All escorted the fallen leader from the governor's palace to his resting place beneath the presbytery of the cathedral. His rivals snubbed their enemy one last time with their conspicuous absence.

The Reformer Arrives

Gálvez had no shortage of adversaries, critics, and detractors in the province during his five short years in Yucatan. When he boarded the frigate *San*

Constantino in the Andalucían port of Cádiz on 22 August 1787, he must have had little idea of how much resistance he would face in implementing and enforcing the Bourbon reforms, laws passed by Carlos III (r. 1759–1788) and Carlos IV (r. 1788–1808) to tighten Madrid's weakening grip on the Americas.[3] His distant cousin, don José de Gálvez, who was rewarded for his administrative acumen with the title Marqués de Sonora by Carlos III, may have had some sway in the young Navy captain's selection as Yucatan's first intendant; don José's signature on the 3 June 1787 royal letter of appointment hints at the role nepotism might have played in his cousin's swift ascent to the intendancy of Yucatan.[4] Don Lucas's ties to the most powerful members of the prominent Gálvez clan were distant yet proudly recognized in an exhaustively researched genealogy commissioned by the Marqués de Sonora in an attempt to establish the distinguished ancestry of the line: don Lucas descended from the Ecija (in Andalucía between Seville and Córdoba) branch of the family, distantly related to the far more prominent Gálvezes of Málaga (on the Mediterranean coast of Andalucía), headed by don José.[5] Though not a close relative, don Lucas followed the family tradition of absolute loyalty to the crown, capable handling of administrative duties, and the characteristic inflexibility in enforcing the absolutist, secularizing policies promoted by the crown.[6]

The memory of Gálvez lives on in Yucatan in the lingering impact of his energetic promotion of public works and regional economic development. Writing in the nineteenth century, when many of the infrastructural improvements Gálvez sponsored still stood, historian Eligio Ancona recalled Gálvez's major projects: the improved roads that linked Mérida to Izamal, Ticul, and Campeche; public lighting in the city center; a new pier in Sisal; and the construction of an alameda in central Mérida.[7] Juan Francisco Molina Solís, Ancona's contemporary, wrote in more detail of the improvements made under Gálvez, including new gateways from the city's walls toward the countryside, new sidewalks, and investment in the development of commercial fishing and rice cultivation.[8] A monument to Gálvez still standing in central Mérida commemorates the intendant's role in the construction of a hospice, the alameda, and several roads and highways. (See figs. 4 and 5.) Under the intendant's direction, the Catalan engineer don Rafael Llovet extensively surveyed and mapped the province with more accuracy than his predecessors, in part to better demarcate Yucatan's poorly patrolled boundaries with Belize.[9] A reinforced armed presence—militia and army divisions deployed along the border with Belize—matched these cartographic efforts. Shortly before his

Figure 4. Full view of La Cruz de Gálvez, monument in between Calles 26 and 28, intersecting with Calle 65, Jardines de Miraflores, Mérida. Photograph by the author.

death, Gálvez began to formulate plans with Llovet to remodel the fortifications of Bacalar and Campeche. In order to better regulate the contraband that economically sustained the British presence, Gálvez reopened the long-abandoned Jesuit colegio as a new customs house. These two final projects were completed after the intendant's death.[10] Today a plaque added in 1974 to one of the few monuments memorializing Gálvez in a city that has largely forgotten him—the so-called La Cruz de Gálvez,—enshrines him as a "progressive constructor of roads" (see fig. 6).

Figure 5. Caption of La Cruz de Gálvez commemorating his contributions to Mérida, the hospice, the alameda, and several new roads and highways. Photograph by the author.

Figure 6. Intersection marker of La Cruz de Gálvez. Photograph by the author.

Figure 7. Caption of intersection marker of La Cruz de Gálvez.
Photograph by the author.

The Reformer's Enemies: The Cabildo, the Soldiers, and the Bishop

Other reforms enacted during the tenure of the first intendant—and his intolerance for any opposition—were not as popular as his infrastructural improvements and economic development schemes. The encomienda persisted as a key economic institution and measure of social standing in Yucatan long after its abolition in all of the other provinces of the Americas except Chile and Paraguay; Yucatecan encomenderos had won a 1721 reprieve from the previous royal abolition of the encomienda of 1718.[11] Despite a gradual decline in the region's dependence on the income from the encomiendas and a dilatory diversification of the peninsula's economy, the encomiendas still provided a significant amount of wealth at the time of the institution's dissolution. In 1785 seventy-seven encomenderos and thirty-nine *pensionistas* received 35,370 pesos of income, or 304 pesos on average.[12] The final and permanent order to abolish the encomienda was passed in 1785, yet it fell to Gálvez to enforce the order upon his arrival in 1787.[13] Yucatan's encomenderos bitterly resisted, as their forefathers had, through appeals, bribes, and, some alleged, threats to the man appointed to carry out the royal will, don Lucas de Gálvez.[14] As the man who personified royal authority in the province from 1787 until his death, his actions alienated one of the most established and powerful factions of the peninsula: the encomenderos.[15]

Litigation over the institution's fate continued until 1803, nearly twenty years after the abolition of the encomienda.[16] Gálvez himself dealt with a number of suits from what he called a "small number of discontented encomenderos."[17] They were likely a more formidable faction than he let on. Seven encomenderos served on Mérida's fifteen-man cabildo in 1785, the year of the institution's abolition. Even though the profitability of the encomienda waned in the eighteenth century, the esteemed social status of the encomendero declined more slowly.[18] Through the final decade of the eighteenth century, Yucatan's elites still used the title of encomendero. As late as 1815, don Antonio Martín de Tovar y Rejón proudly and stubbornly listed "encomendero de yndios" prominently among his other titles of respect thirty years after the institution's permanent abolition.[19] During his term, Gálvez backed the royal treasurer, don Diego de Lanz, in quashing attempts by disgruntled encomenderos to defy Carlos III's *real cédula* (royal decree or authorization) mandating the end of the encomienda. Two attorneys representing the discontented encomenderos—don Francisco Ortiz and don José Correa

Romero—later aided in the defense of the prime suspect in Gálvez's assassination.[20]

The creole-dominated cabildo quarreled regularly with the intendant over other matters as well. Family rivalries frequently mixed with regional politics. Lacking unity, members of the cabildo fragmented into factions based on their support or opposition to Gálvez. Juan Esteban Quijano, together with his son don José Miguel Quijano, led the cohort that opposed Gálvez's leadership. Don Juan Esteban Quijano y Cetina served in a variety of cabildo posts, including regidor, *alcalde ordinario*, and *procurador* between 1780 and 1800. His son don José Miguel followed in his father's footsteps, starting his career in the council in 1789 as procurador before ascending to the post of alcalde ordinario in 1801.[21] Another son, also named don Juan Esteban Quijano, likewise served as a regidor and alcalde in the late eighteenth and early nineteenth centuries.[22] The sons of Quijano held a variety of "honorable ecclesiastical, military, and political posts," constituting a powerful bloc of resentful creoles contained within a single family unit.[23] Besides the two sons who helped the family dominate the cabildo, two others held highly ranked militia posts. Don Ignacio served as a captain of the dragoons, or light cavalry, and don Mariano was an officer with the Battalion of Castile. As was typical for large families of the era, another son, don José Tadeo, entered the priesthood.[24]

Descendants of conquistadors and early colonists, encomenderos dominated the cabildos of the eighteenth century. They were the most prominent rivals of Gálvez in matters involving indigenous labor exploitation, but not the only ones. Prohibitions on the repartimiento and the intractable practice of *servicio personal*, or demands on labor by Spaniards imposed upon marginal Indians, also were reiterated yet widely ignored in the eighteenth century.[25] Through his meticulous efforts to root out these deeply ingrained practices, Gálvez angered middling Spaniards, low-level administrators, and small-time producers who depended on illegal extractions to make ends meet. Many of these mid-level administrators had military backgrounds, which deepened the resentment that militia and army officers felt toward the heavy-handed intendant over matters of discipline.

Many army and militia officers disliked Gálvez in spite of his high standing, extensive martial experience, and numerous titles. He died holding the rank of brigadier and had served as a naval captain before assuming political and military control of Yucatan.[26] Rather than centering on questions of authority or revolving around specific issues, such as the abolition of the encomienda that alienated prominent creoles, Gálvez confronted opposition from military men over disputes of a more personal nature. In these matters as well, Gálvez was better known for a firm hand than a diplomatic mien. In one such instance, the intendant brought charges against don José Sabido de Vargas, the teniente del rey, for his alleged mishandling of a dispute between the militia colonel don Ignacio Rodríguez de la Gala and various officers under his command, including the sergeant major don Rafael Bresón.[27] Usually, a teniente del rey was closely allied with the intendant, but Sabido de Vargas saw the intendant's attempt to mediate as an affront to his public reputation and standing and never forgave him. Insulted honor brought long-standing rancor. A desire to have their honor restored drove men like the teniente del rey to verbally attack Gálvez and nurse grudges against their superior. Sabido de Vargas, who later obstructed prosecutors' progress in pursuing likely leads regarding the assassin's identity, had begun a campaign to exculpate himself by writing letters to the crown objecting to his punishment at the time of Gálvez's death.[28]

Sabido de Vargas's reaction was not uncommon. Minor military matters of discipline metastasized into battalion-wide conflicts and unforgivable stains upon male honor at the personal level. Such slights were not easily overlooked. In a seemingly inconsequential matter, Gálvez chastised two officers for profligate spending on uniforms for the Infantry Battalion of Castile. In what developed into a prolonged dispute over questions of personal integrity as much as financial management, Capt. don Juan José de la Valle and Lt. Col. don Juan O'Sullivan wrote to Madrid in 1790 to defend themselves against charges made by Gálvez and the resulting harm to their reputations.[29] Taints to family honor were not borne lightly, however.

Although the military was an overwhelmingly masculine sphere, women became involved in such questions of honor on occasion. In March 1792, doña María de la Luz de Peña y Aguirre, together with prominent relatives who had served as governors and *oidores* (judges) of the Audiencia de Mexico, wrote to the crown to protest the intendant's treatment of her husband, Sergeant Bresón, in a matter separate from his falling out with Sabido de Vargas. Gálvez brought charges against the sergeant in this separate incident for irregularities in his handling of the battalion's funds. In this case, a reprimand over a minor fiscal matter of a middling Spanish officer became a family-wide question of honor.[30]

These and other complaints lodged by military men and their allies against Gálvez, many of them unresolved at the time of the intendant's death, point to the widespread, yet far from universal, disaffection in the ranks of Yucatan's military men with their commander-in-chief.[31] The Bourbon reforms led to the growth, reorganization, and increasing prominence of the military in the second half of the eighteenth century, which mitigated against full-blown animosity directed toward don Lucas. Yucatan in particular saw increased royal efforts to strengthen its defenses in response to territorial encroachment and economic challenges from the British in the form of a logging settlement in Belize and widespread trade in contraband goods.[32] Resulting reforms led to increasing diversification and specialization among the Americas' armed forces. Organized army battalions directly under the Spanish crown (though rarely composed entirely of peninsulares) grew in number. More rigor and specialization was introduced into the long-established local militias. The reliance upon indigenous militiamen also declined, as the much more disciplined free black militias eclipsed their relatively disorganized ranks. The vast majority of the resistance Gálvez faced came from creole officers in the white militias and battalions of Castile.

Such rivalries often involved more than straightforward questions of military discipline. They also resulted from perceived harm to the professional reputations of Gálvez's antagonists, who often hated him for more deeply personal reasons. Moreover, the tendency of leading families to place their young men in a variety of governmental, military, and ecclesiastical posts meant that the intendant rarely took on one political faction—the military, the encomenderos, the local government, or the clergy—alone. One aggrieved faction nearly always had a close relative in one of the other power blocs. Deeply personal matters—romantic, in this case—and the blurring of lines between two powerful factions, was best personified by don Toribio del Mazo, militia officer and nephew of the bishop of Mérida. His powerful uncle, Bp. fray Luis de Piña y Mazo (r. 1780–1795), who outlasted three governors and often had more influence in Madrid than the secular royal officials, fought tenaciously to preserve ecclesiastical privileges, the latest chapter in a power struggle between church and state that had long divided the province. Animated by matters of jurisdiction and ecclesiastical immunity as much as military rank and romantic rivalries, the bishop and his nephew were the most high profile of all the intendant's antagonists.

Following the bishop's lead, most of Yucatan's clergymen also opposed Gálvez. His faction was a powerful one. Even an ally close to fray Luis, the resident surgeon don Antonio de Poveda, who tended to the cleric during the prolonged illness in the final years of his life, noted that the bishop long had the ability to "ruin governors" and rarely hesitated to do so.[33] By contrast, Gálvez initially held only the position of intendant—not governor—in his first two years as the head of the province, a rather anomalous situation.[34] Gálvez spent these years watching his predecessor in the post of governor, don José de Merino y Ceballos (r. 1783–1789), ousted as a result of the machinations of the province's most prominent prelate.[35] The bishop of Mérida, along with several members of the cabildo, saw their efforts pay off in the form of a royal order recalling Merino y Ceballos to Spain, dated 13 October 1788.[36] Gálvez's path to the governorship was opened, but three of Yucatan's prominent friars—including the former Franciscan provincial fray Fernando Murciano and his successor, fray Antonio Maldonado—sided with Merino y Ceballos to oppose Gálvez's succession.[37] These three men, friars in the influential Franciscan order, were lifelong enemies of the intendant.

The bishop, who supported Gálvez's appointment only as far as it helped him undermine Merino y Ceballos, soon turned on the young intendant. From the time of his 1780 arrival in Mérida until his death in 1795, fray Luis, a peninsular Benedictine friar, had indeed "ruined" the careers of two former governors: Merino y Ceballos and his predecessor, don Roberto de Rivas Betancourt (r. 1779–1783). With a term of service that outlasted two governors and a demonstrated ability to drive at least two of them from office (and maybe a third, by violence, according to a popular rumor), the irascible churchman exercised authority in an array of matters that had little to do with affairs of the church. He intervened in militia assignments and jurisdictional disputes between the governor and regidores of Mérida's cabildo.[38] He frequently wrote letters that included a litany of complaints about the two governors that drew the ire of their superiors, Carlos III and the most prominent and powerful Gálvez, the visitador don José, Marqués de Sonora.[39] One witness wrote that Rivas Betancourt, Merino y Ceballos, and the intendant all ended their careers disgraced or dead at the bishop's urging—or at least his acquiescence in the last case, according to some witnesses.[40]

In dealing with governors, intendants, and other royal officials at a time when the tide was turning against ecclesiastical authority, fray Luis turned to one of the tactics that still mattered: excommunication. Francisco Heredía de Vergara, a militia lieutenant, testified in 1795 that fray Luis's character inclined him to dominate all Yucatecans and especially to subjugate the royal justices through the threat of excommunication. In at least three cases he had carried through with his threats, excommunicating a councilman of Mérida's cabildo, a militia officer, and don José Sabido de Vargas, who, in addition to serving as *teniente del gobernador* (lieutenant governor), was a colonel of the Royal Army.[41] The militia officer, don Ignacio Rendon, earned the ire of the bishop for failing to promote the unqualified nephew of the bishop, don Toribio del Mazo. Excommunication may have been one of the few weapons still feared in the episcopal arsenal, and fray Luis had no reservations about deploying it.[42]

The bishop was as heavy-handed in his approach to matters of popular piety as he was with governors over issues of church power. Without crown approval, in 1780 the bishop began to confiscate the wealth of the *cofradías* (religious sodalities responsible for mutual aid, charity, and annual festivals) of Maya pueblos. This placed him in direct conflict with the governor at the time, Rivas Betancourt. By directly administering the finances of the Maya cofradías, the bishop boosted church revenues while devastating the economic stability and independence of the pueblos. The revocation of the cofradías' autonomy dealt a severe blow to Maya elites and community solidarity.[43] The bishop did not complete this ambitious project. Rivas Betancourt, acting in his capacity as the head of the General Indian Court of Yucatan (usually referred to simply as the Indian Court, or the Juzgado de Indios), first took action to stop the expropriation only after the landholdings of approximately two-thirds of the cofradías had been taken from the pueblos.[44] Once more, fray Luis perceived the actions of the province's secular ruler as an affront to his position as the true head of the province.

The cofradía controversy was just one of the disputes that continued to simmer after the departure of Gálvez's predecessors. No single issue set the bishop against the intendant; rather, a deep philosophical divide over the balance between ecclesiastical authority and royal rule set Yucatan's two most powerful men on an inevitable collision course. In practice, disagreements over the appointment of subdelegados (a newly created position intended to bring more oversight to the countryside), the governor's meddling in marriages of prominent creole families, and the bishop's public criticisms of the intendant emerged as points of contention between the two men.[45] The cofradía issue hampered half-hearted attempts at reconciliation. A letter reprinted in Crescencio Carrillo y Ancona's history of Yucatan's bishops notes Gálvez's opposition to the confiscation of cofradía coffers, which fray Luis justified by publicly declaring that the funds would support the founding of grammar schools headed by rural priests. The bishop's grand project for rural parochial schools never came to fruition.[46] A detailed valuation of his estate upon his death shows that it was not for a lack of funds.[47]

In a related dispute, both don Lucas and fray Luis claimed the right to appoint teachers in the few schools that were founded.[48]

Rivalries ran deeper than simple rifts over the role of royal secular authorities pitted against clergymen jealous of their own privileges. Personal animosities exacerbated their ideological struggle. Letters written by both the bishop and the intendant to the Audiencia of Mexico during the year before Gálvez's assassination suggest that reconciliation was unlikely. In a letter dated 30 January 1792, the intendant decried the bishop's publication of an edict critical of the royal magistrates. In language that echoed his predecessors' failed defense of their administration of Yucatan, the intendant railed against the bishop's "usurpations of jurisdiction."[49] In a seemingly prescient tone, Gálvez warned that any successor faced inevitable conflict with fray Luis. For the bishop's part, the message of a letter he wrote to the viceroy on 8 April 1791 lent credibility to Gálvez's complaints that the bishop arrogated his authority in the province. The bishop criticized Gálvez's appointments of several subdelegados who he saw as unsuitable, a matter that clearly fell under the auspices of crown administrators. He took specific issue with Gálvez's rejection of a candidate for the post that the bishop had supported.[50] Gálvez's approach was in line with the aims of the Bourbon monarchs, especially the anticlerical aims of Carlos III. In Yucatan, the conflict was as intense as anywhere else. The first intendant wrote to the crown during his final years, observing that the priests fought a "war" against the "ministers of the king."[51] Fray Luis also claimed to have the ultimate word in a few rulings made by Gálvez in matters that had traditionally been left to the church: a case of idolatry in Teabo and a dispensation for marriage granted to don José Boves, a suitor of one of the daughters of the powerful Quijano family, against the wishes of the influential patriarch of the clan and his sons (her brothers), who occupied high posts in Mérida's military, economic, municipal, and ecclesiastical hierarchy. For different reasons, neither the bishop nor the Quijanos ever forgave this intrusive meddling in a matter that, by most standards, lay well beyond the bounds of an intendant's authority.[52]

Nineteenth-century historians Molina Solís and Ancona, both born within a generation of Gálvez's death, noted the unyielding approach to authority that alienated many members of Yucatan's upper echelon even in minor matters.[53] His popularity with the lower-status urban residents—the artisans of creole, casta, and Maya ancestry—was markedly better. In Gálvez's own words, in a letter seeking promotion to the rank of brigadier, the intendant claimed that he had contributed to the happiness of the province, alleviated the sufferings of the natives, and saved money for the royal treasury.[54] The actions of Gálvez, an archetypical Bourbon reformer, do in fact demonstrate the multifaceted nature of the eighteenth-century policy adjustments in the territories under the rule of Spain's Bourbons. Not all changes on the ground were harmful to the native population, the majority in Yucatan. Identifying the five major aims of the Bourbon reforms, one notable historian of the eighteenth century noted that along with administrative efficiency, economic development, regulated and reliable revenues, and a reinforced military, Carlos III's agents of change also sought to effect an improvement to the well-being of the lower strata of society.[55] Labeling this era a "Second Conquest" takes a narrow view of the vast project and the various adjustments it went through under the Bourbons.[56] It speaks volumes that the major opponents of Gálvez, and the eventual prime suspects in his murder, came from creole and peninsular backgrounds. As will be shown in later chapters, Maya speakers proved most ready to provide testimony against the likeliest suspect—a peninsular—while his creole allies were much more reticent. Indeed, as a result of the public works and reforms directed toward the Maya majority, few seriously suspected that any members of the rural poor or urban workers harbored any resentment for the intendant, much less any provocation serious enough to inspire murder. But the intendant's occasional meddling in popular festivals did dampen the public's enthusiasm for him. Gálvez's support for the heavy-handed approach of don Juan José de Fierros—then a lieutenant of the battalion of Castile, who broke up a noisy celebration of Our Lady of Pilar in the La Mejorada neighborhood—led to formal complaints to the crown.[57] Gálvez's intolerance of local customs irritated some members of the popular classes who were accustomed to official tolerance of their distinctive ceremonies, processions, and celebrations. However, much of the public had an overall favorable opinion of the intendant. Anyone who hated him enough to want him dead came from elite families.

"Bad Government": Apathy at the Top, Scapegoats at the Bottom

The post of intendant itself developed as a Spanish adaptation of a position that was one of the main innovations of the enlightened absolutism of the Bourbon monarchs. Based on French precedents, Philip V implemented the intendancy system in Spain with guidance from his long-reigning grand-father, the arch-absolutist, Louis XIV of France.[58] Intendancies were first introduced in Spain in 1718 with authority over the *cuatro causas*, or traditional divisions of power in Spanish law: *justicia* (law and legislation), *policia* (local taxes and security), *hacienda* (taxes and revenue), and *guerra* (military administration).[59] Under the Habsburgs, one administrator rarely wielded such broad authority. Before the Ordenanza de Intendentes gave administrators sweeping power over such matters at an intermediate level, authority over the duties entailed by the cuatro causas was in the hands of a more diffuse set of councils and administrators.[60] The introduction of intendants in the Americas came much later as part of a piecemeal process. First introduced to exposed frontiers of the Americas to centralize royal administration in defensive weak points, intendants were appointed to Cuba and Louisiana in 1764 and 1765, respectively.[61] The influential royal inspector (*visitador*) don José de Gálvez, related by a common fifteenth-century ancestor to don Lucas, improvised a workable plan to introduce intendants in frontier areas. Critical support and innovation for an application of the intendancy system also came from the viceroy, Marqués de Croix (Carlos Francisco de Croix). The two coauthored the *Informe y plan de intendencias* in 1768, which led to the creation of intendants for the Californias and the northern provinces of Sinaloa, Sonora, and Nueva Vizcaya. By the time Carlos III introduced the intendancy system to the rest of New Spain with the Real Ordenanza de Intendentes of 1786, the reorganization had already been introduced to the whole of Spanish South America, starting with Venezuela in 1776 and the Viceroyalty of La Plata in 1782.[62] Between the French Bourbons' early seventeenth-century experimentation with absolutist officials known as intendants and the introduction of administrators bearing the same name in New Spain in 1786 and after, Carlos III adopted enlightened absolutism with renewed vigor. In the Americas, intendants headed the new personnel, tightening control in the hands of loyal administrators, further limiting the autonomy and reducing the influence of creole elites.

The Decree of Intendants bolstered the power of provincial authorities at the expense of both long-standing rivals of royal authority and many of the more traditional agents of royal authority. Viceroys, representatives of the monarchs in the Americas, were weakened by a doubling of their numbers and a corresponding division of territory and the transfer of many of their powers to intendants.[63] Moreover, the effort to rationalize rule led Bourbon monarchs to transfer many of the duties involved in the oversight of provincial matters to the intendants, who answered directly to Madrid rather than to their superiors based in viceregal capitals. Reorienting lines of authority to the crown more directly shifted power to the intendants. In a province where the local elite jealously guarded local privilege and the church still wielded unparalleled power, don Lucas de Gálvez personified many of the characteristics that prominent Yucatecans resented. Gálvez and other intendants confronted a "hostile public opinion" as they attempted to carry out the royal will from their respective administrative capitals.[64]

Crown magistrates and cabildo members showed remarkably little interest in uncovering the identity of Gálvez's assassin in the days that followed his death, a sign of just how deep the acrimony ran against the deceased intendant. Notable absences at his funeral gave the first indication of how little respect his rivals had for him, demonstrated in their refusal to attend the last ceremony in the province for the man they so deeply despised. Most conspicuously, don José Sabido de Vargas, the teniente del rey and next in line to the seat of power in Yucatan, defiantly stayed at his post in Campeche for four days after notice of his predecessor's death had reached him, later offering a variety of excuses for his nonattendance.[65] One witness declared that the teniente del rey prioritized attending the feast day of Saint John on 24 June, with friends in Campeche over departing for Mérida in the wake of the assassination.[66] Captain Fierros, a close friend and ally of don Lucas, acerbically noted that the teniente del rey did not contribute one pen stroke to the judicial process of uncovering the assassin's identity and spent ten or twelve days after Gálvez's death socializing with the intendant's enemies in Campeche.[67] Other witnesses reported that Sabido de Vargas had calmly received news of his superior's death with the muttered observation that Gálvez's "execution" was a natural consequence of "bad government."[68] With the line of succession interrupted, the lieutenant governor, don Fernando de Gutiérrez de Piñeres, temporarily took the reins of government, an unconventional step recorded in his letter to the viceroy on 25 June 1792. Piñeres (as he appears in the trial transcripts) had no intention of usurping power, but Sabido de Vargas's failure to report for duty in Mérida disrupted the process of orderly succession and left Piñeres at the head of a new and foreign province.[69]

Piñeres had been on good terms with the intendant but had little appetite for questioning Gálvez's numerous enemies, the most pressing duty for the successor of an assassinated intendant and governor whose killer was still at large. His aptitude for legal matters was lacking and he had little support from many of the magistrates who reported directly to him—men whose talents and familiarity with the province were necessary for the recently arrived young peninsular magistrate. Intimidation no doubt played a part in his ambivalent pursuit of the assassin. Lic. Piñeres did not dare to pursue the most probable candidates for the assassination: men from leading families whose penchant for violence undoubtedly deterred the young administrator who had broken with protocol regarding the line of succession to take power in a leaderless province. During the first days and weeks after the assassination, Piñeres and his assistants only half-heartedly pursued the incriminating leads strongly suggestive of the assassin's origins in Mérida's upper crust—influential and entrenched men who had openly threatened to kill Gálvez in the hearing of numerous witnesses. Instead, Piñeres's closest assistants pursued tenuous rumors linking the murder to Mérida's poorest and most vulnerable residents—as well as outsiders to the province—in spite of the absolute lack of any reasonable motive on the part of those suspects. The breakdown of effective government left Piñeres incapable of imprisoning and questioning far likelier culprits. Instead, he focused on Mérida's urban plebe, the easiest scapegoats. An impromptu measure that restricted travel between Mérida and the surrounding pueblos in the immediate aftermath of the assassination unwittingly contributed to the targeting of the most rootless and transient Yucatecans, regardless of likelihood of guilt, complicity, or any knowledge of the culprits in the assassination.

CHAPTER 3

The Suspects of 1792

Prosecuting the Powerless

~&

~& ONCE THE NIGHT WATCHMEN ON DUTY ON 22 JUNE 1792 FAILED TO find the assassin, after combing the city's central streets early the next morning, Lic. Piñeres commanded his subordinates to distribute official public notices requiring all travelers between Mérida and surrounding pueblos to carry official permissions with them at all times sanctioning such movement. The *bandos* proclaiming the emergency measure were published in both Spanish and Yucatec Maya and posted on all of the major routes leading from Mérida into the countryside or to Campeche.[1] Such travel restrictions led to the first arrests, as enemies with long-standing personal vendettas took advantage of the wide net prosecutors cast to denounce their foes despite their absolute innocence in the killing. The confusing and inconsistent testimony of key witnesses regarding the night of the murder led to even more arrests. Household workers, soldiers, artisans, laborers, and orphaned and ostracized outsiders were the first suspects and material witnesses apprehended. Their crimes usually amounted to little more than being in the wrong place at the wrong time, changing their testimony in the face of pressure and intimidation by their interrogators, having no one to testify as to their whereabouts on the night of the murder, or simply having a reputation for previous criminal activity. Some witnesses blatantly accused their rivals of complicity in the killing to settle personal scores, easy to do during the heightened state of alert that led to at least a short-term imprisonment of their antagonists. Of the suspects and material witnesses incarcerated during the first three months after the assassination, only one had any firsthand connection to the case: a quick glimpse of and a brief conversation with the servant of the man who would later emerge as the prime suspect. While the assassins walked freely through Mérida, one witness remained imprisoned for more than four years, held only for repeatedly changing his testimony in an absolutely failed effort to appease his interrogators.

The bandos, distributed to the local authorities, subdelegados, jueces espa-ñoles, *cabos militares*, caciques, and justicias (Maya cabildo officers) ordered creole and Maya municipal authorities to monitor the entrances to the pueblos within their jurisdiction and apprehend any traveler caught without a license.[2] Although Piñeres ordered their immediate promulgation, local administrators along Yucatan's recently repaired and widened highways (a project champi-oned by the deceased intendant) did not always promptly post the notices. Many of those who unwittingly disobeyed the decree restricting movement had no idea that they were traveling in violation of any law, but the rigorous restrictions regarding travel to and from the city led to some of the first arrests.[3] The suspects of 1792—mostly men and a few women—came from Maya, mes-tizo, Afro-Yucatecan, and low-status Spanish backgrounds and were a multi-racial set of prisoners. Prosecutors exhaustively examined and described eight of them by profession, race, age, and residence: two mestizo butchers, three Maya men living near the center of the city, the sister-in-law of one of the three men, and two pardos (a painter and a fisherman). Two others were Spanish, including a peninsular grenadier identified only by his last name and a reputed cattle thief. A servant of the bishop's medical doctor and a manager of a haci-enda, as well as four other men who appear only as names and time served on a list of prisoners, were not identified by race.[4] Most of the early suspects worked in skilled trades—as artisans, ranch hands, and fishermen—or held low-level military posts. Economically, they lived better than the subsistence farmers or *milperos* of the countryside and unfree domestic workers of the city. Urban workers' marginally better incomes also afforded them more indepen-dence than the slaves and *criados*, unpaid child and adolescent laborers "adopted" into Spanish households to perform unpaid domestic tasks.[5] This relative autonomy often went hand in hand with more freedom of mobility, and their jobs often required frequent travel. Such movement, unfortunately, also caught the attention of authorities looking for even remotely suspicious behavior in the days following the assassination.

Middling Yucatecans who were first arrested came from a class of men who were the easiest targets for colonial agents of the law. The first twenty-one prisoners were better off economically and had more freedom than rural peasants and urban slaves and criados. However, they were outranked by the city's literate professionals: high-level artisans, priests, bureaucrats, officers, and merchants. They were from diverse backgrounds—Mayas, low-level creoles, mestizos, and Afro-Yucatecans. Unlike the better-off, mostly creole professional class, most of them lacked any legal privileges. In their interaction with the courts and agents of the law, they were the Yucatecans most vulnerable to prosecution and imprisonment. This resulted from their alienation from judicial corporate bodies, basic colonial social units that profoundly shaped a subject's legal status in courts of the time period. For instance, although rural Maya campesinos depended upon the unpredictable yearly yield of their milpas for their staples of life, a tenuous existence exacerbated by their heavy tax burdens, they belonged to a well-defined legal body: the Maya pueblo, or the república de indios. This provided some measure of protection from the worst of the harsh punishments commonly meted out in Yucatan. Some rural Mayas had even more legal guarantees of jurisdictional exemptions, tax breaks, and exceptions to sumptuary laws. Such privileges were granted to indios hidalgos, caciques, and justicias who descended from pre-Columbian nobles or ancestors who fought as indigenous allies of conquistadors. This gave them an inherited status above that of the Maya majority in terms of taxes, conspicuous consumption, and legal standing. Not a single Maya from the indigenous pueblo government or with claims to hidalgo status was imprisoned during the entirety of the investigation into the intendant's assassination.

Afro-Yucatecans also suffered imprisonment and interrogation disproportionately. Racial bias no doubt contributed to the high percentage of Afro-Yucatecans imprisoned on flimsy or nonexistent evidence in connection with Gálvez's homicide. However, race was far from the only factor in a subject's encounters with colonial justice. Afro-Yucatecans improved their standing before the law through militia service or affiliation with a prominent household. In much greater numbers than during the previous century, free black officers and soldiers benefited from the much broader application of the protections granted under the *fuero militar* (a privileged legal status granted to officers and enlisted men guaranteeing trial in a usually more lenient military tribunal for most crimes) and an eighteenth-century trend toward a more inclusive interpretation that offered legal coverage to the traditional officer class as well as the rank-and-file militiamen—black, white, and mestizo. Informally, but very effectively, working and residing in an elite Spaniard's home protected many black slaves and Afro-Yucatecan servants against prosecutors' attempts to jail and interrogate them.[6]

Marginal Yucatecans, prominent among those arrested during the phase of the investigation supervised by Lic. Piñeres, appear frequently in trial transcripts, although they are elusive in other types of documents. Because of their lack of significant transferrable wealth and limited literacy, they appear rarely in notarial documents registering property such as wills; records of transactions; correspondence between clergymen, bureaucrats, and prominent citizens; official decrees; affirmations of hereditary privileges; and military paperwork. Court records flesh out the lives of Yucatan's unseen urban and rural wageworkers and craftsmen—its butchers, carpenters, fishermen, coachmen, painters, soldiers, and ranch hands. While the information prosecutors gathered concerning this stratum of Yucatecans is incredibly useful for reconstructing a social history of the late eighteenth century, prosecutors never found any substantial evidence implicating any of the suspects of 1792 in the death of the intendant.

The sweep that followed the assassination uncovered a variety of petty criminals, marginal figures, and miscreants engaged in mildly suspicious behavior, as well as other, completely innocent unfortunates, but nothing suggested that any of them had the audacity or motive to undertake a crime as grave as killing the province's top royal official. One group may have drawn attention due to the heightened tensions in an insurrectionary era and the ties of one member to the epicenter of revolution: France. Three young servants—Pablo Canto, Matías Mayén, and Juan Bautista Chandé—caught in the city's cemetery (or in an exterior corridor of the sacristy of the Church of San Juan, according to another report) at the time of the murder were briefly imprisoned and interrogated on 23 June.[7] Prosecutors never explained what they were doing there. Chandé, described in the summary of the case as "appearing to be of French nationality," likely triggered misgivings on the part of prosecutors due in part to the fear of all things French in the last decade of the eighteenth century.[8] In the late 1700s, French origins raised the specter of insurrectionary conspiracies. In fact, in 1795 New Spain's viceroy, the Marqués de Branciforte, ordered an exhaustive enumeration of all French nationals residing in the viceroyalty, followed by an expulsion of those suspected of subversion. Twenty-one French nationals resided in Yucatan. Only two, Juan Lagrava and Pedro Gaviot, were expelled.[9]

Others were targeted for prosecution because of their reputation for criminal behavior or vendettas on the part of the anonymous informants who went to the authorities to suggest a connection to the crime. In a separate incident, don Joaquín José de Castro, a notary involved in the early years of the investigation, testified that José Bermejo, another prisoner, was a drunk and a cattle thief. Despite the lack of any plausible motive for killing the intendant and no record of animosity toward Gálvez, the notary's allusions to Bermejo's sordid past served as a pretext for his imprisonment.[10] Two mestizo butchers, Antonio and Isidro Medina, had done nothing more than live and work temporarily at Bermejo's house, butchering and selling cattle owned by Bermejo and his wife. Yet this was enough for the prosecution to jail them alongside Bermejo on 23 June.[11] To the north of Mérida, along Yucatan's coast, the mayordomo (overseer) of the Hacienda de Santa María near Dzemul, Pedro Ferrera, sat in jail in Telchac for an indeterminate period. His imprisonment likely stemmed from nothing more than a personal grudge on the part of the soldier who arrested him.[12] Only two witnesses, two additional hands on the hacienda, testified regarding Ferrera's whereabouts on 22 and 23 June. Both confirmed his alibi: he never strayed from the hacienda during the days surrounding Gálvez's death.[13]

The prosecution took little note of the suspects arbitrarily rounded up and briefly imprisoned during the first week after the killing, but a fourth set of witnesses—a group of four Mayas residing near the city center—received much more attention as a result of their firsthand glimpse of a man later believed to be an accomplice to the murder and their heated exchange with him in front of their home. This round of interrogations led to the long-term incarceration of one of the neighbors and an accused accomplice whose alleged involvement in the crime rested upon the testimony of one of the four. Luis Lara, one of the four witnesses who worked for a Spanish widow as a coachman, and a pardo painter and sculptor, Ignacio Matos, were each imprisoned for more than three years.

Lara's difficulties began when María Ventura, a criada who served in the home of don Pedro Rafael Pastrana, mentioned to her master that Lara, a neighbor of her brother, had confronted a "mozo," or young servant, tending a horse on the night of the murder.[14] María and four other eyewitnesses had seen a man, hooded and holding a horse by the reins, outside the house at 10:30 p.m., immediately before the assassination. Lara and the Maya shoemaker Francisco Ek, owner of the house next to the Ventura residence, both confronted the man. Josefa García, the Venturas' sister-in-law, also witnessed the heated exchange.

Ek, Lara's landlord and coworker, and neighbors Luis Ventura and Josefa García, claimed that Lara had the closest look at the young man. Lic. Piñeres noted that the young criado's testimony differed from the testimony of the three other witnesses. Because of the discrepancies, Piñeres jailed all four on 25 June because of their conflicting accounts about the man they saw and spoke with outside Ek's home. Ek, Ventura, and García were released a day later, but Lara's account contained so many inconsistencies that prosecutors kept him behind bars for further questioning. Details Lara provided regarding the physical features of the man with the horse, the man's profession, and his place of origin changed almost every time prosecutors questioned him. He initially said he did not clearly see the man because of the darkness. Next he claimed he had recognized the man as a cattle butcher or *vendedor de suela*, a vendor of low-grade meat and leather, and that he identified him by his voice and a mole on his cheek.[15] Still later he said that the mole was on the man's nose. To clear up the confusion, the prosecution arranged two lineups of suspects that included all of Mérida's cattle butchers, tanners, and vendedores de suela. Lara did not recognize any of them.

Finding themselves at a dead end, prosecutors heading the case in 1792 began to fabricate evidence and tamper with the sole witness they believed had given them their only likely lead. By this point, the investigators blatantly had begun to search for a scapegoat, not a probable suspect. Lara's inconsistency and susceptibility to recant his prior declarations enabled the prosecution team to ensnare the pardo Ignacio Matos. Matos had traveled to Mérida at an inopportune moment to sell a small parcel of land in Mérida's Barrio de Santiago. During most of the year, he resided in distant Maxcanú while working in the nearby pueblo of Calkiní. Don Victoriano Cantón, juez español of Uman, jailed him based only on the order to apprehend and imprison anyone who had left Mérida without a license from the government, not due to any suspicions of wrongdoing. A later prosecutor noted that the bandos were posted on 28 June 1792, three days *after* Matos's arrest.[16]

After the first two lineups of suspects produced no results, prosecutors conducted a third that included Matos. They broke with normal protocol in their unconcealed efforts to pin the crime on Matos by any means; to reveal a mole on Matos's face that his beard usually covered, the prosecutors shaved him, then guided Lara by the cell where Matos was imprisoned. Directing Lara's gaze toward Matos, they asked him if it was possible that he had seen the pardo painter holding the horse on the night of the murder.[17] Lara affirmed that he had.

Lara obviously altered his version of events under the prosecutors' pressure. Once Lara's testimony had served its purposes, the prosecution team conveniently forgot about him. Yet those same inconsistencies—"variations" as they were called in the trial transcripts—were the justification for his long incarceration. For repeatedly changing his testimony, the unfortunate Maya coachman served a total of four and a half years in jail. The other unlucky suspect who suffered from Lara's rapidly changing testimony served a disproportionately long sentence as well. In spite of the fact that Matos's prison sentence stemmed from nothing more than Lara's inconsistent testimony, he spent a total of three and a half years in prison. The miscarriage of justice was obvious: as early as 22 August 1792, Piñeres had written that the charges against Matos and another pardo suspect, Rafael Luna, amounted to nothing more than conjecture.[18] Only years later did an outside prosecutor free him. Matos was released on 17 February 1795. Lara won his freedom on 17 December 1796.[19]

The uncharacteristically long sentences these two men served, strangers before the assassination but irrevocably linked to each other by Lara's constantly changing version of events, underscores the vulnerability of Yucatan's free workers as they entered the legal arena of the colonial court system. Movement between one's home and work, which often involved travel between pueblos or between Mérida and the countryside, invited scrutiny. Absent from most documents, these transitory working men and women of Yucatan appear frequently in court records, though rarely in other forms of colonial documentation. The exhaustive inquiries into the lives of the early suspects and witnesses in the cause célèbre of 1792, then, shed new light on the individual lives, family networks, and communal organizations of the kind of colonial subjects often missing from the historical record. The biographical backgrounds of individuals like Matos and Lara add depth to the rough sketches of Mérida's wageworkers, artisans, servants, and soldiers while calling into question some long-held notions about colonial Yucatan's social history. Most of all, the wide variety of sentences and treatments of suspects and witnesses from this class strongly hints at an underappreciated range of judicial conditions and legal know-how by individuals long viewed as part of an undifferentiated plebe.

Suspects from this first year were just as susceptible to rumors and denigrations of their reputation as later defendants. What courts dismiss today as hearsay and gossip weighed heavily upon the judgments meted out in colonial courts. In spite of the flimsiness of the evidence, Matos's alleged role in the murder gained currency in popular rumors that circulated far and wide. In Veracruz, an unnamed ship captain reported to that province's governor that a "mulatto painter" with the last name of Matos had been tending a horse at the gate of the home of a shoemaker on the night of the murder. According to this third-hand account, the murder weapon had been discovered among Matos's possessions.[20] Rumors of this nature no doubt contributed to the long and unjustified imprisonment of a man who had no connection to the crime.

Matos was not the only Afro-Yucatecan who suffered imprisonment based on rumors. Acting on the bando's orders, don Cristóbal de la Cámara arrested Rafael Luna, a pardo apprehended for traveling through the territory under his jurisdiction within the Partido de la Costa without a license on 30 June 1792. As the slow wheels of the Spanish bureaucracy turned, the interrogation of Luna began in Mérida on 28 July.[21] Luna, held for three months, had fled through the backyard of his landlady's house when authorities moved to arrest him for an unrelated incident.[22] Neither his flight nor his apprehension by local authorities had anything to do with Gálvez's violent end. Instead, both Luna and his pursuers recognized that his status as a suspect stemmed only from his fear and subsequent flight from a confrontation with local law enforcement agents over his adulterous affair with his married landlady.

Luna drew the attention of authorities for having previously evaded arrest for another matter: his "illicit friendship" with Juana Llanos, his landlady and the wife of his employer, Ignacio Nagera.[23] A militia lieutenant, don José Pérez, had heard rumors from a number of people of the adultery (or "concubinage," according to the sources) committed by Luna (who was also married), which prompted Pérez to attempt to arrest him.[24] Luna had already escaped from don José Ignacio Bautista, the juez español of Panabá, who tried to apprehend him in May.[25] This evasion of arrest did more harm than Luna could have imagined. Taken into custody after the assassination of Gálvez, Luna's exact whereabouts at the time of the intendant's death were unknown, leading to more intensive scrutiny and a longer jail term than he would have suffered for simply carrying on an affair with his boss's wife. Don Cristóbal de la Cámara, subdelegado of Tizimín, managed to catch up with Luna in Tizimín and sent him to Mérida for interrogation, until he was cleared of any connection with the assassination.[26] All witnesses, even those who provided lurid details of Luna's illicit romance, concurred that he could not have been in Mérida on the night of the murder.[27] After three months of imprisonment, Lic. Piñeres finally freed Luna on 3 October 1792.[28] The lieutenant governor admonished him to bypass Tizimín, Panabá, or Rio Lagartos en route to his home in Laguna de Terminos to live a court-ordered honest life with his wife.[29]

Afro-Yucatecans and the Law

Rafael Luna and Ignacio Matos differed in the stability of their employment and residence, with Matos living a relatively more established existence compared with Luna's wandering ways. A skilled artisan with family ties to Mérida, Matos traveled anywhere his abilities were needed while keeping in touch with his kin in Mérida. Matos's journeys to visit relatives and sell a small property to pay off a debt were viewed as legitimate, legal activities, but prosecutors and judges frowned on Luna's peregrinations. He made his living by fishing—a less prestigious job, but one that entailed regular travel between coastal towns. While bias against blacks no doubt played a part in the groundless apprehension of these two pardos in connection with Gálvez's assassination, justices and magistrates also perceived their job-related geographic mobility as transience and vagrancy. Under questioning regarding his whereabouts in the previous months, Luna told his interrogators that he went to Tizimín to attend the fiesta of San Pedro, where the subdelegado imprisoned him.[30] Lic. Piñeres tore into the Luna with the first question, a charge not included in the interrogations of other defendants: "What vices do you have that have caused you to be idle for such a long time?"[31]

Matos's and Luna's incarcerations point to the probability that racial bias had some impact on how magistrates and attorneys of the Spanish colonial courts viewed suspects. Their presence among the first suspects imprisoned for relatively long sentences—one for having had rotten luck in timing his travel and the other for an adulterous affair—seems to indicate that Afro-Yucatecans suffered the harshest punishments of colonial justice. Matos clearly had a relatively high status for a pardo, owning property in both Mérida and Maxcanú and having been commissioned to work on specialized projects, such as a retablo, or altarpiece, in Calkiní. Luna lived a more marginal existence. But both seemed absolutely defenseless before the law. This legal vulnerability was not as common on the part of Mérida's free black population as might be expected, however. Matos's long list of friends and relatives included officers and soldiers of the pardo militia corps. Other pardo militia officers briefly appear in the trial transcripts as witnesses and possible accomplices. The far more respectful treatment they received, taken together with contemporaneous cases involving defendants who were pardo militia officers, demonstrates that militia service significantly improved the legal standing of free Afro-Yucatecans.

Economic standing and respectability did not help the trial's most prominent Afro-Yucatecan defendant in court. As prosecutors pored over Matos's travels, family, work, and friendships, a picture of a respectable, tenuously middle-class free black subject emerges. At the time of his arrest, Matos was working on an altarpiece for Father Commissioner fray Francisco Rodríguez, Calkiní's top Franciscan.[32] In addition to painting and sculpting, Matos also worked at times as a gilder, a specialized craft considered a "highstatus" artisanal profession.[33] Questioned intensively regarding his personal associations, Matos listed a white militia corporal and a brother of the leading Franciscan of Calkiní among his friends. His three closest friends were respectable residents of Maxcanú: Juan José Mayor, his compadre and a corporal in the Eighth Company of the white volunteer militia; don José Rafael Rodríguez, the brother of the father commissioner; and a fellow sculptor, Pedro Escalante, his business partner. All of them stated that Matos had no violent tendencies, had never possessed a knife resembling the murder weapon, and had always made a modest but reliable living with his own hands.[34] Other respectable locals—such as white militia corporal don Felix Antonio Bolio, interpreter don Blas Torres, and juez español don Esteban de Sosa—knew him well enough to state without a doubt that he had never owned a knife nor had ever owned any of the clothes that the murderer supposedly wore. Prosecutors linked him to only two minor infractions: the evasion of a tax on his sale of land in Mérida (an action recommended to him by the *cabo de justicia* of the Barrio of Santiago) and a small outstanding debt to the senior priest of Maxcanú, Dr. don José González, which he intended to pay off with the proceeds from the sale of his unused urban property.[35] In spite of his respectable status, Matos's plight highlights how even middleclass blacks fared poorly in their dealings with the law, especially if they did not serve in the free black militia.

Matos's activities on the night of the murder, verified by every single witness he cited, were far from suspect. At 10:00 p.m., Matos and a group of pardo artisans and militiamen, their wives, and doña Magdalena Cisneros, a creole woman whose connection to the gathering is unknown, had been together praying a rosary to Nuestra Señora de los Dolores in the house of Ignacio de Lara, Matos's cousin.[36] After the informal devotional meeting broke up, Matos returned to his parents' home to eat supper and was in bed by around 11:00 p.m. On the way out of town, he stopped by the house of a fellow pardo sculptor to say good-bye before beginning his ill-fated and incomplete journey homeward. Not one witness called to verify his itinerary and whereabouts that night and the following days cast any doubt on his version of events.

His social network in Mérida was likewise quite respectable. Three of the fourteen witnesses who verified Matos's alibi served in the pardo militia, two of them as officers. Two female witnesses were wives of officers. Juan Pinzón, a relative of Matos and sub-lieutenant of the Fourth Company of the pardo militia testified first, confirming that Matos had indeed attended the informal prayer service on the night of 22 June. He saw him again on 24 June at the home of Pedro Juan Valdez, a sculptor, where Matos dropped in before departing for Maxcanú.[37] Bernarda Valdez, Juan Pinzón's wife and the sculptor's sister, corroborated Matos's alibi. Valdez the sculptor, Matos's cousin, was the third of the worshippers to confirm Matos's alibi. His wife followed, confirming the testimony of the previous three witnesses.[38] Ignacio de Lara, a blacksmith and first sergeant of the pardo militia who owned the house where the praying of the rosary took place, testified next. He was Matos's closest relative in the group, a *primo hermano de afinidad*, or first cousin.[39]

Interrogated again three days later, Matos provided his questioners with a longer list of worshippers attending the evening rosary, including another Juan Pinzón and several women. The second Juan Pinzón, also a cousin, served in the pardo militia.[40] Most of the women present were kin of one kind or another of Matos. Two female witnesses were his cousins, and a third called Matos her compadre.[41] The last two female witnesses to testify differed from the others not only in their apparent lack of blood ties or fictive kinship links to Matos but in social rank.[42] Judging from her use of the honorific prefix doña, Magdalena Cisneros was apparently a member of the Spanish-descent elite. She furnished testimony suggesting at least some familiarity with Matos. Although she never saw him due to the crowds, she had tried to find Matos to ask him to deliver a letter to her brother, a resident of Maxcanú.[43] María Carrasco, the final female witness, may have been a criada of doña Magdalena since they shared a residence.[44] Matos's Mérida-based social network thus included an upper-class Spanish woman, respectable artisans, and militia officers. However, none had the sway or status necessary to secure his release in spite of the evident veracity of his alibi. Yet the militia service and accompanying protection of the fuero militar guaranteed that none of them were imprisoned, unlike many other low-status witnesses who were often held behind bars while providing testimony.

Multiethnic Guilds and Interracial Workplaces: Mérida's Artisans

The fine-grained image of the social and religious lives of the Afro-Yucatecan artisan and officer class, aptly described as the "Black Middle" elsewhere, combined with descriptive militia rosters and guild rolls from the final decades of the eighteenth century, provides one of the most detailed portrayals of Mérida's urban craftsmen during the colonial era.[45] Afro-Yucatecans were numerically prominent but were not the only artisans and low-ranking militiamen of the city. Luis Lara's wavering testimony led to an enumeration of the city of Mérida's meat trade workers' guilds—including butchers, tanners, and vendedores de suela—leading prosecutors to undertake two separate registers of Mérida's tanners, butchers, and meat trade workers. Prosecutors also examined and questioned blacksmiths and other specialized metalworkers as a result of their possible involvement and expertise in fabricating the knife. Because some eyewitnesses said paint was found on the knife, investigators also examined sculptors and painters but did not record their names.

Two *peritos* (experts) had determined that the knife used to kill the intendant was made in Mérida and not an imported blade, resulting in an investigation into the blacksmiths who might have made the knife, repaired it, or purchased it.[46] Although few Mayas apparently belonged to the blacksmiths' guild, Mérida's metalworkers were overall a mixed, multiethnic lot. Afro-Yucatecans seemed to be the most numerous, but the guild list recorded during the days immediately following the assassination included Mayas, mestizos, Spaniards, and Afro-Yucatecans.[47] On 25 June 1792, ninety-nine men were hauled in front of Lic. Piñeres and questioned whether they had forged the murder weapon; if not, did they know who did; and if they had any further insights about the knife's origin. Once gathered, Piñeres then decided to parade each man individually past Luis Lara on the off chance that he might identify one of them as the man watching the horse on the night of the assassination. Lara did not recognize any of them.[48]

Militia rolls from both the so-called white and free black divisions, which included professions of the officers and militiamen, provide more background on the race of many of the guildsmen of the blacksmith profession. Twenty-six pardo militiamen appear on the list of blacksmiths, more than twice as many as the twelve soldiers of the so-called white volunteers, which actually included mestizos and creoles.[49] Most likely, this list included only master artisans, since the guild list includes just twenty-five of eighty-seven Mérida-based pardo militiamen identified as blacksmiths on militia rosters. Although Afro-Yucatecans likely outnumbered creole blacksmiths, Spanish-descent metalworkers worked in some of the most specialized posts: The two peritos who ascertained the knife's domestic origin, don Antonio Vecino and don José Antonio Zavala, were Spaniards.[50] Don Domingo Álvarez, the master armorer of the Castle of San Benito, was another Spaniard in a prominent blacksmithing position.[51] Fewer Mayas worked as blacksmiths. The list includes only two men easily identifiable as indigenous by their surnames: Marcelo Cen and Juan Ascencio Poot. However, other Mayas labored in the workplaces of Afro-Yucatecan and Spanish master blacksmiths at a less specialized level.

If Matos's meticulously recounted alibi demonstrates a notable amount of socialization across racial lines, the two guild lists derived from the extensive questioning of blacksmiths, butchers, tanners, and other meat workers point to a high level of workplace integration. The workers in the meat trade were at least as multiethnic as the blacksmiths. The lists include Spaniards, Afro-Yucatecans, mestizos, and Mayas. Mayas were more prominent among the tanners and butchers than they were among the blacksmiths, constituting somewhere between 6 and 24 percent of Mérida's meat workers. The two separate enumerations of butchers, tanners, and low-grade meat and leather vendors in 1794 yielded eight of 123 men, or 6.5 percent of the meat trade workers with Maya surnames in the first examination, and 23 percent, or twenty of 86 men, in the second.[52] Judging from their appearance on one of the two lists and the militia rosters, where they are identified by profession, there were at least fifty-nine pardo tanners and twenty-eight white and mestizo tanners. Mestizos, less easily detected in the colonial records, also worked in the meat trades. At least two of the early suspects, the Medina brothers, were mestizo butchers.

The blacksmiths' guild—which included Spaniards, Afro-Yucatecans, and Mayas—also points to a high degree of workplace interaction among eighteenth-century Mérida artisans and their corporate affiliations.[53]

Judging from the inquiry into the weapons repaired at a blacksmith shop owned by Juan Antonio Argais, an Afro-Yucatecan master blacksmith, integration prevailed inside individual foundries as well. When prosecutors began to hone in on the supposed owner of a particularly suspicious knife, they exhaustively interrogated Argais after they surmised that he had repaired the murder weapon shortly before its use in the crime. Prosecutors had first questioned the high-ranking Spanish artisan who taught him the craft—don Domingo Álvarez, the province's master armorer—and the Maya laborer who worked the forge in his shop, Leonardo Chan. When discrepancies emerged between the testimony of both men, prosecutors once again undertook a more intensive interrogation regarding the alleged murder weapon, its repair, and, most critically, its owner. This round of probing examinations of witnesses illuminated a microcosm of Mérida's working class: Argais's blacksmith shop.

Argais, a pardo militiaman in the Fourth Company of Mérida's free black battalion, lived and worked in a multiracial profession. As one of the ninety-nine blacksmiths rounded up in the days following the assassination, he belonged to the apparently exclusive guild of master craftsmen.[54] He owned his own foundry and employed at least one worker, Leonardo Chan. He also worked with both Mayas and Spaniards; Argais had learned the trade from don Domingo Álvarez, a highly specialized metal worker. Other witnesses further illustrate the multiethnic nature of urban workspaces. Besides Leonardo Chan, investigators also questioned his cousin, Tiburcio Chan, a frequent visitor to the workshop. Argais's network also included Afro-Yucatecans; his closest friend, the pardo Tomás Trejo, also testified.[55]

Argais's respectful treatment by prosecutors highlights how militia service substantially improved one's lot when dealing with agents of the law. Like Matos, Argais was a relatively successful and sought after master artisan with no shortage of work. Unlike Matos, Argais's questioning contrasts sharply with the arbitrary imprisonment, pressure, occasional torture, and verbal abuse that other Afro-Yucatecan, Maya, and mestizo wage laborers and artisans suffered. Comparing the considerable leniency Argais faced with the harsh and unjustified punishment imposed on Matos underscores the importance of the fuero militar when Afro-Yucatecans came face-to-face with the law.[56] The militiaman resembled Matos in many ways. Both were Afro-Yucatecan artisans, specialized enough to have a reputation for quality among local elites; both had roots in Mérida's Barrio de Santiago; and, while not wealthy, both earned a modest living working independently and possessing their own tools of the trade. Socioeconomically similar to Matos, possibly the investigation's most unfortunate and blameless scapegoat, Argais entered the legal arena with a distinct advantage, even when he flagrantly tampered with a witness in front of the prosecutors. Argais's militia service, beyond adding an element of respectability, garnered him the protection of the fuero militar, making it much harder for prosecutors to peremptorily imprison him, although they found inconsistencies in his declarations under oath.

Discrepancies in testimony often resulted in brief stints in jail while prosecutors undertook *careos*, three-party interrogations in which the prosecutors summoned two witnesses who had provided contradictory declarations. Argais's testimony differed from Álvarez's and Leonardo Chan's, but none of the witnesses were imprisoned. One knife in particular was the subject of dispute, and Argais's account of the weapon in question differed in terms of its width, length, markings, and whether it was moldy, twisted, or cracked.[57] The variations in the witnesses' statements led to three careos between the witnesses to sort out conflicting statements. First, Argais faced Álvarez, the man who taught him the art of blacksmithing. Each man stuck to his story; prosecutors were unable to resolve the inconsistency.[58]

The second and third careos involved Argais's Maya employee, Leonardo Chan, and Leonardo's cousin, Tiburcio Chan. Both initially contradicted Argais's version of events but retracted their testimony in the careo. At first, neither remembered ever having seen the knife that Argais claimed to have repaired, even though Argais insisted that both Chans had seen him working on the weapon. Leonardo made his statements in Maya through interpreters don Blas Torres and don Enrique Gonzáles, but the presence of his employer—and nonverbal cues from across the room—apparently persuaded him to recant his earlier declarations. Once in the presence of his employer, he suddenly remembered that he had indeed seen the knife in question. The prosecutor observed that Leonardo looked perplexed and may have changed his testimony to avoid angering Argais.[59] Tiburcio also retracted his previous declaration. Placed in the same room as Argais, he too suddenly remembered seeing the weapon, even though just a few minutes earlier he claimed that he never saw it.[60]

Despite his suspicions of witness tampering, don Manuel de Bodega y Mollinedo, the prosecutor who took over from Lic. Piñeres, did not jail Argais. Bodega did attempt to limit Argais's communication with other witnesses not yet questioned before he interrogated the final witness for

verification of Argais's version of events. According to Argais, one more witness had seen the knife as well: Felipe, the criado of the weapon's owner. In
an attempt to prevent Argais from contacting Felipe, Bodega confined the
pardo blacksmith to his home. But even when he feared witness tampering,
he did not incarcerate a pardo militiaman.[61] This temporary house arrest
differed drastically from the treatment Ek, Lara, and the Venturas received
when prosecutors sought to limit their communication. In that case, all four
Maya witnesses were imprisoned.[62]

Afro-Yucatecans saw their financial fortunes and social standing
improve during the eighteenth and nineteenth centuries, but as the jailing of
Matos and Luna demonstrates, many of them remained legally vulnerable.
Only pardo militiamen saw a significant improvement in their legal standing, accompanying their rising economic and social status.[63] This expansion
of legal privileges and the reinforcement of boundaries between ordinary
civil and criminal courts and military jurisdiction went against the grain of
an overall jurisprudential trend of bringing as many subjects as possible
under the auspices of royal justice and simplifying the labyrinthine system
of competing courts. In many cases, it did make black militiamen loyal subjects of the crown, one of the aims of the broadening of the reach and con-
sistency of the fuero militar. In 1814, when many of Yucatan's leading citizens
voiced pro-autonomy sentiments, the bishop of Mérida wrote to the crown
praising the loyalty of the pardos serving in Mérida's militia. In a time of
turmoil in the Spanish world, when many representative bodies sought to
deny citizenship to the descendants of Africans, Monseñor Pedro Agustín
Estévez y Ugarte recommended to the crown that they receive the full rights
of citizenship in the Spanish Empire.[64] The limits placed upon the colonial
criminal and civil courts' ability to try and punish with impunity no doubt
played a role in their loyalty to the crown.

Argais's confinement to his home rather than the jailing faced by most
problematic witnesses was not atypical for pardos who served in the militias.
Two other contemporary cases involving pardo militiamen—one a habitual
drunk and the other suspected of receiving property—demonstrate that the
fuero did offer legal protection from the worst abuses of colonial justice to
pardos in Mérida. The fuero militar, granted to pardo militiamen in a much
broader interpretation of the privileges than in previous centuries, guaranteed protection from trial by the courts of ordinary royal justice. It also
granted the right to a trial in a military court for most minor crimes. In
practice, it meant that pardo soldiers were unique among low and middling

nonwhites in facing a lesser risk of arbitrary treatment. In many cases, their fuero afforded them the benefit of the doubt—akin to a presumption of innocence while matters were investigated—without the peremptory jailing that most suspects of low status faced during the colonial era. The case of Julián Pérez, a shoemaker and soldier in the Second Company of the pardo militia of Mérida, highlights how militia service merited more respectful treatment from justices and agents of the law in cases involving several castas and Mayas.

In 1803 Juan Lino Angulo, the mestizo cabo de justicia, or barrio constable, confronted Pérez over suspicions that he received stolen property.[65] In 1803 two Mayas from Xcaucelchen went to Mérida to recover two pigs that had been stolen from them. They found the pigs in Pérez's possession. Afraid to confront a pardo soldier, the men instead asked for assistance from Lino Angulo. Despite having found Pérez holding stolen property, local authorities did not jail him. Benefiting from the fuero militar, Pérez's legal status protected him from immediate incarceration by low-level law enforcement agents such as Lino Angulo. Questioned without duress, Pérez admitted that, unaware that the pigs were stolen, he had purchased them from a habitual thief, the Maya Francisco Canché.[66] Although possession of stolen property was certainly grounds for imprisonment until the innocence of the accused could be proven in typical circumstances, Pérez escaped such treatment because of his service in the pardo militia.

Canché was a habitual thief; a previous livestock-rustling incident shows how castas without the fuero fared. During the fall of the previous year, Canché had stolen a mule from another Maya man, Casimiro Chay. Under interrogation, he initially told the solicitor for the Indians, or *procurador de los indios*—a magistrate of the General Court of the Indians, Juan Estevan Meneses—that he had sold the mule to Pedro Castillo, a casta resident of nearby Hunucmá. In contrast to Pérez's treatment, Meneses immediately sent an order to the authorities of the nearby pueblos to arrest Castillo. On 13 January 1803, he was hauled into the royal jail. Castillo was completely innocent; he testified that he had never met Canché. Under questioning, Canché recanted and admitted that he had lied, basically pulling "un tal Castilla, o Castillo" out of the air to satisfy his interrogators.[67] However, unlike Pérez, prosecutors did not treat him with the presumption of innocence and kept him in prison for eight days after unceremoniously dragging him off in chains from the hacienda where he worked, releasing him on 24 January 1803.[68]

Lesser offenses involving only rank-and-file militiamen were tried by their own superior officers. Punishments meted out tended to be less severe in cases where pardo militiamen were tried by men with whom they fought, drilled, and lived for much of the year. Contrasting punishments for drunkenness, a crime that pardos and other castas were tried for disproportionately, effectively demonstrate the discrepancy between the comparatively lenient military tribunals and the sentences imposed by ordinary criminal courts. Juan Rosa Estrella, a pardo militia lieutenant of the Third Company was tried for drunkenness in 1797. The entire trial and punishment—overseen by Sgt. Eugenio Cano and the subinspector of pardos, don Eugenio Rubio—took place within the military hierarchy.[69] Cano and Rubio demoted Estrella to the rank of soldier, but he faced neither imprisonment nor expulsion from his division, despite his reputation for repeatedly being intoxicated while on duty. Cano and Rubio had overlooked earlier incidents and only began proceedings against then Lieutenant Estrella after previously confronting him about his behavior privately and off the record, a fact borne out by the testimony of five witnesses. Estrella's relatively light sentence differs significantly from the punishments imposed on other castas tried for public drunkenness who faced trial without the legal guarantees of the fuero militar. Most of the urban plebe were tried by regular civil authorities, the alcalde ordinario of Mérida in most cases. When apprehended by authorities for public (and even private) intoxication, urban Mayas such as Esteban Coyí or the criado Juan Cauich and castas such as Diego Zapata and José Trejo were jailed promptly on the first offense as they confronted civil judges without the benefit of corporate legal privileges, such as the military fuero.[70]

A Multiethnic Middle: Working Women, Mestizos, and Mayas in Mérida

The critical roles played by Argais, Matos, and Matos's circle of friends and relatives give readers an intimate look at urban Afro-Yucatecan artisans whose status was somewhere in between that of the mostly Spanish upper class and the multiethnic slaves and servants examined in the next chapter. But Afro-Yucatecans were not alone in this multiethnic middle. Mestizos, Mayas, and poor Spaniards—such as master painter José Yanuario Salazar, examined in chapter 8—worked side by side in the same trades. Women worked inside and outside the home in gender-determined roles such as market vendors, cigar makers, and laundresses.

Little social distance separated the middling creoles and mestizos from Afro-Yucatecans who served as rank-and-file soldiers and low-level officers in their respective units. In spite of long-held notions among scholars of a rigid social hierarchy in which colonial subjects of European extraction invariably held a better socioeconomic position than mestizos (who likewise had an advantage over African-descent inhabitants of Americas), only minimal distinctions separated the races in occupational status. A comparison of the top five professions reported by white and mestizo militiamen and pardo volunteers demonstrates a striking similarity across racial lines. Four of the five top professions predominated among craftsmen of both races, including shoemakers, blacksmiths, tanners, and tailors. There were, however, differences. Far higher numbers of pardo militiamen worked as *labradores*, or agricultural laborers, while greater numbers of whites and mestizos worked in lucrative silversmith shops.[71]

While militia rosters did not distinguish between mestizos and low-status creoles, one of the few surviving demographic sources from the late colonial era, an 1809 census of the Barrio of San Cristóbal, does include detailed information on the race and profession of its inhabitants and is relatively intact.[72] The barrio was thoroughly integrated with street-by-street descriptions, including blacks, mulattos, mestizos, Spaniards, and Indians living side by side. In some cases, they even shared living quarters, as was the case with the indio hidalgo couple Rafael Canul (a weaver) and María Cantun, who resided with the pardo Julián Casanova and his wife, María Gertrudis Canul, another india hidalga. Rafael Canul, like a smattering of other indios hidalgos, served in the white militias, demonstrating the diversity of the supposedly segregated militia units. The barrio had an Afro-Yucatecan majority, but sizeable numbers of mestizos, Spaniards, and indios hidalgos also resided there. A few Spaniards in this plebeian neighborhood, such as don Miguel Mezquita, worked as upper-status professionals, like merchants. The two priests residing in the barrio were also Spaniards. Likewise, the only students registered in the barrio—José Antonio Domínguez, Pedro Prebe, and Bartolo Araoz—were identified as "españoles." Others held distinct professions usually reserved for creoles and Spaniards, such as scribes (*escribientes*) and the interpreter general don Vicente de Avila. However, many others worked in the same middling professions as their Afro-Yucatecan and mestizo neighbors, as hacienda mayordomos, carpenters, lamplighters, musicians, militia officers, and fishermen.[73]

Mestizos in the Spotlight

Examining Mérida's artisans only in terms of black and white omits the numerous Mayas and mestizos who worked as artisans alongside the more visible white and pardo militiamen and fails to take into account the mutable and malleable nature of casta categories in late colonial Yucatan. Many low-status militiamen in the white divisions may well have been mestizos by ancestry yet were reputed to be Spaniards by their peers. Little space in the social scale separated low-status Spaniards (such as Salazar, the master painter) and mestizos (such as two barbers, Tiburcio Carvajal and another only identified by his profession—barber—and his last name, Ventura). These two mestizos and the Medina brothers were among a very few residents of Mérida identified in the trial transcripts as mestizo, in contrast to far more labeled with racial descriptors for indigenous, European, and Afro-Yucatecan ancestry. Allegations of their complicity took place as associates of the bishop, both ecclesiastical and secular allies, sought to deflect attention from the growing suspicion regarding a member of the bishop's household who many believed was the intendant's killer and sworn enemy.

Opposition from such powerful quarters deterred the ambivalently committed men who headed the prosecution during the first nine months after the assassination. Under the lackluster leadership of the teniente del rey Sabido de Vargas and the perfunctory undertakings of the lieutenant governor, Lic. Piñeres, investigators' cursory efforts amounted to little more than an attempt to find a plausible scapegoat. Their desultory paper shuffling continued despite the fact that evidence was building in the court of public opinion against a close relative of the bishop. Murmurs of a widely held belief in the complicity of someone close to the cathedral in the intendant's murder grew louder and more assertive as months passed. To stem this tide of rumors against one of their own, cronies of the bishop sought to divert the masses' attention by stifling suspicious gossip and countering it with salacious insinuations. Men and women close to fray Luis de Piña y Mazo spun webs of intrigues, spreading rumors of a seemingly limitless number of fabricated conspiracies that prosecutors dutifully investigated while postponing their inevitable confrontation with the province's most formidable and intimidating household: the episcopal palace. Spurious accusations and counter-rumors eventually traced back to the bishop led to more arrests, inadvertently providing detailed descriptions of the professions and lifestyles of mestizo and Maya artisans.

Two of the earliest, and entirely innocent, suspects caught up in the bishop's machinations were Agustín and Isidoro Medina, mestizos who worked and briefly lodged in the home of the creole José Bermejo, an alleged accomplice targeted by allies of the bishop's household. Their only connection to the case was their temporary residence in Bermejo's home shortly before the murder, slaughtering cattle that Bermejo and his wife, doña María Pérez, had recently purchased. Despite having only passing ties with Bermejo and no motive for killing the intendant, they were jailed together in the early days of the trial.[74] Another mestizo, a barber, Tiburcio Carvajal, was accused of complicity in the assassination on equally flimsy pretense by the priest don Manuel Correa. Fingered as an accomplice in a spurious conspiracy invented by Correa, Carvajal had more luck than the Medina brothers. Carvajal had the fortune to face specious allegations from the bishop's palace at a later date—1794—when a less easily swayed outside prosecutor had taken over the case. The more qualified successor to Sabido de Vargas and Piñeres immediately recognized Father Correa's allegations as nothing more than a ploy to shift attention away from associates of the bishop, though the Medina brothers had no such luck.[75] Fray Luis's coterie did not only use mestizos as scapegoats; others collaborated with the bishop's household. The final mestizo questioned in connection with the assassination, identified only as the "barber Ventura," served as a key conduit of information when other channels of communication were blocked. In 1795 jailers caught Ventura passing messages between a prisoner close to the bishop and his allies when a suspect from the episcopal palace was held incommunicado.[76]

The appearance of a few mestizos identified by race in the trial transcripts is not surprising. While all casta labels were mutable identities, "mestizo" was an especially malleable, even a "disappearing" category.[77] During the early urban-focused phase of the investigation, prosecutors only questioned four suspects and witnesses labeled as mestizo, but there were likely more men and women with Hispanic surnames who appear without any racial designation. Some of the "white" militiamen were likely as not mestizos passing as Spaniards—or at least accepted as Spaniards by their neighbors and acquaintances.[78] Soldiers working as labradores in the rural communities nearest Mérida—like militiamen Juan de Dios Burgos, José Concha, and Antonio Guillermo of Tixkokob (lodgers in Francisco Ek's posada on the night of the assassination)—were probably among the many mestizos who served in the white militia divisions.[79] Laureano Concha, another lodger and likely a relative of José Concha (both were from Tixkokob), did not even speak Spanish; two interpreters, don Vicente de Ávila and don Estevan de Castro, translated his testimony from Yucatec Maya to Castilian.[80] While speaking the province's indigenous language as his sole idiom did not necessarily mean he was a mestizo, Laureano Concha's monolingual use of Yucatec Maya increased the likelihood that he was of partial indigenous ancestry. Many Spaniards did speak Maya, but most of them were bilingual.

The ambiguity over the racial classification of the soldiers and officers in the so-called white militias is not surprising. "Mestizo" and "Spaniard" were far from fixed categories. Indeed, a leading scholar identified mestizos in Colombia in the earlier colonial period as a disappearing category, a situation in which "under particular circumstances people classified as mestizos dropped out of the mestizo slot and into other categories."[81] The frequency with which mestizos and even an occasional Maya served side by side with creoles in "white" militia units demonstrates that rigid segregation was far from the norm. Indeed, in some cases, individuals even changed their legal status from "mestizo," a category by which they were labeled at birth, to "español." In a case from Valladolid in 1801, María Juliana Herrera officially changed the status of her two sons from mestizo to español on the basis of testimony from three witnesses.[82] With enough friendly testimony, one's status could change with ease. However, middle-status mestizos from surrounding pueblos were far more likely to be jailed and interrogated with impunity than upper-class Spaniards and creoles from Mérida. Financial well-being and a central location within one of Yucatan's urban centers mattered as well.

Although working women are more easily identified in colonial-era documents than laboring mestizos, they are likewise often described only in passing in the transcripts of colonial court cases. None served in the militias nor did any evidently belong to the guilds, two major sources of information on men of the laboring classes. However, a few women who worked as laundresses, cigar makers, and market vendors were caught up in the proceedings of the trial. Little more than their names and professions identify them. Their lives and involvement offer only a brief glimpse of the skilled female laborers whose underappreciated efforts kept Mérida clean, provisioned, and in possession of a hand-rolled cigar at the right moment.

The Medina brothers were not the only innocent victims of the allegations lodged against José Bermejo. His wife, doña María Pérez, made cigars at home despite having a name that indicates elite status. Doña María's husband never appears as a "don" however, and, if gossip of the time was accurate, his role as a ne'er-do-well spouse may have meant that she needed to work in spite of her respectable ancestry. Their home, a place where numerous men stopped by to purchase cigars and briefly chat with its occupants, attracted the attention of prosecutors after rumors with origins in the bishop's palace linking Bermejo to the assassination gained currency.[83] Doña María's customers included the treasurer, don Clemente Rodríguez de Trujillo, as well as an unnamed mestizo who may have simply been an invention of the conspirators affiliated with doña Narcisa Suárez, an ally of the bishop.

As mentioned above, prosecutorial efforts gradually shifted away from the unlikely scapegoats targeted during the first months after the assassination. As attention centered on don Clemente Rodríguez de Trujillo (who accompanied don Lucas on that fateful night) and his wife, doña Casiana (who was suspected of a pivotal role in a fatal love triangle), prosecutors interrogated all members of their household and even those who performed domestic work there but did not reside there, including laundress Baltasara Argais.[84] Another laundress, the widow Isidora Carrillo, also provided critical testimony based on her intimate knowledge of the internal workings of the bishop's palace as a source of rumors about the illicit nature of the relationship between doña Casiana and her highly placed paramour.[85] Don Francisco de Heredía y Vergara, weighing in on reports he had heard about the suspect's whereabouts during the days surrounding Gálvez's death, repeated rumors that the bishop's nephew had been hiding at the house of his unnamed laundress, possibly Isidora Carrillo.[86] Another version of the same tale placed him in the house of the laundresses of don Antonio Poveda, the bishop's medical doctor, shortly after the murder.[87]

While widows and laundresses affiliated with the household of the bishop or his close allies attracted the attention of prosecutors, other rumors reached their ears via secondhand reports from women who added their two cents from a geographic, linguistic, and socioeconomic distance. Doña Narcisa, the preeminent busybody who fabricated rumor after rumor to deflect suspicion surrounding don Toribio del Mazo, reported hearing Maya vendors gossiping over their wares of their nearly unanimous belief that the bishop's nephew was the killer. "La Suárez," as one prosecutor dubbed her, unwittingly became a bilingual medium, transmitting gossip across the linguistic divide separating the prominent peninsular Spaniards from Maya laborers. She reported what she perceived as shameless disrespect for don Toribio when she overheard a group of Maya market women, aware that the peninsular protégé of the top prelate could not understand their language, openly declare their belief—in Yucateca Maya—as he walked by that he had murdered Gálvez. As one of her many futile attempts to stifle the rising tide of rumors tying the bishop's nephew to the crime, Doña Narcisa reported the rumor in the hope that the Maya women would be punished. Yet despite her own prominent role in the gossip circulating at the time, the Maya market women voiced the increasingly widespread opinion circulating in both Maya- and Spanish-speaking circles: don Toribio was the assassin.

Urban Mayas such as the market women are frequently overlooked in the history of the city despite their numeric predominance; they were the provincial capital's ethnic majority for most of the colonial era, including the short years of Gálvez's brief tenure as intendant.[88] Several of them became involved as witnesses but were never suspects in the case. While Mérida's Maya population is often viewed as marginal, at least two Maya households attracted the attention of prosecutors due to their eyewitness accounts of a suspicious man tending a horse around the time of the murder. Luis Lara, the Maya coachman, comes across as a pathetic figure in the trial proceedings; other Mayas occupied more prominent places in the city, both economically and spatially. For example, Lara's sometime employer, Francisco Ek, owned a centrally located *posada*, or inn, near the center of the city, with the front gate of his yard facing the sacristy of the cathedral.[89] The central location of Ek's inn served as one sign of his success. His residence, which also served as a *zapatería*, or shoemaker's shop, was well within the zone traditionally reserved for Spaniards. Law and tradition prohibited Indians from the *traza*, or the thirteen-block-square central zone, but prosperity eased men like Ek past such restrictions.[90]

Other Mayas were even more visible in their centrality to public life in Mérida. At least one Maya man made his living as one of the most visible, or at least audible, figures in the colonial capital. Isidoro Xix, a Maya described as an *indio ladino*, fluent in Spanish, served as the *pregonero público*, the town crier or auctioneer, during the last two decades of the eighteenth century.[91] In a mostly oral culture, in which only a minority of the urban population read or wrote in either Yucatec Maya or Spanish, Xix played a critical role in spreading news of auctions, bids for contracts on public projects, the imposition of new taxes, publicity for prominent shops, and important cabildo decisions.[92] Xix and other Mayas—such as the town crier of Izamal, Juan Ek, whose service as town crier coincided with Xix's long tenure—were also rare Maya functionaries of a town government composed almost entirely of creoles and Spaniards.[93] Apparently, indios ladinos filled the role of town crier and auctioneer in Mérida and other head towns (*cabeceras*) more often than not during the late eighteenth century. Before Xix held the post, at least one other indio ladino had serve as a town crier in Mérida. In a 1768 auction of contraband goods seized in the Barrio of Santiago, Simon Be acted as the town crier announcing the upcoming auction.[94] Smaller towns also counted on indios ladinos to serve as pregoneros. In 1788, in the aftermath of the same extended trial involving Lucas de Vargas, pregonero Pascual Balam made the formal announcement of an auction of the confiscated goods of one of Vargas's accomplices.[95]

While relative prosperity allowed Francisco Ek to live in the city center and Xix's role as town crier made it necessary for him to work in the heart of Mérida, convenience likely motivated other urban Mayas to circumvent restrictions on residence in the provincial capital's traza. Ek's neighbors, who were also Mayas, apparently worked in Spanish homes, as did Luis Lara. In a province where few Spaniards had the financial resources to own slaves, Mayas known as criados worked in Spanish homes as unpaid child laborers who performed a variety of domestic tasks. Criados could be of any background, but in late colonial Yucatan they tended to be of Mayan ancestry. Upon reaching adulthood, many continued to serve in Spanish homes, but some began to live and work more independently. Luis Lara, for example, continued to work as the coachman for the Spanish widow doña María Josefa Pérez, who continued to refer to him as her criado.[96] But he had more independence than many criados, especially younger ones. He lived independently of doña María Josefa as a permanent lodger in Francisco Ek's posada. Ek had also hired him as an assistant to his shoemaking business. Ek's neighbors also included criados. Luis Ventura, possibly a criado who had gained his own freedom, came to the attention of prosecutors as a result of his sister's reports to her *amo*, or master. Maria Ventura served as a criada in the household of don Pedro Rafael Pastrana.[97]

Maria Ventura was the first of many slaves and criados questioned in connection with the assassination. However, shifting the focus of the

investigation away from independent artisans to the domestic staff of prominent households fell to Lic. Piñeres's successor, the first outside prosecutor
appointed to the peninsula, Lima-born creole don Manuel de la Bodega y
Mollinedo.[98] Appointed in October 1792 to speed up the resolution of the
case, don Manuel arrived from Guatemala in January 1793.[99] Soon he directed
the investigation away from the innocent urban workers toward those who
lived in the homes of the prominent Spanish rivals of the intendant: the
Quijanos; don Clemente Rodríguez de Trujillo, the treasurer who accompanied Gálvez on the night he was killed; and, above all, the bishop and his
nephew. Finally, the investigator's efforts were in tune with the bilingual
rumor mill and its incessant refrain: Don Toribio did it!

CHAPTER 4

Neither Free nor Family

Criados and Slaves in Spanish Households

⮷ THE FIRST TWENTY-THREE ARRESTS OF 1792—ARTISANS, FISHER-men, hacienda hands and overseers, low-ranking soldiers and militia officers—provide a fine-grained image of the social, economic, and kinship networks of Mérida's multiethnic middle. Their arrests did not, however, move the case toward its resolution in any significant way. In hindsight, none of the suspects jailed during the first six months had more than a tangential connection to the events of 22 June 1792, and their testimony offered no vital leads regarding the assassin's identity. Moreover, their arrests and prosecution highlighted the dissonance between the dead-end leads dutifully pursued by Lic. Piñeres and his associates and the nearly unanimous *voz común* (common voice), the rumors that swirled around the man with a far more plausible motive for killing the intendant: don Toribio del Mazo.

The viceroy of New Spain, the Second Count of Revillagigedo, under pressure from Madrid to resolve the matter quickly, observed that Piñeres effectively only third in the province's chain of command, was in over his head.[1] He soon ordered a more experienced magistrate from the neighboring province of Guatemala to travel to Yucatan to relieve Piñeres of his duties as chief investigator. Lic. Manuel Antonio Bodega y Mollinedo's proximity to Yucatan may have had some part in his selection, based on the idea that the short distance between the two provinces would permit him to arrive quickly. Instead, the new prosecutor's inauspicious start to a stint in Yucatan that lasted less than a year opened with a dispute between Lic. Bodega, an oidor of the Audiencia of Guatemala, and Guatemala's top crown official, don Bernardo Troncoso, the president of the audiencia. President Troncoso declined to provision the armed escort of ten to twelve men that Bodega requested to travel through Petén, a region claimed by Spain. Bodega fretted about the threat of "rebel Indians," Mayas who evaded colonial impositions by living in small peripatetic groups that defied periodic attempts to resettle them under Spanish rule and Catholic religion.[2] Viceregal orders directed Troncoso to ready an armed escort to accompany Bodega. As the headstrong and arbitrary leader of a distant province, he ignored the directives.[3] In October 1792, Troncoso wrote that the province's few militiamen under arms had more pressing matters to occupy them. Bodega would need no more than a small contingent under Capt. Salvador Tavalois, and only to the border of Campeche rather than the entire trip to Mérida, he wrote.[4] Frustrated, Bodega offered to cover the cost of the troops and reduced the number of soldiers requested to seven or eight. Still, the president of the audiencia put off taking any action.[5]

With a reduced escort, Bodega finally departed for Mérida in late November, arriving after an uneventful journey on 17 January 1793.[6] His travails were far from over. President Troncoso's noncompliance foreshadowed Bodega's treatment in Yucatan, where royal authority met the limits of its reach. Here an ingrained sense of regional privilege and a regional identity that increasingly diverged from any association with the imperial metropole, coupled with a lack of cooperation on the part of the province's elite Spaniards and leading creoles, stymied Bodega's progress toward convicting the killer. Beset by personal tragedies and failing health, Bodega's resolve began to waver by July 1793. Despite the loss of his infant daughter, failing eyesight, and swollen joints that made writing excruciatingly painful, the former oidor had made some small, faltering steps toward gathering evidence. Turning his attention away from the series of hapless scapegoats, seemingly chosen at random from Mérida's casta, creole, and Maya laborers, Bodega slowly began cutting a path for his more determined replacement toward don Toribio's conviction. Since most of the elite Spaniards and creoles with firsthand knowledge of don Toribio's sordid personal life and penchant for violence kept up a guarded silence in the presence of the first outside prosecutor, Lic. Bodega turned to the members of prominent households who had nothing left to lose—not even their freedom. Beyond helping

Bodega build the beginnings of his case against don Toribio, the prime suspect in the assassination for the following eight years, his intense questioning of criados and slaves helps construct a comprehensive picture of the often invisible but essential live-in domestic workers of middle- and upper-class homes.

Slaves and criados often offered critical pieces of information in their interactions with authorities, beginning with José Antonio's discovery of the murder weapon at the foot of the carriage on the night of the murder. A wall of silence and a lack of cooperation on the part of the city's high society, resulting from a combination of intimidation, political ties, and bonds of blood and fictive kinship, meant that only a few Spaniards dared to go on the record to share their observations on the suspicious behavior and the probable motive driving the assassin's shockingly brazen attack. On the other hand, the lowest members of households were often the first to break the silence about the suspicious activities that went on within the walls of the homes of Mérida's merchants, nobles, administrators, and officers. Disgruntled slaves and criados, smarting from years of abusive and condescending treatment from masters in elite households, often served as the best conduits of information from beyond the veil of secrecy that shrouded Spanish homes from prying eyes. Relied upon to cover up the sexual affairs and unseemly behavior of elite families and often pressured into doing the dirty work of the political and familial feuds of the province, slaves and criados were not always dependably discreet when questioned about such activities. By the time 1794 brought a second, less easily cowed outside prosecutor, reams of paper recording the incriminating statements of slaves and criados suggested that what the public believed all along was true: Don Toribio, in a pique of jealousy and spite, had slain his erstwhile friend and companion in the capital's life of leisure.

Pursuing New Leads

Lic. Piñeres had given a cursory examination of the first Spaniard who broke the unwritten code of silence, the militia cadet don Lorenzo del Castillo, and the slave who verified his version of events, Cristóbal del Trujillo, usually referred to as Tobi. Under pressure from the leading men of the province— including its leading cleric, don Toribio's uncle, and the interim governor, don José Sabido de Vargas—Piñeres soon shifted his focus elsewhere. Allegations regarding the impropriety of his own love life may also have deterred him from pursuing don Toribio with too much determination. The eighteen-year-old cadet revealed just enough to provide Piñeres with a rough outline of the tawdry romance that potentially spurred don Toribio's rash action against the intendant. A much more lurid tale of illicit love, straight from a period-piece telenovela, emerged in the testimony of Tobi, the coachman serving in the household of don Clemente Rodríguez Trujillo. Subsequent prosecutors, including Bodega and his successor, Dr. don Francisco de Guillén, went back to question Tobi and his wife, María Candelaría, as well as other criados, adding layer upon layer of scandalous detail.

Other witnesses reluctantly revealed more information, but no one served the ends of Bodega's prosecutorial drive to convict don Toribio more than Tobi. The two most forthcoming witnesses—don Lorenzo and Tobi—gleefully recounted the lurid details and conspiratorial sneaking around that surrounded the affair. A torrid tale of a love triangle developed out of the declarations of dozens of usually circumspect but occasionally verbose witnesses. For years, don Toribio had been carrying on a secret sexual relationship with doña Casiana de Melo under the nose of her unaware or possibly unconcerned husband. The relationship became more complicated when a third party intervened—and not doña Casiana's husband, don Clemente Rodríguez Trujillo.

Within two years of his arrival, the new intendant became a second suitor of the already-married woman. The early camaraderie of the two young peninsulares, companions in the nightlife of Mérida's upper strata, descended into open animosity as they underhandedly and viciously competed for the attentions of doña Casiana. Outranking his romantic rival in Yucatan's military hierarchy, don Lucas reassigned don Toribio initially to Tixkokob, a pueblo sixteen miles away from Mérida. This short distance did little to deter don Toribio, known for his equestrian skills, from repeatedly defying orders and regularly galloping into town for forbidden nighttime visits with doña Casiana. Thwarted and angered by such defiance, the intendant reassigned don Toribio to a more distant pueblo—Tihosuco—located in the modern-day state of Quintana Roo, just across its border with the state of Yucatan. After reports reached him that the bishop's nephew defiantly continued his breakneck night rides for secret rendezvous with his paramour, Gálvez took the unprofessional, very personal step of posting his romantic rival to the farthest reaches of his authority: Bacalar. Bordering Belize, the fortress at Bacalar was such an undesirable location that many of its residents were convicts banished to the remotest corner of the province to work on maintenance and expansion of the tropical outpost. Many Yucatecans believed that this final step provoked don Lucas's rival into the murderous fury that ended with the intendant's death. Popular accounts placed don Toribio, dressed as a vaquero, or cowboy, at the site of the murder to dispatch the unwelcome interloper and end his meddling forever. Suspicion also lingered over the husband of the woman at the center of the love triangle—don Clemente Rodríguez de Trujillo—who accompanied the intendant on the night of the murder yet emerged from the attack unscathed.

Young don Lorenzo del Castillo, the first confidant of don Toribio to break the silence, recalled that on 18 June 1792, Gálvez had contacted him in secret to ask if he had seen or spoken with the bishop's nephew. He had not but volunteered that doña Casiana had departed that day for the Hacienda de Miraflores, the site of many a tryst between "la Tesorera," (the female form of "the treasurer") the public's nickname for her, and don Toribio. Eight days after the intendant's death, del Castillo's testimony gave the hesitant criminal investigation team headed by Piñeres its first lead. His incriminating declaration, made with no pressure from his questioners, hints at don Lorenzo's dislike for either doña Casiana or don Toribio. But his freely given testimony, first noted on record on 30 June 1792, was frustratingly vague.[7]

In the next round of interrogations, the cadet's fiancée, doña María Trinidad, provided prosecutors with no further clues. Doña María, doña Casiana's eighteen-year-old confidant and likely accomplice in keeping the affair somewhat secret, accompanied her on the trip outside the city.[8] Just days before his death, Gálvez had questioned doña María.[9] Piñeres, shortly after Gálvez's assassination, followed suit. She contradicted her fiancé's account of the secret rendezvous, but her testimony did little to dispel the whiff of scandal that hung about the two alleged lovers. On Sunday, 10 June 1792, doña Casiana secretly departed for the hacienda, accompanied by doña María. En route, she had an unplanned run-in with her other suitor, the intendant. Unnerved by the encounter, doña Casiana ordered Tobi to turn around and return home. Doña María watched la Tesorera descend from the carriage, approach her mounted coachman, and whisper something to him. She did not hear what was said.[10] Two other prominent female witnesses— identified as intimate friends, doña Francisca Domínguez and doña Luisa Lara, both later identified by Tobi as collaborators in facilitating the forbidden encounters between don Toribio and doña Casiana—believed that the two lovers' friendship was "licit and honest."[11]

Tobi, a slave with an insider's view of the inner workings of the household, contradicted the testimony of doña Casiana's three friends.[12] He offered a far more scandalous series of anecdotes that created an incriminating image of a brazen, public, and adulterous affair. La Tesorera frequently traveled without a male companion, drank beer, and carried on a publicly known affair with don Toribio, he said. All the while, she flirted with his rival, don Lucas, despite being married to Yucatan's treasurer of the Real Hacienda. Tobi and his wife, María Candelaría, evidently unhappy with the treatment they received at the hands of don Clemente and doña Casiana, gave the most damning details of the affair from firsthand experience, testimony that weighed heavily against don Toribio in his quest to absolve himself of any wrongdoing related to the intendant's murder.[13] Tobi began by readily recognizing his role as the carriage driver and confirmed the Hacienda de Miraflores as the intended destination of the trip in question, a place where doña Casiana and don Toribio had met in secret in the past.[14] Regretting her decision at the last moment, doña Casiana ordered him to turn the carriage around, apparently flustered by her run-in with Gálvez. She stepped down from the carriage to tell her slave in confidence to pass on a message to doña Luisa Lara, inventing a last-minute excuse to avoid an awkward meeting suggested by the intendant. She told Tobi to relay the message that she had an appointment to drink beer with unnamed friends at a gathering at the Castillo de San Benito.[15] The intendant, then, should not wait for her.

Tobi went on to state that while stationed in Tixkokob, don Toribio had abandoned his post for several unsanctioned visits to la Tesorera.[16] He mentioned an earlier rendezvous between his owner and don Toribio at the Hacienda de Teyá. He opined that these visits led Gálvez to reassign don Toribio to the more distant Tihosuco. Tobi claimed that after the reassignment he no longer knew whether or not the secret visits had continued.[17] Tobi's initial interview with don Fernando Antonio Gutiérrez de Piñeres, a man whose own love life was made awkwardly public by a criado in 1795, was circumspect, especially when compared to his rambling interviews with both don Manuel Antonio Bodega y Mollinedo and Dr. Guillén. In his 1793 interview with Bodega, Tobi elaborated upon his eyewitness account of sexual misconduct between the treasurer's wife and the young peninsular militia officer, describing their frolicking (*retozos*), tickling, and "games with the hands" during their time together. This he witnessed firsthand, but he noted that even he had not seen everything. In doña Francisca Domínguez's house, the two often locked themselves in a room together during their "continual appointments." Together with their coconspirators, they took pains to keep their meetings secret from the treasurer, don Clemente. They met in the homes of willing accomplices doña Luisa Lara and doña Juana Castro, as well as don Toribio's hacienda, Wallis. Tobi, who shuttled them back and forth between their homes and their secret encounters, saw it all. But a criada acquaintance of Tobi, inexplicably never interviewed, saw more than any of the domestic workers of the house, Tobi declared. He ended his deposition in the 1793 interview with Bodega by reporting that a criada named Simona had seen don Toribio "en la cama con su Ama doña Casiana," or "in bed with his owner, doña Casiana." Wrapping up his lengthy conversation with the outside prosecutor, Tobi characterized the friendship as, in fact, "illicit," contradicting any claims of innocence.[18]

Other slaves and criados added their voices to Tobi's incriminating testimony. Tobi's wife, a slave in the same household, stated with more authority that the relationship between her owner and don Toribio was sexual in nature. Unlike Tobi, who had never witnessed anything firsthand beyond "tickling" and "frolicking," María Candelaría had no doubt about the nature of the friendship. One day she walked into doña Casiana's room by accident ("por casualidad") and found the two in an indecent situation ("en una disposición indecente"). On a separate occasion, doña Casiana posted María as her lookout, making sure that her husband did not catch the pair alone in the bedroom behind closed doors.[19]

Two final witnesses with connections to both households weighed in with their own opinions on the nature of the friendship between don Toribio and doña Casiana. First to testify was Silverio Muñoz, a dragoon who had been a relatively highly placed and trusted criado and who worked as the mayordomo of three of the treasurer's haciendas at the time of the murder. He had fallen under suspicion and was one of the first twenty-three suspects jailed as a result of a completely spurious connection to Ignacio Matos. Now free and released from any obligation to the treasurer's household, he too agreed that don Toribio and doña Casiana were involved romantically and most likely sexually.[20] On several occasions, he had noticed the militia lieutenant lurking about the house, waiting for don Clemente to leave for his office in the mornings. According to Muñoz, don Toribio often spent the entire morning with la Tesorera while don Clemente was at work. He made much shorter, formal visits to the treasurer's home on holidays, when don Clemente stayed in.[21]

Finally, a member of don Toribio's household confirmed the scandalous version of the visits provided by the domestics in the employ of the treasurer.

Felipe Morales, one of don Toribio's criados, had acted as a spy for his master, in a capacity that complemented María Candelaría's duty as the lookout for doña Casiana. The bishop's nephew regularly sent Felipe to see whether or not don Clemente was still at home. Eagerly awaiting news of the treasurer's absence, don Toribio dashed out the door and mounted his horse for a quick gallop over to the treasurer's house the moment his criado returned with news that don Clemente had left for work. In addition to this task, don Toribio also assigned this criado the duty of delivering messages to doña Casiana, which, given the quantity of letters confiscated later, must have meant quite a lot of secret errands beyond the standard domestic duties of a criado. Not surprisingly, Felipe also opined that the close friendship between doña Casiana and her compadre was a sexual love affair. He declared that he spoke on behalf of all of the criados of the bishop's palace: they too viewed it as an extramarital romantic relationship.[22] Other more temporary workers in the household also weighed in on the matter. Even the widow Isidora Carrillo, who worked for three months as a laundress in the household, testified that she concurred with popular opinion—that don Toribio had killed don Lucas in a heated rivalry between doña Casiana's jealous lovers.[23]

The households of don Toribio and doña Casiana were not the only homes of prominent Spaniards that saw the curtains swept aside by resentful slaves and criados, revealing the illicit sex lives of their inhabitants. Privy to the parlors and the bedchambers of the prominent homes in central Mérida, slaves and criados often leaked such information to authorities at inconvenient moments for their masters. Otherwise discreet and well-concealed affairs surfaced when slaves and criados reported their intimate details to authorities or passed along their knowledge via cross-class gossip. Such revelations moved the rumors making the rounds of the prominent households from the realm of conjecture to established fact—or at least gave both ecclesiastical and civil authorities enough evidence to pursue suspected adulterers and fornicators.

Neighborly Relations: A Noblewoman's Visits and Piñeres's Departure

Although don Toribio's affair with la Tesorera was without a doubt the most sensational and widely discussed extramarital affair of late eighteenth-century Yucatan, disclosures about the frequency and casualness of visits between two neighboring homes allowed the bishop to briefly shift the spotlight to the sexual indiscretions of other prominent citizens of the provincial capital. Earlier, Lic. Piñeres probably had hesitated to probe too far into the personal matters of don Toribio out of a fear that anyone digging deeply into his own private matters might uncover his peccadilloes. Indeed, three years after the murder, don Toribio's uncle caused a scandal with his highly public accusations of Piñeres's involvement with a prestigious neighbor of the lieutenant governor. One single African slave, never mentioned by name, was the sole source behind the allegations.

On 4 May 1795, fray Luis visited the home of doña María Antonia del Castillo y Aguirre, condesa viuda de Miraflores, to deliver a notarized, public, formal censure, admonishing her to break off contact with her prominent neighbor, Lic. Piñeres. As the holder of the highest-ranking title of nobility in the province, the countess stood her ground against the bishop and his allegations. Rather than beat a humiliated retreat into the confines of her home—likely the bishop's desired outcome—she reprimanded the bishop for his own shortcomings. She defended her visits to her much younger bachelor neighbor, which she said took place at legitimate hours, as being motivated by Christian sentiments of charity. She ended her harangue with an insult to the bishop's character: "Very little or not at all do men so pious understand the rules of charity."[24]

In support of her defense against accusations of indecorous behavior, eighteen of Mérida's leading citizens came forward to testify on behalf of the condesa viuda and the lieutenant governor. Many of them were well-placed royal and municipal administrators, doctors, prominent merchants—even two priests—who attended her *tertulias*, the social gatherings usually hosted by high-status women like the condesa that typically involved educated men discussing cultural and occasionally political matters. Even so, this was not enough to dispel completely the suspicions regarding the relationship between the charitable widow and her young neighbor. The conflicting reports emanating from the household, repeated by three female witnesses, were traced to the same source: an unnamed female slave who had left the household before 1795. From her, they passed to the bishop the particulars of the relaxed wardrobe worn by Lic. Piñeres in doña María Antonia's home, their carriage rides and attendance of mass together, the evening visits and late night slamming doors, and rumors of secret plans for a wedding that may or may not have already been consummated.[25] In her defense, the condesa viuda had claimed that she had only looked after her neighbor during his illness. A neighbor, twenty-two-year-old doña María Tomasa Anguas, mentioned that during Piñeres's convalescence, the condesa viuda had applied the medicines with her own hands.[26] One enslaved woman's firsthand glimpse of the condesa's private life was sufficient for the bishop to challenge the testimony of eighteen of Mérida's leading citizens in favor of a noblewoman's reputation. Mostly a matter that had more to do with upper-class factional fighting and slights than the fragile honor of upper-class Spaniards, it is worth noting that a slave whose name was not even recorded by the notaries had the power to tarnish her reputation. Criados and slaves were ubiquitous and underappreciated members of Spanish households. Seemingly powerless, they turned on their masters when opportunities arose.

The Wages of Betrayal

Vengeance alone did not motivate Tobi, María Candelaría, and the nameless slave who served the condesa viuda. In fact, slaves and criados occasionally used depositions as a strategy to force the hands of prosecutors who were obligated to remove them from hostile households, especially if they were threatened with retaliation for the condemning content of their testimony. Slaves' status in eighteenth-century Spanish America was little better than those in colonies elsewhere. But their marginal legal personhood, which consisted of little beyond the ability to testify in a court of law and not much more in terms of redress, did offer them occasional opportunities to improve their condition. In other circumstances, slaves used the Inquisition, which considered them fully Christian and responsible for behaving accordingly, to have themselves removed from abusive households—to be freed, at least for a moment, from the harsh working conditions they endured.[27] In a similar manner, judges and governors often removed slaves and criados from hostile homes in return for key testimony in high-profile cases. Tobi, María Candelaría, and the criado Silverio Muñoz were all removed from the treasurer's household in the aftermath of their testimonies, apparently avoiding retribution. In other cases, slaves and criados provided incriminating testimony only after an abusive master was jailed, likely hoping that more evidence might keep a cruel head of the household incarcerated.

The number of household workers who came forward to testify against doña Casiana hints that they suffered harsh treatment from her or her husband. From the household slaves to the mayordomo of don Clemente's hacienda, to a laundress who only lived in the home for three months, servants and slaves spared no lurid detail as the testified, providing insider accounts of la Tesorera's long-standing involvement with don Toribio.[28] No witness matched Tobi in the extent of his cooperation with and usefulness to prosecutors as they built their case against don Toribio. Beyond his elaborate firsthand account of the lovers' play, Tobi had disobeyed doña Casiana's orders to burn all of the letters she had received from don Toribio, saving a few from the fire that he provided to prosecutors.[29] (Don Toribio ignored her repeated requests to burn her letters, leaving us with at least two years of correspondence that give a week-by-week account of the affair.)[30] Tobi obviously risked his masters' wrath, but reporting his indiscretions was a calculated risk that paid off. Prosecutors removed both Tobi and his wife from the treasurers' house for their own safekeeping. Lic. Piñeres ordered the army's captain of engineers, don Rafael Llovet, a trusted outsider and reliable bureaucrat, to take custody of the two as a protective measure. Llovet, one of the first Spaniards to go on the record regarding his firm belief that don Toribio had killed Gálvez, had a vested interest in protecting Tobi and María Candelaría.[31] The pair apparently never returned to their master's house. Moreover, they managed to remain together in their new household with no threat to their permanent cohabitation. Possibly under duress, the treasurer sold the two absent slaves together to the new intendant, don Arturo O'Neill, for the impressively low sum of 460 pesos in August 1793.[32]

Household Violence and Domestic Resistance

Don Toribio's slaves and criados were by no means safe from their master's notorious violent outbursts, and they were more reluctant to go on the record with less than flattering accounts of his vengeful and aggressive behavior until he was safely behind bars and unable to harm them. After 1795, for example, the elderly, deaf Canary Islander, the criado Juan Ramos, finally divulged his firsthand experiences with decades of arbitrary abuse endured by those who ran afoul of the entitled nephew of Mérida's most powerful man. Tío Juan, as he was commonly known, had come to Mérida as a criado of the deceased peninsular don Rafael Castillo y Sucre, vicar general, or the head ecclesiastical judge of the province. The octogenarian criado, now working in the service of the bishop, remembered that his former master had dared to confront don Toribio over his visits to a previous lover, doña Ignacia Cavera. Shortly afterward, the ecclesiastical judge suffered from such a severe case of diarrhea that he died from it on 12 May 1783.[33] Tío Juan believed that the young peninsular nephew of the bishop had poisoned Castillo y Sucre. While nothing concretely linked him to the ecclesiastic's death, the eighty-year-old criado described in detail don Toribio's penchant for violence. Among his everyday atrocities, don Toribio enjoyed the pastime of shooting stray dogs from his balcony and had once tied a dog to a horse's tail for entertainment.

Not surprisingly, many of don Toribio's slaves and criados held their tongue until the young lieutenant was jailed. Felipe Morales, the first of don Toribio's criados to testify against his master, did so with trepidation. As one of the household domestics who accompanied don Toribio on a daily basis, he had seen his master's wrath. In an attempt to absolve himself of any guilt for his role as the involuntary interlocutor for the bishop's nephew, Felipe told prosecutors that he reluctantly passed notes between don Toribio and doña Casiana only due to the threat of physical punishment had he refused to pass on secrets or stand guard during their trysts.[34] Darker rumors of don Toribio's deep-seated rage reinforced the impression criados and slaves must have had of him as a master who acted with impunity when punishing domestics in his household for even the slightest of infractions. Several officers—including Captain of Engineers Llovet, Col. don Alonso Manuel Peón, and Sub-lieutenant don Luis Durán, as well as don José Rivas—recalled hearing that don Toribio had clubbed to death an unnamed Catalan boy who had been in his service.[35] Whether true or not, testimony from a variety of sources painted a picture of a master prone to violence that no doubt silenced many potential witnesses until he was securely behind bars.

While some slaves and criados took advantage of don Toribio's incarceration to unburden themselves of years of arbitrary abuse and cruelty witnessed or experienced firsthand, others took more drastic steps and fled. In the chaos that followed his jailing, two slaves and a criado ran away from the household and apparently eluded recapture. In 1793 Lic. Bodega ordered his legal assistants to ascertain the whereabouts of two slaves purchased by don Toribio the previous year—Plato and Gaius—shortly after his imprisonment.[36] The two may have avoided detection en route to Belize, where they had previously worked as loggers for Thomas Robertson, an English Bayman, before their capture and resale in Yucatan.[37] It is also possible that they found refuge in two maroon communities in Belize or in the recently established black community, San José de los Negros, in Petén, Guatemala.[38] Flight, better known as a form of resistance on the part of slaves, was also a strategy for disgruntled criados. Santiago Kuyoc, who became a criado of don Toribio in Chikindzonot in 1792, ran away when his master was jailed. He took refuge in the house of his grandfather, the cacique don Gregorio Yama. The cacique began caring for the boy after his 1794 arrival; apparently, he never returned to his master.[39] Criados familiar with Yucatan's landscape probably escaped Spanish households more easily than slaves. In a later phase of the investigation, the criado of don Esteban de Castro, one of Yucatan's two interpreters general, fled as well. Hipólito, a Maya criado identified only by his first name, fled Castro's home long before 1801, when his master mentioned his criado's absence to the authorities.[40]

The Ties that Bind: The High Price of Paternal Bonds

Slaves and criados were not always coerced accomplices spying and delivering illicit messages under duress or captives looking to escape at the earliest opportunity. Deep bonds of paternalism tied a minority of slaves and criados tightly to their masters; loyalty led a few of them to enthusiastically involve themselves in even the most underhanded dealings. In return for their blind obedience, even when they followed directives that were illegal and occasionally violent, such slaves and criados were kept at a safe distance from authorities. The immunities of Spaniards from the most privileged classes of individuals—priests especially—often extended de facto to all household members. When prosecutors overcame these legal barriers, though, criados and slaves suffered disproportionately for their complicity in the crimes of their masters. In a few cases, they suffered imprisonment and even death in dank cells alongside their masters as punishment for a loyalty that led to them to perjure and break other laws.

In spite of his sadistic treatment of criados, animals, and probably slaves, don Toribio's residence was typical of prominent Spanish households in its reliance on the most trustworthy domestics to do dirty deeds, carry out secret errands, and pass along forbidden correspondence out of sight of the prying eyes of prosecutors and nosy neighbors. Not all were as eager as Felipe to paint a negative image of their master. A slave named Tomás and a criado named Toribio stand out from other household domestics who readily recounted decades of violence and sexual misconduct

when finally given a chance to unburden themselves on the record, with
don Toribio behind bars.

Surprisingly, slaves and criados often threatened and intimidated enemies of their masters with an audacity shocking for its defiance of racial
norms of the time. Tomás, a slave of the bishop, threatened Sgt. Eugenio
Cano and Cpl. Juan Esteban Rosado, low-ranking officers who stood guard
at the entry to don Toribio's cell, with retaliation from his powerful master
when the two thwarted his attempt to break through the isolation imposed
on don Toribio by a line of sentries, a cell, and shackles. Responsible for
bringing don Toribio his food, Tomás berated Sergeant Cano in a hoarse
whisper, "Why haven't you allowed a barber to enter [don Toribio's cell] and
give my master a shave?" Supposedly, Cano had refused don Toribio's request
to be shaved six or eight times—a problem, Tomás told him, that would come
to the attention of the bishop, who would soon resolve the matter. Walking
away, Tomás told Sergeant Cano, "You are a bad man."[41] The Afro-Yucatecan
militia corporal Juan Esteban Rosado had similar run-ins with the same
slave while serving guard duty, Cano reported. Tomás made the same threats
about retaliation from the bishop and hurled outrageous insults at Rosado.
Apparently, Rosado had done nothing more to provoke Tomás's anger than
confront him while he tried to pry open the windows of don Toribio's cell.[42]
In spite of his brazen attempts to break a court-ordered gag rule and the
audacious insults he launched at ranking officers, Tomás evidently never
faced any punishment for such acts.[43]

In contrast to his overall reputation as an abusive master, don Toribio's
relationship with his criado and namesake, Toribio López, shows how, in
other instances, paternalistic bonds closely tied heads of households to the
resident domestic dependents who dwelt within the same walls. Toribio
López showed extreme reluctance to testify against his master long after
most other slaves and criados had turned on their incarcerated amo. His fate
highlights how loyalty and familiarity motivated some criados to perpetrate
crimes on their master's behalf. In his recorded statements, López disputed
the incriminating testimony of a number of witnesses against don Toribio.
He contradicted them by averring that while stationed in Tixkokob, his master had only traveled to Mérida when the intendant had granted him a license
to travel. Upon his return from the city carrying clean clothing and chocolate for the bishop's nephew, Toribio the criado stated that he always found
his master in Tixkokob, having never strayed from his post. He rejected José
Moran's accusations that portrayed him as a deeply implicated accomplice,

the mysterious man tending don Toribio's two horses at the Arch of the Mejorada who Luis Lara confronted while don Toribio snuck around town visiting doña Casiana and other lady friends.[44] He denied any knowledge of his master's whereabouts or clandestine visits to the city after don Toribio's reassignment to Tihosuco, noting that he had returned to Mérida without his master to get married and remained there to look after mules in the bishop's stables.[45] In both of his lengthy depositions—in 1792 with Lic. Piñeres and in 1794 with Dr. Guillén—Toribio López staunchly defended his namesake and master against charges of any wrongdoing.[46] Finally, in 1795, after Guillén jailed him, the criado broke down and confessed, recanting his earlier testimony. By then it was too late.

Until 1795, Toribio López had been lying. That year, he belatedly admitted to his role as an accomplice, which went far beyond tending the horses while his master skulked through the city on his prohibited visits. Along with the reluctant criado Felipe, López also had the risky duty of delivering letters between the lovers. Tobi's calculated steps to incriminate doña Casiana inadvertently implicated Toribio in the whole affair. The wife of the treasurer had better sense than don Toribio regarding the letters; she or Tobi, acting under her orders, had burned all but one. With impressive foresight, Tobi also saw the potential for revenge in the voluminous amorous correspondence between his mistress and don Toribio. Surely, doña Casiana would not notice if he saved just one letter from the fire. This sole surviving letter, turned over to prosecutors at the earliest opportunity, ensnared López along with his master. The letter from don Toribio to doña Casiana referred to other letters that Tobi and doña Casiana did burn and cited a letter delivered by "T," a thinly veiled reference to Toribio the criado.[47] The young criado, having denied all knowledge of any contact between doña Casiana and don Toribio, very clearly did know more than he admitted.

The households of the bishop and the treasurer were not unique in pressing slaves and criados into service as proxies in their feuds with other prominent families. The treasurer and his wife's dishonor and the loss of most of their domestic workers, as well as the imprisonment of don Toribio and the flight of many of his slaves and criados did not end the factionalism exacerbated by the deep rifts that opened during Gálvez's term as intendant. Nor did it end the use of slaves and criados to carry out the petty crimes that accompanied the rivalries. As the epicenter of activity related to the assassination investigation (or inaction, according to critics) shifted to Mexico

City in 1796, following don Toribio's removal to the viceregal capital, hostilities continued between the associates of the late intendant and the incarcerated suspect in his assassination. A staunch supporter and persecuted ally of Gálvez in the darkest days following his death, Lic. don Justo Serrano, defender of the Indians of Yucatan's Indian Court, kept sparring with don Miguel Magdaleno Sandoval, the acting assessor of war and partisan of the bishop's palace. Much of their bickering consisted of disparaging letters and legal wrangling, but occasionally the tension ratcheted up a degree or two with threats of aggression that punctuated the war of words.[48] Even with their powerful benefactors gone from the scene, the two sworn enemies continued to antagonize each other well into the first decade of the nineteenth century.[49] The men never resorted to violence against one another; instead, their slaves and criados stood in for them as vandals and brawlers on their behalf.

In 1797 the simmering feud erupted into the severe beating of a mestizo criado boy in the house of the defender of the Indians by one of the slaves of don Miguel Magdaleno Sandoval. The incident, noteworthy enough that news of it eventually reached the viceroy in Mexico City, serves as a final example of the involvement of slaves and criados in their masters' disputes and illustrates the responsibility often taken by patriarchal household heads in efforts to extricate their domestic dependents from legal trouble. Each side presented a contradictory version of the row, and Sandoval concluded his litany of grievances against Lic. Serrano by suggesting that Serrano's reckless behavior leading up the fight precipitated the brawl. In the Barrio of Santa Ana on a crowded Sunday during a fiesta, Sandoval said, Serrano had spotted him and a lieutenant of the dragoons, don José Román, in the midst of the festive crowd. According to Sandoval, Serrano goaded his coachman into charging toward them at a full gallop, most likely aimed to give his rival a good scare rather than actually injure him. Sandoval praised his own restraint in the matter—especially for his forbearance with the criado coachman, who he opted not to reprimand publicly in order to avoid causing a scene.[50]

Serrano countered this version of events by focusing on the more recent incident, where the black slave coachman of his rival had beaten his eleven-year-old criadito, or young criado, with a stick or a whip for doing nothing more than loitering behind Sandoval's carriage. The whipping, which left welts and bruises, was not only unjustified but went against racial norms of the era. He demanded a severe punishment for Sandoval's slave, named Tomás, based on a racial hierarchy in which a mestizo outranked a black man. "Does a black slave, vile according to the order of men, have the power to punish a mestizo boy?" asked Serrano. He stated that offenses suffered by criados were insults shared by their masters. Serrano argued that Tomás merited harsh treatment both because a black slave attacking a mestizo disrupted the racial order and because the beating of a criado was an affront to his master's person.[51]

Sandoval fully approved of his slave's attack on his rival's criado, a just punishment in his view. While visiting Lieutenant Román, the two heard a ruckus from the alley near where they were standing and moved closer to see what was happening. Tomás informed him that he had just beaten a boy he found trying to pull out a nail from the carriage with a rock. Tomás identified him as the eleven-year-old criado of Lic. Serrano. Sandoval then reiterated his support for his slave, suggesting that the only improvement would have been to inflict an even more brutal beating on the young criado.[52] Sandoval's dismissal of Serrano's complaint made no mention of race. The assessor never discussed the ethnicity of Serrano's second "servant," a coachman who stood by and watched the event unfold, probably the same criado who drove Serrano's carriage in the first incident. Sandoval, omitting any mention of caste or ethnicity, emphasized the young criado's disrespect toward magistrates and superiors—including himself—who were appointed by God and the king. His argument emphasized social hierarchy regardless of race.

Royal and viceregal authorities rejected Lic. Serrano's race-based argument and declined to punish Tomás. The main thrusts of the competing arguments presented by two of the province's top legal scholars reflect contrasting viewpoints of how society should be arranged, especially in legal matters. Sandoval emphasized an individual's station in life regardless of race while Serrano argued for the importance of a racial order, a hierarchy of castes, as the basis of one's place in society.[53] The social distance between a mestizo criado and a black slave was hardly significant enough to make an altercation between the two household domestics seem like a grave violation of a rigid caste system to most Yucatecans.[54] And in terms of removal from family, loss of kin ties and workday activities, and absolute dependence on the often capricious heads of households, slaves and criados indeed resembled each other quite closely.

Slaves and *Criados* in Colonial Yucatecan Society

By the eighteenth century, slaves such as Tomás were a small minority within Yucatan's population, outnumbered by a larger free mixed-race Afro-Yucatecan population and Maya majority. Late colonial Yucatan was a society with slaves, not a slave society.[55] Like Tomás, most of Yucatan's slaves lived and worked in a domestic setting. Maya campesinos shouldered the burden of producing a scant agricultural surplus for the benefit of a European-descent upper class, unlike slave societies in the Americas in which enslaved Africans bore the brunt of productive work. In Yucatan, slaves and the ubiquitous criados usually toiled in Spanish homes cooking, washing, gardening, driving carriages, keeping stables, tending livestock and horses, working as porters, and bartering for food and other items in the market. Despite their varied racial, ethnic, and geographic backgrounds, Yucatan's slaves and criados lived and worked in close proximity and occupied a similar position toward the bottom of Yucatan's social pyramid.

Slaves almost inevitably worked in Spanish households doing domestic tasks, while criados worked in a wider range of occupations, some of them with more independence than others.[56] Ambiguous in terms of race, legal status, and personal autonomy, criados remain a poorly understood social category, despite their widespread presence in colonial Mérida.[57] The word *criado* does not translate well into English. "Servant" does not adequately convey the prominent role Spanish households played in the upbringing of criados from a young age and the incorporation of criados into their new households at the expense of extended kin networks left behind in the countryside. At its root, *criado* has its origin in the Spanish verb "criar," to raise.[58] In most cases, criados were raised from a young age in the house of their master. Unlike other regions, Yucatan's criados varied a great deal in racial background, ranging from Indian to Spaniard to mestizo to free black.[59] The independence, prestige, and standing within the household hierarchy did depend in part on one's ancestry, but race did not necessarily consign one to a specified place within the domestic pecking order.

The numerous servants, slaves, overseers, and retainers working for the bishop and his nephew aptly illustrate the differentiation of occupations and the status of slaves and criados in Yucatecan society. At the top of the hierarchy of household domestics were criados from respectable peninsular Spanish backgrounds, some of whom were addressed with the honorific title don. Some resided with their masters while others lived more independently.

Spanish criados often worked as mayordomos, overseers of haciendas who only rarely had contact with their masters, or as scribes and other trained professionals. To give one example, don Nicolás Domínguez, a criado of don Toribio, worked as the mayordomo of the hacienda of a priest identified only by his surname, Padre Campos.[60] His formal title don suggests a higher status than most of the criados of the household, distinguishing him from other household servants. Furthermore, he appears in the record identified as don Toribio's "compañero y escribiente," or companion and scribe, almost as often as he is referred to as a criado.[61] Even when they continued as retainers in prominent households, criados from more prominent backgrounds received an education, had more specialized skills, and moved about with more freedom and less direct oversight than most slaves and criados. However, the association of Spaniards with privileged positions in elite households was not a hard and fast rule. Some Spaniards worked at household chores under the watchful eyes of their masters, similar to casta, Indian, and black domestics. Tío Juan, for example, came from the Canary Islands but served as a doorman in the bishop's palace.[62]

Below the independent, trusted criados selected for an independent life of clerical or managerial assistance for prominent clergymen or bureaucrats, criados and slaves closely resembled each other as they performed many of the same domestic tasks, lived in the same residences, and often suffered the same abusive treatment as household dependents. As one of the wealthiest men in Mérida (in spite of a vow of poverty taken as a member of the Benedictine order), fray Luis had a large multiethnic mix of slaves and criados working in his household. Plato and Gaius, the two slaves of a Belizean Bayman who were captured after they chased a stray ox into Spanish territory, had their housekeeping skills listed repeatedly by the town crier, Isidoro Xix, at the auction and in previous announcements leading up to their sale. Xix, an indio ladino, announced that Plato worked as a coachman, knew how to "work in the house," and had a novice's knowledge of the cooper's trade. Gaius had learned how to comb, shave, cook, and drive a coach.[63] Black slaves frequently worked as coachmen, such as José Antonio Betancur, Gálvez's black carriage driver who witnessed the assassination. Tobi had a particularly thorough knowledge of doña Casiana's whereabouts at all times as another enslaved coachman who figured prominently in the trial. Slaves were not the only coachmen, though. Mestizo and Maya criados, such as Luis Lara, also worked as carriage drivers. Lara, one of the unluckiest criados in Mérida's history, drove a carriage in addition to performing other domestic tasks, including shopping for meat and vegetables. At least one of four criados living and working in the household of the subdelegado of the Partido de la Costa, don Manuel Antolín, served as his coachman. The two long-standing rival *letrados* (formally educated, literate bureaucrats and administrators, often of middling origins), Lics. Serrano and Sandoval, had coachmen from differing racial backgrounds. A mestizo criado drove Serrano's carriage, while Tomás, a black slave, worked as Sandoval's coachman.

Criados and slaves divided up housekeeping chores in no way based specifically on race. Gender played somewhat of a role, judging from the regular presence of María Candelaría and the unnamed female slave in the private spaces of the house of the condesa viuda. Each had a much more intimate knowledge of the interior rooms of Spanish households, while male slaves and criados were more likely to accompany their masters and mistresses outside of the house. Male criados and slaves also cooked and shopped; Luis Lara seemed to recognize the man with the horse outside the house of Francisco Ek as a cattle butcher or vendor of meat by-products, since one of his regular errands was shopping for meat for his ama, or head of the house, doña María Pérez. "Negro Tomás," the slave who came to the attention of the authorities for his threats against the men guarding don Toribio, cooked the food and brought it to his master.[64] Other criados, such as Luis of don Manuel Antolín's household, also worked as cooks, as did a criado in the house of the alcalde don Fernando Rodríguez de la Gala.[65] Don Justo Serrano's household included at least one other criado working as a coachman.[66] Other tasks included Tío Juan's work as a doorman in the bishop's palace.[67] Criados' work differed little from that of Yucatan's household slaves, with the exception of most Spanish criados—usually peninsulares—who accompanied high-ranking priests and government officials in their entourages and experienced more mobility in terms of occupation and independence.

Into Spanish Homes: *Criados*, Slaves, and Disparate Routes to Servitude

Doing roughly the same tasks, residing in prominent households, and comparable in their freedom of movement, slaves and criados did differ a great deal in their origins. Unlike the diverse backgrounds of criados, slaves in Yucatan were inevitably of African descent due to a long-standing and mostly enforced ban on Indian slavery after 1542 in Spain's American territories.[68] Like elsewhere in colonial Latin America, slaves were purchased, baptized, and placed into Spanish homes, where they faced lives of servitude. Compared to elsewhere, though, slaves in eighteenth- and early nineteenth-century Yucatan came from British territories (especially after 1760) in higher numbers than elsewhere in the Spanish Empire, and many of them were taken by force.[69] The proximity of slave traders in Jamaica and slave owners in Belize undoubtedly led to Yucatan having a greater percentage of slaves of English origin. The asiento, or the monopoly on slave trading in the Spanish colonies conceded by Madrid to another nation or private company, had passed to the British in 1713.[70] By 1792, the proportion of Francophone slaves had diminished, a trend accelerated by the Haitian Revolution of 1791–1804, which led to severe restrictions on slaves from French territories. Fears that French slaves brought revolutionary ideas and experiences with them led most colonists in Yucatan to adhere to such restrictions. During the Age of Atlantic Revolutions (ca. 1776–1850), they were frequently turned away from Spanish ports in the Americas, including Sisal and Campeche.[71] Sporadic outbreaks of war with England, by contrast, did not cause such alarm. Slaves displaced in such conflicts were not perceived as potential agents of insurrection. Instead, they were seen as fair game for capture, reenslavement, and, in many instances, asylum and manumission.

Yucatan was never a rich province. It had a relatively minuscule slave population. Few Yucatecans owned more than one or two slaves, and only a narrow stratum of the province's wealthiest residents could afford to buy them. Campeche, its largest slave trading port, was never a major center for the sale of slaves. Yucatan's limited resources led many of the province's would-be slave owners and small-time slave traders to resort to one of the oldest methods of slaving in the history of the world: capture in warfare, specifically border raids and small skirmishes. The capture, imprisonment, and sale of Plato and Gaius, a process in which the intendant and his alleged assassin played a prevalent role, illustrates how slaves from British Belize wound up as slaves in Spanish households. In what might have been the last of his mundane administrative tasks, don Lucas de Gálvez ratified the legality of the capture of two slaves from Belize, rejected the appeals of the English slave owner to have them restored to his possession, and approved their sale to the highest bidder. That purchaser, who bought the slaves after Gálvez's death, was none other than don Toribio del Mazo.

Despite the bitter enmity between the intendant and the bishop, Gálvez made a decision shortly before his death that benefited the bishop's household, including his nephew. Despite posthumous charges from Gálvez's critics that he spent most of his time stirring up controversies and chasing women, more mundane affairs absorbed at least some of his final hours. On 21 June, in his last forty-eight hours of life, don Lucas wrote the final word in one of the small international incidents that occasionally erupted along Yucatan's southern boundary with the English territory of Belize. He approved of the capture of two Anglophone slaves and the slaughter of two oxen that had crossed the porous and poorly guarded frontier region between Salamanca de Bacalar and Belize. Originally from Africa's Guinean coast, "Pleito and Coiys" (Plato and Gaius), identified as bozales in the colonial terminology, had crossed the controversial and unclear boundary to cut wood and retrieve two escaped oxen.[72] After a small army patrol from Bacalar under Capt. don Juan Bautista Gual and Cpl. Juan Frith apprehended the two in Spanish territory, the fate of the cattle and the men took a turn for the worse. Corporal Frith and five soldiers slaughtered the oxen for the slaves' defiance of the treaty terms of 1786 and sat down to eat the meat.

Plato and Gaius were imprisoned for trespassing on Spanish territory, by the terms of the recent accord that ended one of the frequent but never successful Yucatecan attempts to drive the British from Central America.[73] Upon hearing of their capture, the superintendent of the English settlements in Belize wrote in support of their owner and his petition to recover the slaves. In a surprisingly humble tone, William Penn begged for the two slaves to be returned to their master, Thomas Robertson. He even suggested that Robertson might be willing to buy them back.[74] Gálvez rejected the request and consigned the two slaves to a status as royal property, with proceeds from their sale going into crown coffers.[75]

The weak bargaining position of Penn and Robertson was further undermined by the slaves' admission that they had entered Spanish territory on earlier occasions. Plato and Gaius confessed that they had previously crossed into Yucatan to harvest caoba (mahogany) wood, a hardwood variety that was an economic mainstay for the British settlers.[76] Corporal Frith brought up this additional violation of the terms of the 1786 treaty in his parley with Robertson at the neutral point of Boca de Talova, in which the corporal served as interpreter and bearer of bad news for the English settler. Robertson did not deny the charges. Informed of the decision that his appeal to recover Plato and Gaius had been denied, he asked Corporal Frith to pass a message to his former slaves that they were no longer in his power; he could do nothing for them now.[77]

Robertson's loss was don Toribio's gain. Following the completion of all relevant paperwork, the process of selling the slaves began about six months after their capture. First, Isidoro Xix made nine announcements of the availability of the slaves, beginning on 15 October 1792.[78] Finally, almost a month and a half later, a buyer stepped forward. Don Toribio, still free despite rumors that circulated about his involvement in the intendant's death, went about his business, which included purchasing the slaves on behalf of his powerful protector and uncle, Bp. fray Luis de Piña y Mazo. Fray Luis was too ill to attend the auction in person. On 29 November, don Toribio went to the auction house where don Miguel Magdaleno Sandoval, interim assessor of the intendancy, presided over the sale. The sale briefly brought together Sandoval; don Toribio; the treasurer, don Clemente Rodríguez de Trujillo; as well as don Justo Serrano, in his capacity as *promotor fiscal*, a prosecuting attorney.[79] Suspects, enemies, and erstwhile friends of the deceased intendant briefly united for routine business shortly before they all were caught up in a divisive and protracted assassination investigation. Each man signed the document one by one.[80] Of those in attendance, only Xix's signature does not appear.[81]

Plato and Gaius were not the only slaves who made their way involuntarily into Spanish homes from British territories, often captured in the warfare that broke out from time to time between the Spanish lands and English settlements in the Greater Caribbean region in the eighteenth century. Tobi also had English ties, captured in the 1770s from an English boat taken by Havana-based Spanish forces under the command of Capt. don José Victor off the coast of Cozumel.[82] Three more slaves captured in a similar border incident were sold just three years before don Toribio's purchase of Plato and Gaius, in 1789, in a nearly identical process.[83] An 1802 decision regarding the fate of seven slaves who escaped from English territories ended when three slaves who had made their way to Yucatan in the hope of gaining their freedom were resold into slavery as well.[84] Capturing and selling slaves from Belize for border infractions or during outbreaks of war was commonplace in Yucatan from the middle of the eighteenth century until the early nineteenth century.[85]

Other slaves arrived through more mundane transactions, also via the British, who were the most active traders in the eighteenth century.[86] Demand was limited, and sellers often waited months for any buyers to make offers. Plato and Gaius saw a month and a half and nine *pregones*, or official public announcements, pass before an interested buyer made a bid.[87] Sometimes it seemed that no purchasers would step forward, leaving the slaves in a state of limbo. Of the three slaves captured in 1789, one waited over a year for a buyer.[88] This unfortunate slave, Jorge—known as *el Viejo*, or "the old one"—was sold to don Santiago Bolio for just 80 pesos on 16 May 1791. Slave prices dropped precipitously in central New Spain and less sharply in Yucatan during the eighteenth century.[89] The timing of this decline in the price of slaves correlates with the demographic recovery of rural Mayas and an upsurge in the population of rural castas. Coming from the countryside often too parched or poor to feed all of its inhabitants, many nominally orphaned children made their way to cities and Spanish households as a poorly understood side effect of this demographic recovery. Frequently found in middling and elite Spanish homes, even in many households too poor to purchase slaves, the ready availability of criados might well have further depressed the demand for slaves. While the entry of slaves into Spanish homes is a thoroughly understood and well-documented process, the ways in which heads of households "adopted" criados requires more discussion.

Criados entered upper- and middle-class Spanish households in three main ways. First, free black and Spanish criados accompanied preeminent peninsular priests and administrators to Yucatan as part of an extended household unit that crossed the Atlantic Ocean together. Second, at least some criados—usually of mixed race—were illegitimate offspring living with the publicly unacknowledged father or some close relative. Finally, and most frequently, rural priests and administrators rounded up ostensibly orphaned rural Maya and casta children and later allocated them to Spanish households. In such cases, the young were referred to as "orphans" and even "gifts." Criados ensnared as suspects, called upon as witnesses, or otherwise entangled in the assassination investigation in spite of their young age, often provided prosecutors with extensive biographic details, providing a better understanding of a ubiquitous but little-known category of household servants whose very existence is often overlooked.

The best-documented criados in Mérida's principle households were Spanish and free black criados who accompanied peninsulares to Yucatan to take up prestigious posts within the priesthood or royal government. Listed by age, place of origin, race, and freed or enslaved status, most passenger lists included an entire household as they embarked. For example, when don Clemente Rodríguez del Trujillo departed from Cadíz in 1777, he was accompanied by his wife, his brother don Balthasar Rodríguez del Trujillo, and another young, single male relative, don Nicolás Madrid y Postigo, as well as two criados—Justa Fernández and Antonio Cavezas—each listed with age, marital status, and specific town and parish of origin.[90] Passenger lists of peninsulares arriving to assume the post of bishop or governor or other high-ranking ecclesiastical or secular governmental positions generally included two to four criados. Peninsular criados usually accompanied royal and ecclesiastical officials from Spain, but a few free black criados also accompanied high-ranking priests and administrators. The passenger lists emphasize their status as *negros libres* (free blacks), differentiating them from slaves; when Dr. don Rafael del Castillo y Sucre, *maestrescuela* (master of divinity), brought the former slave José Ganga with him to Mérida, he exhibited both a certificate of baptism and the 1775 grant of liberty his criado Ganga had received from his deceased master, don Gerónimo Borrego y Alba.[91]

At least five free blacks traveled to Yucatan from Spain as criados of Spaniards either departing for or returning to Mérida.[92] Of the five, the three who had their place of origin listed hailed from different parts of the Americas. Ganga came from Havana, while another major Greater Caribbean port—Cartagena de Indias—was the birthplace of Melchor de la Torre, who accompanied the Dominican bishop-elect Maestro Antonio Alcalde to Mérida in 1763.[93] The other free black accompanying the entourage as a criado was Antonio de Arcos, listed as an unspecified native of the Indies, who had apparently spent time in both Guatemala and Havana. Sra. doña Francisca Sancho, "presidenta" of Guatemala, granted Arcos his freedom to accompany fray Vicente González to Spain to avoid suffering under the British who had captured the port.[94] Both de la Torre and Arcos took advantage of the opportunity to return to the Americas as criados, not slaves.

Such detailed background information on criados who crossed the Atlantic contrasts sharply with the indistinct and forgotten paths of Yucatecan-born criados into Spanish homes. Juana Canto, an Afro-Yucatecan criada, lived a life that poignantly illustrates the alienating experience and loss of identity experienced by criados torn from rural homes at young ages to serve in Spanish households. Her history reaches us via the record of her painstaking and twice-failed efforts to simply receive permission to marry in a Catholic church in 1801. All Yucatecans under Spanish rule—free, slave, Spanish, Maya, Afro-Yucatecan, casta, noble, and commoner—passed three major life events in a church: baptism, marriage, and a funeral mass. In order to marry, one had to demonstrate that they had taken the first step of initiation into the religion of the Spanish monarchs and their subjects: baptism. Although Juana was born in Yucatan and most likely never left the province, she had been so thoroughly uprooted and cut off from her past and her family that Mérida's clergymen did not even know if priests in her anonymous birthplace had indeed sprinkled her with holy water to formally bring her into the Catholic faith, and if so, in which parish her baptism had taken place.[95] Juana, a Mérida criada—probably a *vecina de color*, or person of at least partial African heritage—illustrates the most extreme case of alienation as a true "genealogical isolate."[96]

Two suitors had already given up any hope of marrying Juana and walked away from their proposals to marry her when she finally found a household head willing to aid her in her search for her baptismal record. Magdalena Mijangos, the female head of the third household in which the orphaned or abandoned criada dwelt, tried to help her criada find the documentation of her Christian baptism, a prerequisite for Catholic marriage. Although she succeeded in overcoming the obstacles to her pending wedding, her past remained a mystery. Like slaves, many but not all criados became outsiders residing in Spanish homes completely cut off from their families and birthplaces, an experience described as "social death" in the context of slavery.[97] The tangled and ultimately futile attempts to confirm Juana's Christian baptism reveals the callous disregard with which other Spaniards oversaw a criado's transition to elite households.

Aided by Mijangos, Juana retraced her past, seeking information on her roots and forgotten early childhood. Doña Rosalia Calderón of Valladolid, Juana's former "owner," remembered receiving Juana Canto as a "gift" from don Juan Francisco Muñoz, lieutenant governor of Valladolid, ten or eleven years earlier.[98] Doña Rosalia knew nothing of Juana's parentage or place of origin before Muñoz turned over the young orphan to work in her household. Muñoz himself recalled that he had allocated many orphans to prominent Spaniards during the governorship of don Roberto Rivas, but he insisted that he had always done so with records of their baptisms. He denied having placed any criada in the care of doña Rosalia and said that he knew nothing of Juana's past.[99]

In the end, Dr. Santiago Martínez de Peralta, the vicar general (*provisor vicario general y governador del obispado sede vacante*, a church position second in command to the bishop and the highest ecclesiastical official, who in effect acted as bishop after his death while the seat remained empty), decreed that Juana should be baptized *sub conditione* (conditional baptism) so that her third suitor did not walk away empty-handed.[100] Other than hints that Juana was at least partially of African ancestry, based on a reference to a government notary's visit to the "pueblo negro" and Muñoz's insistence that he had never placed a "vecina de color" in the care of doña Rosalia, Juana, Mijangos, the clergymen, and the notaries never discovered any documentations of the criada's parentage and exact place of birth. The term *criados* implies that, rather than being adopted, these children, given as gifts, were unpaid, captive juvenile laborers, with little to distinguish them from the household slaves alongside whom they toiled.[101]

On the other hand, Mijangos's concern for her criada during Juana's dogged pursuit of matrimony shows the maternalistic side of some criada-ama relationships. Criadas in female-headed households—especially in homes headed by widows and childless single women—apparently fared better than most of these nominally orphaned child laborers. Often with no families of their own to inherit their property, widows and childless women often willed and donated impressive amounts of property and money to criadas, showing uncharacteristic concern for their servants' well-being. For example, the widow doña Bernardina Cabrera donated half of a *solar* (an urban house-plot) in the barrio of San Juan Bautista to her criada Nicolasa Chan and her *crianzas* (criadas under age seven).[102] Another indigenous criada, Theresa Mex, received the impressive sum of 400 pesos in the testament of her ama, doña Josepha Pinto Cabero. Doña Josepha's other two criadas, Feliciana López and Manuela Panti, received 200 and 150 pesos, respectively.[103] Men tended not to be so generous with their criados, judging from the records they left in notarial records.

Unacknowledged kinship ties might have motivated at least some of the affection amas felt for their criadas. The strong bonds between the most infamous criada-ama duo involved in the trial—Juana Martínez, the criada, and her namesake, doña Juana Martínez—derived in part from unacknowledged family connections. The two shared a name, gossip, a social life, and apparently blood ties. Close relationships between criadas and amas meant that the gossip running rampant in Mérida's elite houses involved members of Mérida's high society as well as their closest and favored servants and retainers. Through their connections to powerful families, criados and slaves influenced public opinion through rumors that spread well beyond the limits of their own race and class. These whispered tales of complicity, criminality, and illicit love affairs, passed on by slaves and criados, often originated with their masters. In spite of a solid alibi and no apparent motive for killing the intendant, reports of the complicity of José Bermejo circulated even after don Toribio was incarcerated and public opinion widely held him to be the killer. In an attempt to stifle the scuttlebutt, the second outside prosecutor, Dr. don Francisco de Guillén, uncovered the origin of the campaign of whispers that implicated Bermejo in the assassination: the criada Juana Martínez. Guillén's line of questioning led back to the source of the rumors exonerating don Toribio, the criada, and Toribio López, don Toribio's namesake and criado. López, "the most inseparable" of don Toribio's criados, likely urged on by his master, passed the rumor to the criada. She in turn passed the hearsay to the sister of doña Juana Martínez, doña Narcisa Suárez. La Suárez, one of the leading gossips of her day, insisted to anyone who would listen that prosecutors were pursuing the wrong man; José Bermejo, not don Toribio, was the assassin.[104]

With increasing certainty, Guillén also traced Juana Martínez's parentage to a close relative of doña Juana. Along with revealing Juana Martínez as the source of rumors circulated by La Suárez, Dr. Guillén took it upon himself to investigate her ancestry, writing with increasing certitude that young Juana's unnamed father was a close relative of doña Juana. Juana Martínez, described as both "india" and "mestiza" in the space of two paragraphs, probably owed the confusion over her ethnicity to doubts about the identity of one of her parents.[105] Born and raised in the house of her namesake, the criada Juana Martínez had married Toribio López, the most loyal of don Toribio's servants. Dr. Guillén, writing in 1797, noted that doña Juana Martínez "also had living with her a Juanita Martínez who took her surname because she was born and raised there and was probably sired by a relative of hers."[106] A year later, he wrote with more certitude that Juanita was indeed the daughter of a relative of doña Juana, fathered in an illicit affair.[107] Juanita, as he called the criada, and doña Juana, were on more familiar terms than most criadas and amas. Juanita did not behave as a humble and unseen domestic servant but instead participated actively in social events at the house, judging from the fact that many of the rumors intended to cast doubt on don Toribio's guilt were traced back to her.[108]

Between the extremes of the two Juanas—one who had moved from house to house to the point she did not even remember her place of birth and another who seemingly lived in reasonably happy circumstances with a close, if unacknowledged relative—were more typical criadas like María Ventura, the young criada of don Pedro Rafael Pastrana, who lived in the capital but held the post of subdelegado of Tihosuco. These girls and women lived and worked in the homes of their masters but enjoyed some freedom and kept their family connections intact.[109] Ventura apparently lived in the home of her master, but she enjoyed enough liberty to visit her Mérida relatives frequently. On the night of the murder, at least, she had been permitted to travel freely, even at night, to visit her brother, Luis Ventura, and sister-in-law, María Puc.[110] Less is known about male-female master-criada interactions, but don Rafael was at least on familiar enough terms with his criada that she had no hesitation in reporting to him the strange incident on the night of her visit: an offhand conversation that landed her unfortunate neighbor Luis Lara in jail for over four years.

Tied to the Masters' Fates: *Criados*, Slaves, and the Law

Lara, who enjoyed far more autonomy than most criados, working as a shoemaker in his spare time and living in the house of Francisco Ek instead of with his main employer, doña María Pérez, did not benefit from this relative independence in his dealings with the law. The tribulations of Lara, working in the home of a middling if respectable Spanish widow rather than the more elite residences of most of the criados listed above, highlights just how closely criados' and slaves' fates were bound up with the status, position, and sway—and most likely gender—of the heads of the household in which they dwelt. In spite of her pleas that prosecutors release her only criado, upon whom she depended for basic housekeeping and errands, doña María Pérez did not have enough clout to free her sole, indispensable domestic worker. Although she was referred to as a "doña," she clearly was not among Mérida's most prestigious women, along the lines of doña Casiana or the condesa viuda. Only one criado served in her household, and he lived outside her home, working as a shoemaker to make ends meet.

Both slaves and criados faced sentences that were inextricably linked to the luck of their masters, especially in the ability of their masters to provide them with effective legal counsel and protection from prosecution. Some masters—like fray Luis, Sandoval, and Lic. Serrano—acted as dedicated and mostly effective advocates of their charges. In the case of both of the slaves known as Tomás, questionable behavior did not lead to punishment—no doubt a result of the prominence of the respective household head. In exchange for their loyalty and willingness to act as foot soldiers in the factional fighting for their masters, both of these slaves escaped jailing and prosecution. Serrano's eleven-year-old criadito did endure a severe beating from one of the two aforementioned slaves, but neither he nor Serrano's other criado faced prosecution for their vandalism and reckless endangerment of bystanders that they undertook at their master's behest.

In rare instances, a family's prominent position was enough to protect their in-house clients from prosecution even when they were relatively autono-mous artisans. Some of the most prominent families provided skilled artisans with permanent and temporary lodging, allowing such craftsmen to operate their shops and sell their wares from their homes. Such individuals were not criados although they were still household dependents to a certain extent. The Quijanos, for example, hosted an unnamed Indian who they never identified as a criado, despite his subservient status and residence in their home. Instead, he worked relatively independently as a candlemaker. Nevertheless, this anon-ymous Indian, brought up in connection with the powerful Quijano family, was identified as an individual who might be willing to commit violence on his benefactors' behalf. He came to the attention of authorities after he mocked the merchant don José Boves, a spurned suitor of one of the Quijano daughters. In the resulting altercation, Boves chased his tormenter down the street and con-fiscated a knife from him, a weapon he felt merited the authorities' attention. Neither Boves nor the unnamed Indian ever faced charges as a result of the altercation, despite prohibitions on Indians' possessing weapons in late eighteenth-century Yucatan.[111] Spanish heads of households did not always make a serious effort to protect their charges from the long arm of the law, though. In a rare instance, at least one master, the cabildo councilman don Miguel Bolio, grew so exasperated with the habitual drunkenness of his criado, Juan Cauich, that he turned him over to authorities to face punishment at the hands of the municipal justices.[112]

Spanish heads of households benefited from an array of legal immunities and jurisdictional exemptions far greater than those of most colonial sub-jects in the Americas. In practice, this distance from and defense against intrusive prosecution and investigation by agents of Spanish courts extended to their household dependents, both servants and offspring alike. At the top of the social pyramid, privileged Spaniards like don Toribio benefited from overlapping layers of immunity; the bishop's nephew and his attorneys argued that as a militia officer he was shielded from prosecution by the likes of Lic. Bodega and Dr. Guillén by claiming the coverage of the fuero militar. His residence in the bishop's palace added another tier of immunity via the ecclesiastical fuero that limited the jurisdiction of civil authorities over members of the bishop's household. The most heated arguments over whether or not the fueros of the masters pertained to their dependents connected to Gálvez's assassination took place in the rural sphere rather than the city and are examined in the next chapter. In the cities, the most loyal criados and slaves usually enjoyed a measure of protection from prosecution by civil judges, but only as long as their masters avoided punishment. When, as part of the Bourbon reforms, ground-level adherents of the secularizing thrust of Carlos III and Carlos IV prosecuted clergymen and gathered evidence in churches and ecclesiastical compounds long considered off-limits, unlucky criados shared in their master's reversal of fortune.

Faithful slaves and criados often bore the brunt of the misfortunes that befell their masters. On some occasions, such shared retaliation was fairly minor. For example, the unnamed eleven-year-old mestizo criado of Lic. Serrano suffered a severe beating for his part in his master's schemes but faced no charges for his vandalism. One of the earliest prisoners—the fifth on the list of those arrested—was an unnamed criado of don Antonio Poveda, the bishop's doctor. His imprisonment was brief and unexplained, likely due to nothing more than the suspicions that hovered around his master, the surgeon, during the early months of the investigation.[113] However, two more criados paid the ultimate price for unswerving loyalty to their masters. These two died in prison, faithfully remaining by the side of their masters until the ends of their lives.[114] Toribio López, the favorite servant and namesake of don Toribio del Mazo, died in prison on 4 July 1798 after more than four years of imprisonment, faithful to don Toribio to the last.[115] After the jailing of the priest don José Tadeo Quijano, whose prosecution was a landmark triumph for Bourbon legal scholars who argued for the precedence of regular royal courts above ecclesiastical tribunals regarding serious crimes by priests, the scion of a leading family went to jail alongside his criado. Juan José Novelo, the thirty-five-year-old Spanish criado died in prison in the company of his master in the Castillo de Perote in 1802.[116] Both masters—don Toribio del Mazo and don José Tadeo Quijano—lived long enough to walk free.

Conclusion

Urban Spanish households were racially diverse, populous living quarters inhabited by upper-class creole and peninsular families, as well as an array of domestic workers, both nominally free criados and slaves. Slaves tended to be overwhelmingly black, although a few were of mixed African ances-try.[117] Criados came from all ethnic backgrounds—mestizo, Maya, black, mixed Afro-Yucatecan, and Spanish alike—although a racial hierarchy that placed European-descent criados in positions of power prevailed for the most part. Even so, this was a rough correlation. Capricious masters showed favoritism to some criados and slaves over others, with little consideration for racial preferences. However, with the exception of skilled Spanish retain-ers who worked in a managerial and secretarial capacity, the lives of Indian, casta, and free black criados differed little from those of slaves. In legal mat-ters, they resembled each other closely as well.

The criados and slaves examined above showed an incredible adeptness in legal matters. At least two slaves and one criado used their intimate knowl-edge of the private transgressions within households under suspicion to bar-gain for removal from abusive homes and, in one case, a likely promotion. Tobi, María Candelaría, Felipe Morales, and Silverio Muñoz took a calcu-lated risk. Criados were not spared physical violence, well documented as part and parcel of slave societies throughout the early modern Atlantic World. Felipe in particular risked the wrath of don Toribio, reputedly one of the most volatile and violent men in the province. The combination of intim-idation and paternalism led other slaves to enthusiastically act as proxies in family and political rivalries and as they circulated diversionary rumors and reliably provided favorable testimony in their interrogations. In the case of Tomás, the slave responsible for cooking and bringing don Toribio his food during his incarceration, his patrons (the bishop and his nephew) had enough influence to keep their trusted slave from being punished for his efforts to break don Toribio's court-imposed isolation and the audacious insults he hurled at the guards. Others, like young Toribio, who endured four years of incarceration and died in prison for his fealty to his master and namesake, paid for their loyalty with their lives. Other slaves and criados took advan-tage of their masters' legal problems and incarceration and resolved their grievances extrajudicially, fleeing to either their pueblos of birth or elsewhere beyond the reach of their masters' abusive hands.

Over the course of the eight-year investigation into the events surround-ing don Lucas de Gálvez's assassination, prosecutors examined several ser-vants, slaves, artisans, and laborers from the lower strata of Yucatecan society with unprecedented scrutiny. The past two chapters have examined individu-als all too often lumped together as an undifferentiated urban plebe instead of a more intricate and granular image of a stratified and variegated urban working population, a perspective made possible by studying society through the lens of detailed legal proceedings. Scholars often separate segments of society in easily divisible fixed categories based on race and class. Race and class did have an impact on one's place in society, but other official and informal affiliations were important determinants of one's station in life in colonial society. The contrast between Juana Canto and Ignacio de Lara, two urban pardos, illustrates the extent to which a wide social distance separated people of the same race, even though both were Afro-Yucatecan urban commoners. Juana Canto, while nominally free, faced a transient life of dependent domestic servitude as she moved from one home to another as a genealogical isolate so cut off from her past that even bozal slaves had a better memory of their homeland than she did of her place of birth. In contrast, Ignacio de Lara, first cousin of the unfortunate suspect Ignacio Matos, was a master blacksmith, a first sergeant of the pardo militia, and owner of his own home—one large enough to host a gathering of neighbors who met to pray the rosary together. Moreover, the list of his visitors showed that he kept close ties with his relatives, many of whom served in the militia and worked as respectable artisans. Indeed, race was far from being the final arbiter of one's place in society.

By the time prosecutors had exhaustively questioned and cross-examined anyone in the urban sphere who they believed had any information relevant for solidifying their case, they had interrogated *emeritenses* rich and poor, from slaves to nobles—Maya, mestizo, Afro-Yucatecan, and Spaniard. A cross-class interracial chorus gradually built toward a crescendo, ever more united: don Toribio was the killer. Undeterred, don Toribio insisted on his innocence. He repeatedly maintained that he had been in Chikindzonot, within the confines of his assigned posting to Tihosuco, at the time of the murder. The pueblo's priest, don Manuel Correa; the local Spanish authority, the juez español of Chikindzonot, don Pedro Gutiérrez; a Spanish resident, or *vecino*, don Juan Gálvez; the cacique, don Gregorio Yama; and Mauricio Pat, who worked in the employ of an assistant priest in Ekpetz, a nearby pueblo all confirmed his presence in the initial and perfunctory verification of don Toribio's alibi.[118] Yet Lic. Bodega did not move beyond Mérida to question the pueblos' hundreds of Mayas and fifty or so casta residents—mostly Afro-Yucatecans—who might verify or contradict don Toribio's alibi. This task fell to his successor.

CHAPTER 5

Into the Countryside

Outsiders, Intermediaries, and the Maya World

DURING HIS SHORT TERM AS THE SECOND PROSECUTOR, DON MANUEL de la Bodega y Mollinedo made halting progress toward the case's closure, far more than his predecessor, Lic. Piñeres. Yet he left much of the work unfinished upon his departure, a task left to his ambitious and energetic successor, Dr. don Francisco de Guillén. The arrival in mid-June 1793 of a much more cooperative and supportive governor and intendant—don Arturo O'Neill—helped the prosecution in the long run but did not immediately turn the tide against those who sought to derail the investigation. Resistance to the prosecution's progress by many prominent rivals of the deceased intendant remained intractable. Only Dr. Guillén, working in tandem with Brigadier O'Neill as co-judge, led to the relentless pursuit of the suspect with the most evidence against him: don Toribio.[1]

By this point, consternation over the lack of a conviction had reached high levels, leading to the appointment of a proven military officer with administrative experience in border regions partnered with one of New Spain's most experienced magistrates, with a record of efficient prosecutions of difficult crimes. The two worked together much better than Sabido de Vargas and Lic. Bodega: the teniente del rey undermined the juez comisionado at every opportunity. The two also made better use of local intermediaries in their evidence gathering.[2] Intermediaries in late colonial Yucatan made themselves useful to administrators not simply by means of their bilingualism but through their experience in and familiarity with a Maya-speaking countryside. Many creoles spoke at least a minimal amount of Maya but had neither the confidence of the prosecutors and intendants who sought to solve the case nor the trust of the Maya-speaking majority. Together, O'Neill and Guillén had a knack for finding reliable go-betweens from the ranks of men immersed in a Maya world yet loyal and trustworthy to their peninsular superiors. Bodega, by contrast, had not managed to do so.

In the last months of 1793, Bodega complained repeatedly to the crown of the passive resistance of the teniente del rey of Campeche, Sabido de Vargas, who, he wrote, "is not capable of taking one step forward in this matter."[3] More active opposition came from the bishop's quarters and his cabal. Fray Luis, long accustomed to dispatching governors, ratcheted up his opposition to efforts to convict his nephew. The clergyman labeled Bodega an "incompetent judge" in a 21 September 1793 letter to the king that called for the outside prosecutor's removal.[4] Demonstrating his influence over Mérida's leading citizens, the bishop sent vaguely threatening letters to twenty-two prominent residents and functionaries involved in the case, stating that the pursuit of his nephew was an insult to the prelate's honor that scandalized his parishioners. Recipients included the newly arrived intendant, don Arturo O'Neill; don José Sabido de Vargas; Bodega himself; Piñeres; the entire cabildo of Mérida; the royal treasurer; and the captain of the Spanish militia.[5] In short, fray Luis made it quite clear that he was personally invested in the case's outcome. Cooperation with the outside prosecutor would have consequences. Moreover, don Toribio had well-placed allies and relatives at the viceregal court who used back channels and diversionary tactics to slow the case's progress in Mexico City.[6] Bodega complained that as long as the bishop remained in Mérida, no case against his nephew could be pursued until either fray Luis was removed from the province or the audiencia changed the venue for the trial and the preceding questioning.[7] This final request had unforeseen consequences later, frustrating the efforts of a third prosecutor in a way Bodega had never intended.

Beset by ill health and insurmountable opposition centered on the palace of the bishop, Bodega's progress in prosecuting the case slowed in the late spring of 1793.[8] Both Bodega and his assistant, the notary don Fernando de Sandoval y Rojas, complained of grave health problems. In an October letter to the viceroy, Sandoval (apparently no relative of the assessor of Mérida, don Miguel Magdaleno Sandoval) complained of cataracts, sending along a certificate from two surgeons who verified his complaints with expert testimony.[9] Lic. Bodega, in turn, sent copies of grim diagnoses of his own severe health problems by four of Mérida's leading doctors and surgeons: Juan Antonio Mújica, don Francisco Galera y León, don José Guillermo Bates, and don Fernando Guerrero Blanco.[10] Bodega suffered hemorrhoids, swollen vertebrae and knuckles, and severe headaches. He also complained in less specific terms about the poor health of his wife, whose condition was worsened by the burning Mérida sun.

If the bishop and the outside prosecutor agreed on one thing it was that there was not room in Yucatan for both of them. Both apparently preferred that Bodega depart as soon as possible. Starting in early July, Bodega sent a barrage of requests to the viceroy requesting to be relieved of his duties. Beset by personal tragedies and failing health, he had effectively ceased serious work on the case by July 1793. Despite the loss of his infant daughter, failing eyesight, and swollen joints that made writing excruciatingly painful, the former oidor had made significant progress by the time he departed the province. On 15 December 1793, the viceroy, Second Count of Revilla Gigedo, finally accepted Bodega's request to resign. In February 1794, Bodega left the province for good on the brigantine *Volador* just a year after completing his arduous journey to Mérida from Guatemala.[11]

In the same letter that grudgingly acquiesced to Lic. Bodega's incessant pleas to be allowed to resign, the viceroy appointed a much more persistent successor, Dr. don Francisco de Guillén, an attorney registered with the Real Colegio with a doctorate and ten years' experience with criminal matters as an assessor with Mexico's Court of the Acordada, renowned for its efficiency in an age of slow justice.[12] This court was, in the words of one historian of the tribunal, "the core law enforcement organization in New Spain."[13] His reputation for working morning and night foreshadowed his tenacity in pursuing don Toribio, a task which required all of Guillén's dedication and legal acumen due to the young militia lieutenant's coverage by both the *fuero eclésiastico* (as a member of the bishop's household) and the fuero militar (due to his rank as a lieutenant in the white volunteers).

From Madrid's perspective and from Bodega's point of view, the obstacles to identifying the killer and prosecuting him were insurmountable. But royal authorities accurately believed that they had selected the right man for the job. Over a decade earlier, when Guillén took over the post with the Acordada, he replaced a deposed predecessor in that court deemed not up to the task by that tribunal's judge and head, don Manuel Antonio de Santa

Maria y Escobedo, in August 1783.[14] No one questioned his own competence during his tenure in the post. Bodega's replacement also proved to be a much more formidable foe for the province's bishop and the jurisdictional encroachments of the leading churchman on royal authority. He was unswerving in his determination to implement the secularizing aims of the Bourbon monarchs over the protests of the obstinate priests of the province. Dr. Guillén, more tenacious than his predecessor and less inclined to seek approval from Mexico for every small step toward convicting don Toribio, had more luck in his interrogations in the countryside. Though the Audiencia de México had been urging a more thorough investigation into don Toribio's whereabouts during the forty-eight hours surrounding the killing of the intendant, Bodega's illness, malaise, and the obstructionism of the bishop's cohort prevented him from doing more than a perfunctory inquiry in the countryside. Bodega had indeed tried to gather evidence that don Toribio had not been in Chikindzonot on the night of the murder but found that the lack of necessary "persons of confidence" between Sotuta and Tihosuco, a route that don Toribio reportedly took on the night of the murder, thwarted his efforts.[15] Guillén, better at interpersonal diplomacy, able to gain the confidence of key creole rivals of the bishop, and successful in turning many of the prelate's allies against him, had more luck in his examination of the pueblos along the alleged route of don Toribio's midnight ride.

Guillén's precise reconstruction of events in the distant pueblo in the weeks surrounding the assassination included the deployment of a team of interpreters, interrogators, and notaries to hunt for clues from the previously overlooked Maya-speaking majority of the pueblo. Unlike Lic. Bodega, the new prosecutor had a penchant for selecting men at home in the pueblos of eastern Yucatan who had no allegiance to don Toribio nor any fear of his powerful uncle. Mostly young military officers stationed in the region, they served as low-level administrators in new posts created in the second half of the eighteenth century as a part of the Bourbon reforms. They owed their positions to the extensive restructuring of rural government and, at least in Yucatan, hewed closely to Guillén's aims to collect evidence unimpeded and root out any local bureaucrats who got in the way. Rural priests, for their part, united to try to thwart the new prosecutor's scrutiny of the countryside in a failed attempt to stop him from poking even more holes in don Toribio's alibi. Pueblo priests and low-level bureaucrats, overwhelmingly bilingual creoles of middling status, squared off in a church-state struggle writ small, a conflict that caught up local Maya elites and rural castas before the case concluded.

From Mérida, peninsular authorities, both secular and ecclesiastical, relied heavily upon the bilingual abilities of creoles in the countryside. Unable to speak or read Yucatec Maya himself, fray Luis depended on creole curates who read, wrote, and spoke the indigenous language fluently to forge documents in Maya, translate testimony selectively, and browbeat and bribe witnesses into making favorable (and false) statements to investigators. Pitted against this cohort of curates, a band of rural jueces españoles, subdelegados, interpreters, pueblo notaries, and rural militia and army officers translated, questioned, and compiled evidence against don Toribio. Several bilingual creoles were available at a moment's notice, prepared to carry out the routine tasks of the investigation on behalf of either the bishop's faction or the representatives of royal rule, Dr. Guillén and don Arturo O'Neill. Yucatec Maya did not in fact divide Mayas from European-descent Yucatecans. Instead, it isolated peninsulares and urban-dwellers from inhabitants of the countryside of all races. Even in Mérida, however, many creoles and castas spoke at least a smattering of Maya. The only true outsiders were recently arrived peninsulares who never bothered to learn the indigenous language that by the eighteenth century had become the lingua franca of the land.

Under pressure from Guillén's intensive interrogation and the weight of the testimony of hundreds of Maya-speaking witnesses against don Toribio's version of events, the foundations of his claims to innocence began to crumble. Besides demolishing don Toribio's credibility, Guillén's team of interpreters and investigators inadvertently constructed a comprehensive image of the social, racial, and linguistic composition of a pueblo whose demographic records are otherwise lost to posterity, destroyed by the flames of the Caste War (ca. 1847–1855) and the desolation of Chikindzonot's abandonment in the wake of that conflict. Their exhaustive survey of the pueblo and its inhabitants reveals a far more complicated rural social situation in terms of race, language, and local politics than general surveys of Yucatan have previously recognized. The simple dichotomies of Spaniard pitted against Indian or peasant against landholder only provide a glossed over, generalized depiction of the reality of everyday interactions in eighteenth-century Yucatan. This chapter highlights the often overlooked importance of the hostility between priests who held to the tradition of extensive ecclesiastical privilege in Yucatan and the secularizing thrust of the late eighteenth century in factional formation at the pueblo level, while taking pains to not portray the church and state divide as the sole determinant in divisions that emerged in the rural politics of the eighteenth century.

Local Rule in the Age of the Intendants

While strong personalities like that of the bishop impeded the progress of the prosecutors as they gathered evidence and constructed a case against don Toribio, changes to the lower echelons of government also muddied the already unclear hierarchy of competing courts and agents of law enforcement. Jurisdictional contests involved a variety of judges and magistrates from an array of tribunals that claimed the right to try, represent, question, and punish Mayas and castas in the countryside. Yucatan's indigenous cabildos governed into the early nineteenth century, trying, jailing, and punishing minor crimes in pueblos. Officers of the cabildo responsible for administering justice and recording its proceedings faced encroachments on their traditional pueblo autonomy from priests who claimed authority as ecclesiastical judges, local Spanish officials known as jueces españoles and subdelegados, and magistrates of Yucatan's Indian Court. Fueros that covered militiamen and priests stationed in the pueblos further complicated questions of jurisdiction. Blurred jurisdictional lines resulted from the fact that Spain's monarchs rarely clarified precedence, and one king's royal decrees often contradicted earlier rulings of his predecessors. In light of such jurisdictional competition and confusion, it is impressive that the pueblos' local Maya authorities managed to maintain a high degree of self-government into the late eighteenth and early nineteenth centuries.

Maya cabildos, the key administrative institution of indigenous municipal self-rule, continued to wield authority over most pueblo matters well into the independence era. Though jueces españoles and subdelegados apparently asserted their authority in pueblo affairs more frequently than their predecessors—the cabos de justicia and *tenientes de guerra*—in many cases, they simply signed off on matters handled by the cabildo. In most cases, the indigenous municipal councils settled disputes between Mayas and dispensed with corporal punishments or short-term imprisonments.[16]

Documents archived in connection with Dr. Guillén's inquiry in Tihosuco shed more light on the judicial function of late eighteenth-century local justice. Two copies of a 1795 list of prisoners from Tihosuco, a Maya-language original kept by the indigenous cabildo of the pueblo and a Spanish translation by the interpreter and militia sergeant Eugenio Cano, are bundled with documents related to the case, though they had little to do with the assassination.[17] Tihosuco and most other Maya pueblos maintained their own jails, with local officials known as *alcaldes de la cárcel*, or *alcaldemascabob* in

Maya, guarding and maintaining the prisons.[18] Sentences meted out by the cabildo and the inmates under the watch of the Maya wardens are listed in detail. Neither the original nor the translation name the crimes committed by the pueblo's inmates but both record the jail terms imposed. Judging by the length of the sentences served by the nineteen prisoners—all for six weeks or less—Maya law enforcement agents adjudicated in minor crimes, imposing relatively short imprisonments without relocating inmates too far from their families.[19] Evidence elsewhere suggests that incarceration was relatively rare. Floggings were far more common.[20] Pueblo justice tended to be quick and brutal but stopped short of the lengthy terms of jail, exile, labor, and occasional mutilation imposed by higher courts. None of the Maya witnesses imprisoned in Tihosuco suffered punishments even remotely comparable to the lengthy imprisonment of the Maya criado of Mérida, the witness Luis Lara, who endured four years and six months in jail simply for changing his testimony once too often for the prosecutors' liking.[21]

Local indigenous rule did not go unopposed, though. Most surviving examples of Maya rule at the pueblo level survive only because of challenges to the authority of the batabs and "justicias." Questions of jurisdiction arose over the extent to which the ecclesiastical fuero covered non-ordained assistants of the priest. The jailing of Matías Dzib, a choir leader (*cantor*) for the church, came to the attention of Spanish eyes only because of the intervention of the village curate, don Jacinto Rubio, who personally walked to the jail with a club in his hand to liberate Dzib in an overt assertion of the primacy of ecclesiastical justice over the Mayas' municipal authority. The subdelegado of Tihosuco, don Mateo de Cárdenas, siding with the Maya cabildo, challenged Father Rubio's intervention.[22] The priest's meddling underscores how deeply the struggle between secular governmental authority and ecclesiastical power ran, even in distant Yucatecan pueblos.

Father Rubio's dispute with the Maya justicias in Chikindzonot was only one of many rural rivalries that pitted secular authorities against the priest and his native auxiliaries. In 1794 Juan Yupit and Juan Yama, two Maya alguaciles, members of the cabildo responsible for pueblo law enforcement, were caught up in a dispute over their right to arrest and jail a resident who claimed that his church affiliation shielded him from secular Maya authorities, in an exceptionally broad interpretation of the fuero eclesiástico. Patrolling the pueblo one night, the two encountered a cook in the priest's household, Francisco Yupit, alone with a woman. The two enforcers ordered him to stop and identify himself. Yupit resisted but identified himself as a dependent of the local curate, don Domingo de Cárdenas (a cousin of the subdelegado but not an ally), implying that the two alguaciles had no authority to detain him. The alguaciles insisted that he stop, but Yupit continued on his way, telling them that he was with his wife and they had no business confronting him.[23] The next day, Father Cárdenas called together the justicias and physically threatened one of the alcaldes of the cabildo of Chikindzonot, Tomás Poot. The priest stated that he alone had the right and responsibility to patrol the streets at night, that he was "the only judge" of Chikindzonot.[24]

The three priests who presided over Chikindzonot's parish during the time of Gálvez's death and the subsequent investigation asserted their authority and argued for ample coverage of ecclesiastical privileges and exemption from civil authority—indigenous and Spanish alike—for a host of the clergymen's auxiliaries. And they were many. The sheer number of assistants, servants, and dependents of the priest—which included eleven sacristans, eleven "mayoles," four singers, a violinist and an organist, four *fiscales*, four patrones, three cooks, three *fiscales de doctrina* (pueblo auxiliaries responsible for enforcing church attendance and education), and four gardeners—also demonstrates the strength of the church in Chikindzonot.[25] Moreover, the list of parish assistants does not include the *teniente de coro* (choirmaster), José Uh; the *maestro de capilla* (chapelmaster), Andrés Dzul; or the organist and shoemaker identified alternately as an Indian and a mestizo, José Rivero.

Literacy translated into power in rural politics; the ability of a surprising number of ecclesiastical auxiliaries to write no doubt gave them an edge in their conflicts with the cabildo. One priest benefited in particular from having a loyal, literate choir director—José Uh—a topic explored in more detail in chapter 6. Along with Dzul, the typically literate maestro de capilla, organist Andrés Yupit, violinist Miguel Citep, sacristan Juan Canche, and singers Manuel Yupit, Pedro Yupit, Toribio Tzuc, and Juan Tzuc all signed their names after testifying.[26] Of the justicias, only Paulino Canche, Gregorio Yama, the former regidor Pedro Yama, and the notaries—the cacique's son José María Yama and Benito Yupit—showed any evidence of being able to write, and the first two may have only been able to sign their names.[27]

Disputes over ecclesiastical and secular jurisdiction divided the indigenous elite of Chikindzonot, pitting justicias of the cabildo against high-ranking auxiliaries of the church such as the cantor (Dzib) or the maestro de capilla (Dzul). The sizeable presence of rural castas in pueblos, many of which were affiliated with pardo militia units, also created a conundrum over the reach of local Maya authority. In Tihosuco, Maya authorities apparently exercised jurisdiction over most castas, at least those who resembled the Mayas in the language they spoke, their rural ambit, and their way of eking out a living by cultivating subsistence plots. The previously mentioned list of prisoners held in Tihosuco names inmates unconnected to the assassination investigation serving sentences for unrecorded crimes. Apparently, petty crimes by castas fell under the purview of the Maya cabildos, or at the very least, Maya-operated jails were suitable places for them to serve sentences, judging by the appearance on the list of inmates of non-Maya prisoners Hilario Muñoz, Feliciana Sánchez, Nicolás Andrade, and Antonio Pérez. One unnamed black man or woman also was imprisoned, identified only as "hun pel h box" (a black man) in the Maya original, but contradictorily described as "una negra" (a black woman) in Eugenio Cano's translation.[28]

The Maya justicias' assertion of municipal judicial authority more than 250 years after the conquest is all the more remarkable when one considers the extent of competition and encroachment of Spanish officials upon circumscribed indigenous spheres of authority. An array of Spanish officials adjudicated and enforced the law one level above the local justice administered by cabildo officers. Long-standing efforts on the part of competing factions to hold sway in rural Yucatan were further complicated by local implementation of empire-wide reforms in the second half of the eighteenth century, which left behind a shifting legal landscape in the countryside. While clergymen such as Father Rubio and Father Cárdenas fought tenaciously to preserve the power of pueblo priests, new officials in the countryside—jueces españoles and subdelegados—brought a forceful assertion of direct rule from Madrid to Yucatan. Encomenderos, long accustomed to wielding power over Mayas, both official and informal, had finally been dissolved as a class in 1785. Their predecessors' appeals to preserve the archaic and repeatedly abolished institution in Yucatan for centuries longer than elsewhere in the Americas had succeeded, but Carlos III and his successor, Carlos IV, refused to acquiesce to their pleas for one more exemption to the abolition of the long-standing institution. Magistrates, judges, and attorneys of the Indian Court, based in Mérida but actively intervening in litigation involving indigenous defendants and plaintiffs in distant pueblos, also asserted competence in disputes between Spaniards and Mayas, intra-pueblo controversies involving members of the cabildo, and conflicts between pueblos. In a time of transition and growing competition between Spanish authorities vying for influence in rural politics, Spaniards rarely presented a unified front in their dealings with the indigenous majority. Likewise, pueblos rarely united in opposition to Spaniards. Rural politics were far more complicated than the simplistic image of European oppressors uniting to exploit downtrodden but resistant natives—an all-too-common portrayal of the transient and convoluted factional rivalries that characterized conflicts in the Yucatecan countryside.

The Reach of the Reforms:
The Decree of Intendants and Provincial Politics

Don Lucas de Gálvez served Carlos IV at a time when Bourbon monarchs enacted major changes to labor arrangements and overhauled rural government as part of the same process that created the office of intendant.[29] While the office of the intendant itself was the centerpiece of the extensive restructuring of government directed by Carlos III and fine-tuned by don Lucas's distant cousin, the Marqués de Sonora don José de Gálvez, rationalizing administration below the level of the intendant also showed the Bourbon dynasty's determination to rule the Americas more efficiently, from top to bottom. Carlos III's ordinance also introduced a new series of local Spanish rulers.[30] Jueces españoles (Spanish judges) and subdelegados (subdelegates) replaced the long-standing positions of intrinsically corrupt corregidors and alcaldes mayores that had long antagonized the indigenous population throughout the Americas.[31] In Yucatan, though known by a different name—capitanes a guerra—the predecessors of the subdelegados made demands on their Indian subjects similar to those of a repartimiento, even if it was not identified as such.[32] Though the major change to the roles of these local administrators was the absolute prohibition of their participation in a repartimiento, the authority of the subdelegados was also more clearly defined than the jurisdictions and privileges of their predecessors.[33] The 1786 *Real ordenanza para el establecimiento e instrucción de intendentes de exército y provincia en el reino de la Nueva-España* was the longest legal text produced for the Americas since the *Recopilación de las leyes de los reinos de Indias* in 1680. The detailed instructions outlined the division of labor and responsibilities of each administrator more plainly than previous laws had done.[34]

Many of these local functionaries had risen through the ranks of the military, another institution Carlos III and his predecessors had greatly expanded and reorganized. Recognizing global reorientations that put Spain on the defensive in eighteenth-century imperial competition, Bourbon monarchs initiated a major reformation of rural militias.[35] Spanish losses in the Seven Years' War convinced Carlos III that a wide-ranging restructuring of defenses and the standardizing of military organization was necessary. Ports and fortifications in disrepair finally received belated restoration and expansion. Specific orders addressed the organization of often improvised and irregular militia units and provided for uniforms, ranks, officer numbers, and, especially, numerous garrisons to bolster defenses in weakly patrolled border territories. While the overhaul of the defensive capacities of the Americas came early in the reign of Carlos III, the top-to-bottom restructuring of provincial administration was one of his final acts as king. Drawing from the same class of men of middling status, many of the newly appointed subdelegados and jueces españoles came from the ranks of these rural militia units. In Yucatan, this meant that the new cadre of administrators brought a high level of familiarity with the Maya world beyond Mérida. Don Arturo O'Neill, who had risen through the ranks of this reformed military and was still recognized as an effective and successful general, purged the ranks of these low-level administrators of anyone under the influence of the bishop who might obstruct the process of gathering evidence against don Toribio.

Accustomed to commanding soldiers and officers, Brigadier O'Neill had a knack for selecting military men familiar with the indigenous countryside who were ready to carry out his orders in his duties as a co-judge with Dr. Guillén. Between the changes enacted by the Decree of Intendants and the purge of men of suspect loyalty by O'Neill, the final ten years of the eighteenth century were a time of high turnover in low-level posts.[36] Those who occupied these posts, however briefly, included many militia officers, some simultaneously serving as officers while holding their low-level administrative posts. Mariano Ancona, juez español of Chikindzonot, also served as a corporal in the Spanish militia. His successor, don Manuel Alcalá, inherited the post from Ancona while also serving as a first lieutenant with the milicias urbanas of Calotmul.[37] Their superior—don Mateo de Cárdenas, subdelegado of Tihosuco—simultaneously served as a captain of the elite grenadier unit of the Mérida-based militia. Close to Chikindzonot, don Cristóbal de la Cámara served as the captain of the militia in Motul and as the juez español in nearby Cacalchen.[38] Farther away, don Francisco de Pereira simultaneously served as a soldier in the militia stationed in Dzidzantun and as the pueblo's juez español, all the while making ends meet as a painter.[39]

While several of the low-level officials in and around Tihosuco and Chikindzonot owed their rapid promotion to don Arturo O'Neill's distrust of many officeholders in place at the time of the assassination, in many pueblos the Decree of Intendants brought a change in the name of the office as well as restrictions on activities and clarified lines of authority without bringing a turnover in personnel. Previous occupants of provincial posts such as cabos de justicia and tenientes de guerra often continued to occupy roughly similar but better-defined positions in the same pueblos after the promulgation of the Decree of Intendants. Don Pedro Gutiérrez and don Juan Esteban Ramírez saw their titles changed from teniente de guerra and cabo de justicia, respectively, to juez español but continued to administer the same pueblos with many of the same duties.[40]

Not all of the aims of the reorganization were enacted as intended.[41] One of the main thrusts of the Decree of Intendants was to eliminate the corrupt practice of selling overpriced goods to Indians, especially the deeply entrenched practice of the repartimiento. The repartimiento was a long-standing practice of forcibly selling low-quality goods to Indians in one's jurisdiction at inflated prices.[42] At the root of the problem were underpaid rural enforcers who had often purchased their offices and operated with little oversight and viewed their positions as an investment. To gain a return on the purchase of offices and to subsidize their low salaries, rural bureaucrats resorted to the repartimiento and other illicit means of recouping their losses. Though the Decree of Intendants made some progress toward eliminating corruption, it did not result in as clear a division between salaried professional administrators and rural profiteers. The juez español of Chikindzonot—don Pedro Gutiérrez, predecessor to Ancona and Alcalá—operated a small store where he sold aguardiente, the strong, cheap firewater popular in rural Yucatan.[43] Such questionable mercantile activities never caught the attention of his superiors. Instead, it was Gutiérrez's complicity in aiding don Toribio's fabrication of his alibi that led to his undoing.

As intendant, Gálvez had wide latitude over the appointments of these positions.[44] And his unflinching determination to enact his wide-ranging reform program in the face of resistance from established creoles earned him even more enemies. Leading families often saw the posts as their birthright, though Gálvez did not view the dispensation of offices as an inheritable prerogative. Although don Manuel Antolín served as the capitán a guerra of the Partido de la Costa before the intendant's arrival, Gálvez passed him over for the roughly equal position of subdelegado, assigning don Gregorio Quintana to the new post in 1789.[45] As he was wont to do, the bishop criticized the decision, ineffectively and inaccurately complaining that the intendant had no authority to displace Antolín.[46] Under Gálvez, occupying a post in one district did not necessarily translate into being confirmed in a new office in the same location under the intendancy system. In the end, the bishop and the displaced official took advantage of Gálvez's death to undermine the will of the deceased intendant. Just three months after Gálvez's murder, the intendant's interim successor and enemy, don José Sabido de Vargas, promoted Antolín to the post of subdelegado on 8 October 1792.[47]

Church, State, and Pueblo: Local Politics in Late Colonial Yucatan

The bishop's attempt to undermine the intendant's authority over appointments was not the only occasion in which rural Yucatan became a battleground between representatives of the colonial church and secular authorities. Such conflicts moved to the forefront when priests and secular sympathizers aligned with the bishop squared off against investigators and local officials appointed by Dr. Guillén and Intendant O'Neill in the pueblos in the vicinity of Chikindzonot. The long-standing contest between proponents of ecclesiastical privilege and advocates of more direct royal oversight—a contentious issue since the earliest years of the colonial period—took on a particularly personal tone in the late eighteenth century. Pueblo priests echoed the accusations of impropriety and incompetence of their leader in Mérida and parroted his claims that their ecclesiastical immunity placed them beyond the reach of small-town agents of royal justice. Following the lead of Guillén and O'Neill, jueces españoles, subdelegados, and their allies asserted their authority and extended the reach of their investigation with unprecedented disregard for the priests' fueros and informal deference to ecclesiastical privilege.

Struggles between the church and the state in the countryside were not simply a matter for European-descent Yucatecans. Castas and Mayas did not watch one of the most divisive contests of the eighteenth century from the sidelines. Rural Spaniards, including both American-born creoles and peninsulares, sought allies in these struggles from a multiethnic power base. Mayas, for their part, often divided into two or three parties, typically centered on the indigenous cabildo and the auxiliaries of the pueblo's parish church or convent, while many remained neutral. Factional divisions also split indigenous cabildos. Likewise, castas in the rural sphere frequently saw those who were employed by the church siding with priests while a growing number of pardo and mestizo militiamen aligned with royal authorities. Pueblo politics were as likely to pit priests and their native and casta auxiliaries and assistants against members of the cabildo allied with jueces españoles as they were to divide rural communities along racial lines.

Don Lucas de Gálvez and his successor vigorously challenged a powerful Catholic hierarchy while clergymen rallied around one of the most obstinate and determined proponents of church power in the history of Yucatan: fray Luis. Yet battle lines between agents of royal rule and priests often blurred. Antolín, the former capitán a guerra who felt cheated out of a confirmation to the post of subdelegado, was not the only secular official to side with the interventionist bishop when it was convenient. More importantly, domineering local curates like Father Rubio, who claimed to "rule alone in this pueblo," often browbeat into submission less assertive local officials, like the juez español don Pedro Gutiérrez.[48] Harshly criticizing don Pedro's dependence on the priest, a later subdelegado, don Mateo de Cárdenas, disparaged Gutiérrez as a "servant of the priest's house" and a "scrounger" (gorrón) of the diocese.[49]

The ecclesiastical faction's domination of Chikindzonot and nearby pueblos blocked the prosecutors' progress for the first years of the investigation. With the juez español dependent on the priest and the head of the indigenous government intimidated, the first cursory examination of the veracity of don Toribio's assertion that he had slept in Chikindzonot on the night of the assassination held up under perfunctory examination. Gutiérrez, along with two other Spaniards and two Mayas, backed up his claim. Father Correa, don Juan Gálvez, don Pedro Gutiérrez, don Gregorio Yama, and Mauricio Pat were the only five men interviewed in the cursory first effort to look into don Toribio's whereabouts on 21 June 1792.[50] Two did not even live in the pueblo in question. Moreover, the ratio of Spaniards to Mayas was far from a representative sample of men in the countryside who might have seen don Toribio in the vicinity. Pat was quite literally a servant of the priest, while critics belittled Gutiérrez as one of Correa's criados. Don Juan Gálvez, no relative of the deceased intendant, was conveniently absent when investigators returned to follow up with additional questions about his testimony. The cacique, as it turned out, had provided favorable testimony only under duress, threatened by both the juez español and the local priest.

At Guillén's urging, Intendant O'Neill replaced both the subdelegado of Tihosuco and the juez español of Chikindzonot. In Captain Cárdenas, the

new intendant found a man who prioritized obedience to his secular supervisors over family ties, remaining loyal even when his cousin, don Domingo
de Cárdenas, replaced Correa as the pueblo's priest. Early reservations that
don Mateo's history of militia service with don Toribio, who had attended
Captain Cárdenas's wedding in 1793, were misplaced; don Mateo methodi-
cally questioned hundreds of witnesses in Maya and Spanish, as evidence
against the bishop's nephew mounted. Men with reputations for integrity
and loyalty to the crown now held the most important posts in Chikindzonot
and its environs. As don Toribio began to lose his sway over the area's leading
officials, his alibi began to unravel. Gregorio Yama, the beleaguered cacique,
finding unwavering support from Captain Cárdenas, came forward to
describe the threats and manipulations the priest used to induce him to testify in don Toribio's favor. Removed from his post in late 1794 for lying under
oath and obstructing investigators' efforts, Gutiérrez languished in prison in
Mérida until his death in 1796. His successors, Mariano Ancona and don
Manuel de Alcalá, cooperated with prosecutors, carefully taking statements
of witnesses in Maya and Spanish, each occasionally translating when the
need arose. Members of the bishop's camp made serious attempts to derail
their line of investigation but met with little luck.

The simmering hostility between clergymen and local representatives of
civil government took on an especially nasty tone as attacks on rivals' characters and reputations became commonplace. The rift also crossed ethnic
lines as it drew in the cacique on the side of the subdelegado and the juez
español while the priests sought support from casta and Maya auxiliaries.
After recanting his earlier verification of don Toribio's assertion that he had
been present in Chikindzonot, the batab of the pueblo found himself a target
of invective from the militia lieutenant's allies. Ordered by Dr. Guillén to
appear in Mérida for further questioning, don Gregorio Yama maintained
that he had been threatened and bribed into signing a certificate vouching
for don Toribio's version of events. Don Toribio acknowledged that the cacique knew him well but disparaged Yama as a habitual drunk.[51] Don Gregorio
responded with a certification by don Manuel de Alcalá attesting to the
batab's clear thinking, sobriety, and integrity.[52] Alcalá, along with Mariano
Ancona and don Mateo de Cárdenas, aligned themselves closely with the
Maya cabildo in opposition to the men whom they perceived as their true
enemies: the priests.

Despite attempting to tarnish the cacique's reputation, don Toribio
admitted that he was on familiar terms with him. Largely unseen but

apparently common interactions between Mayas and Spaniards also surface in the countryside, Spanish-descent creoles inter-acted regularly with Mayas. Rural Yucatan was not a place of strict ethnic segregation. Yet many interactions were intentionally hidden, largely due to the disapproval some relationships might incur from superiors. Unable to halt the progress of the case through the intimidation of his Maya parish-ioners and failing to successfully contest assertions of civil jurisdiction by the subdelegado and the jueces españoles, Father Jacinto Rubio turned to personal attacks. He sent a letter to O'Neill noting that Ancona did not live with his wife; instead, he lived with his Maya concubine, Petrona Dzul of Bacalar.[53] Cárdenas, faced with irrefutable charges of adultery on the part of a trusted subordinate, acknowledged this transgression but downplayed the gravity of Ancona's infraction. A seasoned militia officer with over thirty years of service and eighteen years at the same rank, Captain Cárdenas wrote from experience when he stated that taking a Maya mistress was fairly com-mon for officials and soldiers stationed in the countryside.[54] Once the illicit relationship was brought to light, he ordered Petrona Dzul to return to her husband, Ambrosio Cancino, a soldier stationed in Bacalar.[55]

Charges of inappropriate behavior did not always originate with clergy-men nor were they always aimed at civil or military officials. In one of the most heated disputes, charges of inappropriate behavior leveled against another auxiliary of the bishop—this time unnamed—led to an overtly unauthorized intrusion into civil and military jurisdiction by the village priest. In early August 1794, Chikindzonot's alguacil mayor, the head law enforcement agent of the pueblo's Maya cabildo, Juan Yupit, and another lower-ranking alguacil named Manuel Yama, arrested an unnamed man caught in an indecent act with a woman ("malos pasos con una muger"). Hearing news of this event involving a close relative of one of Father Cárdenas's Maya auxiliaries, the priest ordered the pueblo's militia corporal, Marcos Pacheco, and Sergeant Pablo Gutiérrez to arrest, shackle, and imprison the two alguaciles and two unnamed topiles.[56] Despite the flagrant contravention of the conventional chain of command, the militia officers complied. The four Maya authorities were held overnight. By obeying the local priest and not informing the juez español, Corporal Pacheco and Sergeant Gutiérrez had broken from the established lines of authority.[57] Confronted over the unauthorized arrest and use of force, they said they had not bothered Ancona because he was ill, and the priest had told them not to disturb him. Even so, their obedience to the overbearing priest had its limits.

When Father Cárdenas sent a cook who had been arrested earlier to pass along an order to the militia officers to raise the stocks to the height of the table in order to leave the imprisoned alguaciles suspended with their heads downward, the militiamen told the cook they would comply. However, though they dared not defy the priest outright, once the cook left, they failed to obey the order, which would have imposed extreme suffering on the incarcerated Maya officials.[58]

Since don Toribio's presence or absence from the pueblo was a key piece of evidence for or against his guilt in the assassination, Chikindzonot experienced an intensification of the church-state conflict at the local level. Strong personalities also fed the fire. Father Cárdenas had ruled the pueblo with an iron hand. His successor, Father Rubio, was a veteran of church conflicts waged with civil authorities, his position of power bolstered by a linguistic aptitude in Maya that rivaled if not bettered that of most interpreters. These two priests found a formidable foe in Father Cárdenas's relative, Capt. Mateo de Cárdenas, who shared blood ties but no other affinities for his clergyman cousin. His subordinates, Alcalá and Ancona, showed no signs of questionable loyalty to Captain Cárdenas, even though Ancona's personal indiscretions did cause problems for their superior. After the early vacillation of one or two high-ranking officers, Maya cabildo members bucked the pressure of the priests and threw in their lot with the subdelegado and the jueces españoles. The change in personnel among the priests did little to lessen the conflict between church and state at the pueblo level. For example, when the exasperated subdelegado ordered no one to leave Chikindzonot without a passport from him or the cacique, Father Rubio defied this order and told his lay assistants that they only needed his permission to depart, not the approval of Maya or Spanish governmental authorities. Leonardo Pat did so, carrying only a letter from the priest and defying the subdelegado's ban on communication with Mérida.[59]

The intense investigation that followed the intendant's assassination exacerbated tensions between the priests and civil authorities in and around Chikindzonot, but the rivalry between secular and religious justices at the Maya municipal level was not unique to don Gregorio's pueblo. Two years before Gálvez's murder, Baca (twenty miles east of Mérida) saw two separate but allied cohorts of Maya elites petition civil authorities to remove an exploitative priest. First, "some Indian magnates" (*algunos indios magnates*), distinct from the cabildo, petitioned for an end to unremunerated church construction imposed on the pueblo's men, which took milperos away from

planting their fields and left Baca destitute. The cabildo councilmen, led by
the batab, followed suit with a separate, concurrent petition complaining of
the labor demands of the priest.[60] Their appeals to the subdelegado of the
Partido de la Costa, don José Antonio Dávila, which pitted the reinforced
state apparatus against the weakened church authority, received a quick and
supportive response. Cayetano Cervantes, juez español of Baca, investigated
the situation and confirmed the dire straits of his Maya constituents.
Following Cervantes's recommendation, Gálvez issued an order for the
sought-after suspension of the construction of the church just over a month
after the receipt of the letter, on 20 August 1790.[61]

Standoffs between friars and the officials of the new Bourbon order created by the Decree of Intendants ensnared castas as well as Indians.
Subdelegado don Gregorio Quintana of the Partido de la Sierra took on one
of the most deeply entrenched bastions of ecclesiastical power in Yucatan:
the Franciscans. In 1790 he alerted Madrid to the abuses they supposedly
heaped upon their parishioners in Ticul, especially their tendency to inflict
lashings over what Quintana perceived to be rather small infractions. The
crown weighed in on the side of Quintana's interpretation of the mendicants'
circumscribed authority, writing that the Franciscans were to "educate the
inhabitants and administer their spiritual nourishment" and little else,
undermining their assertions to jurisdiction over an array of sins.[62] Although
the individual identified as the victim of an unsanctioned flogging at the
hands of the friars was Enrique Pérez, a rural casta, the real cédula also
ordered an investigation into reports of the abusive treatment of Indians.[63]
The Franciscans' claims of unsupervised guardianship of indigenous parishioners, long questioned, came under intense scrutiny as part of the ground-
level implementation of reforms. Rather than seeing Spaniards unite to
reassert racial domination of Indians in the eighteenth century, then, much
of the countryside saw an intensification of the standoff between the defenders of ecclesiastical privilege and the agents of a new Bourbon order, with
factional fighting involving not only Spaniards but also Maya and casta
parishioners.

Factional disputes did not, however, inevitably break down along lines
of ecclesiastical parties opposing secular factions. Rural conflicts over land,
property, and authority often divided pueblos and Spanish authorities in
unexpected ways. The turmoil of late colonial demographic movements and
rapid reforms also exposed rifts in Maya cabildos. A 1790 conflict between
two indigenous cabildo officers in the Partido de la Costa provides a final

example of the unpredictable and varied nature of eighteenth-century pueblo politics. In Motul, the cacique don Miguel Qui questioned the authority of a long-standing official, the cabo de justicia turned juez español, don Esteban Ramírez.[64] Ramírez had taken the side of the pueblo's native notary in a dispute, ordering the arrest of don Miguel. The cacique, in turn, petitioned the subdelegado of the Partido de la Costa, don José Antonio Dávila, for his freedom after fifteen days of imprisonment. Dávila overturned his subordinate's sentence and ordered the release of don Miguel.[65]

Spanish authorities did not necessarily close ranks against Maya elites, nor did Maya cabildos completely avoid infighting. Creoles in the countryside also had their share of infighting. In the same year and the same district as the dispute between don Miguel Qui and his notary, the juez español of Temax (don Luis Durán) and Dávila forced a Spaniard, don José Zetina, to pay off a debt he owed to the cacique, don Gregorio Yam, when the merchant attempted to avoid payment.[66] Just as clergymen and provincial administrators did not always see eye to eye on rural matters, commercial interests did not always coincide neatly with the aims of rural administrators.

Interpreters: Men between Worlds

The trial records, which record elusive interactions between Mayas and priests, friars, merchants, interpreters, militia officers, and low-level Spanish administrators stationed in the countryside, show that these creoles shared one trait in common: nearly all spoke Yucatec Maya. Even though most creoles in the countryside were bilingual, Mérida-based officials appointed interpreters to translate proceedings, make sense of the disputes at the municipal level, and communicate royal orders between the capital and the countryside in official transactions. While two royally appointed interpreters, known as the interpreters general, officiated from Mérida, most translation in the rural sphere took place in a more improvised fashion. Convenience likely led Captain Cárdenas and other rural officials to select bilingual brokers residing in the pueblos or passing through on business as *tratantes*, or petty merchants. Suspicions regarding conflicts of interest on the part of at least one of the two Mérida-based interpreters played a role in the prevalence of unofficial translators as well. Competition also limited the participation of the interpreters general in the interrogations in the countryside—both in the assassination investigation and in other criminal proceedings.

The three interpreters general in Yucatan—two based in Mérida and one in Campeche—were officials of Yucatan's Indian Court. Cases under their purview typically were conducted in a manner in which the legal restrictions protecting indigenous witnesses, plaintiffs, and defendants were generally adhered to, while some procedural mandates, including an oft-flouted requirement to have two interpreters translate every interview separately, were not assiduously observed.[67] One offhand comment by Captain Cárdenas hints at the impulse local officials felt to keep municipal matters local. In the midst of his efforts to exert control over Chikindzonot and resolve the grievances of the jailed cabildo topiles and alguaciles, the subdelegado wrote that he hoped to avoid "large numbers" of Mayas traveling to Mérida to complain, doubtless to plead their case before the Indian Court.[68] The jurisdictional bounds between matters resolved at the town level and those meriting the attention of the magistrates of the General Court of the Indians were also unclear. Competition for judicial authority came not only from priests, asserting jurisdiction over a variety of infractions as jueces eclesiásticos, but also military tribunals and, in the cities, the authority of Spanish cabildo magistrates, the alcaldes ordinarios. Indeed, the late eighteenth century saw intensified competition to preserve judicial pluralism.[69] The early stirrings of liberalism's emphasis on reduced jurisdictions had yet to sweep away the autonomy of the separate court systems. Intendants such as Gálvez and their loyal agents, armed with a wide range of powers enshrined in the Decree of Intendants, struggled to exercise authority while magistrates of other tribunals sought to preserve their privileges.

Established in the late sixteenth century, the Indian Court retained its influence in the face of attempts to undermine its authority by other magistrates and justices who competed for the right to try indigenous subjects. The eighteenth century did not see a diminution of its power. Normally not at loggerheads with the lieutenants of the intendant, who was, after all, the nominal head of the Indian Court, Captain Cárdenas's efforts to resolve disputes between the priest and members of the cabildo at the municipal level likely stemmed from a normal desire on the part of authorities to keep matters local and also, quite possibly, a deep distrust of the reliability of two Mérida-based interpreters.

Suspicion fell on one of the two interpreters—don Enrique Gónzalez—because of his ties to one of the leading allies of the bishop. Gónzalez was not one of the three salaried professionals on the Indian Court's payroll, but he did translate key testimony in the early stages of the investigation. Due to his ties to an attorney in the service of the bishop, later prosecutors doubted the credibility of his translations. Gónzalez's compadre don Francisco Ortiz was one of the bishop's most dedicated underlings, serving as the mayordomo of his properties and legal representative of his nephew.[70] While Gónzalez's participation in the investigation was limited, his colleague don Esteban de Castro, one of two interpreters general of Mérida, translated more regularly over the course of the investigation, though the extent and nature of his involvement in the assassination was revealed only in 1800. Neither ventured beyond Mérida with any frequency, suggesting that the original aim of the foundation of the Indian Court—to bring justice to the Mayas in their own pueblos or at least nearby cabeceras—was rarely achieved. Likewise, the royal order that two interpreters be in attendance during interrogations of indigenous-language speakers seems to have been rarely observed.[71] As a result, a variety of interpreters stood in to translate in the countryside, assuring that interrogations and other interactions that took place in Maya were written down in Spanish and sent along to the viceregal capital or the Archive of the Indies, where the records are held today.

An array of translators was often recruited on the spot from the ranks of numerous bilingual creoles residing in rural Yucatan. Most interpreters in the case translated only oral Maya testimony, leaving the translation of Spanish documents for a Maya audience up to the two interpreters general, usually Castro. Most men resided in the pueblos where they translated, served in the nearest militia garrison, or were jueces españoles or subdelegados. Like the subdelegado and militia captain don Mateo de Cárdenas, don Augustín Bernardino Medina, another high-ranking officer in the elite corps, served as a lieutenant colonel in the same unit. He translated early in the case, in 1793, in and nearby Motul.[72] Don José de Castro, a resident of Ichmul, served as a sub-lieutenant in the sixth militia battalion of the "White Infantry," stationed in Motul.[73] He translated in the dispute over tribute between don Gregorio Yama and Tomasa Santos, the widow of the deceased juez español of Chikindzonot, during the early verbal proceedings.[74] Eugenio Cano, who was based in Mérida but spent much of his time in the countryside, provided Spanish versions of Maya documents in the same case.[75] Gónzalez, whose ties to dependents of the bishop's household made his translation suspect, was a juez español of Ixil, twenty miles northeast of Mérida. Castro, the interpreter general responsible for most of the written translations, did not handle all textual interpretation. Cano also translated oral testimony; working in tandem with don José Joaquín Pérez, he translated for witnesses from Chikindzonot taken to Mérida for more extensive interrogation.[76] Don Manuel de Aguilar, a lieutenant with the Campeche-based Infantry Battalion of Castile, translated the written and verbal testimony of the Mayas of the same village when they were interviewed about a feud between the Cárdenas cousins, the priest and the subdelegado.[77] In addition to their duties as jueces españoles, don Manuel de Álcala and Mariano Ancona served as interpreters.[78] Only don Vicente de Ávila and don Esteban de Castro, the two official Mérida-based interpreters general, made their living exclusively from their work as translators.[79]

In all, eighteen interpreters—sixteen in addition to the two official interpreters general of Mérida—translated during the course of the trial. Although apparently all were creoles, the prestige of their full-time work and social standing varied widely. Don Blas Torres, the interpreter with the highest social standing, later served as alcalde, a prominent post within the cabildo of Mérida.[80] Castro did not see himself as especially wealthy and hoped for a promotion within the Indian Court.[81] In his efforts to marry up, examined in chapter 8, he faced scorn and disparagement for his "dark lineage." He and don Vicente de Ávila, the two men who held the post of interpreter general between 1792 and 1804, each received a yearly salary of just 200 pesos. The pay for the position had remained stagnant since Diego de Vargas first received a salary of 200 pesos annually as the better paid of two interpreters general in 1578.[82] It is no wonder that Castro took side work, using his language skills to make extra money. José Miguel Quijano, a member of one of Mérida's wealthiest families, sought Castro's assistance to locate and contract Maya workers for the construction of a new home.[83]

In terms of status, while a majority of interpreters were addressed with the honorific title don, only a few were truly from the upper class. Torres, for example, was a well-off former encomendero whose losses were minimal when the institution was abolished. He remained a wealthy landowner, receiving a pension of 300 pesos for his extinguished encomienda and income from his haciendas and business interests.[84] A few of the interpreters were not, however, addressed with such formality, especially those based in the rural sphere, such as Eugenio Cano, Mariano Ancona, Simeon Caro, Diego Santana, and Juan Gervasio Silva of Cancabdzonot.[85] It seems that every single interpreter was Yucatan-born—the one common thread that united the varied group of translators.

Outward and Upward: Creoles in the Countryside

The ready availability of bilingual creoles capable of translating on short notice stemmed from the growing number of European-descent men fanning out into rural Yucatan. Economic ventures had long relied upon coerced Maya labor; with the end of the encomienda and tighter enforcement of prohibitions on servicio personal, creoles sought opportunities outside the city as income from the indirect exploitation of indigenous labor dried up. The ease of exploiting indigenous labor from afar ended with the abolition of the encomienda and Gálvez's crackdown on servicio personal. Governmental reorganization increased the number of creoles and the occasional peninsular Spaniard administrators beyond the bounds of Mérida, as previously discussed. Functionaries who served as salaried professionals—subdelegados and jueces españoles—replaced the improvised cabos de justicias and tenientes de guerra.[86] Judging from their frequent appearance in extensive trial transcripts, present either to assist or occasionally obstruct proceedings, these new officials tended to live where they were assigned, meaning that more of them actually lived in rural Yucatan. Major legislation aimed at shoring up the defensive capacity of the American provinces led to more militiamen, both pardo and creole, being stationed in distant pueblos as well. Lack of opportunities also pushed many creoles, mostly young men, away from the city in search of economic opportunities as small-town merchants and hacienda administrators.[87] Legitimate commercial activities were often supplemented with illicit trade. In a province with a long Caribbean coastline and proximity to British Belize, contraband trade was endemic. Faced with a situation in which they were no longer the only Spaniards claiming authority or prestige in pueblos, clergymen—the most established power bloc in rural Yucatan—sought to preserve their seniority and influence in pueblo politics.

While the Decree of Intendants regulated and increased the presence of Spanish officials in the rural sphere throughout the Viceroyalty of New Spain, laws were passed during Carlos III's reign restructuring Yucatan's militias as well. These laws, including a set of regulations specific to Yucatan, created more garrisons in the countryside, where militia officers and enlisted men were on hand to quell indigenous rebellions (which were quite rare) and curtail contraband trade in English, French, and, later, Anglo-American goods (which was widespread).[88] In Yucatan, the Bourbon military reforms took place roughly in two stages: First, fortifying and manning uncolonized and exposed frontier areas, where Yucatan bordered either British settlements or unconquered Indian territory. And second, bolstering the military presence in the interior and on the coasts. The first phase, focused on demarcating territory and establishing a defensive presence in unprotected regions, emphasized the construction of fortifications over recruiting militiamen. During the early 1700s, Spain's monarchs ordered that forts be built in locations selected to stave off or limit English expansion. After expelling the English from Laguna de Términos, Spanish forces fortified the Isla del Carmen (starting in 1717) to prevent further intrusions by British loggers. On the other side of the peninsula, English establishments in Belize led the Bourbons to found a presidio in Bacalar ten years later to stave off further English encroachments.[89]

The 1760s and 1770s saw further reinforcement of the province's military, focused on troop numbers and sorting out rank among the officer corps over the architectural emphasis of the first half of the eighteenth century. Though the immediate impetus was the capture of Havana by the English and the loss of Florida, any province perceived as exposed underwent a large-scale reorganization. Between 1765 and 1767, New Spain saw a flurry of legislation to recruit and reorganize a large uniformed and regularly drilled militia. The royal decrees included an extension of the coverage of the fuero militar to both officers and enlisted men, new uniforms and equipment, a standardization of the officer corps, and, critically, significant pay raises, which boosted enlistment. In 1778 Madrid published a military code specific to the province, *Reglamento para las Milicias de Infantería de la Provincia de Yucatan, y Campeche*, which reiterated the provision that all "militia soldiers" were covered by the fuero militar.[90] By the 1780s, permanent nominally white militia units were established in Tixkokob, Hunucmá, Motul, Dzidantun, and Izamal.[91] Two of the top three posts of each militia unit, the captain and the sub-lieutenants (ranked first and third, respectively) were permitted to reside in their private homes away from the barracks. Among the top tier of officers, lieutenants—between captains and sub-lieutenants in the military hierarchy—quite explicitly were required to live where they served, as did lower ranking officers such as sergeants, corporals, and drummers.[92] The anomalous condition of the lieutenants, unique among the top tier of the officer corps in the requirement that they reside where they were stationed, obviously had unforeseen consequences for Lt. don Toribio del Mazo. Slightly over a decade after the passage of the *Reglamento para las Milicias* for Yucatan, the authorities invested in the intendant in a separate decree relating to that office that empowered him to relocate militia lieutenants by fiat. With broad authority over these men, the intendant acted as captain general, giving the top executive of the province broad latitude until 1811, when the intendants lost their military command.[93] Such powers legitimated Gálvez's authority to reassign don Toribio—a much more prominent peninsular than those who usually were garrisoned in more peripheral regions—to increasingly remote posts, antagonizing his romantic rival and subordinate in rank.

Don Toribio was a rare peninsular among a cohort of creole and mestizo officers and soldiers, which likely led to a heightened sense of alienation. In addition to the Milicias de Voluntarios Blancos, in which don Toribio served, milicias urbanas were, despite their name, posted in a series of rural pueblos. A creole officer corps usually headed these units, though their rank and file consisted of indios hidalgos and pardos. Creole-led militia battalions and divisions were stationed in Tecoh, Maní, Ticul, Tekax, Mamá, Muna, Tizimin, Espita, Sucilá, Kikil, Calotmul, Chancenote, Nabalam, Tixcacal, and Panabá, which brought more creoles to the periphery of the peninsula in a martial capacity.[94] The bolstered militia presence pushed growing numbers of men recognized as Spaniards on militia rolls to rural Yucatan.

Merchants and Mayordomos

Commercial revitalization based on the expansion of a hacienda economy, the recovery of an indigenous population with a taste for Spanish goods, and a brisk if often undetected trade in black-market British and French goods drew other Spaniards away from Mérida and Campeche in search of a decent living. Like don Toribio's former criado, don Nicolas Domínguez, positions as top managers of large haciendas pulled young men to the countryside as administrators while scarce offerings in the city pushed many of them to search for new opportunities.[95] Don Nicolas was somewhat of an exception. Typically, hacienda managers (mayordomos) of Spanish descent came from more humble backgrounds—such as Pedro Ferrera, mayordomo of the Hacienda Santa Maria, and Silverio Muñoz, mayordomo and criado of the treasurer's haciendas.[96] These creoles (and possibly mestizos) of modest origins oversaw haciendas dedicated above all to livestock raising, but haciendas of the eighteenth century also cultivated rice, corn, indigo, beans, and (in the southwest) sugar, which soon overtook the traditional sweetener, honey, which also was common in haciendas.[97] A late eighteenth-century expansion of sugar cultivation in Yucatan led to an unprecedented supply of the cane commodity and its most notorious by-product, aguardiente.[98]

Although Yucatan's sugar boom of the late eighteenth and early nineteenth centuries was largely confined to the Partido de Sierra Alta and its cabecera, Tekax, barrels upon barrels of domestically produced aguardiente sated internal demand within Yucatan. Papers confiscated from the deposed and jailed former juez español of Chikindzonot, don Pedro Gutiérrez, show a brisk trade in the highly alcoholic colonial drink in Chikindzonot, over 100 kilometers away from the epicenter of cane production. The embargo of Gutiérrez's personal effects included several receipts for the purchase and sale of barrels of the alcoholic beverage. Spaniards and castas, both men and women, participated in the trade. The purchase and sale of large quantities of aguardiente involved individuals nominally recognized as hidalgos. In the two years leading up to his removal from office, several Spaniards were involved in wholesale selling and purchasing of aguardiente with Gutiérrez, including Juan Pablo Lara, Margarita Espadas, don Ramón del Castillo, María de la Luz Castillo, and Casilda del Castillo. The last three were likely relatives, headed by don Ramón, who apparently was a muleteer as well.[99] Urban Spaniards of more privileged backgrounds also profited from aguardiente at a distance. Don Juan de la Cruz Carrillo and don Pedro Bolio of Mérida, who later served as interim intendant, were also identified as traders in aguardiente.[100]

The aguardiente trade was a respectable venture as long as taxes were paid and production was local. However, strong drinks from British and French sources were also sold, part of an extensive if rarely detected black market. Proximity to British Belize and a poorly patrolled coastline, even after the Bourbon reforms, meant that French and British loggers and merchants traveled, traded, logged, and raided and were rarely apprehended by Spanish authorities.[101] On occasion, lookout posts (vigias) manned by as few as two unpaid Mayas working off tributary labor obligations, performed as intended, interdicting the forbidden trade with the British and the French. Their reports give a glimpse of the underground operations of one of Yucatan's less respectable commercial activities: contraband.[102] Prosecutors in Yucatan had long memories, and one minor suspect's smuggling past came to light in the course of the investigation. Lucas Vargas, who made his home in Tihosuco at the time of the murder, found himself under suspicion for the second time in his life for his passing involvement with don Toribio.[103]

His second brush with the law went better than the first. As part of the investigation into his complicity in the cover-up of don Toribio's whereabouts, Vargas's personal possessions were confiscated but returned to him less than three years later, in early 1795, when it became apparent that his only crimes were the ongoing black market trade that he took more pains to conceal from authorities.[104]

In an earlier incident, Lucas Vargas faced a more severe punishment for his trade in contraband, brought to light by a Maya, Lorenzo Canché of Telá, who worked for Vargas in his modest fishing and salvaging operations. A fisherman and beachcomber, Vargas gravitated to peripheral towns because it facilitated undetected contact with British and French sailors.[105] In 1787, when the capitán a guerra (predecessor to the position of subdelegado) José Maldonado finally apprehended Vargas based on testimony from Canché, Vargas already had a reputation for previous clandestine commercial activity.[106] Vargas and five companions came across a small craft of English mariners on the shore of Yucatan near Bahia de Ascenscion. He and his companions—including Canché and Lucas's brother, Andrés Vargas—boarded the craft and spent six to twelve days fishing for turtles and harvesting honey on Cozumel (accounts varied), which were left in the hands of the English. The British returned them to shore and left Vargas and his crew with a number of boxes. Canché reported that he did not know what they contained, though they appeared to be heavy. His uncertainty suggests that he had been excluded from the spoils.[107]

Vargas's ongoing but more discrete trade in contraband likely would have never caught the attention of investigators if not for the involvement of accomplices who were implicated in the assassination and the subsequent cover-up. In the second instance, prosecutors wrote that they suspected Vargas continued smuggling with the connivance of the soon-to-be-deposed subdelegado, don Rafael Pastrana.[108] The rumor mill that guided prosecutors' early investigations buzzed with hints and allegations regarding anyone who had a criminal past with some connection to don Toribio, which included Vargas. In the trial transcripts, don Manuel de la Bodega characterized Vargas as rough, robust, and aggressive. He repeated a rumor that Vargas had once tried to stab one of his social betters—don José Barbosa—in a fight in Mérida. Barbosa downplayed the event, stating that there had been no physical altercation, but Vargas had shamelessly attacked him verbally.[109] Intense interrogations and the questioning of witnesses confirmed that Vargas indeed had no part in the intendant's assassination. The intendant had even promised him a certificate guaranteeing him free passage in the area around Tihosuco after his earlier arrest, a very lenient sort of colonial probation. But one final comment hinted at his affinity for the British with whom he reputedly traded on a regular basis: evading taxes and defying prohibitions on trade with an enemy nation. In belatedly recognizing that his long conversations with don Toribio were of a personal nature, he admitted that he had suggested to don Toribio that he "go over to the English," possibly reflecting the hopes of many in the province that the intendant would either die or be deposed in the near future, allowing his former rivals to resume their prominent places in society.[110]

A brawler and smuggler like Lucas Vargas and Mariano Ancona, a low-level administrator and militia officer who lived in concubinage with another man's Maya wife, were at the low end of a spectrum of creoles and Spaniards in the countryside. Others, like peninsular scribe and hacienda manager don Nicolas Domínguez or subdelegado don Mateo de Cárdenas, came from respectable families and were marked by the honorific title of don, indicating hidalgo status. But no rural Spaniards were from the very highest strata of Yucatecan society. Truly wealthy merchants, nobles, high-ranking clergymen, scholars, magistrates, and administrators gravitated toward Mérida, Campeche, and, to a lesser degree, Valladolid. Though the nineteenth century saw some of these migrant Spaniards emerge as local elites in wealthier regions, such as the sugar hacendados around Tekax, in the late eighteenth century, only those without opportunities in the city moved into the countryside.[111]

As Spaniards fanned out into rural Yucatan, they did so with ties to various factions in urban areas or in pursuit of their own political or economic opportunities. The upsurge in the number of Spaniards in the countryside, among them many administrators in newly created positions as well as managers for the expanding haciendas, led one historian to refer to the late eighteenth century as a "second conquest."[112] The term *second conquest* implies a wave of Europeans united by a singular purpose of exploiting the Maya population, a unity that never existed. Instead, clergymen tried to preserve the pueblos as a bastion of ecclesiastical power against the onslaught of Bourbon reformers who sought to centralize rule with the twin prongs of a reformed military and a streamlined, professional rural civil administration. Hacienda managers, merchants, and smugglers looked to make money and formed alliances of convenience. Each of these groups sought ties with prominent members of the indigenous population and the mostly African-descent castas whose own demographic expansion into the countryside paralleled that of the creoles. A vast church hierarchy composed of Mayas and castas assisted priests in even the smallest pueblos. Jueces españoles and subdelegados were as likely to align themselves with indigenous cabildos—or at least some prominent officers from among them—as they were to overtly oppose them in power struggles. Spanish officials not only commanded other creoles but also headed units composed of pardos and indios hidalgos, who also formed a critical component of the bolstered defenses of the colony. Intertwined with local interests and atomized into small competing factions, poorer Spaniards, at the low end of the spectrum, often differed little in social status from the mestizos and Afro-Yucatecans around them. Certain positions, such as ordained priests and jueces españoles, were reserved exclusively for individuals of European descent. Other positions were not so closely aligned with certain racial groups. In militia service, small-time commerce, rural artisanal work, and hacienda management especially, poor Spaniards differed little from the castas in the countryside.

Castas in the Countryside: Afro-Yucatecans in a Maya World

Upward mobility through militia service and an indigenous demographic recovery that created commercial opportunities lured both creoles and castas of middling status to the countryside. Other incentives likely appealed more strongly to castas, especially those of African descent. A second look at the pardo blacksmith Ignacio Matos and his associates in both the capital city of his birth and the pueblo where he made his new home demonstrates the advancement in social standing available to skilled Afro-Yucatecans willing and able to relocate.[113] Matos's friends and relatives in Mérida were, without a doubt, respectable members of the "Black Middle," skilled artisans and militia officers. However, his relocation to Maxcanú apparently marked a move upward both socially and economically. He took on specialized projects, including a time-consuming altarpiece. His associations were less circumscribed by racial boundaries as well. Two out of three of his closest companions and favorable character witnesses were prominent creoles of Maxcanú: his compadre and a corporal in the Eighth Company of the white volunteer militia, Juan José Mayor, and don José Rafael Rodríguez, the brother of the Father Commissioner, the pueblo's leading Franciscan.

Fittingly, his return to Mérida for one final errand to sever ties with the city inadvertently led to his downfall.

From the other direction, crown efforts to buttress the defensive capacity of the peninsula led to reorganizing and increasing the numbers of pardo militia units in the countryside. Though some units of the milicias urbanas were composed mostly of indios hidalgos and other hidalgos served in the white militias, royal policy began to favor arming and commissioning Afro-Yucatecans while scaling back the numbers of armed Mayas defending the province. By 1790, pardo rifleman militia units were stationed in Muna, Uman, Hunucmá, Izamal, Seibaplaya, Hool, Poquiaxum, Tenabo, Calkiní, and Maxcanú.[114] Another harder to calculate number of pardos also served in the less regulated milicias urbanas. Pardo companies of milicias urbanas were based in Oxkutzcab, Ticul, Muna, and Maní.[115] Information for the rank-and-file militiamen of the eastern pueblos of Nabalam, Calotmul, Chancenote, Espita, Sucilá, Xcan, Tixcacal, Loche, and Panabá is not available in detail, but as don Rafael Bresón, sergeant major of the Campeche volunteers, noted, "The ranks of every company includes indios hidalgos and pardos."[116]

Though Afro-Yucatecans were often located geographically and socially between Spaniards and Mayas as a mixed-race "intermediary category," their tendency to integrate with the rural Maya majority or closely ally with one of the competing creole factions in Chikindzonot and Tihosuco stands as a microcosm of the intricate forging of allegiances by rural Afro-Yucatecans.[117] Though racially in-between, they tended to associate closely with either Mayas or a particular faction of creoles. Matos, for example, moved from a mostly Afro-Yucatecan circle of family and friends in Mérida to adopting leading creoles as his closest associates in Maxcanú. Matos was also rare among rurally based Afro-Yucatecans in his apparent inability to speak Maya. In Chikindzonot and Tihosuco, with no pardo militia units based there and being relatively close to Belize, the likely point of origin of many Afro-Yucatecans, the vast majority of the pardo population adopted a Maya lifestyle. Most castas in Chikindzonot made milpa, spoke only Yucatec Maya, and married into the local indigenous population. One of the most reliable creole officers enlisted by Dr. Guillén in his pursuit of incriminating testimony, Capt. don Mateo de Cárdenas, described the casta population and the Mayas in the following manner: "The pueblo of Chikindzonot has always been composed of Indians, and some fifty vecinos, mostly mulattos, as rustic and pusillanimous as the Indians, whose language they speak exclusively.

They are not accustomed to travel to other parts of the province, and they pass a miserable life from the scarce yield of their small plots of corn, which they work with their own hands."[118]

While Cárdenas's tone is quite condescending, between the lines of his caustic description one can better grasp a poorly understood phenomenon in eighteenth-century rural Yucatecan society: the Mayanization of Afro-Yucatecans. Out of fifty or so Afro-Yucatecans, two or three worked in the priest's household and one or two served in the militia, but most of the African-descent castas in Chikindzonot were culturally and linguistically indistinguishable from the Maya majority, living among them, speaking their language, and tilling the same subsistence plots, the milpas.[119] Chikindzonot's castas are identifiable by their Spanish surnames and their identification as vecinos rather than indios. All but three of the forty-seven male witnesses with Spanish surnames testified in Maya.[120] Just three of them signed their names.[121] Just as the Maya witnesses did, many Afro-Yucatecans justified the vagueness of their declarations by noting that they were tending their milpas during the time of don Toribio's alleged absence from the pueblo as a pretext for not giving more detailed testimony.[122] They crossed racial lines for marriage partners as well and often fell under the jurisdiction of local Maya authorities in minor crimes, as discussed previously. These Mayanized Afro-Yucatecans represented one of several avenues available to rural castas, especially those of African descent, who effectively became culturally Maya; likely their descendants were indistinguishable from the Maya majority.

Marriage patterns, especially across racial lines, are recorded in the trial transcripts. The 162 Maya men who testified do not appear with their wives' names listed, but the women's testimonies do identity their husbands. Endogamy was the norm, but significant intermarriage between castas and Mayas did take place. Twenty-one women with Spanish surnames, most of them castas, married other non-Indians. Two of the twenty-one women married Spaniards prominent enough to use the honorific don.[123] Four casta women married Maya men, including Michaela Zetina, who married the *escribano* (notary) José María Yama. Apparently, marriage to casta women had no stigma for Mayas since Yama held one of the most prominent indigenous cabildo offices. The frequency of marrying outside one's ethnic group was apparently greater on the men's side: fourteen Maya women listed casta husbands.[124] The discrepancy is less likely due to cultural norms among the Maya and more likely the result of a gender imbalance in Belize, where male slaves greatly outnumbered female slaves.[125] Moreover, male slaves, engaged in logging, likely had more occasions to escape than female slaves, who were employed in household labor.

One result of regular if limited interracial marriages and unions over the course of several generations was a blurring of racial lines. Due to the destruction of the parish records of Chikindzonot, it is unknown what racial category priests applied to the children of couples such as José María Yama and Michaela Zetina. Racial categories were inconsistent, however, especially on the part of castas who were politically or professionally associated with individuals of other races. Felipe Gómez, a shoemaker, and a tailor, Laureano Rivero, residents of Chikindzonot, worked in the church, while Sergeant Rajón served as a militia officer.[126] Two castas in particular associated closely with the clergymen in and around Chikindzonot—likely a factor in the ambiguity that surrounded their racial identity. Two of them appear in the trial records labeled with different, contradictory racial markers. Manuel Vera, a blacksmith from the pueblo of Ichmul, received more prosecutorial attention than he bargained for simply for signing as one of two witnesses to the Maya-language verification of don Toribio's alibi, as did shoemaker José Rivero. In the margins of their testimonies, the two men appear as mestizos, probably the identity they provided to their interrogators.[127] Yet a few pages later in the trial transcripts, the deposed juez español of Chikindzonot, don Pedro Gutiérrez, identified Rivero as an "Indian" and Vera as a "mulato" when discussing their part in the production of the questionable document.[128]

Vera and Rivero apparently placed no premium on their racial identity, but others in a rural sphere did. The two self-identified mestizos whose chosen racial category was contradicted by a creole who knew them well did not generate any controversy. Their choice of the term *mestizo* seems not to have been a case of *passing*, defined as "successfully concealing or minimizing the black and Indian elements" in one's background for the purposes of social advancement.[129] Changing from either Indian or mulatto to mestizo offered little in terms of social mobility. However, passing for social advancement apparently also took place during the eighteenth century, especially in cases of contested marriages. Normally relegated to the background in everyday interactions, one's racial identity became a much more contentious issue when parents used it as a pretext to prevent a marriage of supposedly unequal partners. In Izamal in 1791, María Luisa Herrera objected to Francisco Medina's marriage proposal to her daughter, Manuela Tolosa, who she identified as an "ordinary Spaniard" (*española ordinaria*). Francisco's status as a pardo was never in doubt, and the Spanish local authorities identified Manuela as a mestiza. Manuela did not weigh in on the matter.[130] Herrera's petition to reject Francisco's marriage proposal based on her daughter's purported status as a Spaniard does seem to have been a case of attempted passing, even if Spanish authorities did not accept its validity.[131]

Conclusion

As large numbers of Afro-Yucatecans moved from the cities to serve in militia units or work as artisans, black slaves fled Belize for freedom among Mayas, and creoles sought out professional, military, or administrative advancement, the eighteenth century saw a growing number of outsiders enter the Maya world. These outsiders and intermediaries, more at home in the countryside among the Maya than the upper tier of Spaniards, were critical go-betweens in Dr. Guillén's methodical effort to disprove don Toribio's alibi. As allies of the church or the Bourbon administration, they came under prosecutorial scrutiny, shedding light on the rarely examined lifestyles of rural castas and creoles in Yucatan. The records of the outside prosecutor's activities in the countryside highlight the permeability of racial categories, the frequency of marriage and other unions that crossed racial lines, and the inner workings of the interethnic alliances that predominated in rural Yucatan. However, if the allegiances to priests or alliances with jueces españoles led to cross-class cooperation, such rifts also divided pueblos. The following chapter examines the stratification and divisions of the *cah*, the Maya word for the municipalities that the Spaniards labeled pueblos, during the late eighteenth and early nineteenth centuries.

CHAPTER 6

A Stratified *Cah*, United by Language

Cabildos, Church Auxiliaries, and *Indios Hidalgos*

~≼ THE METICULOUS RECOUNTING OF THE QUOTIDIAN INTERACTIONS
between Mayas on one hand, and priests, militiamen, local administrators,
merchants, rural artisans, and hacienda managers on the other, offers a
nuanced perspective on indigenous interactions with castas, creoles, and
Spaniards in eighteenth-century Yucatan. The voluminous records of Mayas
as they came forward to testify and the records of the investigators' interactions with Maya leadership also offer potential insights regarding Maya life,
with close attention to how connections across ethnic lines among militiamen, clergymen, and provincial administrators reconfigured pueblo politics.
Growing numbers of creoles, Afro-Yucatecans, and other castas in the countryside did not lead to an immediate leveling of Maya society but rather a
reorientation. Studies of Maya local authorities and their increasing interactions with the rising eighteenth-century hacienda agriculture have provided
especially thorough coverage of these topics.[1] Even so, trial transcripts of the
assassination do offer a fresh perspective on two facets of rural life: the status
of indios hidalgos in the late eighteenth century and the deep divisions
between auxiliaries of the church and the indigenous cabildo. Notably, while
this microhistorical perspective brings into focus divisions and stratifica-
tions at the pueblo level, it also highlights how widespread fluency and literacy in Maya were in the rural sphere, regardless of racial background.

While the previous chapters highlighted how rifts between the cabildo and Mayas serving the priest created disunity in the community, the following pages briefly revisit one of the most complicated categories of prominent Mayas—indios hidalgos—in the late eighteenth and early nineteenth centuries before examining the use of Yucatec Maya as a rural lingua franca. This chapter closes by studying the weakening hold priests had over their Maya parishioners as a growing number of nonindigenous Maya speakers moved into the countryside and undermined their authority.

Indios Hidalgos

Indios hidalgos of the Bourbon era remain one of the least understood categories of Mayas in Yucatan. Much of the difficulty in classifying this group of indigenous elites stems from the fact that, unlike many other colonial designations, the rough equivalent for *indio hidalgo* in Yucatec Maya—*almehen*—never became exactly synonymous with hidalgo status.[2] In contrast, by the late eighteenth century, the Maya term *batab* was used interchangeably with *cacique*, the Caribbean term for an indigenous leader adopted by Spaniards as a universal term, or Spanish *gobernador*, for governor.[3] However, not all individuals identified as almehen were necessarily acknowledged as hidalgos. The two strands of indigenous nobility remained discrete—albeit with a great deal of overlap between the two: one an internal indigenous acknowledgment of descent from pre-Columbian nobility and the other a Spanish designation of privileged status within the colonial order. Mayas determined internally who was an almehen while indio hidalgo status required confirmation by Spanish authorities, since bestowing approbation on a lineage's *probanza de hidalguía* (proof of hidalgo status, which included genealogical information and records of previous certifications of hereditary privileges) granted its members several prerogatives in the Spanish sphere: the right to bear arms, ride horses, dress as Spaniards, be addressed as don, and, perhaps most importantly, exemption from tribute. Since many of the traits that distinguished indios hidalgos from the commoners, or macehuales, granted them the privileges of Spaniards, it is no surprise that many of them were at ease in a Spanish orbit, especially in military, social, and judicial matters.

Indigenous hidalguía derived from post-conquest recognition from the crown to *indios conquistadors* and their descendants who fought alongside

Spaniards as allies against unconquered Mayas and, later, prominent Mayas who aided Spanish authorities against indigenous rebels and pirates in the seventeenth and eighteenth centuries. Lineages (*chibalob*) such as the Xiu, Chel, Canul, Chan, and Pech in the west shifted their allegiances to the Spaniards earlier in the conquest era while the prominent dynasties of the east—the Cocom and Couoh—resisted more tenaciously.[4] Recognition of hidalgo status depended upon one's ancestors' aptitude for moving from resistance to strategic affiliations with the Montejos at critical moments in the long conquest of Yucatan. Descendants of Maya nobles who resisted through the 1540s and beyond were not awarded hidalgo status. As a result, the Xiu, Chel, Canul, Chan, and Pech dynasties received recognition as indios hidalgos, while the Cocom and Couoh, though noble, did not. Central Mexican allies of the Montejos who settled in Yucatan also received recognition as hidalgos. Thus, not all almehenob were hidalgos, nor were all hidalgos almehenob.[5] Descendants of Mexican Indians who had settled in Yucatan after the conquest were recognized as hidalgos for their participation in the conquest, but their lack of Maya ancestry would have prevented them from being considered almehenob, though some undoubtedly did achieve such status by marrying into elite Maya lineages.[6] Hidalgo status was not reserved exclusively for the descendants of indios conquistadors. Over the course of the colonial period, other Mayas gained recognition as indios hidalgos, usually fighting pirates or quelling rebellions.

Martial rights and responsibilities remained a key part of the identity of Yucatan's hidalgos into the late eighteenth century, though provincial authorities curtailed the number of Mayas serving in militias after the 1761 Jacinto Canek rebellion. In 1790, at least in the Partido de la Sierra, four pueblos—Oxkutzcab, Tekax, Ticul, and Muna—had indio hidalgo–headed companies of milicias urbanas.[7] Significantly, two of the indios hidalgos had Spanish surnames: Capt. don Santiago Días of Ticul and his first lieutenant, don Pascual Orosco of Muna. The prevalence of Spanish surnames among hidalgos likely derives from the more common usage of Castilian patronymics among central Mexican Indians. Family ties also played a role; three of the sixteen indio hidalgo officers in the district had the patronymic Pech while three of the four officers of Oxkutzcab had the same surname, Nic. All were addressed as "don." In the Partido de la Costa, less information is available, but it is clear that indios hidalgos served in the companies based in Nabalam, Calotmul, Chancenote, Espita, Sucilá, Xcan, Tixcacal, Loche, and Panabá alongside creoles and pardos.[8] In their militia service, both in mixed

units and as autonomous battalions under a supervisory board of white officers (*plana mayor*), indios hidalgos had more contact with Spaniards, a
familiarity that gave them an advantage in their dealings with Spaniards in
a legal arena as well.

Since most Maya-produced documents came from authors associated
with either the church hierarchy or the pueblo council, few texts offer insight
into indios hidalgos who were not affiliated with clergymen as auxiliaries nor
served as councilmen on indigenous cabildos. Fortunately, the inclusion of
five indios hidalgos with neither cabildo nor church ties among the
Chikindzonot witnesses offers some additional insight on hidalgos discrete
from either of these two pueblo factions. In Chikindzonot, five Maya men
with the surname Dzib were identified as indios hidalgos: Juan, Miguel,
Nicolás, Francisco, and Manuel.[9] Though the Dzibs provide one local example of the persistence of this class, the second half of the eighteenth century,
which saw the recovery of the overall indigenous population, also saw a rise
in the number of hidalgos.[10] As is clear by the presence of five indios hidalgos
with the surname Dzib, lineage still served as the basis for the designation of
hidalgo, which was hereditary. Extant militia records are incomplete at best
for eastern Yucatan as a result of the destruction of the Caste War; thus, it is
unknown if the Dzib hidalgos served in the militia. Since these five hidalgos
shared a surname, or chibal, and none of them served on the cabildo or as
members of the ecclesiastical hierarchy, they may well have served in a militia unit whose records are now lost. The order that the five were interviewed—at the same time as the vecinos, or non-Maya, witnesses—suggests
that they were still viewed as a separate class.

In legal matters, indios hidalgos tended to be much more assertive than
commoners. Indios hidalgos begin to appear more often in litigation from
the late eighteenth and early nineteenth centuries, usually in defense of their
privileges. Documentation of reaffirmations of hidalgo status and the accompanying benefits are common from the era, both in military matters and
hidalgo privileges more broadly defined. The indio hidalgo don Roque Pech
lodged a complaint against the juez español of Motul in 1790 for withholding
a military title that conferred upon him the rank of lieutenant.[11] Between
1779 and 1801, don Atanasio Xiu and don Pablo Xiu wrote petitions requesting the reaffirmation of their privileges from Governors Roberto Rivas
Betancourt and José Merino y Ceballos and Intendants don Lucas de Gálvez
and Benito Pérez y Valdelomar, which were granted.[12] Indios hidalgos also
were seemingly more adept in a courtroom in matters unrelated to their

privileged status. Juan Pablo Pacab, "natural de los hidalgos" of the barrio of San Cristóbal of Mérida, became embroiled in a lengthy dispute over land with the cacique of the barrio of Santiago, don Marcelino Bacab, in the 1790s.[13] The suit of a female india hidalga—María Yutan of Chunhuhub, who demanded that Miguel Burgos of Maní comply with his promises to marry her some time before 1795—provides a final example of indios hidalgos who were well-versed in legal matters, this time in a more personal matter. Interestingly, her intended marriage partner was non-Maya.[14]

Yucatec Maya: Rural Lingua Franca

Indios hidalgos moved relatively comfortably in a Hispanic ambit, but intermediaries were necessary for mediation between representatives of royal rule and the mostly Yucatec-speaking majority in many situations. While the need for intermediaries between crown agents and the indigenous populations of several regions of New Spain and Peru has been examined elsewhere, Yucatan stands out for the frequency with which translators were needed with casta witnesses and creoles whose primary language was Yucatec Maya. Interpreters, intermediaries between agents of Spanish rule and a monolingual rural majority, were almost always present during interrogations related to the intendant's assassination when investigators questioned any individual—Maya, casta, or Spaniard—who spoke only Maya or spoke Maya better than Spanish. In nearly all of the interrogations of Maya-speaking witnesses, the team of investigators commissioned by Dr. Guillén typically did so with the aid of an interpreter, following apparently standard protocol for rural evidence gathering.[15]

Apparently, only on one single occasion did they depart from normal procedures. The intent was not to deny Mayas access to translation but to keep working in a rare moment when an impromptu translator was unavailable. They justified the decision by noting that all of the men who were present—the questioner, the two "testigos de asistencia" (witnesses in attendance), and the notary—all spoke Maya, so there was no need for the standard fifth member, the interpreter. In February 1795, the most recently appointed interpreter, Santiago Pacheco, fell ill and Captain Cárdenas proceeded without him because he, jueces españoles Alcalá and Ancona, along with don José Vicente Reyes as the second witness in attendance, were all proficient in both Maya and Castilian. Since all were adequately bilingual for questioning

witnesses, Cárdenas made the decision to move forward, likely to avoid halting the case's recently gained momentum.[16] In most cases, at least one interrogator, outside judge, witness in attendance, or other government official
needed a translator to understand Maya, making them essential in most situations with Mayas or Maya speakers present. In Chikindzonot, distant from
Mérida linguistically and geographically, everyone involved in local government from the subdelegado on down spoke Maya.

Since the killing of an intendant was the highest-profile challenge to
royal authority in Yucatan for decades, protocol for questioning witnesses
was followed more closely than in more routine civil disputes and petty
crimes since superiors were more inclined to review such matters. For local
incidents less likely to generate controversy or reach the eyes of higher
authorities, no interpreters were present when it was understood that both
provincial administrators and the subjects involved understood Maya,
whether or not they all were indigenous. Local justices such as cabos de justicia and jueces españoles bypassed interpreters in more minor criminal
investigations. In an exhaustively examined case of livestock theft, the juez
español of Hocabá, don Juan Patrón, verified the contents of recorded testimony with Maya cabildo members and other Maya witnesses of Cusumá
without anyone formally acting as an interpreter. José Madera, the interpreter, did translate in one surprising instance. Luciano Gómes, the cabo de
justicia of Seyé, required Madera's translation services when he testified.
Pedro Arceo, another casta or rural Spaniard who accompanied Gómes, also
needed an interpreter.[17] In a similar fashion, when a Maya fisherman and
salvage worker, Lorenzo Canché, employed by the previously named Lucas
Vargas, denounced his master for contraband trade with the English in 1787,
one of the "witnesses in attendance," Miguel Sierra, translated Canché's
responses without being named as an interpreter.[18]

Previous examinations of colonial Yucatec speech and writing—especially those from a philological perspective—have led to a more comprehensive understanding of rural indigenous life. However, the omission of
Maya-language documents authored by non-Mayas and evidence of fluency
in the indigenous language across the racial spectrum—from Mayas to pardos to mestizos to creoles—provides only a partial picture of intercultural
interactions. Gradual and far from complete, Hispanicization is an important side of the story, but the Mayanization of the rural sphere, as casta and
creole minorities adopted the language and many of the lifeways of the indigenous majority in the countryside, is missing in these analyses. Examining

evidence of rising bilingualism on the part of creoles and castas, and even the existence of many monolingual castas who spoke only the indigenous language, provides a different perspective on the widely accepted model of gradual Hispanicization as a one-way process. The need for interpreters to translate for witnesses from a surprising range of ethnic backgrounds shows how deeply Yucatec Maya pervaded rural life as a common language across ethnic and racial boundaries.

Creoles, priests, militiamen, local officials, and rural merchants often spoke Maya fluently, and in some cases were literate in the language as well, writing documents in Maya. Castas—especially rural Afro-Yucatecans— also primarily spoke Yucatec Maya in many pueblos, as Captain Cárdenas's derisive commentary on Chikindzonot's casta population mentioned in chapter 5 indicates.[19] While bilingualism was common among creoles oper- ating outside of Mérida, many castas and even a few Spaniards spoke Maya as their primary—and, occasionally, only—language. In 1795 a soldier with the Batallón de Infantería de Castilla of Campeche, Santiago Briseño, was reportedly "awkward in the Spanish language" and needed don Esteban de Castro to translate his testimony from Maya to Spanish.[20] Supposedly, the unit was composed exclusively of individuals of Spanish descent, which meant that at least one creole was nearly monolingual and much more com- fortable in Yucatec Maya than the European language. Others who were close to "españoles" were monolingual, even when in close relationships with creoles. Even Tomasa Santos, the widow of Juez Español don Pedro Gutiérrez, testified in Maya, as did her daughter, who was identified as a Spaniard.[21]

Chikindzonot, on the edge of region known as the *montaña*, or *el monte*, was located at the outer limits of established and permanent Spanish control. Here, far from the influence of Mérida and Campeche, it comes as no sur- prise that Yucatec Maya prevailed as the most commonly spoken language. However, a number of non-natives residing closer to Mérida also communi- cated daily in Maya. On haciendas, zones of the highest levels of intercultural contact, Maya hacienda hands interacted in a daily workplace context with casta and Spanish supervisors. Though the suspicions surrounding suspect Pedro Ferrera turned out to be a prosecutorial dead end, authorities ques- tioned the men who knew him best, a diverse group of creole, mestizo, and Afro-Yucatecan mayordomos and their casta and Maya cowboys and ranch hands. From an investigative perspective, it was a wild goose chase, but the transcripts of the examination of his alibi left behind more evidence of Yucatec Maya's status as the preferred language in rural Yucatan, nearly as

common to castas as it was to Mayas. In the estancias of Chunchacah and
X-Komxan, owned by the treasurer don Clemente Rodríguez de Trujillo and
overseen by his mayordomo and criado Silverio Muñoz, the interpreter don
Francisco Ortega translated not only the testimony of the Maya *mayorcoles*
(overseers of milpa planting on a hacienda), Alexandro Pech and Pedro
Tamay, but also translated for the casta vaqueros Manuel Cuevas and Esteban
Pinto.[22]

Literacy was rare among all but the most prestigious and educated rural
inhabitants; illiteracy was the norm. However, a few non-Mayas wrote a variety of documents in Maya in the course of the trial. Immediately after
Gálvez's assassination, Lic. Piñeres ordered bandos published throughout the
province, calling for the apprehension of anyone acting suspiciously or traveling without a passport on the major routes from Mérida into the countryside. Written in both Spanish and Maya and directed to both Maya and
Spanish authorities, the bandos were distributed to the subdelegados, jueces
españoles, cabos de justicia, principales, and batabes.[23] Don Esteban de
Castro, interpreter general, took on the duty of publishing the documents in
Maya. Local Maya officials of Acanceh and Hoctun responded to Maya versions of the bando in their own language, acknowledging receipt of the
edict.[24] In another instance, the cabo de justicia—Lucas Tolosa, recognized
as a Spaniard—and the Maya batab don Ignacio Yam of Timucuy jointly
affirmed their receipt of a Spanish version of the document in Yucatec
Maya.[25]

Like Tolosa, who was bilingual, provincial administrators involved in
the assassination case also demonstrated an aptitude for reading and, occasionally, writing Maya. An inventory taken as evidence from a deceased rural
administrator sheds some light on communication in Maya in the countryside. After don Pedro Gutiérrez, the deposed juez español of Chikindzonot
died of dysentery in prison, Guillén and his associates perused his personal
effects when they cataloged the deceased official's possessions. They confiscated five Maya-language documents in his possession: three were from
Mayas (two from the cacique don Gregorio Yama and another from Paulino
Canche, one of the two alcaldes. Two were produced by non-Mayas—one by
Eulogio Tomás, likely one of the "fifty or so" Afro-Yucatecan castas described
above; the other was a Maya version of the bando dealing with Gálvez's death
translated by don Esteban de Castro.[26] Beyond Gutiérrez's reading ability in
Maya, other evidence suggests that the deceased juez español was thoroughly
bilingual: his widow, Tomasa Santos, spoke only Maya, increasing the odds

that he spoke a high level of conversational Maya as well.[27] Only a minority of the population read and wrote in Maya, but all who did so were not Mayas.

Gutiérrez had only limited quotidian interactions with Spanish speakers and spent most of his time immersed in a rural Maya world, making him a likely candidate for fluency and literacy in Maya. Other, higher ranking officials also demonstrated an impressive capacity in the peninsula's indigenous language. Gutiérrez's direct superior, the subdelegado don Pedro Rafael Pastrana, also deposed for his unreliable behavior during the collection of evidence against don Toribio, had a variety of untranslated Maya documents in his possession at the time of his arrest, suggesting that he too conducted routine business in the native lingua franca. His confiscated papers included one *expediente de indios*, a certification from the cacique and justicias of Sacalaca regarding the settlement of a small nearby hacienda, and a total of forty-four "papers of Indians."[28]

Further up the chain of command, the lieutenant governor of Valladolid, don Juan Francisco Muñoz, wrote fluently in Maya. Muñoz, mentioned in chapter 4 for his part in placing the criada Juana Canto in the custody of doña Rosalia Calderón of Valladolid, produced an array of Maya-language documents, dispensing with interpreters to reproduce translations of official correspondence himself. As the lieutenant governor of the villa of Valladolid, a distant third in terms of urban centers of Yucatan, fluency and literacy in Maya provided a distinct advantage in communicating with the majority of the population. While none of the documents were included in the Gálvez trial, Muñoz wrote extensive translations of official correspondence, including the ascension of a new governor (1785) and new regulations on pueblo elections (1789).[29]

Yucatan's Mayas held onto their language in both its written and spoken form as a "major medium of resistance" to such a degree that it had become the lingua franca of the countryside by the late eighteenth century.[30] As they did so, they exposed the limitations of Bourbon reforms. The Enlightenment-inspired overhaul of government and society, while wide ranging, fell short of its aims in several respects. In particular, Carlos III's efforts to eradicate indigenous languages and enforce linguistic unity met with little success. The Bourbon monarch's redoubled efforts to eliminate linguistic diversity, embodied by the real cédula of 10 May 1770, announced a renewed effort by the monarchy to make Castilian the universal language of the empire.[31] It did not have as thorough an impact as its author, Carlos III, intended. In most areas where the ravages of the conquest, disease, and forced relocations and concentrations of populations from disparate geographic origins (*reducciones*) had not wiped out the indigenous societies, native languages survived one more assault on their culture. Indeed, the persistence and diffusion of Yucatec Maya from its origins as an indigenous language to the common language of the rural majority of the province underscores the limits of Bourbon policy.

Perhaps no Bourbon monarch perceived the political advantages of the Castilianization of the countryside as well as Carlos III, the most forceful proponent of making Spanish the general language of the Americas. Widespread acceptance of the use of native languages at the local level created a linguistic distance between local government and royal administrators. While intermediaries (frequently creoles) did deftly mediate between these two spheres, the persistence of indigenous languages and their official use at the municipal level excluded royal officials—especially recently arrived peninsulares—from quotidian decision-making and administration. While the decline of indigenous writing presaged the dissolution of indigenous local government, favoring Spanish over indigenous languages also weakened ecclesiastical power. Franciscans played the most prominent role in standardizing Yucatec Maya and its colonial script, but they were not the only clergymen to master the province's native language. Jesuits and secular clergy—parish priests and their superiors who had not taken orders—also usually spoke Yucatec Maya.[32] Such mastery, combined with their moral suasion and daily familiarity with the Maya majority, gave them a distinct advantage in rural power struggles between the reforming thrusts of a regalist dynasty in Madrid and the entrenched influence of Rome's representatives in the Americas.[33] One final study of the activities of the priest of Chikindzonot and his assistants demonstrates the degree to which clergymen abused their power to serve the political ends of their faction.

Priests and Power in the Countryside

The most dramatic display of priestly power through literacy in Maya emerged in the form of a certification signed by several leading Mayas vouching for the presence of don Toribio in their pueblo on the night of the murder that came under increasing scrutiny. Upon closer examination, the document was fraudulent, dictated by one Spaniard and signed by leading Mayas under duress, alternately bribed and browbeaten by a priest with a long history of involvement in rural politics. The document itself, written in Maya and signed by leading principales from the ranks of both the priest's auxiliaries and the indigenous cabildo, confirmed that don Toribio had been in Chikindzonot, ill and bedridden but never absent, on the days surrounding the murder. After a cursory initial inspection, the document seemed credible, since it was written in the indigenous language, evidently in the hand of one of the few literate leaders of the pueblo. A closer examination of the text's creation, however, revealed the fraudulent methods and manipulation behind the alibi's certification, further undermining don Toribio's claims that he had never left Chikindzonot around the night of the assassination.

Several irregularities came to light as Captain Cárdenas and his assistants uncovered the dubious conditions behind the certification. First, the text's author did not hold one of the offices usually responsible for writing formal legal correspondence. The escribano normally handled all official correspondence of the pueblo, though sometimes either an apprentice or an assistant filled in. Less frequently, a *maestro* (choirmaster) also recorded official business. None of them drafted the signed verification of don Toribio's alibi. Instead, one of the literate assistants of the church—the teniente de coro, José Uh—wrote the document in Maya. According to José Guadalupe Uc, the former regidor who passed the certificate to the other principales, Father Manuel Correa insisted that the teniente de coro write it because the notary, José Maria Yama, had bad handwriting ("mala letra").[34] The teniente de coro did not draft the document alone; he transcribed the Maya words of a local creole, Father Correa's nephew don José María Rodríguez. Since the verification was factually false—further questioning revealed that none of the cabildo leaders had seen don Toribio in the days leading up to the murder—Father Correa resorted to threats and coercion to convince cabildo members to sign a document that was not their own creation. According to the witness Uc, the cacique don Gregorio Yama resisted signing the document that he knew his son the escribano had not drafted, but after the priest pressured him and offered each member of the cabildo a bit of aguardiente, he relented.[35]

This final illustration of how creoles' literacy in Maya worked to their advantage in contests with agents of royal authority also underscores the danger of taking Maya documents at face value. Though the signed confirmation of don Toribio's presence in the village was in fact a Maya-authored document, written by a literate Maya church assistant, its content was dictated by a bilingual creole and the signatures were coerced by a creole clergyman with extensive experience representing the church's interests in rural disputes. Recently arrived peninsular officials likely knew nothing of Correa's impressive grasp of Yucatec Maya and his ability to manipulate witnesses on behalf of church interests. In 1767 Correa had acted as a justice of the church (*juez eclesiástico*) investigating claims that the curate of Becal, don Bernardo Echeverría, severely abused the Maya caciques and imposed a harsh labor regime on the pueblos under his watch. Whereas the secular government's investigation had required the services of an interpreter general, don Pedro Cervera, Father Correa acted as both interrogator and translator in the less regulated proceedings of ecclesiastical justice.[36] Father Correa's aptitude in Maya and background in pueblo politics—especially in conflicts over secular and ecclesiastical jurisdiction—came in handy nearly thirty years later.

The removal of Father Correa from Chikindzonot in 1795 did not end the intransigence and meddling by the priests of the pueblo. Two of his successors, don Domingo de Cárdenas and don Jacinto Rubio, as well as a priest of the neighboring pueblo of Ekpetz, were also literate in Maya and equally determined to hinder the efforts of the subdelegado and the juez español to govern the pueblos without interference. Their ability to write in Maya allowed them to communicate through messages secretly passed to leading men of the pueblo. In a tangential dispute, for example, Father Rubio defied an order to limit the number of assistants who owed him tribute in labor, sending two messages in Maya to the cacique, don Nicolás Catzim of Ekpetz, which contradicted the subdelegado's orders forbidding him to exploit the labor of Angel Yam and Pedro Nauat.[37] The priest of Ekpetz, don José Agustín Barbosa, was even more intimidating and much more to the point about his parishioners' testimony regarding the assassination. He concluded a brief letter in Maya to don Nicolás soliciting *paties* (measures of cotton cloth used to pay tribute), a piece of routine business, with a less than subtle comment that he was watching and knew whether or not he was telling the truth! It was one of the most flagrant attempts to sway testimony in the entire trial.[38]

Rural churches, at the geographic center of each pueblo, towered symbolically above the smaller buildings housing the local cabildo (referred to as the audiencia) and secular Spanish magistrates. Clients showed their loyalty and counted on receiving sanctuary when local or outside opponents pursued them.[39] In Chikindzonot, most high-ranking ecclesiastical assistants sided with the priests as the most determined deniers of don Toribio's absence. Priests like don Jacinto Rubio influenced the men closest to the church, such as the fiscal Lorenzo Citep, who insisted that don Toribio was sleeping when all other Mayas stated that the bishop's nephew had left the pueblo.[40] They, in turn, expected and received unofficial legal assistance based on claims of immunity made by the curates they served. Matías Dzib, the singer in the church's choir, sought refuge in the church, since the subdelegado dared not enter to arrest him there. Dependents of clergymen were not always loyal, though. Martín Castro, the mestizo cook who lived directly in front of the sacristy, aired don Toribio's dirty laundry for the interrogators. In addition to other bits of incriminating evidence, he stated that the clothes the bishop's nephew wore on 24 June 1792, the first day he saw him in Chikindzonot after the murder, were thick with dust from the road, evidence of a long ride on horseback and not the illness that Citep claimed don Toribio had been suffering.[41]

Clergymen—especially those who qualified under the standards of canon law as ecclesiastical judges (jueces eclesiásticos)—claimed the authority to prosecute a variety of transgressions, including drunkenness, usury, sacrilege, bigamy, concubinage, and blasphemy. Since indigenous subjects of Spain's American territories were exempt from prosecution by the inquisition after 1571, ordinary ecclesiastical judges jealously guarded their authority over Maya parishioners.[42] Their frequent recourse to physical punishment—usually floggings—and fines gave force to their assertions of authority. Despite the long-standing prohibition on corporal punishment of natives by clergymen, the priest don Domingo de Cárdenas continued to whip his parishioners, not only those who skipped mass but also native enforcers of the law—the alcaldes of the jail and the topiles Eusebio Tec, Matías Pat, Francisco Chimal, and Pablo Dzib—for daring to punish a favored fiscal of the priest, Pedro Canche, for abusing his wife.[43] Jacinto Rubio, a juez eclesiástico, drew on the long tradition of priestly power in the province, deeply rooted in the culture of the peninsula, when he asserted that he was "the only judge" of Chikindzonot.[44] His behavior, and that of many of his fellow priests, demonstrated their belief that they had a separate jurisdictional sphere that rivaled the authority of secular rulers.[45] The power of priests, both under canon law and as a result of their sway over Yucatecan society, created obstacles to prosecuting and questioning suspects and witnesses with ties to the ecclesiastical hierarchy. The difficulty in securing testimony from a cowed population was best captured by Dr. Guillén, writing in 1794: "Many people of this province believe that making statements against a priest, even though it might be true, will incur a curse, or even death."[46]

When the secret messages the priests Correa, Rubio, Cárdenas, and Barbosa sent to their Maya clients failed to effectively deter them from testifying under the prosecutorial pressure of the subdelegado and his associates, the clergymen attempted desperately to send messages to their powerful ally—the bishop—in spite of the prosecution team's attempts to cut off communication between Chikindzonot and the outside world.[47] The letters reveal the tight bonds between the urban ecclesiastical hierarchy and the priests heading the province. Missives that prosecutors collected as evidence demonstrate the tight personal bonds between the bishop and the priests who acted as his nephew's defender. Father Jacinto Rubio, in his July 1795 letter to the bishop, referred to don Toribio as his "querido y amado hermano," or dearly beloved brother.[48] Father Barbosa, unable to dissuade his Maya parishioners from implicating don Toribio with their testimony, conducted a counter-investigation in the countryside, the results of which he sent to Mérida, though to little effect.[49]

Conclusion

Don Toribio found himself banished to a rural post—cut off from his active social life in the city, powerless to defend his romantic interests, and isolated by a linguistic barrier that divided monolingual peninsulares from a population of castas, creoles, and Mayas who all spoke at least some Yucatec Maya. In describing his master's situation, Toribio López detailed his dire straits. While assigned to Tihosuco, the criado stated, his only two friends were the priest of Tixkokob (and his brother), Br. don Santiago Salas, and don Nicolas Domínguez, a mayordomo of the Mérida-based priest don Francisco Campos. Deepening don Toribio's solitude, his powerful patron the bishop died in 1795. Without his protector's pressure, many less loyal allies melted away, changing their testimony in the hope of avoiding further imprisonment and interrogation. Prosecutors believed that don Toribio's recent reassignment to the most remote presidio of the province—Bacalar—was the final provocation. According to the widely accepted version of events, don Toribio, renowned for his equestrian skills if reviled for his violent outbursts, rode in one night to Mérida and dispatched his romantic rival in a fit of passion. With a clear motive and a discredited alibi, magistrates from Mexico City began the arduous process of challenging each of his appeals, moving him inexorably closer to his final sentence: death by garroting, the means by which men of standing met their ends.

The multiple volumes of transcripts recording the proceedings in Chikindzonot reveal the tensions in late eighteenth-century New Spain in microcosm. Priests opposed the Bourbon policies aimed at limiting their influence while the third parties—the local cabildos—sought to achieve their goal of local autonomy in a delicate balancing act. The military, whose officers and soldiers often had ties to all three of the rival parties, presented no united front. Though many studies have played up racial solidarity as a major theme, politics among Mayas were divisive and confrontational as well. In Chikindzonot, the cacique and the entire cabildo sided with the juez español, although this did not occur in every pueblo. Soldiers in Chikindzonot dutifully fulfilled their orders guarding and transporting prisoners, at least most of the time. In other cases, officers such as Corporal Pacheco and Sergeant Gutiérrez in Chikindzonot or soldiers like the guard Juan José Torres in Mérida were intimidated into defying their superiors by bullying priests.[50]

The same extralegal strategies prevailed in both the capital and the remote corners of the province. In Chikindzonot, the priest don Jacinto Rubio notified the intendant of Mariano Ancona's illicit living situation in an attempt to sidetrack the interrogation of witnesses against don Toribio. The bishop fray Luis publicly used a similar ploy in Mérida, admonishing a noblewoman of the city to end her trysts with don Fernando Gutiérrez de Piñeres in retaliation for his part in the prosecution of his nephew, don Toribio. Honor and reputation also influenced one's standing before the law—in the pueblo as well as in the capital. The cook at the convent in Chikindzonot, Francisco Yupit, claimed that as a "hombre de bien," the alguaciles had no right to apprehend him. The priest verified his standing as a respectable man in justifying his interference into pueblo politics. On the secular side, don Gregorio Yama counted on a certificate from the juez español don Manuel Alcalá to counter charges of drunkenness and reaffirm his reliability as a witness. Meanwhile, in Mérida, the bishop pressured many leading citizens into confirming don Toribio's reputation as a peaceful and honorable man in his defense of his nephew.

Rather than a deepening chasm separating the Maya world from the Spanish sphere, rural Yucatan in the late eighteenth century saw growing numbers of castas and creoles adapt to Maya life by speaking the indigenous language, taking on Maya wives and concubines, tending the same crops, and forging alliances with willing Indian associates. If Spanish influence and European influence radiated out from Mérida and Campeche, the Yucatecan countryside remained culturally Maya. Those who moved there from the cities in pursuit of military, administrative, or commercial opportunities acculturated to Maya lifeways rather than the other way around. In such circumstances, the proposed breakdown of rural Yucatan into a class of Spanish exploiters united against steadfast Maya resistance appears far too simplistic. The thousands of pages of trial transcripts produced by prosecutors working in Chikindzonot, Tihosuco, and the surrounding pueblos show a far more complicated situation. Spaniards and creoles vied for the supremacy of ecclesiastical or civil laws, while militiamen and merchants, many of them dealing in contraband, formed alliances of convenience. Mayas, meanwhile, typically sided with the church or the state. Growing numbers of castas often differed little from the Maya majority. In conclusion, disputes in rural Yucatan only occasionally boiled down to simply Spanish-Maya conflicts, but instead were multifaceted disagreements where the major conflict of the Bourbon era—church against state—played out at the local level.

CHAPTER 7

Divided at the Top

Politics of the Personal

⪼ THE ASSASSINATION ITSELF AND THE THREE YEARS THAT FOLLOWED often read like a period-piece romance novel or a script for a telenovela: murder in the darkened heart of the city by a disguised man; a love triangle between a married woman and two prominent Spaniards, one an agent of the king and the other a nephew of the bishop and neither of them the husband of the lady in question; an elaborate alibi and a web of intrigue spun to keep the story plausible; finally, a hard-charging prosecutor brought in to peel back the layers of lies and immunities that protected the accused from a certain conviction. However, had the author been a screenwriter or novelist instead of the series of notaries and prosecutors who dictated interrogations and summarized proceedings, one might have noted an ebbing of creativity while the writer tried to keep the narrative flowing as 1796 and 1797 approached. For our imaginary author, the events of 1798 signaled the onset of writer's block. A complicated cast of characters and too many unresolved plotlines with apparently no progress toward resolution marked these years. Fortunately, our hypothetical writer did indeed have a surprise in store in 1800, allowing the reader to emerge from the entangled, plodding detours of 1796 through 1799. However, to give the full history of the assassination of don Lucas de Gálvez and its aftermath, we must first muddle through these middle years in Mérida and the deep divisions among the city's leading citizens that were exacerbated by the aftermath of the assassination.

The quality of the gripping narrative declines during the slow years of 1796 and 1797, grinding to a near halt by 1798. By that time, Captain Cárdenas had died, possibly of a stroke.[1] Intrigue in the viceregal capital had led to Dr. Guillén's removal from the case. Brigadier O'Neill's affability with Yucatecans and his rank had qualified to him to adjudicate when a suspect's or witness's fuero called for the presence of a military judge, hastening the case's progress in the years immediately following his arrival. But his popularity plummeted after the resounding defeat of Yucatan's militias at St. George's Caye by a ragtag band of outnumbered English Baymen and slaves on 10 September 1798, an event celebrated today as the beginning of Belize's road to independence.[2] Far from the actual battlefield, many of the documents produced in Mérida and Mexico City between 1797 through 1800 include arcane disputes over jurisdiction, allegations of conflicts of interest at the level of the Audiencia de México, and a series of irate missives from the now-sidelined prosecutor, Dr. Guillén. However, while the pace of the narrative slowed during these years, a closer look shows how the aftermath of the intendant's assassination and the subsequent investigation fanned the flames of creole rivalries. While recent historical trends have revitalized scholarship on indigenous and African-descent residents of the Americas, depictions of Spanish-identified Latin Americans have all too often reverted to a caricature of a unified oppressor class. Creoles in Yucatan were anything but united. Downward mobility left many of them little better off than many middling Afro-Yucatecans and mestizos. Indeed, the distinction between mestizos and low-status Spaniards was a tenuous one. Sweeping reforms, implemented with no compromise and no consideration for local sensibilities, seemed to motivate the murder of the man responsible for enacting widespread changes: don Lucas de Gálvez. But the intendant's death did nothing to assuage the anger of creoles or ease economic tensions.

Instead, the invasive probe into the personal lives of leading Spaniards during the investigation aggravated long-standing rivalries. This chapter turns to the years after the assassination and how the scrutiny of the prosecutors damaged reputations and exacerbated antagonisms stemming from more private matters. Rumors, referred to in the transcripts as the voz común, were admissible as evidence in criminal proceedings, which raised the stakes in elites' fraught efforts to project an honorable image.[3] An already politically divided population of Spaniards turned to insults and slights against rivals' reputations when Guillén and his agents turned up unsavory details in the personal lives of suspects and witnesses.

Transitions at the top of the social pyramid also intensified insecurity and competition between leading creoles and peninsulares. The abolition of the encomienda closed one era, an age in which the descendants of conquistadors and early settlers exploited indigenous labor from afar. The late eighteenth century also saw the rise of the hacendados, marking the beginning of a new economic basis for a privileged position that lasted into the twentieth century. Encomenderos based their prestige on inheritance and access to indigenous labor based on royal grants. Expansion of private large-scale landholding and the exploitation of workers drawn by cash payments in an era of rising tax burdens or trapped by debt fueled the expansion of the hacienda and the ascension of the hacendados to the top of the creole hierarchy.[4] Often the two groups came from similar origins, but some long-established families of notable prestige—descendants of conquistadors and early settlers—saw a significant decline in their standing while offspring of middling creoles and recently arrived peninsulares moved up the hierarchy. Socioeconomic insecurities intensified suspicion and competition among prominent creoles and peninsulares.

Centers of Power in the Capital City

Given the ebb and flow of the fortunes of the prominent families of Mérida, one way of tackling the difficulty of defining *elite* for the late eighteenth century is to take a geographic approach. Buildings facing the main plaza vied for power from the city center. From there, alliances radiated from the middle of Mérida into less prominent neighborhoods. Three structures in the city center served as the most secure and permanent seats of power in Mérida's social geography: the governor's mansion, the cabildo or ayuntamiento, and the bishop's palace.[5] These multibuilding compounds often housed leading families, a retinue of criados and slaves, and closely associated professionals such as scribes and notaries. Private homes facing the plaza demonstrated the prominence of their owners. On the one hand, centrally located homes like the Casa de Montejo echoed the past glories of fading lineages of conquistadors. Through a female line of descent, the home of the best-known conquistador of the province—don Francisco de Montejo the Elder—remained tenuously in the family's possession, though not for long.[6] Indeed, though progeny of the conquerors held it, the male line of the homeowners—the Solís y Ancona family—were of much higher standing than the Montejos of the eighteenth and nineteenth centuries.[7]

By 1824, the Montejos' original estate had been subdivided. Descendants of later arrivals to the province now held much of the original central plot of land. Families such as the Cano y Roos, Buendía y Caveros, Rendóns, and Mendicutis purchased parcels of the original Montejo compound during the late eighteenth and early nineteenth centuries.[8] Neighboring homes marked the affluence of their owners, such as El Olimpo, a massive private home that once stood next to the ayuntamiento, occupied at the time of Gálvez's death by the cantor of the cathedral, Dr. don Pedro Faustino Brunet. Another centrally located home—the house of the condesa viuda de Miraflores, doña María Antonia del Castillo—served as a site of political discussions and social gatherings from members of a variety of factions, with the notable exception of most clergymen close to the bishop.[9] Besides the private homes of preeminent citizens, the bastions of royal authority and ecclesiastical power—the cathedral and the attached bishop's palace and the governor's residence, perpendicular to the cathedral—squared off. Yet the power struggle in Mérida was multifaceted, more than a simple rivalry between clergymen and agents of the royal government. Next to the governor's residence, but not aligned with it, lay the cabildo, the seat of municipal authority in Mérida.

During the late eighteenth century, the balance of power shifted as the intendant occupying the governor's mansion gained unprecedented authority while the influence of the church waned and municipal authorities struggled against an assertive policy of centralization from Madrid aimed at reducing their autonomy. The impact of shifts in the ruling philosophy of the metropole was blunted by local conditions in Yucatan. The bishop's blood ties and networks of patronage to magistrates at the viceregal court in New Spain paired with the deference Mérida's citizens showed to clergymen limited the reach of royal authority. Royal appointees, bolstered by the Decree of Intendants, faced resistance from both the bishop's faction and the ayuntamiento, the municipal council long accustomed to acting decisively and autonomously, aided by geographic isolation from the viceregal capital. Personal rivalries or alienation from natural allies led individual priests, bureaucrats, councilmen, and officers to switch sides on numerous occasions. Powerful clans often had family members in high-ranking positions in the church, military, local government, and royal administration, which led kin groups to balance family ties against factional solidarity.

The seat of royal power—the governor's palace—housed a man newly vested with authority from the crown. Gálvez personified Bourbon absolutism. But local opposition slowed the changes he sought to enact swiftly. His steady, quick pace of reform angered prominent creoles and powerful clergymen. The first intendant's position was further weakened by the fact that many of his closest associates were other peninsulares or outsiders to Yucatan who also lacked familiarity, friends, and relatives in the province. Captain Fierros, who spent much of his time at the governor's palace as Gálvez's personal secretary, languished in prison for months with no legal advocate after his friend and immediate superior's murder. The intendant's scribe, don Francisco de Heredía, had traveled from Spain in the company of Gálvez and inherited the intendant's enemies upon his death.[10] Don Fernando Gutiérrez de Piñeres, only twenty-nine at the time of the assassination, arrived shortly before Gálvez's assassination, leaving him little time to cultivate allies. His more Machiavellian rival, don Miguel Magdaleno Sandoval, cultivated friendships with the cabildo and the bishop's entourage. Lic. Piñeres, although he was well connected in Spain, lacked allies at the provincial level, resulting in his hesitant investigation into rumors of don Toribio's complicity in the assassination.[11] Other allies with high-ranking posts but no connections to the entrenched families of the peninsula included the Catalan engineer don Rafael Llovet, Gálvez's associate in his ambitious infrastructural overhaul of Mérida, and don Justo Serrano, the Cuban-born attorney who earned the enmity of Yucatan's creoles as a tireless advocate of the peninsula's Maya majority. The engineer and the magistrate of Yucatan's Indian Court emerged as two of the first witnesses to testify against the bishop's nephew before the prime suspect was jailed, when don Toribio still walked free and the threat of violent reprisal loomed for anyone willing to make statements against him.[12]

Fittingly, the cathedral towered above the adjacent governor's palace as the most imposing structure in the city center. The influence of the dominant figures from within the cathedral and the bishop's palace overshadowed the influence of the royal authority inhered in the governor's palace next door. Based on a long tradition of autonomy and a distinct set of laws governing the church's property and its clergymen, fray Luis sought to prolong and even extend the reach of ecclesiastical authority and immunity during his term of service. Allies of the bishop sought and received refuge inside the ecclesiastical compound, beyond the reach of royal law. Just as Matías Dzib sought sanctuary in the church grounds of Chikindzonot, outside the jurisdictional bounds of the subdelegado who sought to arrest him, the cathedral notary don Antonio Solís fled to the grounds of the episcopal palace to take advantage of its status as a space immune to prosecution by civil authorities.[13]

Dwelling under the protection of this ecclesiastical fortress were a number of dependents, including the mayordomo don Francisco Ortíz, who later served as a defense counsel to don Toribio; at least one scribe; and the surgeon, don Antonio Poveda. In addition to sharing a residence with the ailing prelate, with whom he must have spent much time due to his poor health, one of the surgeon's sons was a godson of the bishop.[14] Don Toribio himself, even during his militia duties in Tixkokob and Tihosuco, kept a room there. All of the inhabitants enjoyed some degree of immunity from prosecution as lodgers in the bishop's palace. In spite of the Bourbon campaign against ecclesiastical authority, the residence of the leading ecclesiastic next to the cathedral remained a source of vast power. Fray Luis also sought to cow witnesses and intimidate rivals, using the ecclesiastical space as his base of operations. With only tenuous legal grounds for doing so, he commanded witnesses who had testified against don Toribio to appear before him and receive a stern reprimand, followed by orders that they recount their depositions and provide no more incriminating testimony. Most of them complied; a few tried to hide, but none openly defied the bishop.[15]

However, the solidarity of the churchmen and their associates fractured in the face of relentless prosecution. The church grounds' place as a space beyond ordinary royal jurisdiction was under siege throughout Spain's empire as policies in Madrid reasserted the primacy of royal jurisdiction above the competing claims of the church. Poveda, the surgeon, and don Antonio de Herrera, the chief ecclesiastical notary, both relented under persistent questioning to provide testimony that contradicted the bishop in the assassination trial. The leading prelate's grasp on the province slipped as the unity of his followers broke down. The territorial integrity of the church also was subordinated to state interests. Imbued with Bourbon ideals of curtailing the coverage of the ecclesiastical fuero and asserting the authority of the state in jurisdictional conflicts, Bodega had ordered his reluctant assistants to enter the church and inventory the personal effects of don Toribio.[16] Bodega's breach of the church's defenses marked a pivotal moment in the Bourbons' jurisdictional assertiveness in matters involving clergymen and their dependents.

Across the central plaza from the cathedral, the cabildo presented a less united front against its competitors for political power. Despite the factionalism that divided its members, all cooperated in their defense of the exercise of municipal authority in judicial and executive matters, a stance that set them against both bishops and intendants. Although the intendants ceremonially presided over cabildo meetings, their presence was largely symbolic, and the councilmen pursued their own agendas. Unlike representatives of royal authority or ecclesiastical privilege, with one man heading both of those factions, the cabildo's power was more diffuse. Two alcaldes shared power with the twelve regidores. Men holding four other posts—the *fiel ejecutor*, the *alférez real*, the *alguacil mayor*, and the *procurador general*—carried out additional executive, ceremonial, law enforcement, and judicial functions of the cabildo.[17] The *depositario general* dealt with disputes over property adjudicated by the cabildo and was responsible for its financial operation. Finally, the escribano took on essential secretarial and legislative duties, recording the proceedings and notarizing official documentation produced by the cabildo with his signature.[18]

For the last hundred years of colonial rule, creoles and a minority of peninsulares uniformly addressed with the honorific title don occupied Mérida's cabildo posts. Mestizos and Afro-Yucatecans were officially excluded from holding positions on the cabildos of the three major population centers of Yucatan: Mérida, Campeche, and Valladolid.[19] Almost all councilmen during the eighteenth century were wealthy creoles, since the office of regidor and others were sold for a price of at least 200 pesos, effectively excluding all but the most financially successful families. Peninsulares were also rare in the one governing body dominated by creoles. The most extensive study of Mérida's cabildos during the eighteenth century found just one peninsular—the alguacil and regidor don José Cano—holding any position of power between 1770 and 1800.[20] Contributing to the ayuntamiento's solidarity—or at least unity among two or three factions—many of the council members came from similar professions. At the time of Gálvez's assassination, hacendados and merchants were the most numerous and influential constituency on the cabildo.[21] All the same, power was more evenly distributed among the members of the cabildo than within any other ruling body. No long-standing single leader, such as the bishop or the intendant, held undisputed authority over the council.

Honor, Nobility, and Ecclesiastical Jurisdiction:
The Bishop and the Condesa Viuda

Despite the high status of the members of the cabildo, the individual with the most prominent position by some measures in Yucatecan society, the only titled person of nobility, was not on the cabildo. This was mostly due to the fact that the one recognized holder of a title of nobility in Yucatan was a woman. However, as the hostess of informal meetings from all factions in Mérida, the condesa viuda de Miraflores opened her home to other elites to hold tertulias, social gatherings of the leading lights of Mérida. Her vast residence was another seat of unofficial power.[22] Her guests included men associated with both the royal government and the capital's cabildo. Notably, few priests were invited, and none of those closest to the bishop attended. When a woman with a legitimate claim to the top spot of Mérida's social pyramid crossed a man who headed Mérida's religious hierarchy, conflict was nearly inevitable.

The tension between the bishop and the condesa viuda de Miraflores came to a head on 4 May 1795. Fray Luis called upon doña María Antonia del Castillo, censuring her formally in a confrontation over her frequent and allegedly indecent visits from her neighbor, the lieutenant governor, don Fernando Gutiérrez de Piñeres.[23] The admonition followed an earlier informal visit. This time, a notary and witnesses accompanied the bishop. Witnesses, neighbors of the noblewoman, were prepared in advance to condemn her behavior in officially recorded testimony. The bishop admonished her to cease all interactions with the lieutenant governor, what the bishop referred to as her "intimate correspondence" ("familiar correspondencia") with her neighbor.[24] The bishop claimed only the purest motivations for the reprimand: "feelings of humanity," concern for her soul, and a desire to halt the bad example she set for his scandalized flock.[25]

A much more likely explanation is that, in his final six months on earth, Bishop fray Luis de Piña y Mazo used allegations of indecency against his political rivals to shame them into silence. Facing affronts to his supremacy in his last years, in no small part due to the overwhelming evidence against his nephew, Fray Luis now squared off against a resolute outside prosecutor building a compelling case against his imprisoned protégé with the unflinching support of a new intendant. Lic. Piñeres's difficulties with the bishop began with his secretive and tenuous investigations regarding rumors of the complicity of the bishop's nephew in the murder. His perfunctory inquiries avoided taking on the bishop directly but laid the groundwork for Lic. Bodega's and Dr. Guillén's more intensive scrutiny. His amiable and widowed neighbor was caught in the crossfire. The bishop's efforts to derail the case against his nephew coincided neatly with the desire of don Miguel Magdaleno Sandoval, *asesor de guerra* (military counsel), to avenge what he perceived as Piñeres's usurpation of his post. Most of the witnesses who knew both men believed that Sandoval had given the bishop the report on Piñeres's socializing with his noble neighbor out of pure spite.[26]

Doña María Antonia del Castillo, widow of the late count of Miraflores, don Juan Nepomuceno Calderón, remained defiant. She fired back, defending her own good name and reputation from his accusations and reprimanding the bishop for his notoriously uncharitable attitude. She defended her visitor's frequent presence in her house: first, the visits occurred at legitimate hours of the day, and, second, Christian sentiments of charity led her to care for her neighbor's everyday needs.[27] Moreover, when at least three priests, subordinates of the bishop himself, had lodged at her home, the irascible prelate had never objected.[28] She concluded by telling the bishop, "Very little or not at all do such pious men understand the rules of charity."[29] She denied his authority over her personal life, even though a censure often preceded the church's most feared weapon in its moral arsenal: excommunication.

This single incident captures in one instance many of the controversies that divided the upper tier of society not only in Yucatan but in much of colonial Latin America. First, the rivalry between Mérida's top churchman and its only noblewoman, who was supported by many of the province's prominent citizens, underscores the fierce factionalism that divided the elite Spaniards who resided in the privileged section of Mérida's city center. Second, it provides a case study of Bourbon administrators' undeterred opposition to church authority. For his part, fray Luis personified the trenchant reaction of clergymen to their weakened position, clinging to the Catholic Church's fading glory as a one-time equal partner in the conquest and colonization of New Spain. The condesa viuda's staunch defense of her own honor, supported by the testimony of eighteen of Mérida's leading citizens, highlights the importance of honor in both social and judicial contexts. Finally, a female slave's role as the source of the most incriminating testimony regarding the nature of the friendship between the two highly placed neighbors demonstrates how household domestics managed to contribute to public opinion that also shaped outcomes of cases brought before colonial courts.

The bishop of Mérida's overbearing and intrusive behavior regarding the condesa viuda and Lic. Piñeres, as well as his nephew's obnoxious comportment and sordid reputation for violence and debauchery, had left them marginalized among other elites. Their disagreeability and haughtiness likely led to their exclusion from the regular gatherings of Mérida's leading lights. Although rivals from different factions met to discuss politics and gossip at the tertulias, those closest to the bishop were not in attendance. Here, on neutral ground, prominent figures—including the captain and inspector of the pardo militia, don Pedro Rivas; merchant don José Miguel Quijano; his brother the alcalde, the younger don Juan Esteban Quijano; notary and later treasurer don Policarpo Echanove (don Clemente's replacement as treasurer); notary don José Bates; Dr. Guillén; regidor don Francisco Brito; and doña María Antonia del Castillo's brother, don Ignacio del Castillo—met to socialize in the evenings, along with Lic. Piñeres, of course.[30] Men of the cloth visited the condesa viuda's home as well, but none were from the inner circle of those clergymen closest to the bishop. Two priests, don Francisco Xavier Badillo and don Manuel Zepeda, attended on occasion as well. She also provided lodging to priests from the nearby pueblos of Muna and Chichimilá— don Juan Muñoz and Br. don Juan José Gómez—when they had business to attend to in Mérida.[31] Yet the most diehard adherents of the bishop's faction—including the ecclesiastical notary don Andres de Herrera; the surgeon don Antonio Poveda; and don Miguel Magdaleno Sandoval, who supposedly said he avoided these gatherings because of Piñeres's attendance—did not attend, nor did the bishop himself.[32] Only a few women, including the condesa viuda's sister-in-law and her sisters, attended the mostly male gatherings.[33] The meetings brought together clergymen, creole cabildo councilmen, military officers, and peninsular bureaucrats, who set aside their differences long enough to socialize, gossip, and share ideas.

Based on a long-standing tradition of priests claiming authority as ecclesiastical judges with jurisdiction over a variety of offenses, fray Luis opened an investigation into the noblewoman's behavior, beginning with the testimony of six witnesses who concurred with the bishop's allegation of inappropriate behavior between the widowed noblewoman and the young administrator. Of the six witnesses brought forward to testify by fray Luis— Br. don Bernardo Baldes, doña Ana Martínez, doña María Tomasa Anguas, doña Ana Martinez, don Miguel Bolio, and don Pablo Vergara—the three women gave the most incriminating accounts. Moreover, they cited an unnamed female slave as the original source of the sordid particulars of the alleged affair. They described enclosed carriage rides and masses they attended together as a couple, nighttime visits and slamming doors at a late hour, and rumors of a secret plan to marry that may or may not have been consummated already.[34] Furthermore, Lic. Piñeres had temporarily lodged at the house of the condesa viuda during a prolonged convalescence. During that time, doña Maria Antonia had personally overseen his recovery and allegedly had not even allowed servants to enter the bedroom where he stayed. Additional details were omitted because the notary or the bishop had decided not to record them, "por ser muy indecorosos," or because of their inappropriate nature.[35] Gender solidarity played no part in the taking of sides. While three women testified against her, a total of nineteen men and just one woman supported her claims to innocence.

Despite the bishop's influence, the widowed countess doña María Antonia del Castillo y Aguirre called upon on her ally and regular tertulia guest Brigadier O'Neill to support her challenge to episcopal authority. The intendant ordered the bishop to suspend his investigation, declaring that the matter did not fall under the bishop's purview. After the bishop initially defied this order, arguing that it did not apply in this case, O'Neill warned him in strong language "not to meddle in my jurisdiction."[36] The intendant had political motivations to defend the personal reputation of one of Mérida's leading ladies as well. Although the condesa viuda bore the brunt of the bishop's attacks, the leading prelate also disparaged the reputation of Lic. Piñeres. In addition to slurs against his moral character, the loyal subordinate of the intendant faced accusations by the bishop over the undue influence of the noblewoman in Piñeres's handling of judgments in his role as auditor of the province. According to five witnesses, anyone hoping for a favorable outcome in any lawsuit handled by Piñeres improved their odds by soliciting her intervention.[37]

Slighting the noblewoman was one thing; impugning the professionalism of a close aide of the intendant was another matter. O'Neill not only put a stop to the episcopal proceedings, he also began questioning the attendees of the tertulias in search of supportive witnesses who would refute the bishop's allegations and restore the noblewoman's honor and Piñeres's reputation. Twenty witnesses, including only one woman, went on record in support of the honorable reputations of the neighbors. The witnesses included most of the tertulianos, as well as other militia officers from varying ranks, two public treasurers, regidores, alcaldes, other priests, the *abogado de indios*, various encomenderos, and even a Franciscan instructor of

philosophy from the Tridentine colegio, fray Miguel Buenaventura del
Canto. In O'Neill's words, "almost all the well-known individuals of the capital" testified to the good character of the alleged lovers in a summary for-
warded to the audiencia in Mexico City.[38]

Apparently, the broad support silenced critics of the condesa viuda.
Lic. Piñeres may not have been so lucky. In spite of efforts by men of such
prominent standing as don José Miguel Quijano, a councilman who asserted
that Piñeres always worked diligently in times of poor health, his tentative
handling of the early phase of the assassination investigation combined with
rumors regarding unseemly personal behavior likely led to his reassignment
within a year of the bishop's inquiry into his behavior. The disgraced young
magistrate, still in his early thirties, received orders to relocate soon after
news of the scandal reached Spain. By the end of 1796, he departed for the
remote Philippines to begin a new phase of his service to the crown as the
fiscal of the Audiencia of Manila.[39]

The Bourbons' regalist aims bolstered Madrid's support for O'Neill's
assertion that the matter pertained to royal jurisdiction despite the bishop's
claims he had the right to investigate reports of an extramarital affair due to
his standing as the province's leading ecclesiastical judge. The procurador,
don Anselmo Rodríguez Balda, interpreted a series of reales cédulas passed
between 1771 and 1786 to mean that the bishop and churchmen in general no
longer had the right to even admonish individuals in private over concubinage or adultery. The policing of morality had shifted from a prerogative of
the church to a duty of the state, and the bishop had overstepped the bounds
of his legal authority.[40] Following the lead of his predecessor, don Lucas de
Gálvez, Intendant O'Neill was equally unswerving in his determination to
put the bishop in his place, ordering him not to "interfere in my jurisdiction."[41] O'Neill's eventual victory over a bishop who had outlasted four governors was hastened by an unexpected turn of events; fray Luis died on
22 November 1795, after suffering declining health for several years.[42]

The Condesa Viuda's World:
The Enlightenment in a Colonial Backwater

Two of the most prominent attendees at the tertulia were a peninsular magistrate and an Irish Hispanic general, a pair who worked in tandem to make
more progress on the case in less than two years than their predecessors had

or their successors would. One of the unexpected consequences of the assassination was the arrival of highly regarded jurists and administrators, dispatched to a normally low-priority area to bring justice to the recalcitrant province. Their presence at the condesa viuda's tertulias seems to have been welcomed by most, and both apparently handled their assignments with more social grace and deference to local customs than their respective predecessors, Lic. Bodega and don Lucas de Gálvez. Indeed, most prominent men in the province received them warmly, with the obvious exception of the clergyman whose status as the most powerful man in the province was challenged by both the guiding philosophies and prosecutorial activities and centralizing thrust of men such as Dr. Guillén and Brigadier O'Neill.

The two men refused to be cowed and expressed their contempt for the clergyman in their writings. Guillén, the former judge of the Acordada, showed unconcealed ire and little deference for Mérida's bishop.[43] He deprecated the bishop's temperament and overbearing manner and also questioned his intelligence. Guillén, giving no more respect for the bishop after his death than he did while he was alive, described fray Luis as a "prelate without solid instruction, irascible, and vengeful" in 1797.[44] He memorialized the bishop as "imbued with erroneous principles" and wrote that he "governed with despotism and domination."[45] As the second outside prosecutor called in to conclude a case that had frustrated his predecessors' efforts for over two years, Guillén confronted the bishop's privileges and immunities head-on. His ten years of experience as a judge of the Acordada, likely the most efficient court in New Spain, prepared him well for difficult legal work. Moreover, don Matias de Gálvez enthusiastically supported Guillén's appointment to the judgeship during his brief tenure as viceroy, providing him with an additional incentive to track down and prosecute the killer of his benefactor's distant cousin.[46]

For two years, Dr. Guillén, a well-read, Enlightenment-inspired jurist, collaborated with the archetypical Bourbon administrator, don Arturo O'Neill. If Guillén embodied Madrid's eighteenth-century emphasis on efficiency and enlightened absolutism, Brigadier O'Neill's experiences typify the centralizing aims of the Bourbons, especially the growing reliance on battle-tested officers as administrators in place of men whose major claim was illustrious ancestry. Due to his rank of brigadier, which enabled him to adjudicate in situations where witnesses or subjects held a military fuero, O'Neill acted as a cooperative co-juez, or co-judge, helping Guillén surmount the thorny issue of officers' legal immunity. As an intendant with a track record of

loyalty to his Bourbon superiors, O'Neill backed Guillén's exhaustive investigation, adding crucial support that both Lic. Piñeres and Lic. Bodega had
failed to receive from O'Neill's immediate predecessor, interim governor
Sabido de Vargas.

Though born in Ireland, O'Neill's fealty to the crown was never in
doubt, and his strategic abilities were only rarely called into question. The
young Irish exile saw major combat for the first time as a lieutenant in the
Hibernia Regiment against Portugal in 1762 during the Seven Years' War,
earning a promotion to adjutant major. His next major engagement, under
Gen. Alejandro O'Reilly, in Algiers in 1775, utterly failed to "punish the
pirates in their own lair."[47] Out of a force of twenty-two thousand, over two
thousand Spaniards died before General O'Reilly ordered a retreat. O'Neill
escaped unscathed, and a string of victories against Portugal in 1777 over
border disputes reversed any damage his reputation might have suffered for
his role as an officer in the Algiers fiasco. His brief appointment as governor of Santa Catalina Island began his appointment to a series of administrative posts in borderlands of uncertain fealty.[48] The entire Hibernia
Regiment, including Lieutenant Colonel O'Neill, proved their worth soon
afterward, this time against the hated English in the American Revolution.
His service in this war—especially in the Battle of Pensacola in March
1781—sufficiently impressed his superiors that they named him to the governorship of Pensacola after the victory. He held this post until he departed
for Yucatan.[49]

Family and Faction

If Brigadier O'Neill and Dr. Guillén felt no need to show traditional deference to the top churchman of the province, they put more effort into building
friendships with prominent creoles, especially the Quijanos. For the two men
heading the assassination investigation, cordial relations with one of the
leading families of Yucatan made for a much more agreeable stay in Mérida.
The Quijanos also benefited. The family's amiability with O'Neill and Guillén
stemmed from both personal and political motivations.[50] Due to their well-
known rivalry with the deceased intendant, many suspected that the
Quijanos had some part in the murder of don Lucas. Entertaining and socializing with the two men responsible for sorting through the rumors and evidence led some to look askance at the friendship, but it did place the Quijanos

on better footing with investigators working on behalf of the crown than their rivals who resided in the bishop's palace.

Mérida's cabildo rarely united behind either the church or the state. Most councilmen sided with the condesa viuda and Lic. Piñeres, but the alcalde don Miguel de Bolio y Paz sided with the bishop. He did so not so much out of loyalty to fray Luis but out of animosity toward the Quijano clan, who in turn allied with Lic. Piñeres and Brigadier O'Neill. With no single, permanent executive heading the cabildo unchallenged, various factions vied for control and influence within the most important municipal government body. While no specific dynasty or coalition dominated the cabildo over the long haul of the colonial period, one faction led by a single extended family held the upper hand in late colonial local politics in Mérida. Due to a combination of patriarchal fecundity, political acumen, and professional success, the Quijanos and their relatives by marriage presented a formidable power bloc in Mérida's ayuntamiento during the late eighteenth century.[51] In part due to the proclivity of the patriarch don Juan Esteban Quijano to reproduce, as well as a result of his political acuity, the Quijanos and their in-laws were a force to be reckoned with. In his own words, his sons occupied "honorable ecclesiastic, political, and military posts" by the late eighteenth century.[52] Moreover, they belonged to the ascendant class of hacendados, large-scale landowners who emerged as the dominant economic class from the late eighteenth through the early twentieth centuries.[53]

Don Juan Esteban Quijano, a high-ranking notary (*escribano de gobernación y guerra*), encomendero, and merchant, served as alcalde ordinario, regidor, and procurador between the years 1780 and 1795 on Mérida's ayuntamiento, as did his son and namesake, don Juan Esteban the younger, and another son, don José Miguel Quijano, who also served as procurador.[54] Don José Miguel, a merchant and militia captain, as well as member of the cabildo, served as his father's lieutenant in the politically powerful Quijano family.[55] Two other sons, don Mariano and don Ignacio, held high-ranking military posts, with each respectively serving as lieutenant of the Batallón de Castilla and captain of the dragoons. Don Joaquín held another influential post as a bureaucrat, as the *juez general de bienes de difuntos*, or judge of the property of the deceased.[56] Two more sons, don José Tadeo and don Manuel, served as priests in Mérida.[57]

If don Juan Esteban's propensity to produce a number of sons allowed him to place many of them in influential posts, he apparently maneuvered to marry off his daughters and sons with prestigious in-laws, creating ties of kinship to other established creole clans such as the Cosgayas, the Laras, and the Elizaldes. Don Ignacio, captain of the dragoons, for example, married doña María Michaela de Cosgaya y Elizalde, which linked them to other members of the cabildo, including the regidor and alcalde don Juan Antonio Elizalde, uncle of the young bride.[58] Don Juan Esteban's seven daughters also played a role in raising the family's profile, though apparently with a bit more reluctance in at least two cases. Doña Nicolasa married the alcalde don Anastasio de Lara, adding another important ally to the Quijanos' faction in the cabildo. Another daughter, Madre Eduarda, took a different route to respectability as a high-ranking nun in the Convento de La Purísima.[59] These family ties allowed creole families to at least partially compensate for their exclusion from the top position of the church and royal government hierarchy. If the Quijanos themselves did not control the senior post in the cabildo as one of the two alcaldes, often someone connected by blood or marriage did.

Such strategic marriages, however, required the acquiescence of don Juan Esteban's offspring, which was not always so easily gained. Two daughters—doña Tomasa and doña Josefa—resisted pressure from their father and brothers who sought to subordinate their romantic pursuits to the Quijanos' political and economic interests. The refusal of doña Tomasa and doña Josefa to recognize don Juan Esteban's authority was not the only opposition faced by the male Quijanos. Their public defiance of their father's wishes and the open affair of another with a man of ill repute fueled their enmity with the first intendant before his assassination. The Quijanos' rivals in the cabildo sought to tie this antagonism to their alleged complicity in don Lucas's death.

The hostility began with small matters with just one of the sons of Juan Esteban. The animosity may have begun in 1789, when Gálvez delivered the news that the crown had denied Capt. don Ignacio Quijano a promotion in rank.[60] Later, the newly arrived intendant confronted Quijano over a matter of militia discipline after he fell under suspicion for misuse of military funds.[61] Shortly after, he reprimanded don Juan Esteban Quijano, serving as alcalde at the time, over ostentatious displays of power, earning the ire of two of the most prominent members of the family early in his tenure. Then the intendant ordered a subordinate—don Leandro Poblaciones, captain of the artillery—to investigate the Quijanos' treatment of their hacienda's *semaneros*, Maya workers paid by weekly wages.[62] The intendant's focus on the financial dealings of the Quijanos, coupled with his efforts to curtail their over-the-top displays of power, led one family member to complain that

Gálvez was an avaricious man who sought to despoil them of their wealth. In an exchange recalled by the interpreter general, don Esteban de Castro, one that must have confounded the peninsular intendant, the translator recounted a heated moment in which don Juan Esteban, serving as alcalde, turned to him and vented in Maya, telling the interpreter that all Gálvez really wanted was money. Viewing Gálvez's treatment of his family as a shakedown, don Juan Esteban defiantly concluded his diatribe in Maya by declaring that the intendant would never get any of his money. Castro and the alcalde both understood Maya; Gálvez, who was present for the exchange, did not.[63]

As the first intendant determined to enforce the royal will with no compromise in matters such as the abolition of the encomienda, the abuse of servicio personal, and curbing elaborate ceremonies and boisterous celebrations, he had many enemies among the creole elite. But for the Quijanos, the final straw was the intendant's interference in their personal affairs. Gálvez's uninvited mediation in a dispute over the marriage of doña Tomasa cemented the ill will this powerful family felt toward him.[64] Gálvez held a position of command that authorized his punishment of Capt. don Ignacio Quijano for military infractions related to his malfeasance in military matters. His administrative capacity gave him grounds to order don Juan Esteban to desist from certain ceremonial displays at cabildo meetings. Yet public opinion and most interpretations of the law did not sanction his intervention in the matter of the marriage choice of doña Tomasa. Many believed such meddling cost Gálvez his life. Marriage and the parental role in decisions regarding a child's choice of spouse were imperative for families seeking to make powerful connections with other prominent lineages.[65] Yucatan was a province where a limited number of prominent families, many of them the descendants of early settlers and encomenderos, dominated the upper tiers of society, and only a trickle of newcomers had arrived to threaten their position, most of whom eventually married into long-established local dynasties.

Don Juan Esteban Quijano's strident denunciation of the intendant, along with the defiance of one daughter and the extramarital affair of another, slowed the family's rise to power but did not halt it entirely. After the departure of the two most sympathetic co-judges—Dr. Guillén in 1796 and Brigadier O'Neill in 1800—scrutiny of the family intensified over suspicions that the Quijanos were involved the assassination, though few believed any of the many sons had individually carried out the attack. Together with the tawdry rumors about the behavior of two of the daughters, the family's reputation suffered. Rivals within the cabildo challenged their domination of the council. Political enemies took advantage of the Quijanos' declining fortunes to oppose the family's efforts to maintain their dominance of the cabildo. In an 1802 letter to the viceroy, Alcalde don José del Castillo and Regidor don Miguel de Bolio—"enemies of the House of Quijano"—opposed the accession of one more Quijano to the post of alférez real of the cabildo based on allegations that the family was implicated in the assassination of Gálvez.[66] Even so, the damage did not completely undo the Quijanos, who recovered somewhat in the following decade. By the 1810s, a namesake and grandson of don Juan Esteban Quijano, son of the militia captain don Ignacio, was a prosperous merchant while his uncle don Joaquín Quijano remained influential enough to win election as one of the regidores in the 1812 Constitutional Ayuntamiento.[67]

Don Toribio's Demise

The Quijanos' struggle to keep their lineage's good name against their many detractors might be considered a draw in the long run. Don Toribio's public opinion campaign, waged for the most part via intimidation by his uncle, failed. From Maya market women to erudite, supposedly anonymous poets who posted their allegations in verse in the street, by 1795, most of Mérida's citizens believed that the bishop's nephew murdered the intendant. Efforts to counter the crescendo of rumors implicating don Toribio failed to stem the tide. The bishop's bullying only worked in the short run. After fray Luis's fatal illness and death, don Toribio's allies deserted him en masse. Voz común did have validity in the colonial legal system, lending credibility to the painstakingly gathered evidence against the "bad lieutenant," don Toribio.

If the Quijanos' political acumen allowed them to neutralize potential opponents in social settings and sway public opinion in their favor, don Toribio's long history of violence, disrespect for prominent locals, and scandalous lifestyle added to resentment of his uncle's meddling and scolding, undermining their campaign to present the militia lieutenant as a blameless and upright man. In the first years after the assassination, the campaign of intimidation had its desired effect. If the bishop's authoritarian ways eventually alienated a majority of the leading citizens of Mérida, the deceased intendant's callous manner also drove many into the bishop's camp, providing the prelate with some much needed assistance in legal matters. With disillusioned bureaucrats who distanced themselves from their superior, Gálvez's personal snubs seem to have played as much of a role as political disagreements.

One of don Toribio's staunchest allies in thwarting the attempts of successive prosecutors to conclude the case against him came from the ranks of the royal administration, the assessor of the intendancy, don Miguel Magdaleno Sandoval. Sandoval's animosity toward don Lucas de Gálvez stemmed from Sandoval's competing claim to don Fernando Gutiérrez de Piñeres's post as auditor de guerra of Yucatan. When Gálvez decided in favor of Lic. Piñeres, don Miguel made the first of his frequent expressions of antipathy toward Gálvez by failing to attend a welcoming banquet hosted by Gálvez; Sandoval himself was the intended guest of honor.[68] Sandoval sought allies in Mérida's cabildo, hoping to find common ground with rivals of the new intendant to undermine his authority and win approval for the position of auditor. He succeeded in deepening the conflict between the municipal council and crown administrators but did not win Piñeres's post. He soon aligned himself with the most steadfast opponent of royal power: the bishop.

Sandoval remained an implacable foe of the deceased intendant's allies decades after don Lucas's death. During the proceedings, Sandoval ignored his obvious conflict of interest as a magistrate charged with solving the crime and a close friend of the uncle of the prime suspect, don Toribio. He frequently leaked information from secret proceedings and even used his insider status to assist don Toribio's defense attorneys, don Francisco Ortíz and don José Correa Romero, with their legal strategies.[69] After Lic. Piñeres's 1796 departure for the Philippines, Sandoval finally ascended to the coveted position at the root of his animosity for the deceased intendant and his departed predecessor, taking over as auditor de guerra in Piñeres's absence.[70] But his resentment lived on. As late as 1807, Sandoval was still criticizing the behavior of his rivals—Captain Fierros, Lic. Serrano, and Gálvez's successor, Intendant O'Neill—for their intervention in a dispute between ships of the nations of the United States and France that occurred in the coastal waters of Campeche.[71]

The bishop benefited greatly from Sandoval's support and that of other defectors from the ranks of the royal government who secretly or openly sided with the cleric to sidetrack or slow the trial's progress. As a scholar of law, Sandoval's regular visits and legal counsel benefited the bishop.[72] In a similar manner, the underhanded dealings of don José Joaquín de Castro, who served as a notary during several stages of the trial's progress, worked to the bishop's advantage. In 1796, as prosecutors' assistants dissected the elements of don Toribio's alibi, Castro faced charges of altering the testimony of don Toribio's criados and was suspected of shifting suspicion away from don Toribio by playing up rumors regarding José Bermejo's supposed complicity in the assassination.[73]

Unfortunately for the bishop, few creole and peninsular administrators who sided with him out of convenience during the intendant's lifetime held grudges with the persistence that matched Sandoval's. Between 1792 and 1796, support for the bishop, and later his nephew, dissipated. The arrival of don Lucas's amiable successor and the diplomacy of Dr. Guillén neutralized much of the resentment of royal rule and undermined sympathy some might have felt for the heavy-handed administration of Gálvez. Witnesses began to testify more willingly against don Toribio and rumors began to swirl openly, even as he still walked freely in Mérida. At first, only a few adversaries of the bishop, most of them so well placed as to have little to fear from him, joined forces with the outside prosecutors. Don Juan Antonio Elizalde, heading the cabildo as the alcalde in February 1793, when don Toribio was still free, was one of the earliest members of the cabildo to unabashedly voice his suspicions that don Toribio was the assassin.[74] Soon a growing chorus revealed their firsthand experiences with a violent, spoiled, and adulterous young man.

The Bad Lieutenant: Sex, Violence, and don Toribio's Reputation

Colonial Spanish law took into account one's public reputation when determining guilt or innocence.[75] Whispered stories of don Toribio's violent outbursts and tales of orgies under the nose of his otherwise sanctimonious and intolerant uncle led prosecutors to pursue him as the likeliest suspect. The bishop's palace, in turn, put incredible amounts of energy into countering gossip with a rumor campaign of their own aimed at changing the tone of the voz común. In the 1790s, Yucatan still had no printing press, but literate members of the middle and upper classes read widely, keeping abreast of the latest developments at the viceregal level and Spain via the government-published bandos as well as satirical poems authored and posted anonymously, many of them making veiled accusations against don Toribio.

Metered verses (*décimas*) mourned the death of Gálvez in the streets, alluding to don Toribio's role as the killer couched in coded language.[76] Four versed, veiled accusations against don Toribio were posted in prominent places: a brief allegory of a stranger in the province conversing with "Truth," a poem by an author identified simply as a "Campechano," and two separate, shorter sonnets.

The poems appeared shortly after the crime, starting in the third week of August 1792. The first poem began by noting don Toribio's stature: "No es el asesino Duende" (roughly, "The assassin is not a dwarf"). "Todos lo están mirando" (All are looking at him) made light of his public presence. Its most pointed accusation came in the last line, which concluded that "la causa viene de España y de España el agresor" (the cause comes from Spain and from Spain [comes] the agressor).[77] Since the majority of the intendant's most implacable foes were creoles and the city had few prominent peninsulares, the poem narrowed the range of suspects if it was taken as a credible source.[78] Likely as not, it was an unambiguous accusation aimed at don Toribio and widely understood by the literate population of Mérida, the anonymous author's target audience. Of all of Gálvez's rivals, don Toribio was certainly the most prominent and able-bodied peninsular.

A longer poem, ostensibly addressed to the "wise, just, and incorruptible" viceroy, the Second Count of Revilla Gigedo, on the surface seemed to be extolling the virtues of the viceroy and assuring its readers that the leading representative of royal rule would soon catch the murderer. Between the lines, the poet insinuated that ties between the suspect and the archbishop in Mexico City might be slowing the proceedings. The poem also hinted at don Toribio's role as a likely suspect. The author of the décimas was even more oblique but presciently alluded to the complicating factors that later hindered the case's progress: the asylum of the church, the competition between jurisdictions (via a mention of the *fuero real*), and the reference to judges as friends, an apparent allusion to the bishop's powerful connections in Mexico City and beyond.[79] In labeling the assassin a "rival," the anonymous author referred to the public feud between don Toribio and the intendant, suggesting that the enmity that drove don Toribio to kill the intendant stemmed from personal rather than political reasons.[80] The final stanza also discussed sin and absolving one's conscience. These final lines of the first page indicated a man with a personal animosity toward don Toribio, while the references to sin and forgiveness hinted at his connection to an ecclesiastical patron. The next two stanzas alluded to specific problems the prosecutors faced, making it even clearer that the author's target was don Toribio. He accurately foresaw an intense struggle over jurisdiction ("una fuerte competencia") and predicted that "even if the church were to shelter him," justice would win out. The next lines foreshadowed that the suspect's efforts to "corrupt witnesses" and "make friends" would do little to shield him from justice.

The least specific of the four rhymed responses to don Lucas's death was the dialogue between a stranger to the province and Truth personified. The stranger ("Forastero") asked questions, providing Truth the opportunity to contradict certain criticisms of Gálvez's rule. Truth lamented Gálvez's passing, praising the deceased intendant with references to classical figures, including Vespasian, as well as describing the deceased intendant as the "Abel of our times." Truth noted, as subsequent historians did, Gálvez's infrastructural reforms—a hospital, a boulevard, and streets—writing that the innocent intendant had been wronged by an ungrateful city. This poem, mostly a general lament and defense of Gálvez's term as the first intendant, made no allegations and only briefly mentioned the early rivalry between Gálvez and the Franciscans.[81] A fourth poem, supposedly penned by a campechano, mourned the death of Gálvez by a "treasonous" hand and hinted at a rivalry between the province's two cities, with a resident of Campeche leveling an accusing finger at Mérida and its "ungrateful people."[82] A short sonnet extolling the deceased intendant and mourning his loss followed each poem.

Witnesses interviewed before don Toribio's imprisonment were reluctant to share their interpretation of the poems, but at least one—Capt. don Enrique de los Reyes—went on record with his interpretation, which he believed pointedly accused don Toribio.[83] Lic. Piñeres, making no headway toward the case's resolution, took offense at the fourth poem, which implicitly held the viceroy and his provincial agents responsible for bringing justice to the man who most of Mérida considered guilty.[84] Only when don José Bates, the English-descent notary, informed him that the third and fourth poems targeted the bishop's palace rather than the royal bureaucracy did Lic. Piñeres relent a bit in his pursuit of the author, who was never definitively identified.[85]

The poems were posted in the streets with no one noticing; at least no one admitted to having seen their distribution. Copies circulated in prominent homes, as prosecutors later discovered. Don Alonso Manuel Peón had at least one copy in his possession, which he gave to Captain of the Engineers don Rafael Llovet.[86] One witness suspected that the author was likely the bishop's political rival, don Nicolás de Lara, a former rector of the cathedral who ended his life far from his birthplace, living as an Augustinian in Mexico City after his fall from grace with Yucatan's top prelate. Captain Fierros believed that the exiled rector might have surreptitiously sent an original copy from Mexico City for distribution in the province probably to exact revenge on the clergyman who destroyed his career.[87] Others identified the author as an enemy of the family with an agenda of incriminating the del Mazos. In order to discredit the statements of the notary don José Rivas, don José Correa Romero alleged that Rivas had authored the poems.[88] By doing so, he hoped to convince the judges and prosecutors that Rivas had made his declarations out of spite for don Toribio. Rivas denied the allegations and said that he had only heard the poems recited to him by another man whose identity he did not recall.[89]

The written evidence provided by the poems only tangentially helped prosecutors who struggled to decipher the coded allegations. Mérida was still largely an oral rather than a print culture. Several witnesses—including don Enrique de los Reyes, don Esteban de Castro, and don José Bates—reported having heard the verses recited but averred that they never saw them in print.[90] The interpreter general, don Esteban de Castro, in a virtuoso demonstration of his verbal talents, recited the first poem in its entirety almost exactly as it appeared in print.[91] As we shall see, Castro may well have had an interest in leveling accusations against don Toribio. During more than seven months between the assassination and the arrival of Lic. Bodega, residents of Mérida—from slaves to councilmen—whispered among themselves, condemning don Toribio as the assassin in the court of public opinion. Such accusations, some of which were made in the house of the condesa viuda, did not go unobserved by the bishop. According to the one firsthand witness to the visit the bishop made to the home of the prestigious widow doña María Dominga Pérez, the bishop mentioned "certain conversations against the honor of don Toribio," in a not entirely relevant example of the scandalous goings on at the condesa viuda's house.[92] Reports of such discussions held in the house of the province's most prominent woman no doubt spurred the bishop to wage his campaign against the reputations of Lic. Piñeres and doña María Antonia.

Lic. Bodega's arrival and the subsequent depositions of hundreds of Mérida's residents allowed them to finally make their whispered accusations public. The beleaguered protector of the Indians, don Justo Serrano, testified first, followed by the two slaves of the treasurer's household, Tobi and María Candelaría. The latter two had previously felt don Toribio's wrath when he accused them of preferring and abetting his romantic rival—Gálvez—in his pursuit of doña Casiana. Next, the regidor don Manuel Bolio characterized the widespread belief of the militia lieutenant's guilt as "public and notorious."[93]

Serrano's and Bolio's testimonies seemed to have opened the floodgates. A number of highly placed witnesses came forward, concurring with the allegations made against don Toribio and doña Casiana. Many early witnesses were from Gálvez's inner circle, such as Llovet and his chamberlain, don José Morán, who had accompanied Gálvez from Spain as a criado. Enemies of the bishop with few ties to Gálvez—such as the assessor of the Indian Court, don Juan Esteban Meneses—also testified against don Toribio.[94] Members of the cabildo, though they had little love for the intendant, also turned against the tyrannical churchman. The regidor don José Domínguez; the alcalde don Juan Antonio Elizalde; the notary don Gregorio de la Cámara of the cabildo of Mérida; the alcalde of Valladolid, don José Ruz; and the militia colonel don Alonso Manuel Peón, a tertuliano and a rare peninsular who integrated with ease into creole high society, figured among don Toribio's more prominent accusers.[95]

The growing belief in don Toribio's guilt crossed lines of language and class as slaves, criados, and Maya market women added their voices to the growing chorus of residents convinced that the bishop's nephew was the killer. In response, the bishop and his allies sought to sway public opinion against the belief in his nephew's guilt. Fray Luis relied upon doña Narcisa Martínez, alias La Suárez, and her household. Doña Narcisa's household was tied to the bishop's palace through marriage, but not in the typical way of a union between offspring. In this case, the two homes were tied by the marriage between criados Toribio López and Juana (Juanita) Martínez. As seen in chapter 4, the female-headed household was the epicenter of the bishop's counterattack on rumors swirling around his nephew. Despite their origins from the humble home of a widow and two criados, the campaign of whispers against José Bermejo, aimed at a diverting attention away from don Toribio, soon began to circulate. With doña Narcisa as the ringleader, Dr. Guillén traced the source of the rumors to La Suárez, her sister doña Juana Martínez, and her niece doña Paula de Sosa.[96] He denounced La Suárez as a "famosa secretista," responsible for calumny and false testimony.[97] The three, although all spinsters, had friends in some of the leading houses, perfect for launching rumors to deflect attention from don Toribio. Doña Catalina Rios, wife of the regidor don José Cano, reported that she heard rumors regarding Bermejo's complicity from Juanita, the mestiza or Indian criada.[98] With ready access to leading priests, La Suárez told the Franciscan fray Antonio Maldonado; the vicar of the Church of Jesús, don Manuel Gonzáles; and a Padre Villa that Bermejo was the most likely culprit.[99]

Bermejo was not the only suspect whose implication in the assassination had its basis in secondhand reports emanating from the household of the prolific rumormonger, doña Narcisa. One of her versions of Bermejo's guilt included the detail that don Clemente Rodríguez de Trujillo, the treasurer and apparently cuckolded husband of doña Casiana, had paid Bermejo to carry out the assassination.[100] With less precision, Dr. Guillén tracked whispered allegations about the complicity of the militia cadet don Juan José Roché and the persistence of accusations against Captain Fierros back to doña Narcisa as well.[101] What may have appeared as innocuous gossip to some was perceived by Dr. Guillén as perjury and obstruction of justice, so he had her imprisoned. Doña Narcisa died in a women's hospital in Veracruz on 20 August 1796.[102]

Reputation

In eighteenth-century Yucatan, a subject's legal reputation became established when rumors of criminal behavior spread widely enough to be considered common knowledge.[103] Prosecutors and judges of colonial Latin America not only accepted unconfirmed rumors regarding suspects' reputations, they actively sought them out. Don Toribio, innocent or not, saw a long list of witnesses describe his aggression and cruelty, establishing him as a man predisposed to carry out violence to avenge slights. Further probing revealed a long history of sexual peccadillos. When a range of witnesses concurred that the intendant and the militia lieutenant had broken off their friendship over a romantic rivalry, don Toribio began to emerge as the likeliest suspect with the strongest motive. Intimidation may have worked in the short run, but once the lieutenant was imprisoned, scores of witnesses stepped up to reveal a widespread resentment for don Toribio that spanned the social spectrum—with everyone from slaves and criados to regidors on the cabildo recounting their own personal experiences with his aggressive nature.

Slaves and criados rarely had a chance to avenge slights, but the interrogations by outside prosecutors gave them an exceptional opportunity to
tarnish the reputations of masters and mistresses of leading households.
Doña Casiana's slaves remembered don Toribio's violent confrontations with
them over their supposed preference for his romantic rival, don Lucas.
Don Toribio's criado Felipe Morales, who frequently accompanied his master, described him as violent as well and voiced his fear of the abuse he might
suffer for failing to carry out his unusual duties of delivering messages
between his master and doña Casiana and standing guard during their trysts
to make certain that no one found out about them.[104] A criado in the bishop's
house—a Canary Islands native known as Tío Juan, who had previously
served in the household of the deceased provisor, the peninsular don Rafael
Castillo y Sucre—remembered that his former master had dared to confront
don Toribio over his visits to another lover, doña Ignacia Cavera. Shortly
after, the provisor suffered a case of diarrhea so severe that it killed him on
12 May 1783.[105] A witness from the other end of the social spectrum, knighted
as a caballero of the Order of Calatrava—don Alonso Manuel Peón—had
heard the same rumor, quite similar in its detail.[106] Both the criado and the
caballero believed don Toribio had a hand in the death of Castillo y Sucre,
one of the few subordinates of the bishop with the audacity to confront his
temperamental nephew over his life of debauchery. Others, including don
Juan Esteban de Meneses, reported having heard don Toribio celebrate upon
receiving news of Castillo y Sucre's death. Meneses reported hearing
don Toribio exclaim, "Thank God! Now we are free from that demon," upon
hearing of his antagonist's demise.[107]

Rumors of his fatal attack on the Catalan criado (discussed in chapter 4)
were only part of a long, storied violent past.[108] The officer and subdelegado
don Mateo de Cárdenas declared that he had heard that don Toribio had
killed an unnamed Indian with a blow from an iron bar.[109] Llovet recalled
that when the two men were stationed in Bacalar simultaneously, don Toribio
enjoyed torturing domestic animals. Capt. don Enrique de los Reyes, don
José Rivas, the criado Tío Juan, Sublieutenant Durán, and Isidoro Romero (a
witness not identified elsewhere) all concurred that don Toribio had a penchant for cruelty to animals. Apparently, one of the accused assassin's well-
known pastimes was shooting stray dogs. Tío Juan added one final anecdote:
Don Toribio had once tied a dog to the tail of a horse, no doubt a horrific and
terrifying experience for both animals.[110] The bishop's nephew never faced
any criminal charges for his crimes against humans or animals. Instead, the

widely reported accounts of cruelty and violence added weight to the charges against him regarding the intendant's death, due to the notoriety of his reputation for aggressive behavior.

The bishop's party also attempted to damage opponents' reputations to misdirect the activities of prosecutors and discredit the testimony of unfavorable witnesses but met with mixed results. In 1797 the alcalde don Miguel de Bolio y Paz, though not a close ally of the now deceased bishop, attempted to cast doubt on the validity of Dr. Guillén's prosecution. Evidently annoyed by the outside prosecutor's friendship with his cabildo rivals, the Quijanos, the alcalde alleged that the former judge of the Acordada spent all his time dancing, playing cards, and relaxing at friends' haciendas. Judging by Dr. Guillén's prolific writing and exhaustive investigation, the outside prosecutor's social life must have been a secondary priority to his investigative efforts, and Bolio's complaint cannot be taken too seriously. The alcalde also tried to undermine the validity of the declarations made by two defectors from the bishop's palace: the mayordomo don Francisco Ortíz and the medical doctor don Antonio Poveda, who had eventually buckled under repeated questioning and testified against don Toribio. Dr. Guillén had used both prosecutorial pressure and amiability; Bolio alleged that Ortiz and Poveda regularly accompanied Guillén out on the town during his supposedly very active nightlife.[111]

Honor

Prosecutors established a pattern of violent behavior on the part of their prime suspect, but don Toribio's history of violence was only one side of the infamous reputation that worked against him in a legal setting. Rumors of the militia lieutenant's volatile temper, along with whispered tales of a dangerous love triangle that incited the killing, damaged the honor of one of Mérida's leading ladies. Honor—especially female honor—depended heavily on a public image of chaste, modest behavior. Although doña Casiana, wife of the treasurer don Clemente Rodríguez de Trujillo and lover of don Toribio, never faced formal charges in connection with the intendant's murder, her reputation never recovered. Over the course of the trial, the social standing of a number of other women was irrevocably tainted by the retaliatory allegations regarding sexual indiscretions that were hurled back and forth between the men closest to the bishop and those determined to prosecute his nephew for the assassination.

A coterie of loyal female friends sought to shield doña Casiana from the inevitable harm to her reputation due to the widespread belief that her involvement with both don Toribio and the intendant—in spite of being a married woman—had driven don Toribio into the murderous rage that culminated in Gálvez's death. Doña Luisa Lara and doña Francisca Domínguez confirmed being her close friends; both qualified her friendship with don Toribio as "licit and honest." According to contradictory reports Dr. Guillén heard from doña Casiana's slave Tobi, these same two women had conspired with doña Casiana and doña María Trinidad López to hide her affair with don Toribio from her husband and abetted their trysts by providing them with discreet locations to meet. Public opinion drowned out the isolated claims of innocence made by the women on behalf of their friend. Even doña Francisca's nephew, don Luis Durán, openly contradicted assertions of doña Casiana's innocence.[112]

Following up on rumors often led to dead ends, as the reports of complicity regarding many of the early suspects such as Fierros, Ferrera, and Bermejo demonstrate. Moreover, Dr. Guillén needed to build a more solid case against such a high-profile suspect with manifold legal protections and a variety of attorneys ready to defend him. To bring more conclusive evidence to bear against don Toribio, Guillén tested the limits of Bourbon resolve to prioritize royal interests over deference to ecclesiastical privilege to do so. If popular opinion was not enough to confirm the passionate feelings between don Toribio and the treasurer's wife, a series of letters confiscated from the two in an audacious and intrusive search Guillén ordered provided racy details that confirmed the rumors. An entire volume of letters written by doña Casiana (and other prominent women of the city) to don Toribio, which addressed him as "beloved owner of my heart" and signed "yours forever, with all my heart, Casiana," bore out the illicit nature of the affair and gave credence to suspicions that don Toribio had flaunted military regulations issued by Gálvez requiring him to remain in his increasingly remote assignments. The dates of several of the letters referring to frequent nocturnal visits to Mérida coincided with the period don Toribio was stationed in Tixkokob.[113]

Doña Casiana, obviously the more discreet of the two lovers, had burned the letters don Toribio wrote to her, which left just one half of the correspondence available to enter as evidence.[114] Only one of don Toribio's letters to doña Casiana had survived, saved from the fire by the slave Tobi and transcribed by Dr. Guillén. Like doña Casiana, don Toribio signed with unambiguous romantic affection: "I wish to please and serve you with the truest and firmest love and the most lasting, with the love that will be yours until my death, all yours with soul, life, and heart, always." He also kept a journal, which Dr. Guillén read, interpreting its shorthand as the militia lieutenant's coded recounting of the intimate details of the relationship.[115] A small collection of don Toribio's personal writings, most of them written in the months before the intendant's assassination, was also catalogued in 1796. The first documents—two letters dated 26 April 1792 to don Baltazar Peraza and don Manuel Ortiz—consist of nothing more than missives updating two colleagues of his undertakings in Tihosuco, specifically investigating whether don Pedro Rafael Pastrana needed to be relieved of his service for reasons that were not mentioned. Other pages—a series of poems set as dialogues between two separated lovers, one of them in Bacalar and the other remaining behind—show don Toribio's unexpectedly softer and romantic side. Though these five poems did seem to allude to don Toribio's separation from doña Casiana, he took care to never mention her by name. Still, his frequent references to her "captivity" and "jail" and his "barracks" seem to fit the description of her marriage and his increasingly distant postings as a militia lieutenant. Finally, his references to a "competitor" for her affections and a threat to "give him a cruel death" caught the investigators' eyes. They underlined passages that seemed to indicate premeditation of a violent attack by the author. Evidently swept up in the gathering of papers without careful attention to their relevance, the collection of rather amateurish poems ends with one written much earlier, in 1780, dedicated to a woman named Barbara.[116]

The affair and the intrusive examination of the two parties' personal effects sparked a prolonged feud that drew in figures from all of the major factions of Mérida: the church, Bourbon bureaucrats, the cabildo, and the military. In 1794 don Lucas's secretary, don Francisco Heredía y Vergara, a native of Andalucía who accompanied the intendant from Spain, alleged that the bishop himself oversaw a permissive palace tainted by lax morals in a place that should have been a paragon of righteousness. He stated that don Toribio's outrageous behavior included bringing "libertine women" to the bishop's residence for illicit visits right under the prelate's nose. Others close to the bishop also faced charges of indecency. The bishop's medical doctor, don Antonio Poveda, confronted accusations of a long-standing affair with an unnamed woman, with whom he had fathered two illegitimate sons.[117] Another witness, don Luis Durán, declared that one of the bishop's allies—the subdelegado of the Partido de la Costa, don Manuel Antolín—was an adulterer whose transgressions were conveniently over-looked by the normally judgmental bishop. Antolín's affair with Maria Escalante had produced two illegitimate children as well, according to Durán.[118] Durán said that priests (referring to the Franciscan fray Francisco Mata) in the subdelegado's partido had begun proceedings against Antolín, but the bishop had intervened and the charges were dropped.[119] The most blatant example of the bishop's shielding of adulterers within his household came from the procurador de los indios, don Juan Esteban de Meneses. Meneses recalled that the notary of the Curia Eclesiástica, don Antonio Solís, flaunted his privileged position by carrying on an adulterous affair with a young girl known only by her surname, Guzmán ("Niña Guzmán"), whom he had impregnated. Confronted by secular authorities, Solís fled to the bishop's palace, where he often smugly defied the judges by strutting about casu-ally on the balcony, in plain view of the prosecutors but beyond the reach of punishment.[120] The array of allegations of decadence within the bishop's pal-ace undermined one of the bishop's most effective political weapons: the moral authority of the church.[121]

Shaming upper-class women typically did not take place as publicly as the humiliation inflicted on doña Casiana did. Indeed, if her indiscretions not been seen as the prime motive for the assassination, it is likely that she would have been shielded from some of the worst embarrassment. In many cases, an implicit code of honor prevented a man from naming the woman in question, especially women from among the elite. The young woman with the surname Guzmán, for example, is never identified by her first name. Doña Casiana frequently appears in the transcripts named only as "una Señora de esta Ciudad" (a woman of this city) in the trial transcripts. The notaries dictating the proceedings omitted her name and referred readers to one of the few citations that actually did name her, referring to her as the "covered [or hidden] woman."[122] In the first interrogations, in 1792, don Juan Estevan de Meneses, don Felipe Santiago del Castillo, Col. don Alonso Manuel Peón, and don Rafael Llovet all referred to her as a "certain woman." The notaries recording the proceedings also protected her anonymity.[123] Authorities regularly sheltered prominent figures from the upper strata of Mérida from public scrutiny when they faced accusa-tions of infidelity. When don José Peón, militia commander of the Partido de la Sierra, accused his wife, doña Felipa Maldonado, of cheating on him with don José Carreño, notaries set aside the 1806 proceedings in a separate section—"Reservada"—to keep the already damaged reputations of the spurned husband and his unfaithful wife from further harm.[124]

Such concern for reputations rarely extended to the lower classes. Investigations involving women without such prestige were conducted without any concern that a prominent woman's indiscretions might be known. When Rafael Luna, a pardo, faced accusations of an affair with his landlady (and the wife of his boss), Juana Llanos, prosecutors did not hesitate to name her. When Spanish rural administrators, such as the juez español Mariano Ancona and the subdelegado don Manuel Antolín, were accused of concubinage and affairs with lower-status women—the Maya woman Petrona Dzul in Ancona's case and Antolín's alleged lover, Maria Escalante, a woman who appears without the honorific doña—notaries recording the accusations made no effort to protect the identities of the accused women.[125]

As his censure of doña María Antonia del Castillo and don Fernando Gutiérrez de Piñeres makes clear, the bishop never hesitated to deploy charges of sexual misconduct against his political enemies, especially those who aided the prosecution of his nephew and protégé. Beyond humiliating Lic. Piñeres and the condesa viuda, the bishop also turned on Capt. don Pedro Rivas Rocafull, accusing him of having an affair in retaliation for having overseen don Toribio's transfer from one prison to another.[126] Neither of the two witnesses questioned about the accusation—Capt. don Domingo de Zapata and the regidor don Manuel Bolio—believed the allegation.[127] According to Rivas Rocafull, a veteran officer, the bishop had attacked the reputations of two secretaries in the employ of Gálvez's predecessor, Governor Merino y Ceballos: don Juan Antonio López and don Juan de Aguilar, using the same term for cohabitation—*amancebados*—he had previously deployed to attack don Toribio's enemies.[128]

As don Toribio's prolonged and poorly concealed affair with doña Casiana moved beyond whispered rumors to widely accepted knowledge in the public realm, the bishop's faction struck back. Don Francisco Heredía y Vergara, secretary of the governor, faced accusations of an indiscrete affair with doña María Josefa Escudero, a widow who was younger than twenty-five years old.[129] Doña María Josefa's own uncle—don José María del Puerto, a high-ranking priest and ecclesiastic judge of Tahdziu—had denounced the liaison to the authorities. When the priest went to complain about his niece's behavior, O'Neill allegedly mocked the curate, offering him the use of his sword to kill Heredía.[130] Frustrated by O'Neill's flippant response, the priest turned to a more receptive member of the cabildo. The alcalde who lodged the formal complaint against don Francisco, don Juan Crisóstomo Mimenza, wrote that the two carried on their illicit affair so scandalously and shamelessly because don Francisco benefited from the patronage of Intendant O'Neill.[131] Heredía staunchly stood in the intendant's camp, having first arrived in the province as Gálvez's scribe.[132] Mimenza, on the other hand, often allied with the clergy and identified with the faction of the cabildo that resented and opposed Bourbon restrictions on municipal prerogatives.

Mimenza's appeal to the crown had the impact he hoped for, at least in the short run. Orders from Madrid mandated the creation of a commission to investigate the allegations. However, Carlos IV appointed Intendant O'Neill as its head. Using a defense that echoed the protestations of don Toribio, O'Neill noted that Heredía was a compadre of doña Josefa María, which justified the frequency of their visits. He also charged that the charges against Heredía stemmed from animosity from the ayuntamiento, specifically from the public enmity between don Miguel Bolio, Mimenza's ally, and Heredía, who supposedly interfered in the council's elections. In the end, the matter ended without further investigation. Benefiting from Intendant O'Neill's patronage, Heredía saw that the case was dropped in 1798 with no charges filed.[133]

Male honor suffered less from rumors of romantic indiscretions, but sexual behavior did have some impact. Both don Toribio and Lic. Piñeres worried that their reputations might suffer from the rumors surrounding their sexual behavior.[134] Don Toribio's second defense attorney, don José Correa Romero, complained of the negative consequences Dr. Guillén's supposedly unjustified accusations against his defendant had on the "honor . . . and noble circumstances" of the militia lieutenant.[135] Likewise, the accusations the bishop leveled at the condesa viuda and the lieutenant governor led Lic. Serrano to declare, "If I were Piñeres, I would never return to the bishop's palace after the way he just humiliated him."[136] Yet for Piñeres, the charges ran deeper than simple accusations of an illicit affair. The five witnesses for the bishop recited a list of mundane-seeming indiscretions, including the length of the nighttime visits; the sewing, washing, and ironing of Piñeres' clothes; and rumors of a secret marriage. But the insult to Lic. Piñeres's masculinity—accusations of the influence the condesa viuda had over him in judicial affairs—might well have led to his transfer to the Philippines.

Race and Social Standing: Masculine Honor in Mérida

For Yucatecan creole men, honor depended on legitimate birth, a vice-free lifestyle, political office, economic status, and racial reputation. Most elite men in the city descended from Spaniards, although other Europeans integrated into high society. On rare occasions, mestizos and Afro-Yucatecans moved in elite circles, though very tenuously. African or indigenous ancestry could be and was used against political rivals. Even so, race was far from the only factor that led to stratification among Spanish- and other European-descent Yucatecans. A personal history of crime, illegitimate birth, work in manual trades, and a vague perception of ordinariness all worked against Spaniards who sought to elevate their social status by marriage, career, or political appointment. A variety of titles, honors, and deferential forms of address distinguished the upper tier of Spaniards and creoles from a growing number of less prominent creoles and European-descent Yucatecans. While the upper tier of Mérida's residents were Spaniards, a handful of other Europeans—French, English, Italian, and others—occupied prominent posts. The Bolios, mentioned earlier, were descendants of the Genovese captain don Santiago Bollio y Justiniani.[137] More recently arrived Europeans from outside Spain typically worked in respectable professions requiring a high level of education or specialization, such as the London-born medical doctor don José Bates and the French surgeon don Bartolomé Gouyon. Others made a living as merchants, like the Englishman don Roberto Tomson and the Irishman don Juan Hore.[138] As resident foreigners, they had a precarious position in Mérida's professional and upper classes, coming under suspicion when Spain went to war with the countries of their birth. French-born residents of Yucatan received especially close scrutiny. In one extreme case, Intendant O'Neill expelled young French bachelors Juan Lagrava and Pedro Gaviot; the two were never accused of any crimes but were deemed unproductive, idle singletons who contributed nothing to Yucatan's overall welfare.[139]

Most social markers of elite status were usually reserved for Spaniards and other Europeans who tended to hold correspondingly high posts in commercial, bureaucratic, and ecclesiastical activities, though a few urban Indians still held titles of distinction, and Afro-Yucatecans on rare occasions penetrated the invisible barrier that excluded them from prominent commercial and governmental positions. Out of an Indian population of 14,751 in 1794, 153 were identified as indios hidalgos (or *indios nobles*, according to the census), which entailed an exemption from tribute.[140] By the late colonial period, however, hidalgo status no longer invariably corresponded with being addressed as a don.[141] Batabes of the barrios were still addressed by both Mayas and non-Mayas with corresponding titles of veneration, such as don Marcelino Bacab of the barrio of Santiago. A few others, such as don Pablo Pacab and his father, don José Pacab, appear in the documentary record as almehen; they were also addressed as don and held significantly more property than most Mayas.[142] But for the most part, the indios hidalgos and almehenob had little in terms of property or status—even the title of don—to distinguish them from the middle strata of Mérida's society.[143]

Afro-Yucatecans entered the upper ranks in even fewer numbers, and they did so only by being recognized socially as Spaniards by the late eighteenth century.[144] The most striking case of social mobility during the late colonial period comes from the quick ascent and subsequent humiliation of don Miguel Duque de Estrada, a prominent merchant based in Mérida and, later, Campeche. Don Miguel's socioeconomic climb began in Tabasco, where he served on the Tribunal of the Acordada and the law enforcement society Santa Hermandad and held the lucrative post of collector of tithes during the 1780s. By the 1790s, he was a prominent merchant in Mérida's commercial guild. He then had his *limpieza de sangre*, or cleanliness of blood, confirmed in 1802, which officially recognized his descent from Europeans, free of Jewish, Moorish, African, or Indian ancestry. From this privileged and respectable station in society he was selected as a representative to the Cortes de Cádiz in 1811. In spite of his established reputation as a Spaniard, political opponents objected to his election, citing his heretofore undetected African ancestry. Although his economic status suffered little harm, the humiliation of his subsequent rejection from the Cádiz Cortes temporarily halted his rapid social rise.[145]

Ancestry, whether racially mixed or purely European, was one of several factors that figured into one's place in the hierarchy of Spanish-descent elites. The eighteenth century was a time of change not only in the economic bases of elite status and the balance of power between the institutions that wielded influence but also in the families that held these offices. Decline had long set in for the descendants of the conquistadors, most spectacularly for the Montejos and their relatives. Families with shallower roots in Yucatecan soil had risen more quickly than the established dynasties, many of them established by progenitors who had arrived in Yucatan in the late seventeenth and early eighteenth centuries. The Bolios descended from a late seventeenth-century migrant to the province. Their rivals, the Quijanos, had similar origins, tracing their descent to a peninsular merchant, Juan Quijano, who first appears in the Yucatecan records in the early eighteenth century. Other families, such as the Peones, also began their rise from middling creoles to powerful regional dynasties in the early eighteenth century. Through sheer numbers and political acumen, the Quijanos likely held more sway in the province than rival families such as the Bolios.[146] Moreover, don Juan Esteban ruled his family with a firm hand. Descendants of peninsular arrivals of the late seventeenth and early eighteenth centuries, families like the Peones, Quijanos, and Bolios dominated creole politics by the end of the century, surpassing the descendants of conquistadors and the original settlers.

Yet illegitimacy cast a long shadow on the Quijanos, likely leading in part to their decline after 1800, while one branch of the Peones outstripped them in wealth and landed property in the early nineteenth century, when Manuel José Peón emerged as one of the hacienda era's "land barons."[147] Don Juan Esteban, adopted son of Juan Quijano, became the most prominent member of the family and a prolific patriarch in spite of his humble origins. He was the illegitimate son of the former governor Antonio Figueroa and Isabel Ávila Ancona and was adopted by don Juan, the dynasty's founder. Apparently, Ávila Ancona was a relative of don Juan's wife, meaning that don Juan Esteban maintained kinship ties with his parents, however remote. In spite of his status as a bastard, his influence in the late eighteenth century outstripped his brother, the legitimate son Juan Francisco Quijano.[148] But his illegitimate birth may have predisposed him to being especially sensitive over his status. Illegitimacy made "natural children" easy targets. Even the normally professional Dr. Guillén, exasperated with the threats made by churchmen and their assistants toward compliant witnesses, disparaged the work of the ecclesiastical scribes, labeling the notary don Ignacio Ruz the "bastard son" of don José Ruz in the official record.[149]

Staying on Top: Precarious Prestige

By the late eighteenth century, an unspoken policy of marrying his children to prominent citizens aided the paterfamilias of the Quijanos, Juan Esteban, in overcoming any setbacks to his social standing. However, if marriage of acquiescent offspring to sons and daughters of important dynasties gave him an advantage in solidifying ties to long-standing lineages of the peninsula, the behavior and defiance of two of his daughters outraged him due to his belief in the family's superiority to the two suitors. The Quijanos, a clan of jealous and elitist brothers matched in their resolve by two strong-willed sisters, highlight the stratification and possible ethnic animosity that separated European-descent Yucatecans from different backgrounds. Don José Boves, who married doña Tomasa Quijano over the objections of her father and brothers, was an Asturian merchant, hinting at a rivalry not only between peninsulares and creoles but between different regions within Spain, even across the Atlantic Ocean. Even so, Boves, a respectable if recently established merchant, resembled the patriarch's own progenitor in his early years as a peninsular on the make. The other rejected suitor—don Esteban de Castro, one of the two interpreters general of colonial Yucatan—endured insults to his ancestry, with ambiguous hints of either Maya or African heritage on the part of his forebears. While accusations of non-European blood were never substantiated, the insinuations that he led a life of vice were borne out. The Quijano men also subtly disrespected the interpreter by omitting *don* in front of his name when they mentioned him, though nearly everyone else did use the honorific form of address.

The Quijanos successfully resisted the entreaties of Castro, who had more than a passing connection to the family. However, they failed to prevent don José Boves from marrying doña Tomasa. Gálvez had intervened on behalf of the Asturian merchant, likely the biggest misstep of his career and a clear case of jurisdictional overreach.[150] Rumors abounded that don Miguel José Quijano, who managed the affairs of the household, had paid an Indian to murder Boves rather than accept such an affront to their honor.[151] Other witnesses, like the priest don Miguel del Castillo, a friend of Boves, believed that the Quijanos plotted to poison their rival.[152] Many witnesses also believed that Gálvez's intervention had led to his death at the hands of a Quijano or someone from within their extended household. The story circulated widely through Mérida that the Quijanos wanted vengeance for having abetted their daughter's defiance of patriarchal rule.

While a shift in the ruling philosophy during the second half of the eighteenth century legitimated the vast majority of don Lucas's decisions that his rivals perceived as obnoxious, his meddling in a contested marriage contravened crown policy. Bourbon policies regarding matrimony actually strengthened parental choice and freed their hands to intervene. The right of fathers to reject the marriage proposals of their daughters' suitors, authorized by the Royal Pragmatic on Marriage of 1776, empowered parents—including Yucatecans—who sought to prevent marriages of children to suitors they perceived as their social inferiors.[153]

Nearly everyone perceived Castro as a creole and Boves's status as a Spaniard was never in doubt. Racial difference motivated many parents to reject pretenders, but class differences also mattered. When Juan Sanzol proposed marriage to doña Mariana Echeverría, her mother, doña María de Ancona Carrillo, and brother, don Rafael de Echeverría, appealed all the way to the viceroy in 1792 to confirm their rejection of Sanzol. They made no allegations of non-European ancestry against Sanzol. Instead, they argued that he was a social inferior in occupation, "hierarchy," and blood.[154] In a deviation from royal policy—in Yucatan at least—intendants and governors continued to occasionally intervene in marriages in favor of the rejected suitor. Such decisions usually involved non-elites on both sides—such as the marriage between Julio Puerto and Urbana Palma of Motul—but meddling in marriage choices by members of the upper tier of society had the potential to incite retaliation against authorities, as Gálvez learned.[155]

Conclusion

Before his death, don Lucas de Gálvez did not take on the more difficult task of advocating on behalf of the second suitor rejected by the Quijanos, don Esteban de Castro. Castro's unruly lifestyle and association with a group of compatriots of ill repute gave the up-and-coming dynasty more grounds for rejection, but Esteban, as they called him, had a personal history intertwined more tightly with the Quijanos than outside observers suspected. Just how deep their ties ran became a subject of intense scrutiny between 1800 and 1803. On the one hand, the Quijanos held the interpreter general in low regard, refusing to address him as don Esteban and disparaging his ancestry with the epithet "linaje oscuro," (dark lineage) and, of course, rejecting his pretensions to wed their daughter and sister. Other interactions were far from hostile. As mentioned earlier, the militia officer and merchant don José Miguel, one of Juan Esteban's sons, sought Castro's assistance in hiring Maya workers to help him build a new home. In another informal moment of confidence, don Juan Esteban, normally unfriendly to Castro, vented to him in a moment of anger that the intendant sought to despoil the family of their wealth.

But the closest tie that shamed the family was not Castro's own "dark ancestry" but the fact that he had fathered two grandchildren of Juan Esteban. Don Juan Esteban, hoping to escape from the infamy of his own illegitimate birth, no doubt disapproved of Esteban de Castro's long-term extramarital affair with his daughter doña Josefa Quijano and their two out-of-wedlock children. Doña Josefa had, in fact, married a more suitable partner, at least to her father's eyes: the merchant don Tomás Baldos Murciano, an encomendero before the institution's dissolution.[156] Apparently, don Tomás was frequently absent, and he died in 1800 in Tabasco. An astute observer might have noticed that the time frame for the conception of her first two children did not coincide with her husband's brief visits to Mérida. Upon Baldos Murciano's death in July 1800, the dissolute interpreter general appealed to the Quijano patriarch for permission to wed doña Josefa. With a third illegitimate son on the way, he hoped that by marrying his longtime partner, he might help them to avoid the stain of an out-of-wedlock birth and that the process of legitimation might begin.

Faced with the Quijanos' adamant refusal to consider his proposal, Castro sunk into despair and began to drink more heavily. In September of that year, apparently under the influence, he took a drastic step that altered the outcome of the case against don Toribio, which had slowly progressed toward sentencing in the years leading up to 1800. Castro's drunken outburst in a church on 15 September 1800 stemmed from nearly a decade of disappointment as well as a deeply held secret that created intense tension between Castro and his circle of friends. While Bourbon reforms restricting local autonomy and long-held traditions that limited creole participation in top posts antagonized upper-class creoles like the Quijanos, Peones, and Bolios, frustration at declining opportunities drove men like Castro to dramatic action. Men of middling standing, facing constant disparagement from wealthier peers and few prospects for advancement, also felt dissatisfaction over the failure of the new order to bring any substantial improvement to their lives. After Castro's unexpected eruption, the interpreter and his closest companions came under intense scrutiny, providing a case study of low-status creoles who vented their frustration against the crown in acts of unexpected aggression with unforeseen consequences. The final chapter examines four frustrated creoles and their well-concealed part in Gálvez's death.

CHAPTER 8

A Strange Turn of Events

⇥ IN MID-JUNE OF 1792, DON ESTEBAN DE CASTRO, ONE OF TWO INTER-
preters general based in Mérida, gathered with his friends Lt. don Bernardo
Lino Rejón and the master painter José Yanuario Salazar to watch a fourth
compatriot, Manuel Alfonso López, try to kill a chicken.[1] The "friends of a
disorderly lifestyle" had met to test the efficacy of a poison with which López
planned to kill the intendant. Supposedly following the advice of don Manuel
Antolín, the subdelegado of the Partido de la Costa, López had procured a
poison colloquially known as "puta de noche" (whore of the night), and tested
its strength on a barnyard fowl in front of his friends.[2] At López's request,
Castro sent his ten-year-old Maya criado, Hipólito, to go outside the city and
gather the toxic root. Lieutenant Rejón watched as López presented a jar of
what appeared to be colored water, which he called "milk of a toad."[3] Then,
after boasting that this poison would not only kill the intendant but that it
would also make his eyes pop out of his head, he demonstrated its potency by
administering a few drops to a chicken. Instead of falling over dead, the
chicken stumbled about as if drunk, they recalled. But it lived. Rejón, Salazar,
and Castro laughed at the shamefaced would-be assassin. Enraged and humiliated, López settled on a different approach. His next target would not be as
lucky as the chicken.

1800

Eight years later, don Toribio had probably given up hope of exoneration. He and only a few others maintained his innocence in the face of overwhelming evidence and a belief in his guilt that united nearly all Yucatecans. His conviction and sentencing was a foregone conclusion. His documented history of violence lent credibility to the charges against him. The informal and legal protections that had hindered prosecutors' progress had been whittled away in the years between 1792, when he walked freely through the streets, and 1800, when he languished in the dank prison of San Juan de Ulúa (in modern-day Veracruz). By 1800, don Toribio and his most faithful allies were in prison. A few had died. Most of his friends and supporters had confessed to their complicity in constructing a false alibi that buttressed his claims to innocence. In all likelihood, the young lieutenant had indeed made the midnight ride to Mérida and back in the wee hours of the morning. But he had not killed his rival.

In March 1800, Dr. Guillén put the final touches on a seven-volume summary of all of the proceedings, held today in the National Archive of Mexico. The meticulous prosecutor spared no detail in constructing an airtight case against don Toribio. Following Guillén's massive undertaking, Lic. don Antonio López Matoso, the clerk of the court (*relator*) responsible for the sentencing, requested nine months to review the evidence before recommending a sentence for the prime suspect. Despite don Toribio's prominent standing, many believed he faced capital punishment.[4] His future looked bleak. Few of the priests and ecclesiastical clerks who had steadfastly supported him remained alive and free.[5] Only two minor supporters—the priest of the cathedral, don Francisco Xavier Badillo, and the ecclesiastical notary don Juan Andrés de Herrera—remained free in 1800 despite Dr. Guillén's suspicions and attempts to imprison them. Don Toribio's most dedicated patron and protector, the bishop, was dead. His two staunchest defenders—don Francisco Ortíz and his successor, don José Romero Correa—had served brief jail terms. The imprisonment deterred them from any further advocacy on behalf of the prime suspect. Although don Toribio's defender in Mexico City later rose to prominence, don Carlos María de Bustamante was an unknown and untested lawyer in his mid-twenties in 1800. In the first year of his law career, the liberal intellectual giant of the nineteenth century had passed the bar less than a year before he found himself defending don Toribio's life.[6]

The case against don Toribio seemed solid. Only the priest of Chikindzonot, don Manuel Correa (also the uncle of don José Romero Correa), persisted in denying don Toribio's guilt. Over two hundred Maya-speaking residents of the pueblo said otherwise. Don Toribio denied his affair with doña Casiana until the end. But hundreds of pages of letters spelled out in voluminous detail the depth of their involvement and the frequency of their visits, in defiance of social norms (she was married to the treasurer) and military orders stationing him far from Mérida. Dozens of witnesses, from slaves to regidores, contradicted his claims to innocence as well. Innovative and determined magistrates and judges, from Dr. Guillén to the fiscal of the audiencia, don Francisco Xavier Borbón, improvised solutions to demands that they prosecute individuals protected by a nearly impenetrable web of legal immunities. The jailing of a bishop's nephew showed that the Bourbon monarchs and their American councilors no longer showed the deference once afforded to the sacrosanct space of the episcopal palaces and cathedrals in New Spain. But in 1803, cleared of all guilt in the assassination, don Toribio walked free. Taking a sympathetic tone toward don Toribio, Bustamante noted that upon his release, the deceased bishop's nephew had to be gradually exposed to sunlight after his imprisonment in the dark cell to avoid damaging his retinas.[7]

The Interpreter's Confession

Although contemporaries credited the novice defender's prowess in court, the militia lieutenant's sudden reversal of fortune had less to do with the legal aptitude of Bustamante than the unexpected confession of a less prominent court functionary in Yucatan who had escaped detection for nearly eight years. Esteban de Castro, interpreter general of Yucatan's Indian Court, had been briefly imprisoned for fifteen days in January 1797. A priest, don Francisco Xavier Badillo, who had some inkling of his involvement in the assassination, denounced him to the authorities. Father Badillo's determination to protect don Toribio at all costs led prosecutors to disregard his allegation as one more ploy to divert their focus from the actual assassin. Prosecutors quickly verified Castro's alibi; since he had not personally killed the intendant, but instead was the crime's intellectual author, he had indeed been at home with his family on the night of the murder, as he calmly stated.[8] But Badillo had been right. Castro had indeed played an instrumental part in the elaboration of a complicated plot that ended in Gálvez's death.[9] Between 1800 and 1804, Castro—"a man, vice-ridden, stupid, and given to inebriation," according to Bustamante—gave several contradictory versions of how he masterminded the murder and his associates had undertaken the assassination.[10] Only two key pieces of the story stayed consistent throughout: he himself had played a central role in plotting the assassination and his "friend of a disorderly lifestyle," Manuel Alfonso López, had killed the intendant.

At around 4:00 p.m. on 16 September 1800, Castro declared that he wanted to unburden his conscience and called for one of Mérida's two alcaldes, don Anastasio de Lara, to come immediately to the atrium of the cathedral in the presence of two notaries. His confession gave don Toribio a new lease on life but also nearly brought a leading family to ruin. "I know how the assassination of Sr. Gálvez happened, and to relieve my conscience, I will reveal to you [how it took place]," he stated. Castro implicated several conspirators—among them don José Tadeo Quijano, don Ignacio Quijano, a Franciscan friar named Manuel Antonio Armas, don Manuel Antolín, Manuel Alfonso López, and the master painter José Yanuario Salazar.[11] Alcalde Lara initially was skeptical, noting that he caught a whiff of aguardiente on Castro's breath.[12] Yet the interpreter insisted. Calling two notaries, Lara dutifully took his confession, which the notaries recorded.

Don Esteban de Castro had no intention of going to prison alone. According to the astonishing chain of events he first described for the alcalde, the conspiracy to kill the intendant had involved a number of Mérida's citizens in a convoluted plot, including everyone from the wealthy Quijanos down to the master painter Salazar and Castro's Indian criado, Hipólito. Castro initially portrayed himself as a somewhat reluctant intermediary between the Quijanos, who sought to have Gálvez killed, and his hapless drinking and gambling companion, the murderer, Manuel Alfonso López. In his first telling, after Gálvez had intervened to permit José Boves to marry doña Tomasa Quijano against the wishes of her father and brother, the Quijanos offered a 2,000-peso reward for the intendant's death. The Quijanos, anticipating the inevitable assumption of their guilt because of their public disputes with Gálvez, sought out intermediaries to hire the killer to distance themselves from his death and deflect suspicion. Despite his own antagonism with the Quijanos over his long-standing affair with doña Josefa Quijano, Castro claimed that he acted as the primary go-between.

In Castro's initial version of events, don Manuel Antolín, angered by the intendant's decision not to appoint him to the post of subdelegado, also served as a liaison, representing the Quijano family in face-to-face dealings with Castro. In his capacity as intermediary, Castro first notified don Bernardo Lino Rejón and, later, Manuel Alfonso López of the bounty. Rejón, a lieutenant with the Ninth Company of Mérida's urban militia, turned down the offer. López jumped at the chance.[13] Salazar was identified in an early version of events as a lookout for López on the night of the assassination.[14] If so, his presence would have explained the fleeting glimpses two witnesses saw of two men running down the street shortly after the murder, one urging the other on by yelling, "Corre, pendejo!" (Run, dumbass!) at the other.[15]

Castro also implicated the Franciscan fray Manuel Antonio Armas and don Joaquín Garrido as complicit in their silence during the days leading up to the assassination; he alleged that they were fully aware of the plot's progression.[16] Of all the accused coconspirators, Castro only made vague allusions about Fray Manuel Antonio's involvement. In one version, he hid Antolín in his cell following the murder, using the protective shelter of the Franciscan monastery to shield the subdelegado from prosecution.[17] In another version, López accused Armas of acting as an intermediary who paid him a small fraction of the hush money the Quijanos never delivered in its entirety.[18] At least one of the accomplices, Lieutenant Rejón, believed that the Franciscan had masterminded the conspiracy along with Castro, Antolín, and the Quijanos.[19] Unfortunately for the prosecutors, Armas died less than a month after Castro's wide-ranging, rambling denunciation. Prosecutors never had a chance to question him about his involvement in the plot.[20]

Women were not spared in Castro's ever-widening and elaborate web of conspiracy, dutifully transcribed by the notaries. He alleged that López's wife, doña Ana Rejón, and Rejón's wife, doña Cayetana Díaz, must have been aware of the plot.[21] As the interrogations continued, it also became clear that doña Josefa Quijano had at least some inkling of Castro's machinations.[22] Determining exactly how much the rest of her family knew about the conspiracy consumed the energies of several investigators over the next four years.

Hatching a Plot

Castro recounted the events leading up to the night of the assassination for his rapt audience of the alcalde and the two notaries and repeated it in varying versions on several occasions for prosecutors in Yucatan and Mexico City. This was the first version: In March or early April of 1792,

Subdelegado Antolín had approached him to make the initial offer of 2,000 pesos. Castro claimed that he and Antolín also discussed the method of assassinating Gálvez. Both preferred poisoning; eighteenth-century forensic science had few means of determining who had carried out a killing when toxins were used.[23] Tempted by the reward but unwilling to take the drastic action himself, Castro mentioned the offer to his impoverished friends. During an afternoon of drinking anisette together, Castro suggested to the poor militia officer that he might make some money by poisoning an unnamed person. Since the alcohol-fueled session also loosened the interpreter's tongue regarding his affair with doña Josefa Quijano, Lieutenant Rejón assumed that the target was don Tomás Baldos Murciano, doña Josefa's husband, whom Castro feared. Rejón brushed off Castro's proposal, considering it idle talk.[24] Following Rejón's rejection, Castro met with López in his home on 22 April 1792 to notify him of the offer of murder for hire.[25] López said it would be easy and announced his intention to locate a sufficiently toxic poison. Antolín met with them later, concurring that it would be best to poison Gálvez; he even suggested a type of herb that might be dropped into the intendant's milk or chocolate drink undetected.[26]

Castro gave vivid descriptions of the two months of plotting leading up to the late-night attack. Following Antolín's recommendation, López sought the poison.[27] Hipólito, just ten years old at the time, headed into the brush outside the city walls to find the puta de noche, which was not even strong enough to kill a chicken. Abandoning the idea of poisoning Gálvez, López settled on a more direct method. On 19 June 1792, López tapped on Castro's window with a knife attached to a stick that soon would serve as the murder weapon. By now Castro had begun to have reservations about the assassination plot; he hoped that López's two months of inaction meant that his friend had abandoned the idea as well. In this version of events, Castro attempted to distance himself from the murder. He recalled that, at this moment, he asked López, "Are you crazy?" More than a month had passed since Castro had met with Antolín or any of the Quijanos, and he quickly ran to warn Antolín that López planned to kill Gálvez that very night. After two days passed with no harm done to Gálvez, they assumed that López had again lost his nerve. Castro met with Antolín, and the two dismissed López's threats of violence as "the lies of López." Yet López remained as resolute as ever in his determination to kill the intendant.[28]

Figure 8. Second artist's rendering of the murder weapon sketched from the original. Courtesy of the Archivo General de la Nación, Mexico.

By the early morning hours of 23 June 1792, it was obvious to all of the conspirators that López had indeed carried out the attack. According to Castro's account, the Quijanos immediately cut off all contact with the four men to keep up the appearance of innocence and retreated behind the walls of their family's well-guarded home. López, Castro, Rejón, and Salazar began to turn on each other, fearing that one of them might confess or commit another murder to keep the plot secret. López was the first of the conspirators to threaten to kill one of his accomplices. Two days after assassinating Gálvez, he came to collect his promised reward from Castro. "Come on now, pendejo [roughly, 'dumbass,' or a vulgar term for a stupid or contemptible person]," López demanded, "give me the money; the work is done." Castro, repentant and lamenting his complicity in the assassination, burst into tears. An unsympathetic López insulted his masculinity, asking in a belittling fashion, "Man, are you a puta?"[29] He then repeated his threat to kill Castro if he did not receive the money and left.[30] Despite his unease, Castro passed the rest of the day translating the bandos seeking information on the killer's identity and whereabouts from Spanish into Maya, although he knew full well exactly who the assassin was.[31]

López's intimidation of his coconspirators did not go unanswered. Castro and Rejón, frightened by López's violent behavior and threats against Castro, conspired to lure him into the wilderness outside Mérida to kill him. Salazar, evidently less prone to violence than his three friends, convinced Castro and Rejón to spare López.[32] Rejón soon began to suspect that the interpreter and the master painter, plotting with López, had turned against him. Rejón's nickname, "Locutus," was a reference to his verbosity, suggesting that his compatriots perceived him as the most likely to let slip the secret of their conspiracy.[33] Rejón's wife, recalling an unexpected visit from Salazar, Castro, and López to their home, remembered that he whispered to her to not let him out of her sight to go for a walk with them.[34] Rejón also avoided eating any food his three friends might share and advised his wife to take the same precaution.[35]

The tension between the former friends proved too much for Rejón. Less than a month after Gálvez's death, he recalled that he felt the need to "flee from the fire of the crimes of his friends."[36] Unlike his compatriots, he looked after his wife before departing. Unable to permanently silence Rejón by killing him, Castro had offered to bribe him to keep his silence. Rejón accepted and insisted that Castro pay his wife 8 pesos a month in his absence.[37] After attending to his wife's well-being, and having told her that he had business to look after in the distant valley of Hopelchen, Rejón decamped to a pueblo over a day's ride from Mérida. There he remained in hiding for the next eighteen months.[38]

López also absconded from Mérida for awhile. Three or four witnesses had seen him run from the scene of the crime: a priest identified as Father Evía, a young servant from whom he had requested a bit of aguardiente, an Indian named Marcelo Chan, and possibly Luis Lara.[39] Afterward, López rode to Opichen, the pueblo of residence of his Maya compadre, Tiburcio Ek.[40] His horse, which had been seen by witnesses, died in Ek's care shortly after López's flight from Mérida. Ek buried the horse, leaving investigators with one less piece of evidence.[41] López only stayed away for two days, impatient to return to Mérida to confront don Esteban de Castro over the promised payment of 2,000 pesos.

Castro contemplated his fate with a pessimism that rivaled Rejón's paranoia. He considered a more drastic escape, fearing both his friends and the authorities. Before Lieutenant Rejón departed, Castro showed him a bottle of poison that he planned to drink if he were arrested.[42] López, having demonstrated his willingness to kill, apparently never feared that his friends might turn against him. He spent much of his time during the intermittent years harassing Castro and insisting that the intermediary pay him the 2,000 pesos.[43] Salazar's friends must have considered him a man who could keep his own counsel, a well-earned reputation. In the earliest phase of the trial, in 1792, Lic. Piñeres had asked him if he recognized the knife he had seen in López's hands only a few days earlier. He calmly told the lieutenant governor he did not. Salazar never mentioned the incident to his friends.[44] Nor did he ever report fearing any retaliation from Castro, Rejón, or López.

The New Trial

The viceroy in Mexico City heard of the unexpected turn of events in Yucatan through unofficial channels. A few days after taking over as viceroy, don Félix Berenguer de Marquina (r. 1800–1803) received notice of the emergence of the new allegations.[45] The news came from two separate pieces of correspondence: an anonymous letter and an official notification from don José Castillo y Aguirre, the other alcalde of Mérida. On 5 November 1800, the oidor of the Audiencia of Mexico, don Emeterio Cacho, passed on the anonymous missive to the viceroy.[46] He wrote that news had reached him that

Castro had fallen out with the Quijanos, which led him to confess to his role in the crime.[47] Given the slow pace of official correspondence, the unattributed message was likely intended to prevent don Toribio's execution in the hope that a late-breaking development might postpone his sentencing and possible execution. Two months later, official notice arrived. On 7 January 1801, a letter from Alcalde Castillo y Aguirre, dated 29 November 1800, arrived in Mexico City to belatedly inform the viceroy of the stunning new revelation regarding the intendant's murder, over five months after Castro's confession drastically altered the course of the investigation.[48]

Both Oidor Cacho and Castillo had separate but obvious motives for implicating the Quijanos, leading to initial skepticism about the report's accuracy. Don Emeterio Cacho was one of the most powerful allies of don Toribio and among the few who remained loyal after the death of don Toribio's influential uncle. Cacho's access to the highest echelons of power in the viceroyalty made him a formidable if initially ineffective supporter of the bishop and his nephew. Family alliances also played a part in Cacho's loyalty to don Toribio; the oidor's sister was married to an uncle of don Toribio, don Pedro de Piña y Mazo.[49] Cacho had been a brother-in-law to the bishop's brother in the years leading up to his death. Despite the lack of true blood ties, he remained loyal to don Toribio long enough to see him walk free. Cacho's influential post as oidor and his friendship with the viceroy, Marques de Branciforte, made him one of don Toribio's most influential connections at the viceregal court.[50] For his part, don José del Castillo y Aguirre, the alcalde, was a widely reputed enemy of the Quijanos. He and others in a rival faction opposed the control of Mérida's ayuntamiento by the Quijanos and their in-laws and associates.[51]

The viceroy needed to appoint a qualified magistrate to begin prosecuting the case. He drew lessons from the first, rudderless phase of the investigation under Lic. Piñeres: the case required an outsider, yet one familiar with the idiosyncrasies of the province. Don Juan Tabat, who served as a naval captain of the frigate *La Saeta*, knew the province due to his frequent travels from Yucatan to other Caribbean ports such as Veracruz, Havana, and New Orleans.[52] No respecter of social class, Tabat resembled his predecessor, Dr. Guillén. Neither had any reservations about jailing the most privileged members of Yucatecan society.[53] Captain Tabat immediately ordered the imprisonment of two Quijanos—doña Josefa and her brother, the priest don José Tadeo—along with Antolín, López, Salazar, and Rejón.[54]

The wives of two of the men associated with the conspiracy also went to prison.[55]

The new stage of the trial involved many of the same jurisdictional obstacles as the earlier investigation. This included the fuero eclesiástico held by the priest don José Tadeo Quijano. In one of his first acts as the Quijano family's legal representative, Procurator don Ignacio Covarrubias demanded a change of venue, insisting that Father Quijano's trial be adjudicated by an ecclesiastical court.[56] To deal with this potential drawback, the viceroy resorted to the same jurisdictional compromise that had been used previously. The viceroy appointed Dr. don José María Bucheli, vicar general of the archbishopric of Mexico, to serve as the ecclesiastical co-judge overseeing the interrogation and investigation of the wealthy provincial priest.[57]

On 12 January 1801, Captain Tabat commissioned don José Cano, alguacil mayor and regidor of Mérida's ayuntamiento, to go to the house of don Juan Esteban to confiscate the belongings of doña Josefa and don José Tadeo, identified in the initial version of Castro's confession as the financial backers and instigators of the assassination. The ensuing confrontation pitted a powerful creole hacendado, don Juan Esteban, against the only peninsular on the ayuntamiento, Regidor Cano—both formidable figures on the city council. In the end, Esteban compromised by allowing Cano to confiscate his daughter's goods but not those belonging to his son.[58] With Cano unwilling to prolong the standoff, the compromise between the rivals of the cabildo stood.

Learning from previous setbacks, the viceroy ordered Tabat to undertake a preliminary and perfunctory investigation before transporting the prisoners to Mexico City. Shortly after, he ordered the incarceration of all of the suspects, accomplices, and additional members of their households to the dungeons of Veracruz, Perote, and Mexico City. In Veracruz, don Manuel del Castillo Negrete, a high-ranking justice (*alcalde del crimen*) of the Audiencia de México, took over the proceedings.[59] Even with this foresight, one major problem threatened to interfere with the progress of the justices charged with overseeing the new phase of the trial. Lic. don Miguel Magdaleno Sandoval, who had delayed the trial in Mérida, had not only escaped imprisonment, but happened to be in the viceregal capital on unrelated business at the time of the new prosecution. To forestall any unforeseen meddling by Sandoval, the viceroy banished him to twenty leagues from Mexico City, with strict orders not to interfere.[60]

Sorting Out the Truth

The passage of eight years and the compilation of most of the forty-plus volumes of contradictory testimony tested the abilities of Tabat and Castillo Negrete as they assembled evidence for the new trial. Deceased witnesses and faded memories made it harder to find reliable firsthand recollections of the night of Gálvez's death. Many witnesses and suspects had died in prison before testifying. Others, such as the criado Hipólito, had fled and managed to evade authorities. The motives of the suspects also appeared much more ambiguous than in the previous case. Castro, Rejón, López, and Salazar changed and retracted their testimonies so often that not one of them gave a consistent version of events. The accuracy of their testimonies was hardly helped by their levels of intoxication at critical junctures. All recalled drinking aguardiente or anisette during many of the major decisions or confrontations. Their memories of dates, times, conversations, and participants were, at best, cloudy.

Castro's companions recounted the interpreter's drunkenness at crucial points of the assassination plot. He was drinking anisette when he first suggested to Lieutenant Rejón that the Quijanos would pay a large sum to see the intendant dead. Since Castro was inebriated, Rejón never took the offer seriously.[61] The interpreter was also drinking with López when he made the offer that persuaded López to kill Gálvez. López found Castro intoxicated on Sunday, 24 June 1792, when he came to collect his reward.[62] Finally, Alcalde Lara hinted that Castro was probably drunk when he confessed to his role in the crime in September 1800. Bustamante rightly identified don Esteban de Castro as "vice-ridden and prone to inebriation," a personality trait that would have made it hard for the interpreter to give an accurate rendering of events in his testimony, even if he had wanted to.[63]

If alcohol limited witnesses' and suspects' accuracy, death silenced others who never provided prosecutors with their version of events. Key figures in the new conspiracy died before the justices in Mexico City had the chance to verify their statements through interrogation. The accused Franciscan, fray Manuel Antonio Armas, died in 1800 without defending himself against Castro's accusations of complicity. Other suspected conspirators and witnesses followed him to the grave. Tiburcio Ek, the compadre of Manuel Alfonso López who had tended his horse in Opichen, died before Captain Tabat had a chance to interview him.[64] Subdelegado Antolín, who had seen his fortunes improve after Gálvez's death, now suffered a precipitous fall from grace that ended with his death. Banished to the remote Castle of Perote, near the border between the modern-day states of Veracruz and Puebla, and suffering from asthma and leg pain, he died just a few days after Castro admitted that he had fabricated Antolín's role in the assassination, on 21 February 1802.[65] Prosecutors also had more difficulty questioning the criados of major figures in the plot, potential sources of inside information. Hipólito, Castro's criado, had fled years before Castro's imprisonment in 1800, and the criado of don José Tadeo, named Juan José Novelo, died in prison at the priest's side in 1801 before he was questioned.[66]

Prosecutors were not always able to find a plausible motive for each of the conspirators. Castro, the author of the assassination, had no obvious reason to want the intendant dead. Interrogated in the humid prison of Veracruz, he incongruously admitted that he likely would have benefited from Gálvez's continued tenure at the head of the provincial government. Castro owed his position as interpreter general to the deceased intendant, he said, and he had hoped that Gálvez's favorable disposition toward him would lead to a promotion to procurator or defender of the Indians.[67]

Although the ringleader's reasons for plotting against the intendant are unclear, the Quijanos, Antolín, and López all held grudges against Gálvez. The intendant had passed over Antolín and appointed another man to the post of subdelegado of the Partido de la Costa. Antolín felt the post was rightfully his. The bishop's open opposition and meddling in matters beyond his jurisdictional authority exacerbated a situation that might have been resolved more quietly. The Quijanos' antipathy for Gálvez was notorious, but don José Tadeo had less of a clear motive than his father and brothers for hating the intendant. There was no evidence of a previous dispute between the intendant and the priest Castro fingered as the brother who offered the reward of 2,000 pesos. Only López had a clear motive for killing the intendant. Besides providing a quick remedy from his poverty, Manuel Alfonso López had a less public but no less heated rivalry with Gálvez. Before the intendant's arrival, López had a small number of Indians working for him in defiance of long-standing but often flouted proscriptions on servicio personal. A Maya woman who worked for López complained to Gálvez that López mistreated and whipped her, a fact confirmed by López's wife.[68] Gálvez recognized the mistreatment as one of the ongoing abuses related to the outlawed but still operational servicio personal (an informal system of labor tribute) and freed her from López's service. He prohibited López from ever having access to Indian labor again. López, irate over Gálvez's intervention, called the intendant a "son of a whore." He perceived the slight as a harsh insult, complaining that Gálvez held native workers in higher regard than himself, a Spaniard.[69]

The timing of Castro's denunciation led to suspicions that he overstated or even fabricated entirely the complicity of the Quijanos. After doña Josefa's absent husband, don Tomás Baldos Murciano, died in Tabasco in July 1800, Castro had some hope that the Quijanos might allow their daughter to marry him. But, just as they had resisted Gálvez's interference in the marriage arrangements of their daughter doña Tomasa to don José Boves, so they refused to allow Castro to marry doña Josefa. Shortly before his drunken admission of guilt on 15 September 1800, Castro had appealed to the alcalde of Mérida—don José del Castillo, a powerful rival of the Quijanos—to intervene on his behalf. Castillo gladly took on a family whose influence in the ayuntamiento he sought to curb, despite apparently being only an acquaintance of Castro. Approaching the Quijanos, Castillo formally requested a private audience with doña Josefa in order to ascertain her feelings about the disputed marriage. At her age, he argued, the Royal Pragmatic of 1776 no longer impeded her marriage choice. Her father, don Juan Esteban, and her brothers don Joaquín and don José Miguel, barred the door and refused to grant Castillo an audience with doña Josefa.[70]

The Quijano men resoundingly rejected Castro's pretensions, even though they knew he had fathered three illegitimate children with doña Josefa, regardless of the fact that the affair had gone on for nine years, and in spite of the death of her husband. The Quijanos justified their refusal of the interpreter's proposal due to his low social station. Their objections centered on his "humble" status and his occupation as interpreter, which they viewed as inferior.[71] The Quijanos did refer to his "dark lineage," a vague term that denoted non-European ancestry, but they used this denigrating expression only once and did not elaborate upon it. They also alluded to his habitual drunkenness, charging that the interpreter had the audacity to ask for their daughter's hand in marriage after drinking sizeable quantities of aguardiente.[72] Doña Josefa admitted to their affair, confessing that their relationship had begun in 1791 and that in 1792 she had declared her love for Castro and would be "his forever."[73] During her marriage to Baldos Murciano, she had three children by Castro, which she somehow managed to hide from her father. Baldos Murciano was often away from Mérida in Tabasco, and his frequent absences from the province made it nearly impossible for him to have fathered doña Josefa's children. If any doubts lingered, the last child was conceived after Baldos Murciano's death.[74] Castro and doña Josefa did their best to hide the children from the Quijano family patriarch don Juan Esteban, with Castro raising two of the children and doña Josefa raising the third as a supposed orphan.[75] But the ruse was transparent, and doña Josefa's father and brothers eventually learned the truth. Castro himself admitted that he had fathered the three children.[76]

The Quijanos saw Castro's subsequent denunciation as a desperate attempt at retaliation for their resounding rejection of his nuptial pretensions. On 19 September 1800, Capt. don Ignacio Quijano explained his interpretation of Castro's motives for denouncing the family as masterminds of the murder to Intendant O'Neill: the charges were groundless, and Castro had accused them as accomplices solely out of a spirit of vengeance.[77] O'Neill believed the Quijanos, and, much as Gov. Sabido de Vargas had done with don Juan José de Fierros, he placed Castro in solitary confinement in an attempt to silence his accusations of the Quijanos. Although news of the surprising development in the assassination trial did not immediately reach the viceroy, the damage was done. Mérida's citizens now murmured against the Quijanos as they had once whispered accusations against don Toribio.[78]

Between 1800 and 1802, Castro himself gave several inconsistent accounts of the Quijanos' role in planning the assassination. In his first confession, he identified don Ignacio and don José Tadeo as the two Quijano brothers involved in the plot. Confronted by a series of interrogations to address inconsistencies in his testimony, Castro equivocated and backed away from his earliest accusations against the family. He later admitted that he had only assumed that Father don José Tadeo had been aware of the plot because he accompanied Antolín in the carriage in which the subdelegado met with the interpreter to discuss the conspiracy. Finally, he admitted that the only substantial expression of ill will toward the intendant he heard from any of the Quijanos was a "vague" complaint by don José Tadeo.[79] In the penultimate scenario described by the interpreter, the Quijanos appeared less like a family seeking an assassin and much more like grumblers whose complaints inspired overzealous action by a man hoping to gain favor with the influential clan.

The interpreter also frustrated his interrogators by providing varying accounts of his familiarity with the Quijano men. He initially described frequent talks with don José Tadeo and don Ignacio, but don José Tadeo denied any personal contact with him. Doña Josefa gave the most credible account of Castro's acquaintance with her brothers, stating that Castro knew her brother don Juan Esteban because both regularly attended ayuntamiento business that required an interpreter.[80] Castro concurred, stating that don Juan Esteban spoke with him casually on various occasions.[81] Doña Josefa said Castro also knew don José Miguel from Castro's unofficial work in finding Maya workers to help in the construction of a house.[82] And, despite efforts to distance themselves from the interpreter, don Juan Esteban Quijano Sr. had loaned Castro, supposedly a total stranger, 200 pesos in 1786, a significant sum.[83]

In his final version, Castro retracted all of his earlier declarations, stating that only doña Josefa was aware of the plot, but none of her brothers were involved in the assassination. Doña Josefa admitted that Castro had told her of the plan to kill Gálvez three or four days before his death and that she later became aware of López's role in the murder.[84] In Mexico City, on 12 February 1802, Castro admitted that he had never discussed Gálvez's assassination with any of the Quijano brothers and only kept up the ruse because he had told his actual coconspirators the version that implicated the Quijanos.[85] On 19 February 1802, Lieutenant Rejón concurred with Castro's retraction, stating that he had parroted Castro's allegations against the Quijanos, Antolín, and fray Manuel Antonio only because Castro had told him to do so.[86] Salazar stated that he had known Father José Tadeo from his youth and doubted that he was involved in the assassination despite Castro's insistence that he was.[87]

Yet a cloud of suspicion lingered over the Quijanos, due in part to their inexplicably suspect behavior. Though Castro eventually recanted, the suspicious activities of the family and their associates were never satisfactorily explained. For example, four Franciscans testified that Antolín stayed in the cell of the implicated Franciscan, Armas, in the two months leading up to the murder and often left the building disguised as a member of their order.[88] They strenuously denied knowing Castro at all, though all other witnesses concurred that they had regular contact in routine governmental business and informal translations. Moreover, the Quijanos, who claimed that they did not know Castro or his associates, provided the imprisoned suspect López with food and clothing.[89]

Castro himself admitted that his motives for accusing the Quijanos were twofold. In a convoluted explanation that suggests he was not acting entirely rationally, the interpreter admitted that he had initially hoped to blackmail the Quijanos into acceding to his demands and to pressure doña Josefa into continuing her affair with him. When he failed, Castro implicated them and exaggerated or fabricated their involvement in the plot.[90] He had told doña Josefa the same version of events to hint that he had won the favor of her father and brothers and to pressure her to stay with him out of the fear that he would implicate them in the crime.[91] In the volumes of testimony, he never satisfactorily explained why he connected Antolín or fray Manuel Antonio to the murder. Once the two had died, prosecutors lost interest in exonerating them or reaching an understanding of why Castro incriminated them as well.

No Way Up and Out: Creole Frustration in the Time of the Intendants

While members of the Quijano family saw their fortunes rise from the time of the arrival in Yucatan of their progenitor, an ambitious but middling peninsular in the early 1700s, to become the most powerful clan of creoles in 1800, few other creoles saw such a spectacular improvement in their social standing. Indeed, stricter enforcement of prohibitions on servicio personal had deprived López from ever having unpaid Mayas in his service again. Though López was irked by what he felt was a personal affront, the assassin also suffered economically from losing ready access to Indian labor.[92] After the killing, he hoped to gain revenge as well as favorable treatment from Gálvez's triumphant (and, ideally, grateful) enemies. López hoped to receive both a 2,000-peso payment for killing the intendant and to be rewarded with a post as a *teniente de subdelegado* (likely a misnomer for juez español), or at least command of a lookout post for killing a widely hated government official.[93]

His close compatriot Castro also had a hard time making ends meet and suffered the condescension of more fortunate creole families. The Quijanos, for example, pointedly omitted the term of respect don when they mentioned him.[94] The 200-peso salary paid to interpreters also barely covered the daily living expenses he incurred raising a large family (as well as three illegitimate children). As previously mentioned, he had hoped for advancement to a higher position within the Indian Court to either procurator or defender of the Indians.[95] In the eight years that transpired between Gálvez's death and Castro's imprisonment, the interpreter did not receive either of his desired promotions. Though he denied any animosity toward the intendant,

having being previously passed over undoubtedly did not improve his feelings toward Gálvez.

Castro had hoped to receive favors from Gálvez and found his ambitions
thwarted. López, on the other hand, hoped that one of Gálvez's many enemies might reward him for killing their primary antagonist. Both were disappointed, in Gálvez's lifetime and after his death. López, the frustrated
ne'er-do-well, and an interpreter facing limited future prospects for were
joined by two other men in their close circle of friends who also lived on the
margins of respectable creole life. José Yanuario Salazar worked as a painter,
the same profession as the early pardo suspect Ignacio Matos. In socioeconomic terms, little distinguished him from the middling mestizo and Afro-
Yucatecan craftsmen who dominated many of the trades and filled out the
ranks of the pardo and blanco militias. Less is known about Rejón, identified
as a lieutenant in the milicias blancas; but Castro stated that he suggested to
Rejón that he kill the intendant due to the dire financial straits in which
Rejón found himself in 1792. Witnesses also noted that he was frequently
found in taverns.[96]

The Fates of the Prisoners

Castro's confession and later partial retraction, corroborated by testimony
from Rejón and Salazar, altered the fate of several prisoners incarcerated
during earlier phases of the trial. The priest don José Tadeo was released from
prison shortly after Castro's abjuration. The few remaining prisoners charged
as accomplices in attempting to prove don Toribio's discredited alibi went
free as well, one by one. Though prosecutors had been able to disprove Don
Toribio's assertion that he had been in Chikindzonot at the time of the murder, magistrates presiding over the final phase of the case no longer believed
that don Toribio's insubordinate abandonment of his post meant that he had
killed the intendant. As a result of this change in the prosecution's direction,
Father Manuel Correa, the priest whose imprisonment set a precedent in the
treatment of suspects covered by the ecclesiastic fuero, was released from
prison in 1801.[97]

In 1803, after ten years of imprisonment, don Toribio walked free too,
absolved of any guilt in connection with the murder itself. Like Captain
Fierros before him, he not only insisted that his freedom was part of the debt
the royal government owed him but demanded that the viceroy repair the

damage to his reputation. He claimed that the general "bad concept" that the public held regarding his role in the killing of don Lucas—which reached as far as Europe, he asserted—required royal redress to undo the harm to his status.[98] The viceroy concluded that the severe treatment don Toribio suffered was indeed unwarranted and ordered that he be compensated financially, since his personal assets had been seized to cover expenses incurred by his stay in prison.[99] The crown, in turn, offered him a promotion in rank in a new destination. Don Toribio, abandoned by all but his staunchest allies and left without a powerful patron, likely had no desire to return to Mérida. In 1807 King Carlos IV awarded him the post of subdelegado of the Partido de Tehuantepec in Oaxaca. Here the nephew of the bishop apparently lived out his days.[100] However, the restitution offered by the king, the viceroy, and the Audiencia of Mexico had limits. In July 1802, the Audiencia of Mexico rejected a petition by don José Correa Romero demanding that the possessions of the recently deceased Dr. Guillén be confiscated and given to don Toribio in compensation for the juez comisionado's relentless pursuit of the wrong man.[101]

Castro's confession and subsequent disavowal of his previous allegations made against a vast number of accused conspirators came too late for some of the suspects and prisoners. Fray Manuel Antonio Armas and Subdelegado Antolín were exonerated postmortem. Antolín died in prison on 22 February 1802.[102] Cleared of charges, his confiscated possessions were passed on to his designated heirs.[103] Other minor suspected accomplices and perjured witnesses—including don Pedro Gutiérrez, the juez español of Chikindzonot; doña Narcisa Suárez; don Ignacio Ruz; Lorenzo Citep; and the criado Toribio López—had their names cleared posthumously as well.[104] Many long-released former prisoners were officially absolved of any wrongdoing in the wake of Castro's confession. Most of the eighty-six prisoners from the first eight years were pardoned in one sweeping decree, but a few merited special attention. Those suspects most closely aligned to don Toribio—the signers of the certification of his alibi, for example, or his hacienda workers—were declared free but not innocent. Others from the upper tier of Yucatecan society, such as don Pedro Bernardino Elizalde and the militia cadet don Mariano Carrillo, received a specific mention by the viceroy that their imprisonment should have no impact on their honor. However, when the Audiencia of Mexico cleared don Clemente Rodríguez de Trujillo and his wife, doña Casiana, of any wrongdoing, they pointedly made no mention of restoring their honor.[105]

Punishment, Imprisonment, and Death

Salazar, Rejón, and López—who never denied drinking, gambling, and plotting with Castro—did not go free. After harboring some early doubts, the alcalde del crimen Castillo Negrete became convinced that López had indeed carried out the murder of the intendant.[106] Rejón and Salazar concurred with Castro that López was the assassin. Doña Josefa Quijano recalled López's panicked visit to her during Castro's brief imprisonment in 1797, which she interpreted as evidence of López's guilt.[107] Even López's wife, doña Ana Rejón, concluded that her husband was the assassin, and her descriptions of his violent character coincided with the testimony of others regarding his aggressive disposition, including reports of him beating his Indian servants. In her testimony, provided in March 1802, she described him as "hard and vengeful."[108] Shortly afterward, she died in prison. Along with López's own reluctant confession, the confused and often contradictory accounts provided by witnesses concurred only in the accusation that López himself had actually killed the intendant. Castillo Negrete began to review the case carefully to make sure that he had properly followed all procedures before sentencing López.[109] Proceeding with caution, he began to take López's testimony, but the accused assassin followed his wife to the grave, dying of tuberculosis on 21 May 1802. He never completed his own version of events, nor addressed inconsistencies in his testimony.[110]

Of the conspirators who remained imprisoned, doña Josefa fared best, apparently benefiting from a new "illicit friendship" she formed during her incarceration with the warden of the prison, don Jaime Alzubidé. As a result of their romance, she received better treatment than most of the inmates. Alzubidé gave her keys that allowed her to leave her cell as she pleased and provided access to the kitchen to prepare her own meals. He ordered his criado, José Díaz, to look after her needs, providing the type of domestic service that she was accustomed to receiving in Mérida. Yet prisoners enjoyed little privacy, and the affair was well known to the other inmates, including her erstwhile lover, Castro. The relationship finally came to light when doña Josefa gave birth to her fourth out-of-wedlock child, the offspring of her affair with her jailer. Resorting to a tried-and-true strategy for disgruntled criados, José Díaz testified against Alzubidé, motivated by annoyance over the additional workload that serving doña Josefa entailed.[111] His superiors were incensed; Alzubidé was severely reprimanded over his relationship with doña Casiana.[112] Ordered to look after the infant's well-being, Alzubidé was jailed himself and released after eight months. Doña Josefa suffered no severe consequences and was released from prison on 5 November 1804, freed by a royal pardon.[113] Her dispute with the law was not yet finished, though. Doña Josefa's legal battle to recover her extensive holdings, both real estate and personal possessions, lasted until 1807.[114]

Her lately scorned lover, don Esteban de Castro, served the longest and harshest sentence of any of the suspects. Rejón and Salazar, his two surviving coconspirators, walked free in 1808.[115] Castro spent his time in jail writing appeals to the Audiencia of Mexico for his freedom. One such appeal, from 1806, exemplified a strategy he frequently used. He downplayed his own role and played up that of López. Castro said that he intended his offer to be a joke and never expected López to carry out the assassination. López had killed Gálvez, he said, because of the dispute over his Indian laborers, not because of the offer of 2,000 pesos, made in jest.[116] His appeal failed. In 1812 King Ferdinand VII ordered Castro to be transferred to the Presidio de Zanguanga in the Philippines, a remote tropical prison that amounted to a death sentence.[117] Castro benefited from the political chaos of the struggle for independence, and the order was never enforced. In later appeals, Castro emphasized the torture he had suffered, which left him permanently crippled, as well as his illnesses, to appeal for a pardon.[118] On 10 December 1802, Castro suffered thirty-five uninterrupted minutes of torture as prosecutors, frustrated with the frequent changes he made during his testimony, sought to torment him to get at the truth. He suffered a dislocated vertebra, which left him crippled for life and unable to sleep lying down because of the pain.[119] Prison authorities noted that he slept in a posture that resembled a chicken. According to one source, Castro spent his sentence as a chastened man, teaching Christian doctrine in prison and serving as a sacristan in the prison's chapel when not filing appeals for his freedom.[120] Finally, on 9 January 1821, Castro was freed, the last prisoner convicted in the case of don Lucas de Gálvez's assassination.[121]

New Spain went through a tectonic shift as it broke away from Spain, but the magnitude of the impact on society from the assassination and the independence movement was much smaller in Yucatan. Within the peninsula, the assassination altered the balance of power between the church and the state, aggravated animosities between rival families, and deepened internecine divisions within leading clans. In 1812, for example, Col. don Ignacio Quijano, executor of the testament of his brother, the priest don José Tadeo Quijano, sought to exclude the least favorite sibling, doña Josefa, from the inheritance. To add insult to injury, she complained that he refused to turn over the contested plot of land. Instead, he allotted the plot to an unnamed, unrelated Indian who took up residence there against her wishes.[122] But no family was completely destroyed. In 1817 doña Josefa's son don Felipe Baldos (who may or may not have been the biological son of Tomás Murciano Baldos) served as a regidor on the ayuntamiento. In spite of his mother's bad name, his likely illegitimate parentage, and the rift with his powerful uncles, the Quijanos retained some influence.[123]

The death of don Lucas de Gálvez, one of the most audacious affronts to the Bourbon crown and its agents, did not significantly alter Yucatecan society. The Quijanos, the most prominent creole family implicated in the attack, suffered a setback in their rise to power, but their descendants continued to hold prominent positions in local government. Don Felipe Baldos served as regidor, and his uncle, don Joaquín Quijano, served beside him as a fellow regidor in 1812.[124] Don Ignacio Quijano Escudero (a nephew, not the son of the don Ignacio accused of complicity in the assassination) served as a deputy in Yucatan's chamber of deputies in the 1840s.[125] Even the scion of one of the families most tainted by the scandals of the early phase of the investigation—don Clemente de Trujillo y Melo, son of doña Casiana and her husband the treasurer—served as regidor. Both the Quijanos and the younger don Clemente belonged to the more conservative faction in municipal politics of the independence era.

In Yucatan, ascendant creole families did not, for the most part, reject the socioeconomic structure of society so much as they accepted independence from without, as almost a by-product of the war for independence that ravaged much of the rest of New Spain. Resentment of royal rule gave way to disenchantment with Mexican authorities, from the first emperor to the series of presidents who ruled for brief terms. Local society itself changed little. While the Quijanos themselves never attained the same level of dominance over Mérida that marked their prominence in the cabildo in the last decade of the eighteenth century, their class—the hacendados—continued its rise. The primacy of henequen as Yucatan's first wildly profitable export, first produced as naval cordage and later used to bind wheat for mechanical reapers in the United States and Canada, secured hacendados' position at the top of the pyramid.[126]

Mayas and rural castas, on the other hand, suffered enormously. In the words of one contemporary observer, "The hacendado intervenes constantly in the existence of the 'indebted' Indian, from his birth until he dies, not to educate him, not to improve him, but to keep and prepare him for the service of his property."[127] Scholars of nineteenth-century Yucatan noted the hardships of the Mayas, including arbitrary floggings, sales of indebted "servants" as part of the property of haciendas in land transfers, severe malnutrition and related diseases, and dire poverty.[128] The gap between the descendants of creoles and those of indigenous and African ancestry widened, leading to tensions that erupted with the Caste War of 1847–1853. Though never unified, the common speech of Yucatec Maya, spoken in most shared workplaces and professional associations, diminished as the lingua franca, reducing the shared devotional spaces, friendships, militia service, and ties of compadrazgo that brought together European-descent, indigenous, and Afro-Yucatecans, documented throughout the preceding pages. But for a time, the social tensions that erupted in nineteenth-century Yucatan's Caste War waned as resentment, resistance, and apathy toward Spain and its agents pervaded the province, tenuously uniting the peninsula in the conspiracy of silence that allowed one peninsular to suffer imprisonment for the murder of another while a cabal of creoles who had actually carried out the crime escaped punishment.

Conclusion

A conspiracy of down-and-out creoles, all hoping to benefit from the new intendant's reforms but who were sadly disappointed, planned and carried out a crime that shook the province, slowed the pace of reforms, and frustrated the efforts of the prosecutors and investigators they evaded for eight years. Resistance to the overhaul of the government and the efforts to rein in regionalism and rationalize rule deserves a closer look, beyond the most audacious affronts to crown administrators. Many of the alleged and actual assassins and accomplices chafed at the rapid changes imposed by Gálvez, a man marked by qualities sought after in Bourbon-era administrators. Previously, no historians have yet attempted to examine this critical event in its entirety or explore its deeper implications. Creole resentment of eighteenth-century reforms ran deeper and was expressed in more ways than has been recognized. And this violent incident, remembered by history buffs in Yucatan but forgotten elsewhere, did indeed impact the future direction of the peninsula.

Mérida, Yucatan, had changed only gradually in the first quarter of a millennium of Spanish rule, but its course had been altered for future centuries. The decades immediately before and after don Lucas de Gálvez's death saw an accelerating rate of change—one resisted by the deeply entrenched power blocs in the province. At a regional and viceregal level, the unrelenting advance of some of the principal dynasties came to an abrupt halt. The surnames of the leading families of the colonial era were rare among the henequen-based landed elites of the nineteenth century. Even so, the transition to a land-intensive hacienda economy, with its far-reaching impact on society—barely perceptible at the time—had begun to move forward. Furthermore, power blocs had begun to employ patronage networks to draw Indians, mestizos, and Afro-Yucatecans into their orbit, creating multiethnic, though still hierarchically rigid, creole-led cabals. This arrangement of factions, often armed, persisted into the nineteenth century, until one cohort of Maya-speaking campesinos unified against Mexican national rule and launched the Caste War.

In this clannish environment, the leading families most deeply entangled in the assassination never recovered from their implied involvement, even when they were declared innocent. Careers and reputations were inevitably tarnished—with notable exceptions—especially among administrators who performed well. Don Carlos María de Bustamante, for example, "made so able a defence as to save [don Toribio's] life," launching a career as a successful lawyer and leading liberal intellectual of nineteenth-century Mexico.[1] Bustamante's able defense of a suspect widely believed to be the "next to mount the gallows" between 1801 and 1803 offers a counterpoint, a rare success story in a series of trials that ruined the careers of many leading men who often dragged their subordinates down with them.[2] If don Toribio's last defense attorney added a particularly able defense to his burgeoning résumé, the first jurist to prosecute him fared much worse.

Don Fernando Antonio Gutiérrez de Piñeres saw his uninspiring performance as the first investigator to hesitantly take on the bishop and his nephew end his rapid rise through the ranks that characterized his family's status as favorites of the Bourbons.[3] Gingerly attempting to compile evidence against don Toribio in a remote territory with no allies, Piñeres faced disapproval and a faltering career for his negligence in the early stages of the investigation, from June 1792 until his successor's arrival in January 1793. Under thirty and new to his position as the lieutenant governor and legal counsel—he started just a month and half before his superior's sudden death—he had neither the connections nor the experience to adequately carry out an investigation. His dilatory inquest amounted to jailing marginal members of society, some of whom were suspected of petty crimes and others who had committed no infraction whatsoever, along with a few faltering steps toward investigating the likeliest suspect with the most plausible motive. His targets for incarceration and interrogation—an assortment of Mayas, mestizos, Afro-Yucatecans, and low-status creoles who primarily worked as domestic servants, laborers, or artisans—were unconvincing. During his de facto exile in Manila, beginning in 1796, he repeatedly sought a promotion and return to Mexico. In 1807 Carlos IV finally conceded and named him to the Audiencia of Mexico as fiscal del crimen, the same post held by the now dead Dr. Guillén. But due to the great distances and turmoil of the era, Gutiérrez de Piñeres never left the Philippines to occupy his new post. In 1811, as his biographers noted, "He died in Manila, the graveyard of judges, before hearing of his promotion."[4]

A few had better prospects after the case's conclusion. Gutiérrez de Piñeres's successor, Lic. don Manuel de la Bodega y Mollinedo, continued to serve in respectable posts in Mexico. The only setback in his career was a suspension for an unrelated incident: marrying without permission from the crown.[5] His poor health earned him more sympathy from his superiors, despite their reluctance to permit him to leave. The viceroy who watched his lack of progress from afar, the Marqués de Branciforte, blamed his illnesses, "strange occurrences," and "suspicious partiality and connections" for the snail's pace of his investigation rather than any personality defect or professional shortcoming.[6] In the face of such resistance, Bodega did make significant steps toward the case's resolution. He began to gather evidence first from a few domestic servants and later from a few leading creoles and peninsulares who broke the silence and turned on the leading suspect, though his successor compiled much more evidence against don Toribio. In spite of his poor health, he continued working as a crown bureaucrat through the independence era, starting with an appointment as oidor once again in 1796, this time with the Audiencia of Mexico. He ended his career as a ministro togado of the Council of the Indies, starting in 1814.[7] Bodega's investigation, marked by fits and starts and health crises that crippled him and his notary, Fernando Sandoval, did bring focus to the investigation. Don Toribio emerged as the prime suspect. Although he remained free for the duration of Bodega's term in Yucatan, the once and future oidor effectively set the course for his dogged successor, Dr. don Francisco de Guillén.

Dr. Guillén's inquiry was exhaustive. Skeptical of the honesty of the few witnesses who attested to don Toribio's alibi—that he had never strayed from Chikindzonot—the fiscal dug deeper. Less than ten Spanish-speaking witnesses and just four Maya-speaking witnesses had testified on his behalf, while hundreds of Maya witnesses waited until 1794 through 1795 for Guillén to ask them to weigh in. None had seen don Toribio during the days surrounding the murder. His alibi, built on shaky foundations, was demolished. Guillén's pursuit led his superior to single him out for praise in a case that did little to flatter anyone's reputation. The Marqués de Branciforte, viceroy of New Spain at the time of the transfer of venue, singled out Dr. Guillén as an "able lawyer," a public servant characterized by "zeal, talent, rectitude, and probity."[8] Guillén, an apt jurist schooled in the new jurisprudence of Bourbon letrados, placed the interests of the state above those of the church.

In the wake of the reordering of jurisdictional bounds, he took bold steps, entering the bishop's palace to collect evidence and trying a member of the top prelate's household and several loyal priests under royal jurisdiction, signaling a new low for the protection offered by the fuero eclesiástico. Despite his accolades, his dedicated pursuit of the truth of the matter, and his sterling reputation, Dr. Guillén soon was removed from the case, in 1796.

Though Guillén had earned nearly everyone's confidence, don Toribio's allies at court, including don Emeterio Cacho, managed to scale down his involvement once the trial moved to Mexico City, placing day-to-day management of the case in the hands of don Nicolas de Olaez, the relator. Although Guillén was frustrated by the change of venue and being sidelined from heading the case, he returned without a hitch to his post as assessor of the Acordada in Mexico City in 1797. He apparently suffered no retaliation in spite of his hard-charging approach to taking on a powerful family. Don Toribio's eventual exoneration did little to harm Guillén's reputation. In the *Calendario manual y guía de forasteros en México, para el año de 1800*, he is listed as the assessor of the tribunal, residing in Calle de los Donceles.[9] He died less than two years later. In 1802 don Toribio filed a civil suit petitioning for an indemnity from his estate, singling out Dr. Guillén as the primary culprit in his long imprisonment for a crime he did not commit.[10] Even posthumously, Guillén's reputation earned him a reprieve. Don Toribio's suit was rejected.

One final minor player—don Manuel del Castillo Negrete, the alcalde del crimen of the Audiencia of Mexico, who headed the prosecution of the changing cast of creole conspirators—also went on to more success. In 1806, possibly in reward for his tenacious pursuit of the truth in a mind-bogglingly complicated case, he was named to the Council of the Indies.[11] If anyone came closest to the truth of the matter—that a cohort of down-on-their-luck, dipsomaniac creoles had killed the intendant based on a fabricated promise of a huge payout from another family—it was Castillo de Negrete.

Consequences were more severe for the dozens of suspects imprisoned, questioned, and charged with false testimony, witness tampering, complicity, or the crime itself. The prime suspects and collaborators pursued by Lic. Bodega and Dr. Guillén—don Toribio, his uncle, and their extensive network of political allies—suffered tarnished reputations and stalled career advancement at the least and imprisonment in many instances. Few nineteenth-century authors remembered don Toribio's bishop uncle fondly. Quoted by a normally pro-clerical author, Justo Sierra wrote of him as

Figure 9. Hacienda Wallis's main building, now a neighborhood community center in Mérida. Photograph by the author.

"wrathful, harsh, selfish, and miserly."[12] Despite vehemently protesting that the prosecution had never disproved don Toribio's alibi, the illustrious creole historian Eligio Ancona described the bishop as "irascible" and prone to meddling in matters outside of his purview, the bane of the existence of at least three governors.[13] Fray Luis's nephew, once a highly desirable and eligible bachelor of the town, took a post elsewhere, small compensation for nearly a decade of imprisonment. His belated appointment in 1807 to the post of subdelegado in Tehuantepec, Oaxaca, was small compensation for the years he spent in prison.[14] Character witnesses and their horrific accounts of don Toribio's violence against subordinates and domestic animals meant that even if he was exonerated in the killing of his romantic rival, he never recovered from the disrepute. Apparently, he never returned to his beloved Hacienda Wallis, the site of his "orgies and feasts."[15]

In 1803 he requested permission to return to Spain shortly after his release from prison, and a real cédula from late December of that same year gave him license to return to the Iberian Peninsula.[16] He evidently returned in early 1804. From there he crossed the Atlantic Ocean once more to New Spain in 1807 or 1808 to take the new position of subdelegado in distant Tehuantepec.[17] He never set foot in Yucatan again.

If what remained of don Toribio's life was saved by the inebriated confession of the hapless interpreter in the nick of time, it ushered in the beginning of the end of the Quijanos' zenith during the last decade of the eighteenth century. The decade's early years had been hard. In 1791 don José Boves married doña María Tomasa, in defiance of the paterfamilias's efforts to marry most of his fifteen children to powerful or wealthy men and women. His other daughter, doña Josefa, was having an affair with don Esteban de Castro, a man of notable talent but low social standing. Gálvez forbade the younger Juan Esteban Quijano from using his ceremonial staff of office.[18] Don Ignacio faced charges over his abuse of power in his role as a militia colonel. The intendant's death could not undo doña María Tomasa's marriage, but it removed the threat of any further actions against two of the sons. Despite the murmurs against the Quijanos, who clearly had a motive for wanting Gálvez dead, Dr. Guillén's well-known and occasionally criticized friendship with the family effectively deflected attention away from the Quijanos.[19] Moreover, the Quijanos had been less vocal about their motives than don Toribio, a suspect who many believed had already committed a homicide at least twice before.

The dawn of the nineteenth century brought their upward trajectory to a halt. Two family members, doña Josefa and the priest don José Tadeo, were imprisoned for their supposed role in the killing in 1801. Don José Tadeo likely blamed his sister's ill-advised affair with Castro for his imprisonment. The two never reconciled.[20] The second decade of the nineteenth century, which followed Juan Esteban Quijano's death in 1808, brought more division to the family. In 1812 doña Josefa sued her brother Ignacio, executor of the will of don José Tadeo, over possession of La Quinta Miraflores.[21] Don Ignacio likely concurred with his brother the priest in holding their sister responsible for José Tadeo's incarceration. Political divisions also emerged in the second decade of the nineteenth century. Joaquín, the ninth of fifteen children and the second youngest of the sons, showed liberal leanings. Although his father and several other brothers never compromised in their regalism, Joaquín Quijano was the only member of the traditional cabildo who actively participated in the constitutional ayuntamiento of 1813. Meanwhile, his brother Miguel demonstrated barely concealed anticonstitutionalist sentiments. Only Joaquín managed to serve on the traditional cabildo, the constitutional ayuntamiento, and the post-independence town council in 1822.[22] He was the last of the sons of Juan Esteban to serve in the cabildo. Just as the bishop's loyal and regimented cabal disintegrated shortly after fray Luis's death, so too the Quijanos became a less formidable family and began their slow descent from the upper strata of Yucatecan society after Juan Esteban's death. Camarillas (patron-client family or political networks revolving around a dominant figure) often only endured for the lifetime of their creole leaders before fragmenting.

No such leadership marked the last of the cohorts examined here. The "friends of a disorderly lifestyle"—Castro, Manuel Alfonso López, don Bernardo Lino Rejón, and José Yanuario Salazar—had never been anything close to an influential power clique. But they too fractured under questioning. Whatever tenuous ties they had to the Quijanos—which likely amounted to nothing more than Castro's affairs with doña Josefa, a bit of translation for the father, and a loan—were definitively severed. After her affair with the prison warden don Jaime Alzubidé, doña Josefa managed to marry well once again. Her second husband—don Fernando de Quijano y Bustamante, likely a peninsular cousin—supported her efforts to regain La Quinta Miraflores in 1812.[23] This remarriage likely signaled the end of her involvement with Castro. We know less about the fate of the four men who planned, carried out, or colluded by their silence in the case, who all confessed their role in the crime. Unlike the Quijanos, their part in the assassination or its subsequent cover-up was never in doubt. Such men rarely came to the attention of authorities or are recorded in the histories of the province. Their appearance was brief, as were their careers and their lives, for the most part. López, the accused murderer, died in May 1802.[24] Castro emerged from prison crippled. Even if he had not faced the difficulty of convincing authorities to let him return to his post after twenty-one years of inactivity, the position of interpreter general was abolished the year of his release, in 1821. Of the surviving conspirators, Salazar is evidently the only one who returned to his career with notable success. Freed in 1808, he returned to work as a painter with little loss of talent during his years in prison. He was hired to oversee the painting of the cypress baldachin built to cover the altar in Mérida's cathedral, a task for only the most talented artisans.[25]

Salazar also stands out in the record for being one of the rare men of humble status and artisanal work who resurfaces in the official record after the trial. Others—such as the coachman Lara or another notable painter of retablos, Ignacio Matos—disappear without a paper trail to follow. Occasionally, repeat offenders such as the contrabandista Lucas Vargas resurface in the archives across time. But, despite such allegations, Matos and Lara did not. Their fates after years of unjust imprisonment are unknown.

Indeed, the crime opens a window on relationships that often escape other historians. Without the decade of investigation into the murder trials and the transcripts that resulted from it, many of the relationships between creoles and mestizos, Mayas, and Afro-Yucatecans would remain invisible. These records highlight blood ties, fictive kinship, and racially mixed workplace and religious spaces. Francisco Ek, a Maya, owned an inn that lodged militiamen serving in one of the units composed of white volunteers, who were called as witnesses. When Manuel Alfonso López, a creole, feared retaliation or apprehension immediately after the murder, he fled to the home of Tiburcio Ek, a Maya resident of Opichen and his compadre. Ignacio Matos, likely the most wronged victim of the early misdirected stage of the investigation, had several respectable artisans and officers firmly established in Mérida's black middle testify in his favor; others who testified on his behalf included a number of well-placed creoles, such as don José Rafael Rodríguez, brother of Maxcanú's priest; Cpl. Juan José Mayor; and doña Magdalena Cisneros, who vouched for a his presence at a mostly Afro-Yucatecan religious gathering. Professional relationships also were far less segregated than has been assumed. Juan Antonio Argais, the artisan suspected of repairing a knife used in the murder, trained under the creole don Domingo Álvarez, the province's master armorer, and employed a Maya assistant. Maya laborers worked and lived in Spanish-owned homes and workplaces as well, such as the Maya candlemaker who resided in the Quijanos' household and María Ventura, the Indian criada who lived in the home of don Rafael Pastrana.

Other instances of interethnic intimacy were intentionally hidden from authorities and mentioned only as a way of discrediting the declarations or participation of witnesses and investigators. Supporters of don Toribio pointed out Mariano Ancona's affair with Petrona Dzul to undermine Ancona's able assistance in compiling testimony that discredited the militia lieutenant's alibi in Maya-speaking towns. Conversely, Dr. Guillén pointedly included the unacknowledged blood ties between the two women named Juana Martínez—one a Spaniard and the other a mestiza—to downplay their credibility. The records of the trial were rife with other unproven accusations of interracial affairs, including charges leveled against the militia sublieutenant don Luis Durán y Domínguez, who challenged rumors of an affair with an unnamed "mulata."[26] Without the prolonged investigation, relationships of this nature would never have come to light.

The preceding chapters have examined how individuals experienced such changes, focusing on Yucatecans who moved outside of their traditional ambit: Mayas living and working independently in the city, monolingual Maya-speaking castas in the countryside farming small plots, and Europeans lacking long-standing ties to the province. By this time, many Mayas, castas, and Afro-Yucatecans had experienced some degree of upward mobility. Mayas moved into occupations and geographical spaces that traditionally were the domain of Spaniards, such as the indio ladino Isidoro Xix, Mérida's town crier, and Francisco Ek, the innkeeper and shoemaker who lived across the street from the sacristy of the cathedral. Afro-Yucatecans such as the painter and gilder Ignacio Matos and the blacksmith Juan Antonio Argais, who owned his own shop and had at least one Maya employee, were far better off economically than their slave ancestors. Such interpenetration of supposedly separate spheres meant that various creole-headed factions were indeed multiethnic bands, relying on an assortment of mayordomos, criados, slaves, compadres, auxiliaries, and other allies from various racial backgrounds. Patronage required at least some degree of inclusion, even if it was hierarchical. Creoles learned that bolstering their numbers by being inclusive had its advantages.

Creole elites had learned another lesson: defiance went unpunished. Viceregal authorities' perspective may have differed. For them, the message received was a cautionary one: they needed to redouble their efforts to integrate Yucatan and other peripheral provinces. During the colonial and early national period, the intention to do so by Mexico City largely failed. Yucatecan creoles implicated in the assassination, wrongly or rightly, had learned to resent outside authority but had not been punished so severely that the castigation of Gálvez's killers acted as a deterrent. Within New Spain and its independent successor, Mexico, the course was set for the century of breakaway and autonomist movements that followed. Yucatecan creoles had defied the royal authorities and nearly all of them lived to tell about it, albeit in conflicting, contradictory, and inconsistent testimonies. On a broad scale, the peninsula's populace had used geographic isolation to thwart royalist attempts to rein in regionalist impulses. A confabulation of resentful creoles had killed the intendant and went undetected for eight years. Ambivalence toward the dead governor undermined attempts to solve the case, as normally effective jurists came up against a wall of noncompliance.

Downward mobility sparked such resistance. The rapid changes of the late eighteenth century did not leave the upper tiers of Spanish society untouched. The loss of encomiendas, stricter enforcement of the prohibition on repartimientos, and the decline of ecclesiastical privilege and municipal autonomy bred resentment on the part of the privileged classes of Mérida. Moreover, the Spanish-descent population grew more quickly than opportunities for economic advancement. Many Spaniards no longer could be considered economic or social elites, in spite of their sense of entitlement to a privileged position as a birthright of European ancestry. Lacking opportunities in the traditional ambit of creoles and peninsulares in Latin America, some Spaniards moved from the city into the mostly Maya countryside—such as the militiamen from Tixkokob or the subdelegado of Tihosuco, don Mateo de Cárdenas—often bolstering the military and bureaucratic presence there. Migration of both peninsular Spaniards and other Europeans to Yucatan accelerated during this time. The demographic face of the province changed, and the extensive trial records from the Gálvez assassination provide an opportunity to examine the effects of this mobility, both social and geographic, as they played out in a legal forum.

By the late eighteenth century, Yucatecan society had evolved well beyond a set of cohesive corporate entities composed of Mayas, Spaniards, and Afro-Yucatecans, each isolated from one another—the system that theoretically governed Spain's American colonies. In the face of such changes, the legal structure of Latin America continued to function well in some settings while it utterly failed to keep up with the transformation of Spain's colonies in other cases. The protections afforded to holders of a fuero, for example, mostly remained in place until the end of the colonial period. Suspects who escaped prison sentences or evaded interrogation and incarceration for long periods of time invariably benefited from such fueros or from the extralegal protection of powerful patrons. For Mayas who remained in the countryside or slaves who resided in prominent households, layers of protection shielded them from arbitrarily harsh punishments.

However, Yucatan in the late eighteenth century no longer functioned as a system of two republics, with Afro-Yucatecans serving in Spanish households. Mayas and Afro-Yucatecans who sought to better their status by moving outside the homes of Spaniards or the república de indios were the ones who ran the greatest risk of unjust rulings from the colonial courts. Economic and social improvement involved risk in the legal sphere, as the case of the painter Ignacio Matos illustrates. Living in Mérida as a free man certainly offered him more opportunities than those available to his likely enslaved forefathers, but the urban area also entailed more surveillance and scrutiny from an array of law enforcement officials. Creole elites, unsettled by such rapid changes elsewhere in the Atlantic World and the threat of such disorder spreading to Yucatan, where a large percentage of the population no longer fit into the categories created for them at the outset of the colonial experiment, were hesitant to adjust the legal framework to the shifting social structure. Upper-class Spaniards resisted legal reforms that threatened their privileged position in society, whether the threat came from lower classes encroaching on their geographic space and political dominance or from the top in the form of crown orders that limited their autonomy and legal immunities. Such resistance often resulted in violence, such as the attack on Intendant Gálvez. The oidores, viceroys, and their subordinate judges and magistrates responded quickly during such outbreaks of violence. But instead of resulting in an efficient and exemplary punishment that demonstrated the displeasure of Carlos IV with such an act of treason, the crown's surrogates oversaw a series of trials that unjustly punished a number of innocent men whose treatment stemmed from nothing more than their vulnerable status before the law. Rather than giving a convincing demonstration of authority over Spain's American colonies, the directionless and frequently suspended series of trials in pursuit of don Lucas de Gálvez's assassin highlighted the degree to which local conditions and traditions limited the reach of Bourbon rule in the Americas.

Glossary

alcalde Prominent position on the city and pueblo councils.

alcalde de la cárcel Head guard of the town jail (*alcaldemascab* in Maya).

alguacil mayor Cabildo member charged with the execution of sentences.

almehen Maya term for the native nobility.

asesor de guerra Military counsel of the province.

audiencia A court and advisory council to the viceroy of New Spain; its judicial duties were carried out by the *sala del crimen*.

batab A hereditary Maya municipal-level ruler who unofficially headed the indigenous cabildo of his pueblo.

cabecera Head town; the political capital of a subdivision in Yucatan known as a *partido*.

cabo de justicia A rural-based low-level policing official of Spanish descent, similar to that of a *juez español*.

cabo del barrio An urban-based low-level policing agent of non-Maya ancestry.

cacique An Indian authority who headed a local native government.

cantor Singer; a leading church auxiliary office in rural Maya society.

careo Face-to-face confrontation between witnesses intended to sort out conflicting testimony.

casta A person of multiracial ancestry.

criado/a A household domestic servant who usually resided in and was raised from a young age in the household of their master.

criollo The term used to describe people of European, and especially Spanish, descent, born in the Americas.

encomenderos Holders of encomiendas.

encomienda A royal concession to conquistadors and early colonists that entitled them to tribute in labor from the native population of a specific geographic area.

estancia A medium-sized parcel of land devoted to raising livestock.

fiscal Crown attorney serving the audiencia, or a high-ranking lay native assistant to the priest, in a rural colonial context.

fuero A special legal right entitling an individual belonging to a privileged corporate entity to trial in a separate court.

gremio A guild of craftworkers of the same profession.

hacendado An owner of a hacienda, or medium-sized plot of land usually used for raising cattle or other large livestock.

herrero Blacksmith or other metalworker.

indio hidalgo A member of the native nobility, it included descendants of the central Mexican Indians who assisted in the conquest and members of the Maya nobility of Yucatan.

intendant A position created in 1786 with the Decree of Intendentes that brought Spanish-held provinces under tighter control.

juez comisionado A specially appointed judge, assigned to preside over extraordinary or difficult cases, much like an outside prosecutor in the US legal system.

justicias In a rural Yucatecan context, the term referred to the high-ranking Mayas who served on the cabildo of the pueblo.

labrador An independent small farmer.

licenciado An individual who held a university-level degree within the Spanish educational system.

maestrescuela Master of divinity, a high-ranking educator who taught priests their duties.

milpa Small plots of land usually held by natives devoted to subsistence farming.

montaña Literally, mountain; in colonial Yucatan it referred to the uncontrolled region beyond the limits of established and permanent Spanish control.

pardo The most commonly used term in late colonial Yucatan for Afro-Yucatecans of mixed ancestry.

peninsular A Spaniard born in Spain.

pícaro A rascal or scoundrel.

procurador Solicitor or attorney general.

regidor A councilman on either a native cabildo or a Spanish ayuntamiento.

relator Counselor of a court charged with reading briefs of the cases that are to be tried; court reporter.

solar Urban house-plot.

teniente del rey The second-highest ranking official in the royal government of the province after the governor.

tertulia A literary and social gathering of prominent citizens, popular throughout Latin America, many of which became politically charged settings hosted by women during the independence period.

topil Low-level law enforcement official in Maya pueblos who were not part of the cabildo.

vecino Resident of a city, sometimes used to distinguish a non-Maya resident from Mayas in rural locales.

vaquero Cowboy who worked on a hacienda.

vendedor de suela Vendor of low-quality meat and low-grade leather often used for making shoes.

zapatero Shoemaker.

Notes

PROLOGUE

1. "De la causa formada en averiguación de los agresores," 1794, Archivo General de Indias (AGI), México 3036, no. 120, test. 1, cuad. 3, ff. 2–4, includes one of the earliest accounts of the attack, written by Auditor and Lieutenant Governor (*Auditor de Guerra y Teniente de Gobernador*) don Fernando Gutiérrez de Piñeres immediately after the murder.
2. "Declaración del Tesorero," 1795, AGI, México 3036, no. 115, test. 1. This statement was made in 1795, nearly three years later. The earlier version recorded in "De la causa" did not mention Gálvez chasing his attacker.
3. "Documentación relativa al proceso sobre el homicidio de Lucas de Galvez," 1792–1802, Archivo General de las Simancas (AGS), Secretaría del Despacho de Guerra 7219, test. 3, no. 650, f. 91.
4. Matthew Restall coined the term *Afro-Yucatecan* to encompass all Yucatecans of African descent in *The Black Middle: Africans, Mayas, and Spaniards in Colonial Yucatan* (Stanford, CA: Stanford University Press, 2009). *Campechano* refers to a native of Campeche.
5. "De la causa formada en averiguación de los agresores," 1794, AGI, México 3036, no. 120, test. 1, cuad. 3, ff. 3–6; and "Se hace relación del resultado sobre Coartada en el plenario," 1794, Archivo General de la Nación (of Mexico) (AGN), Criminal 294, f. 110.
6. "De la causa formada en averiguación de los agresores," 1794, AGI, México 3036, no. 120, test. 1, cuad. 3, f. 5.

CHAPTER 1

1. In most territory under Spanish rule in the late colonial era, locally born creoles and mixed-race Latin Americans spoke Spanish while many indigenous groups retained their native language. By contrast, the use of Yucatec Maya had become

commonplace among most rural *castas*, and many creoles spoke at least rudimentary Maya by the late eighteenth century. See Mark W. Lentz, "Castas, Creoles, and the Rise of a Maya Lingua Franca in Eighteenth-Century Yucatan," *Hispanic American Historical Review* 97, no. 1 (February 2017): 29–61.

2. The term *juez comisionado* translates literally to "commissioned judge," but the activities of the two magistrates overseeing the investigation (who arrived from Guatemala and Mexico City, respectively) resemble those of outside prosecutors more than actual judges.

3. Gilbert M. Joseph, "Rethinking Mexican Revolutionary Mobilization: Yucatán's Seasons of Upheaval, 1909–1915," in *Everyday Forms of State Formation: Revolution and the Negotiation of Rule in Modern Mexico*, ed. Joseph and Daniel Nugent (Durham, NC: Duke University Press, 1994), 158.

4. In his account of his journey from Italy to Mexico, the Capuchin friar Ilarione da Bergamo recorded eight days of sailing from the "Sound of Campeche" to Veracruz. Robert Ryal Miller and William J. Orr, eds., *Daily Life in Colonial Mexico: The Journey of Friar Ilarione da Bergamo, 1761–1768* (Norman: University of Oklahoma Press, 2011), 71.

5. Nancy M. Farriss succinctly wrote, "The long and stable history of the *encomienda* in Yucatan is symptomatic of the region's backwardness in general and most especially its feeble economic growth," in *Maya Society under Colonial Rule: The Collective Enterprise of Survival*, 2nd ed. (Princeton, NJ: Princeton University Press, 1984), 39.

6. Manuela Cristina García Bernal, *La sociedad de Yucatán, 1700–1750* (Seville: Escuela de Estudios Hispano-Americanos de Sevilla, 1972), 33–40. García Bernal's section on the encomienda set the standard for future scholarship, especially in the legal and institutional aspects of the tribute arrangement.

7. Juan Antonio Valera and Francisco de Corres, "Discurso sobre la constitución de las provincias de Yucatán y Campeche," in *Descripciones económicas regionales de Nueva España: Provincias del centro, sureste y sur, 1766–1827*, by Enrique Florescano and Isabel Gil (Mexico City: Secretaría de Educación Pública-Instituto Nacional de Antropología e Historia, 1976), 205.

8. Antonio de Ciudad Real, "Relación de las cosas que sucedieron al R. P. Comisario General Fray Alonso Ponce. . . . ," in *Colección de documentos inéditos para la historia de España* (1588; Madrid: Imprenta de la Viuda de Calero, 1872), 58:590, noted that, in the late sixteenth century, Yucatan exported maize to Florida, Cuba, and Veracruz.

9. Among the products that Valera and Corres suggested should be further exploited in their description of Yucatan, they praised the virtues of "Geniquén" for use in making ropes. "Discurso sobre la constitución," 248.

10. Under an encomienda system, indigenous inhabitants retained the land but owed tribute and labor to an encomendero. With the rise of the hacienda, Spaniards turned to landholding, as rural estates emerged as the economic engine of the

mature colonial period. See James Lockhart and Stuart B. Schwartz, *Early Latin America: A History of Colonial Spanish America and Brazil* (Cambridge: Cambridge University Press, 1983), 134–42.

11. Robert W. Patch, *Maya and Spaniard in Yucatan, 1648–1812* (Stanford, CA: Stanford University Press, 1993), 100–6.

12. Ibid., 100–2.

13. Ibid., 140–42.

14. Christopher M. Nichols, "Solares in Tekax: The Impact of the Sugar Industry on a Nineteenth-Century Yucatecan Town," *Ethnohistory* 50, no. 1 (Winter 2003): 161–89.

15. See Valera and Corres, "Discurso sobre la constitución," 225–26 and 257–58 for contemporary observations on fraudulent commerce with the English in the 1760s.

16. Jorge Victoria Ojeda examines the reorganization of Yucatan's defensive capacity in *Mérida de Yucatán de las Indias: Piratería y estrategia defensiva* (Mérida: Ayuntamiento de Mérida, 1995). Restall provides comprehensive coverage of Afro-Yucatecan officers and militiamen in *Black Middle*, 155–78.

17. Valera and Corres, "Discurso sobre la constitución," 216–17.

18. Thomas Kitchin, *The Present State of the West-Indies: Containing an Accurate Description of What Parts Are Possessed by the Several Powers in Europe* (London, 1778), 39–40.

19. "Lucas Vargas y complices—Polvora," 1791, AGI, México 3069, exp. 1.

20. *An eye draft of Logger-head Cay near to Cape Catoche in 21 de: 20 mi: N: L:* (ca. 1760) can be found in the John Carter Brown Map Collection, cabinet Ef760 /1 Ms.

21. Allan J. Kuethe and Kenneth J. Andrien, *The Spanish Atlantic World in the Eighteenth Century: War and the Bourbon Reforms* (Cambridge: Cambridge University Press, 2014), 305–6. Don Arturo O'Neill, Gálvez's successor, utterly failed to drive out the English in 1798, marking the last armed attempt to reclaim Belize that was launched from Yucatan. For the most recent discussion of Belize's frontier with Yucatan and the flow of slaves across the border from English to Spanish territory, see Matthew Restall, "Crossing to Safety? Frontier Flight in Eighteenth-Century Belize and Yucatan," *Hispanic American Historical Review* 94, no. 3 (August 2014): 381–419.

22. Alexander Grab characterizes Charles IV as a king who "showed more interest in hunting and carpentry in state affairs and was influenced by his domineering wife, Maria Luisa," in *Napoleon and the Transformation of Europe* (New York: Palgrave Macmillan, 2003), 124. Charles IV left routine matters to Manuel Godoy, the prime minister.

23. "Branciforte sobre los franceses existentes," 1796, AGI, Estado 24, no. 19, 1j.

24. "Desembarco de desterrados negros y mulatos franceses," 1792, AGS, Secretaría del Despacho de Guerra 7237, no. 52, f. 284; "El Señor Governador e Yntendente

de aquella provincia sobre venta de 15 negros esclavos," 1809, AGN, Civil 2152, exp. 11; and "Sobre 115 negros de tropas auxiliares," 1796, AGI, Estado 35, no. 13.

25. Charles F. Walker provides the most recent and thorough treatment of the Great Rebellion in the Andes in *The Tupac Amaru Rebellion* (Cambridge, MA: Harvard University Press, 2014). John Leddy Phelan, *The People and the King: The Comunero Revolution in Colombia, 1781* (Madison: University of Wisconsin Press, 1978) remains the authoritative work on the Comunero Uprising.

26. One example of lenient treatment for creole conspirators includes the Quito Rebellion of 1765, in which suspected creole leaders went unpunished. Anthony McFarlane, "The 'Rebellion of the Barrios': Urban Insurrection in Bourbon Quito," *Hispanic American Historical Review* 69, no. 2 (May 1989): 283-330. McFarlane concluded: "This conciliatory policy seems to have worked well" (319). Creole clergymen implicated in the uprisings in northern and western New Spain following the expulsion of the Jesuits were also treated with more leniency than indigenous participants. See Felipe Castro Gutiérrez, *Nueva ley y nuevo rey: Reformas borbónicas y rebelión popular en Nueva España* (Zamora: Colegio de Michoacán, 1996), 177-79.

27. Patch, *Maya and Spaniard*, 33, 100-2.

28. Restall, *Black Middle*, 219-26.

29. Ibid., 143.

30. Patch, *Maya and Spaniard*, 159-68, provides an in-depth account of the abolition of the repartimiento in the 1780s and 1790s.

31. Stanley J. Stein, "Bureaucracy and Business in the Spanish Empire, 1759-1804: Failure of a Bourbon Reform in Mexico and Peru," *Hispanic American Historical Review* 61, no. 1 (February 1981): 10.

32. Ibid.

33. For an extensive exploration of the subdelegados within the wider project of the creation of the intendancies, see Rafael Diego-Fernández Sotelo, María Pilar Gutiérrez Lorenzo, and Luis Alberto Arrioja Díaz Viruell, eds., *De reinos y sub-delegaciones: Nuevos escenarios para un nuevo orden en la América borbónica* (Zamora: El Colegio de Michoacán, 2014).

34. Restall, *Black Middle*, provides a notable exception, depicting the pardo minority especially as middle class.

35. Once taken as the authoritative work on colonial Yucatan, Farriss's *Maya Society* argued that late colonial society in Yucatan had actually moved toward greater separation between Mayas and the Hispanic population, asserting: "The boundary of caste that had been solidifying in don Fernando Uz's time [the early seventeenth century] had become a Berlin Wall by Canek's [the 1760s]" (100). For more recent scholarship that takes a more binary view of society, using the division between the *república de indios* and the *república de españoles* as a point of departure, see recent works on Oaxaca by Yanna Yannakakis, who emphasize the divide between indio and Spaniard. Here I

argue that the sharp lines between racial categories blurred more than previous scholars of colonial Latin America have recognized. However, there are some important differences in scope. In *The Art of Being In-between: Native Intermediaries, Indian Identity, and Local Rule in Colonial Oaxaca* (Durham, NC: Duke University Press, 2008), Yannakakis highlights the legal distinction between indios and Spaniards, a difference that retained its importance throughout the colonial era, at least in Oaxaca.

Urban residence did complicate legal categories for indigenous Yucatecans, especially in Mérida. However, the institutions of native rule retained their sway in the rural sphere. Such blurring of jurisdictional lines did not necessarily occur elsewhere. Though Oaxaca is comparable with Yucatan in terms of the persistence of the indigenous majority's language, customs, and local autonomy, comparisons have limits. First, the corregidores (or *alcaldes mayores*) who acted as lightning rods for indigenous grievances did not have counterparts in Yucatan. Second, unlike multiethnic, polyglot colonial Oaxaca, Yucatan had just one major indigenous language, facilitating Spanish, casta, and Afro-Yucatecan adoption of Yucatec Maya as a primary or secondary language, which eroded boundaries between the two repúblicas. Finally, this work confines itself chronologically to the late colonial era, when boundaries between ethnic groups broke down, unlike the broader time frames of Yannakakis's monograph. Finally, Yannakakis focuses on Villa Alta. *Murder in Mérida*, by contrast, has a broader geographical scope, encompassing both the city of Mérida and the pueblos of Tihosuco and Chikindzonot in depth and other rural zones in passing. Finally, no work analogous to Restall's *Black Middle* has dealt in any depth with Afro-Oaxacans or other groups that do not fit neatly in any of the "poles" of the casta system—negro, indio, and español—for colonial Oaxaca. Mérida's more diverse population saw the geographical and social (if not legal) divisions blur more quickly. While Mérida was not a viceregal capital like Mexico City, Gabriel Haslip-Viera's description of New Spain's largest urban center holds true for Yucatan as well: "Certain social realities made estate and ethnic categorization largely meaningless." *Crime and Punishment in Late Colonial Mexico City, 1692–1810* (Albuquerque: University of New Mexico Press, 1999), 22. Comparisons with secondary cities elsewhere are also relevant. In Martin Minchom's *The People of Quito, 1690–1810* (Boulder, CO: Westview Press, 1994), the author examines "Declarations of Mestizo" to demonstrate a similar degree of racial ambiguity among Quito's urban commoners. Racial lines blurred more extensively in urban centers than in the countryside, but a black minority often integrated into a Maya majority in Yucatan's pueblos as well. As Restall wrote, "In smaller towns and villages . . . free-colored settlers were more likely to become part of the local Maya community" (222). See Restall, *Black Middle*, 222, and Yannakakis, *Being In-between*, 15, for a discussion of Oaxaca's version of the caste system.

36. Corregidores, rural officials with the most quotidian contact with indigenous subjects, were targets of Andean revolts and uprisings. In Peru, these attacks were often provoked by the abusive repartimiento. Ann M. Wightman mentions an early example, the 1726 assassination of the Corregidor of Carabaya, near Cuzco, in *Indigenous Migration and Social Change: The Forasteros of Cuzco, 1570–1720* (Durham, NC: Duke University Press, 1990), 51. Nicholas A. Robins, Charles F. Walker, and Sinclair Thomson examined late eighteenth-century violence that marked the opening salvos of Andean indigenous rebellions. Thomson studied increasing indigenous upheavals in the decades leading up to the Great Rebellion, finding rising resistance and a push for self-rule that preceded the Great Rebellion, in *We Alone Will Rule: Native Andean Politics in the Age of Insurgency* (Madison: University of Wisconsin Press, 2002). During the Great Rebellion, indigenous rebels killed the corregidores of Tinta, Paria, Carangas, and Lipes. See Nicholas A. Robins, *Native Insurgencies and the Genocidal Impulse in the Americas* (Bloomington: University of Indiana Press, 2005), 78, 175–76. Rebel mestizos also targeted corregidores; headed by the mestizo militia sergeant Luís Lasso de la Vega, the rebels of Tupiza captured and executed the corregidor, Francisco García de Prado, in March 1781. See Nicholas A. Robins, *Genocide and Millennialism in Upper Peru: The Great Rebellion of 1780–1782* (Westport, CT: Greenwood Press, 2002), 128–29. Walker's treatment of the execution of Antonio de Arriaga, corregidor of Tinta and nemesis of Tupac Amaru II, is among the best. See *Smoldering Ashes: Cuzco and the Creation of Republican Peru, 1780–1840* (Durham, NC: Duke University Press, 1999). In times of turmoil, corregidores avoided going in person to defiant communities and sent agents to collect taxes or restore order in their stead. Corregidores' assistants were targeted too. In 1769, vexed by the widely hated corregidor Marqués de Villahermosa's repartimiento demands, Indians led by the cacique of Sicasica, Alejandro Chuquiguaman, killed Manuel Solascasas, Villahermosa's collector, after the corregidor retreated to the safety of La Paz. Thomson, *We Alone Will Rule*, 114–16.

37. Walker, *Smoldering Ashes*, 53.

38. Francisco Javier Cevallos-Candau, Jeffrey A. Cole, Nina M. Scott, and Nicomedes Suárez-Araúz, eds., *Coded Encounters: Writing, Gender, and Ethnicity in Colonial Latin America* (Amherst: University of Massachusetts Press, 1994), 119.

39. Kevin Gosner, *Soldiers of the Virgin: The Moral Economy of a Colonial Maya Rebellion* (Tucson: University of Arizona Press, 1992), 129–55.

40. Robert W. Patch, *Maya Revolt and Revolution in the Eighteenth Century* (Armonk, NY: M.E. Sharpe, 2002), 177.

41. Castro Gutiérrez, *Nueva ley y nuevo rey*, 183–95.

42. Robins, *Native Insurgencies*, 47.

43. Jay Kinsbruner, *Independence in Spanish America: Civil Wars, Revolutions, and Underdevelopment* (Albuquerque: University of New Mexico Press, 2000), 25.

44. John Leddy Phelan, *The People and the King: The Comunero Revolution in Colombia, 1781* (Madison: University of Wisconsin Press, 1978), 206–7.

45. Phelan, *People and the King*, is one major exception to the tendency of historians to provide only cursory coverage of creole-led uprisings. Other creole-headed revolts and conspiracies have received far less attention from scholars. For example, Venezuela's first stillborn movement for independence, headed by creoles Manuel Gual and José de España, has received only a paragraph of coverage in Kinsbruner, *Independence in Spanish America*, 25.

46. As Phelan noted in *People and the King* (67), the Tupac Amaru rebellion, a largely indigenous uprising, provided the most immediate inspiration for the creole-led Comuneros in 1781 in New Granada.

47. John Charles Chasteen, *Americanos: Latin America's Struggle for Independence* (Oxford: Oxford University Press, 2008), 10.

48. "Resumen del antecedente extracto," 10 December 1792, AGI, México 3039, no. 51, s/f.

49. James C. Scott, *Domination and the Arts of Resistance: Hidden Transcripts* (New Haven: Yale University Press, 1990).

50. Michel Bertrand, *Grandeza y miseria del oficio: Los oficiales reales de la Real Hacienda de la Nueva España, siglos XVII y XVIII*, trans. Mario Zamudio (Mexico City: Fondo de Cultura Económica, 2013), provides the most extensive treatment of the role of family networks in appointments to royal positions of power in eighteenth-century Mexico.

51. Works dealing with insurrectionary and subversive activities in eighteenth- and early nineteenth-century Yucatan include Patch, *Maya Revolt*; Pedro Bracamonte y Sosa, *La encarnación de la profecía Canek en Cisteil* (Mexico City: CIESAS, 2004); and Victoria Reifler Bricker, *The Indian Christ, the Indian King: The Historical Substrate of Maya Myth and Ritual* (Austin: University of Texas Press, 1981).

52. The most extensive trial records are held in forty-four bound volumes in the Archivo General de la Nación of Mexico City. The trial transcripts are found in AGN, Ramo Criminal, nos. 287, 291, 292, 293, 294, 295 and sections of 299, 300, 301, 302, 309, 310, 311, 316, 317, 322, 323, 324, 325, 328, 329, 330, 331, 332, 335, 336, 337, 341, 342, 343, 344, 345, 348, 349, 372, 389, 391, 392, 469, 471, 484, 546, 619, and 726. Five thick volumes summarizing the case that contain notarized copies of much of the proceedings are held in the Archivo General de Indias in Seville. They are found in AGI, Audiencia de México, nos. 3036, 3037, 3038, 3039, and 3040. Lastly, two volumes dealing with matters of military immunity and martial justice related to the assassination are found in the Archivo General de las Simancas, Secretaría del Despacho de Guerra 7219 and 7218.

53. Maya-Spanish conflict has served as the theme for much of the scholarship of the past forty years. By reducing Yucatecan history to struggles between Spaniards and Mayas, scholars overstate racial solidarity among Europeans against the

indigenous majority. Earlier studies fail to examine the cross-class and interethnic alliances that come to light in the minutiae of the trial transcripts and in
other criminal cases that will be examined. Times of heightened animosity
between Spaniards and Mayas did generate frantic reports and records of punishment of ringleaders of revolts, mass flight, and religious defiance, leading to a
preponderance of archival texts written during times of conflict.

Two of the three most-consulted monographs on colonial Yucatan, by
Nancy M. Farriss and Robert W. Patch, have taken a bifurcated approach to
Yucatecan society, foregrounding Maya-Spanish conflict. Farriss's *Maya Society*
considered environmental conditions, ethnographic analogy, the Maya world-
view based on translated religious writings and upstreaming based on (then)
current Maya religious practices, using extensive archival research in Spain and
Mexico, to depict Maya cultural survival as a conscious product of Maya unity
in the face of Spanish colonization. Patch's *Maya and Spaniard* emphasized
Yucatan's economic ties with the outside world and the coexistence of an emerging capitalist market alongside the archaic encomienda, challenging the idea that
Yucatan was an isolated backwater during the colonial era, with Spanish economic exploitation of the Mayas receiving exhaustive coverage. Matthew
Restall's *The Maya World: Yucatec Culture and Society, 1550–1850* (Stanford, CA:
Stanford University Press, 1997) provided a more comprehensive picture of Maya
society that downplayed conflict and emphasized Maya cultural survival, using
thousands of mostly unexamined "mundane" Maya-language documents,
including Yucatec wills, cabildo election records, land titles, and petitions.

Although Restall's work is doubtless the most exhaustive investigation of
Maya documents, he built on a tradition of using Yucatec Maya writings pio-
neered in Bricker, *Indian Christ*, and Philip C. Thompson, *Tekanto, a Maya Town
in Colonial Yucatan* (New Orleans: Middle American Research Institute, Tulane
University, 1999), based on research originally published in a 1978 doctoral
dissertation.

These works, of course, generally overlooked the prominence of mestizos and
Afro-Yucatecans, a situation in no small part corrected by Restall's *Black Middle*.
Recent scholarship focused mostly on the nineteenth century has brought
nuance to the bifurcated society of Spaniard and Maya, demonstrating the blurring of ethnic boundaries and identity formation that involved far more than
identifying as Spanish or Indian. See, for example, Wolfgang Gabbert, *Becoming
Maya: Ethnicity and Social Inequality in Yucatán since 1500* (Tucson: University
of Arizona Press, 2004). Long viewed as a marker of indigenous identity, the
automatic identification of Yucatec Maya speakers as essentially "Maya" by earlier historians met a serious and scholarly challenge in Gabbert's concise and
imaginative work. Gabbert examined the matrix of characteristics that informed
one's identity: patronymic group, fluency in Maya, dress, rural or urban residence, occupation, and economic status. In a similar manner, Restall showed that

during the colonial period, *Maya* was often used to refer to the language, other people, or as a descriptor for objects but rarely as a self-identifier during the colonial period. "Maya Ethnogenesis," *Journal of Latin American Anthropology* 9, no. 1 (2004): 64–89.

54. Afro-Yucatecan militiamen—especially the officer corps—were notable exceptions to this rule. The bishop of Yucatan, Pedro Agustín Estévez y Ugarte, wrote a letter to the crown in 1814 in support of the pardos' loyalty, advocating their inclusion as citizens with full rights. "Memorial del Obispo de Mérida de Yucatán," 1814, AGI, Estado 41, no. 5.

55. By contrast, Bertrand, *Grandeza y miseria*, points out that in other regions of New Spain—especially before 1750—marrying into prominent creole families was commonplace on the part of recently arrived peninsular administrators.

56. For a contrasting view, see Adrian J. Pearce, *The Origins of Bourbon Reform in Spanish South America, 1700–1763* (New York: Palgrave Macmillan, 2014). Pearce asserts that "important change and innovation came to the Spanish colonies during the first decades of Bourbon rule" (9). While certain regions of Spanish America—especially South America—did experience significant changes, peripheral regions changed less. Indeed, most major changes imposed on Yucatan—the restructuring to the militias, limits on the clergy, extinction of the encomienda, and the imposition of the intendancy system—took place after 1763.

57. Stanley J. Stein and Barbara H. Stein, *Apogee of Empire: Spain and New Spain in the Age of Charles III, 1759–1789* (Baltimore: Johns Hopkins University Press, 2003), 27.

58. Restall, *Black Middle*, 155–77. See also Ben Vinson III, *Bearing Arms for His Majesty: The Free-Colored Militia in Colonial Mexico* (Stanford, CA: Stanford University Press, 2001).

59. Patch, *Maya and Spaniard*, 204–5.

60. Farriss, *Maya Society*, 355.

61. To provide just one of several examples that will be examined in more depth, in 1790 the juez español and subdelegado of Baca sided with the Maya cabildo in petitioning Gálvez to suspend construction on the church due to the destitution of its indigenous parishioners. Gálvez ruled in favor of the Mayas allied with the Spanish authorities and ordered a halt to the construction. "Petición de las autoridades y vecinos para que suspende la fabrica de la iglesia por su mucha pobreza y necesidad que tienen de dedicarse a sus labranzas," Baca, 1790, Archivo General del Estado de Yucatán (AGEY), Colonial, Ayuntamientos, vol. 1, exp. 3, ff. 1–6.

62. Tulane Latin American Library Manuscript Collection (T-LAL/MC), Viceregal and Ecclesiastical Manuscript Collection (VEMC) 50, 1795, exp. 2, f. 22v.

63. "Expediente Reservado, que comprehende ciertos procedimientos observados en el Padre Cura del Pueblo de Chiquinsonot," 1796, AGN, Criminal 335, exp. 2, cuad. 56, f. 161.

64. Three previous authors provided concise narratives of the assassination that were more literary than historical. Dramatist and novelist Angeles Rubio-Argüelles found the material in the case fascinating enough to write a short, dramatic—but far from complete—account of the murder trial. *Asesinato en Yucatán: Verídica historia del alevoso asesinato cometido en la ciudad de Mérida el año 1792, en la persona de don Lucas de Gálvez, Gobernador, Capitán General e Intendente de la Provincia de Yucatán* (Ediciones A. R-A., 1956). One of the cofounders of PAN (Partido Acción Nacional), Gustavo Molina Font, provided a more accurate summary of the main events in *Gesta de los Mayas: Y otros relatos del Viejo Yucatán* (Mexico City: M. León Sánchez, 1965). Molina Font's brief sketch omits a few key names, events, and individuals—such as the identity of doña Casiana Melo and Dr. don Francisco de Guillén's key role in the prosecution—and makes a few other errors that will be discussed but provides a fairly accurate summary. In his preface, Juan de Dios Pérez Galaz qualified his own concise recounting of the killing of don Lucas as "not a final work," based exclusively on sources available in Mérida, without access to the documents in the AGN or the AGI. Even so, his book provides an adequate general outline of the events of 22 June 1792 and after, with the added benefit of providing a twentieth-century local historian's perspective on Gálvez's legacy. *El asesinato de dn. Lucas de Gálvez (Un pasaje de la historia de Yucatán)* (Campeche: Talleres Linotipográficos del Gobierno del Estado de Campeche, 1942), n.p.

CHAPTER 1

1. His full title, as it appears in the passages recording his death, was "Señor don Lucas de Gálvez Montes de Oca, Comendador de Ballaga y Algarga en el Orden de Calatrava, Yntendente Governador y Capitan General."

2. "De la causa formada en averiguación de los agresores," 1794, AGI, México 3036, no. 120, test. 1, cuad. 3, ff. 15–16.

3. "Expediente de información y licencia de pasajero a indias del capitán de navío Lucas de Gálvez," 1787, AGI, Contratación 5531, no. 4, ramo 20.

4. Ibid. Don José de Gálvez used his influence to place many distant relatives, close associates, and prominent men who married relatives into power. Horst Pietschmann, "Protoliberalismo, reformas borbónicas y revolución: La Nueva España en el últimom tercio del siglo XVIII," in *Interpretaciones del siglo XVIII mexicano: El impacto de las reformas borbónicas*, ed. Josefina Zoraida Vázquez (Mexico City: Nueva Imagen, 1991), 33–34. Another Gálvez did have a role in an earlier promotion granted to don Lucas: Don Matías de Gálvez, as governor of Louisiana in 1784, did intervene on behalf of his cousin in his appointment to commander of the *San Felipe*. Rubio-Argüelles, *Asesinato en Yucatán*, 11–13. In her short account, Rubio-Argüelles only used sources from Spain's Archivo General de Indias rather than the more detailed record of the case found in Mexico's AGN.

5. "Blasón y Genealogía de la casa de los Gálvez de Macharaviaya, Don Ramón Zazo y Ortega, Cronista, y Rey de Armas Numerario de la Catholica Magestad del Rey nuestro Señor (que Dios guarde) Don Carlos III, Rey de España, y de las Indias," AGI, Manuscritos. The two branches shared the same ancestor—Antón de Gálvez—"common father of the various branches of this family that have established themselves in distinct places in Andalucia" (D3). The more famous Gálvezes included the marqués de Sonora, don José de Gálvez; his brother, the viceroy of New Spain, don Matías de Gálvez; and his nephew, don Bernardo de Gálvez, who succeeded his father, don Matías, in the position of viceroy.

6. For a detailed study of the role family networks played in the placement of royal officials in the Americas, see Bertrand, *Grandeza y miseria*.

7. Eligio Ancona, *Historia de Yucatán, desde la época más remota hasta nuestros días*, vol. 2 (Mérida: Imprenta de M. Heredia Argüelles, 1878), 487.

8. Juan Francisco Molina Solís, *Historia de Yucatán durante la dominación española*, vol. 3 (Mérida: Imprenta de la Lotería del Estado, 1913), 309.

9. The summary of Ing. Llovet's inspections are held in "Visitas de inspección a Belice," 1790, AGS, Secretaría del Despacho de Guerra 6949, no. 19, ff. 146–81.

10. "Se le concedió el grado de Brigadier que solicita," 1791, AGS, Secretaría del Despacho de Guerra 7219, vol. 2, no. 118, f. 60.

11. García Bernal, *La sociedad de Yucatán*, 38–40.

12. Ana Isabel Martínez Ortega, *Estructura y configuración socioeconómica de los cabildos de Yucatán en el siglo XVIII* (Seville: Diputación Provincial de Sevilla, 1993), 127.

13. The original decree, the Reglamento Provisional, Mérida, 28 June 1786, is found in AGN, Civil 1358, and is reproduced in Edmundo O'Gorman, ed., "Incorporación de encomiendas en la provincial de Yucatán y Tabasco," *Boletín del Archivo de la Nación* 9, no. 4 (1938): 597–609.

14. Manuela Cristina García Bernal, *Desarrollo agrario en el Yucatán colonial: Repercusiones económicas y sociales* (Mérida: Universidad Autónoma de Yucatán, 2006), 275–305, explores the abolition of the encomienda and creole resistance in more detail.

15. Martínez Ortega, *Estructura y configuración*, 127.

16. "Pleito del cavildo Rex[or] y Alferez Real D. Bernardino José del Castillo y Aguirre. . . . ," 1794, AGN, Civil 847, exp. 1; "Expedientes formados en la Real Audiencia, sobre Yncorporacion a la Real Corona de las encomiendas de Yucatan y Tabasco y reglamento para la recaudacion de Tributos," 1787, AGN, Civil 1358, exp. 6; "Testimonio de una Representazion de los ministros principales de Real Hazienda de Mérida de Yucatán. . . . ," 1791, AGN, Civil 1358, exp. 9; "Real Cedula ganada por el Apoderado de los Cavalleros Encomenderos de esta Provincia sobre haver decharado su Magestad desde quando deve entenderse el abono del exceso de la alta," 1794, AGN, Civil 2152, exp. 2; "Autos seguidos a pedimento de los Encomenderos de esta Provincia de Yucatan," 1801, AGN, Civil 2152, exp. 6;

and "Sobre la cantidad que debe entregarse a los Encomenderos," 1803, AGN, Civil 2152, exp. 9.

17. "Expedientes formados en la Real Audiencia, sobre Yncorporacion a la Real Corona de las encomiendas de Yucatan y Tabasco y reglamento para la recaudacion de Tributos," 1787, AGN, Civil 1358, exp. 6, f. 1.

18. Martínez Ortega, *Estructura y configuración*, 127, 217–19.

19. "Juzgado del Alcalde. Diligencias promovidas por Antonio Martín de Tovar y Rejón, en defensa de los bienes concursadas de Juan José Rojo, cura que fue de Maxcanú," 1816, AGEY, Colonial, Judicial, vol. 2, exp. 14, f. 106. Don Alonso Manuel Peón, for example, used the title "del Orden de Calatrava Coronel de Exercito, y del Batallón de Milicias disciplinadas de esta Capital y en ella Encomendero de Indios" when giving testimony in 1795. T-LAL/MC, VEMC 50, 1795, exp. 2, f. 106.

20. "Real Cedula ganada por el Apoderado de los Cavalleros Encomenderos de esta Provincia sobre haver decharado su Magestad desde quando deve entenderse el abono del exceso de la alta," 1794, AGN, Civil 2152, exp. 2, ff. 1–40; and "Autos seguidos a pedimento de los Encomenderos de esta Provincia de Yucatan," 1801, AGN, Civil 2152, exp. 6. Ortiz represented the encomenderos in 1791 during Gálvez's tenure, and in 1794 Correa Romero represented the encomenderos of Mérida.

21. Martínez Ortega, *Estructura y configuración*, 260; and "Quinto Estado de la Causa de Homicidio," 1801, AGI, México 3037, no. 167, sub-no. 1.

22. Ibid., no. 167, sub-no. 3.

23. Ibid.

24. Ibid.

25. As late as 1795, Carlos IV needed to reiterate the abolition on servicio personal in a real cédula of 1795, at the behest of the attorney and protector of Yucatan's Indian Court and their complaints that previous decrees went unenforced. "Participando estar dispuesto por las leyes y reales cédulas cuanto conduce a la libertad de los indios, y ordenando se cuide de reformar los abusos introducidos," 1795, AGEY, Reales Cédulas, vol. 1, exp. 41. Scholars continue to debate the degree of coercion involved in the repartimiento. Foremost among economic historians taking a revisionist approach, Jeremy Baskes wrote that indigenous involvement in the system of production and credit was not forced but that "Spanish officials did not have to coerce the Indians to participate at all. Peasants partook of their own free will." *Indians, Merchants, and Markets: A Reinterpretation of the Repartimiento and Spanish-Indian Economic Relations in Colonial Oaxaca, 1750–1821* (Stanford, CA: Stanford University Press, 2000), 6. By contrast, in her more recent book, Yanna Yannakakis continued to refer to the repartimiento as a Spanish "system of *forced* production." Yannakakis justified her position arguing: "Baskes's economic analysis reveals much about the previously unknown particulars of the repartimiento, but it does not take into account sufficiently the

politics of the repartimiento and the underlying coerciveness that defined Spanish-indigenous relations in Oaxaca. Further, Baskes acknowledges that in the collection of repartimiento debts, alcaldes mayores (Spanish magistrates) and their intermediaries often resorted to violence and coercion." *Being In-between*, 19 (italics mine).

26. "Relaciones de los méritos y servicios del Capitán de Navio D. Lucas de Gálvez," 1787, AGS, Secretaría del Despacho de Guerra 7219, vol. 1, no. 3, ff. 1–5. Gálvez was promoted to the post of captain of the frigate *Santa Dorotea* in 1771 and ascended to the position of captain of the Navy in 1777. Much of his military experience took place in the Mediterranean theatre.

27. "Disciplina Militar," 1792, AGS, Secretaría del Despacho de Guerra 7208, no. 14; and "Ignacio Rodríguez Gala. Disciplina militar," 1788, AGS, Secretaría del Despacho de Guerra 7206, no. 12, copias nos. 8, 9.

28. "José Savido Vargas. Disciplina militar," 1790, AGS, Secretaría del Despacho de Guerra 7207, no. 48. The teniente del rey brought in two alcaldes and four notaries of Campeche, who testified, in a recorded contradiction of Gálvez's ruling, to his honorable behavior and contradicted Gálvez's characterization of the teniente del rey's actions.

29. "Premios. Invalidez," 1790, AGS, Secretaría del Despacho de Guerra 7207, no. 15.

30. "Antonio Bolo. Disciplina militar," 1792, AGS, Secretaría del Despacho de Guerra 7209, no. 13, ff. 64–65. The intendant died before his superiors were able to resolve the matter. These petitions reached Spain after Gálvez's death, which explains why the file includes no response to the letters.

31. Other cases include the complaint of the sergeant major of Campeche's militia, don Juan de Ojeda, over procedural irregularities involved in Gálvez's orders to bring charges for desertion against the soldier, Santiago Jiménez. "Quejas de Juan de Ojeda, sargento mayor, contra Lucas de Gálvez," 1790, AGS, Secretaría del Despacho de Guerra 7207, no. 24, ff. 134–39.

32. Jorge Victoria Ojeda described the eighteenth-century defensive reorganization of Yucatan in *Mérida de Yucatán*, 53–61. Sergio Quezada and Elda Moreno Acevedo highlighted the strategic importance of Yucatan, noting that by taking possession of both Florida and the coast of Yucatan, the English might take Spanish America "by the horns." "Del déficit a la insolvencia. Finanzas y real hacienda en Yucatán, 1760–1816," *Mexican Studies/Estudios Mexicanos* 21, no. 2 (Summer 2005): 315. The teniente del rey of Campeche, Enrique Grimarest, writing in his proposal to fortify Bacalar, emphasized the peninsula's importance in preventing contraband and defending Guatemala against English incursions. "Aumento de tropa del Presidio de Bacalar," 1787, AGS, Secretaría del Despacho de Guerra 7210, no. 67, sub-no. 25.

33. T-LAL/MC, VEMC 50, 1795, exp. 2, f. 22v.

34. "Expediente de información y licencia de pasajero a indias del capitán de navío Lucas de Gálvez," 1787, AGI, Contratación 5531, no. 4, ramo 20. In eight of the

twelve provinces, intendants automatically took over the authority conceded to governors and began holding the title of intendant and governor simultaneously. Only Guadalajara, Mexico City, Veracruz, and Yucatan retained separate governors. In addition to his limited power, Gálvez was the lowest paid of all of the intendants. Intendants in Mexico City and Veracruz were annually paid 4,000 pesos, nine of the remaining ten were paid 3,000 pesos. Only Yucatan's intendant received less, an annual salary of 2,500 pesos. Marina Mantilla Trolle, Rafael Diego-Fernández Sotelo, and Agustín Moreno Torres, eds., "El Régimen de Intendencias en la Nueva Galicia," in *Real Ordenanza para el establecimiento é instrucción de intendentes de exército y provincia en el reino de la Nueva España* (Guadalajara: Universidad de Guadalajara, 2008), 35, 41.

35. The most strident voices raised in opposition to the new governor came from the members of the ayuntamiento (another term for cabildo)—especially the regidores (councilmen) don Ignacio Rendón and don Manuel Bolio—and don Enrique de los Reyes, a militia captain. They complained of his disrespect for them and his unwarranted harsh punishments. "José Merino Cevallos. Empleos," 1788, AGS, Secretaría del Despacho de Guerra 7218, no. 3, f. 21.

36. Ibid., ff. 26, 27.

37. Ibid., ff. 23, 24. Not surprisingly, this cohort found allies in the Quijanos.

38. Molina Solís, *Historia de Yucatán*, vol. 3, gives a critical account of the influence of fray Luis in secular affairs, while Crescencio Carrillo y Ancona's *El obispado de Yucatán: Historia de su fundación y de sus obispos desde el siglo XVI hasta el XIX, seguida de las constituciones sinodales de la diocesis y otros documentos relativos* (Mérida: Imprenta y Lit. de Ricardo B. Caballero, 1895) gives a more sympathetic treatment of the bishop by a contemporary of Molina Solís.

39. "Representacion del Juez Comisionado," 1793, AGI, México 3039, no. 82, s/f; and "Testimonio de lo Contenido en el Quaderno Reservado num° 42," 1795, AGI, México 3040, no. 7, ff. 36–38.

40. "Testimonio de lo Contenido en el Quaderno Reservado num° 42," 1795, AGI, México 3040, no. 7, ff. 51–55.

41. T-LAL/MC, VEMC 50, 1795, exp. 2, ff. 62v–68.

42. Ibid., ff. 81v–82.

43. Patch, *Maya and Spaniard*, 188.

44. Ibid., 188.

45. "Reservado. Sobre el actual gobierno en Yucatan," 1791, AGN, Civil 1454, exp. 6. As part of the major reorganization of government in New Spain under the intendancy system in 1786, Carlos III created the position of subdelegado as one of the new administrative posts to oversee sections of territory known as *partidos*. Late colonial Yucatan had twelve partidos. They answered directly to the intendants.

46. Carrillo y Ancona, *El obispado de Yucatán*, 2:945–46.

47. The bishop enjoyed at least 25,000 pesos of net worth at the time of his death. "Sobre los explios del señor arzobispo que fue de Yucatán, don fray Luis de Piña y Mazo," 1809, AGN, Obispos y Arzobispos 9, ff. 361–67.

48. Carrillo y Ancona, *El obispado de Yucatán*, 2:945.

49. "El Capitan general Yntendente de Yucatan sobre que se determinen prontamente varias representaciones que tiene dirigidas a la Real Audiencia," 1792, AGN, Civil 1519, exp. 26.

50. "Reservado. Sobre el actual gobierno en Yucatan," 1791, AGN, Civil 1454, exp. 6. Fray Luis complained that Gálvez had not named don Manuel Antolín, a popular (according to him) *capitán a guerra*, to the position of subdelegado of the Partido de la Costa despite being well liked by his military subordinates. In October 1792, just four months after Gálvez's death, the bishop's sway eased Antolín's appointment to the previously denied post. "Manuel Antolín. Empleos," 1793, AGS, Secretaría del Despacho de Guerra 7210, no. 18, f. 55.

51. "El Capitan general Yntendente de Yucatan sobre que se determinen prontamente varias representaciones que tiene dirigidas a la Real Audiencia," 1792, AGN, Civil 1519, exp. 26.

52. Ibid. Authorities moved too slowly to resolve either suit before Gálvez's death. The fiscal of the Audiencia de México, don José de Yturrigaray, noted in the margins of the concluding paragraphs of the intendant's complaint in 1804, after an inexplicable delay, that both protagonists were dead. Fray Luis's complaint appears without any official response whatsoever. Ibid.

53. Ancona, *Historia de Yucatán*, 2:488, and Molina Solís, *Historia de Yucatán*, 3:307.

54. "Lucas Gálvez. Grados," 1791, AGS, Secretaría del Despacho de Guerra 7219, no. 3.

55. Horst Pietschmann, *Las reformas borbónicas y el sistema de intendencias de Nueva España*, trans. Rolf Roland Meyer Misteli (Mexico City: Fondo de Cultura Económica, 1996), 4.

56. One example of Madrid's trial-and-error approach to the reorganization of its American territories comes from the changing policies of the eighteenth century toward the repartimiento. In 1751 Ferdinand VI legalized the institution before his successor, Carlos III, prohibited it in 1786. Baskes, *Indians, Merchants, and Markets*, 42–46.

57. "Antonio Rodríguez de Cárdenas, teniente gobernador, se queja del capitán general por el modo de llevar un recurso, contra Juan José de Fierros, interpuesto por aquel," 1791, AGS, Secretaría del Despacho de Guerra 7207, no. 70.

58. Pietschmann, *Las reformas borbónicas*, examines the implementation of the intendancy system and the influence of French precedents and the Enlightenment, as well as Spain's own imprint on the Bourbon institution. Other subsequent works—Pietschmann's work first appeared in German in 1972—have placed greater emphasis on the Spanish influence rather than the French origins.

59. Pietschmann, *Las reformas borbónicas*, 29–35. The *Ordenanza de 4 de julio de 1718 para el establecimiento, e instrucción de Intendentes, y para Tesorero General, Pagadores, y Contadores de los Exercitos, y Provincias* established the post in Spain. Though predecessors to the intendants—governors—had exercised some limited control over financial and military matters, the Real Ordenanza de Intendentes granted the intendants more direct authority over such matters than their predecessors. Pietschmann, *Las reformas borbónicas*, 251.

60. Ibid., 34.

61. Beatriz Rojas, "Orden de gobierno y organización del territorio: Nueva España hacia una nueva territorialidad, 1786–1825," in *Las reformas borbónicas, 1750–1808*, ed. Clara García Ayluardo (Mexico City: Fondo de Cultura Económica, 2010), 144.

62. Luis Navarro García, *Las reformas borbónicas en América: El plan de intendencias y su aplicación* (Seville: Universidad de Sevilla, 1995), 84–89.

63. Pietschmann, *Las reformas borbónicas*, 134–42.

64. Ibid., 258.

65. Sabido de Vargas wrote the first letter to reach the viceroy informing him of the assassination, dated 26 June 1792. He wrote that he was setting off immediately to take possession of the intendancy, though four days had passed since the assassination. "Asesinato de Lucas de Gálvez Capitán general de Yucatán," 1792, AGI, Estado 35, no. 1.

66. "Sobre el homicidio de D. Lucas de Galvez Capitan Gral. de Yucatan," 1793, AGN, Criminal 471, f. 155v.

67. "Representación de Fierros," 1793, AGI, México 3039, no. 82, s/f.

68. "Quinto estado de la causa de homicidio cometido en la persona de Dn. Lucas de Gálvez," 1793, AGI, México 3037, no. 33, s/f.

69. "Da cuenta a V. M. del homicidio alevosamente executado en la Persona de Su Gobᵒʳ Yntendente y Capitán General Lucas de Gálvez," 25 June 1792, AGI, México 3037, no. 41, s/f.

CHAPTER 3

1. "Cúmulo de Bandos Promulgados," 1792, AGN, Criminal 302, no. 8, ff. 332–33.

2. "Quaderno numero 32 formado en virtud de lo mandado en Auto de 15 de Abril," 1794, AGN, Criminal 322, parte 1, exp. 1, f. 38. An original copy of this bando was included in the confiscated papers of a subdelegado imprisoned later in the case. Justicias were the other members of the Maya ruling class who assisted Piñeres on the native cabildo. The lowest-ranking non-Maya local authority in the countryside, the juez español, answered directly to subdelegados. Cabos militares served in a position similar to juez español, with both military and law enforcement functions.

3. "Memorial ajustado de la causa formada sobre el homicidio del Sr. Don Lucas Galvez," 1800, AGN, Criminal 287, f. 235.

4. "Memorial ajustado de la causa formada sobre el homicidio del Sr. Don Lucas Galvez—Lista de Reos," 1800, AGN, Criminal 287, f. 1.

5. While most criados that appear in the trial records were children and adolescents, some criados continued in a state of servitude into adulthood. Chapter 4 discusses criados in greater depth.

6. "Memorial ajustado de la causa formada sobre el homicidio del Sr. Don Lucas Galvez—Lista de Reos," 1800, AGN, Criminal 287, f. 1.

7. Ibid.; and "De la causa formada en averiguación de los agresores," 1794, AGI, México 3036, no. 120, f. 22v.

8. Ibid., f. 22v.

9. "Branciforte sobre los franceses existentes en aquel reino," 1796, AGI, Estado 24, no. 19, sub-no. 9.

10. "Parte 4ª del Memorial ajustado de la causa formada sobre el homicidio del Sr. D. Lucas de Galvez," 1800, AGN, Criminal 291, f. 170v. Castro, the notary, testified that he was a man of "extragadas costumbres" (f. 170v).

11. Ibid., f. 175. The notes taken at the time of their arrest were deemed unimportant and do not appear in the trial transcripts.

12. "Testimonio de varias diligencias practicadas en la causa sobre el homicidio que se executó en la persona del Señor don Lucas de Gálvez," 1793, AGN, Criminal 310, cuad. 2, letra B, ff. 188–89. Even fewer details exist for the arrest of Felipe Cárdenas, "alias Sancho," whose name appears on the Lista de Reos. Prosecutors later complained of the absolute lack of information regarding his imprisonment.

13. "Diligencias para averiguar el Agresor, y complices de la alevosa muerte executada en la respectable persona del Sr. Intendente don Lucas de Galvez," 1792, AGN, Criminal 302, no. 5, ff. 240–42.

14. "Testimonio del Quaderno 2º de las diligencias practicadas en la Causa sobre el homicidio del Sr. Dn. Lucas de Gálvez," 1794, AGI, México 3036, no. 119, f. 2.

15. "De la causa formada en averiguación de los agresores," 1794, AGI, México 3036, no. 120, ff. 41–42.

16. "Memorial ajustado de la causa formada sobre el homicidio del Sr. Don Lucas Galvez," 1800, AGN, Criminal 287, f. 235.

17. Ibid., ff. 246–50. The later outside prosecutor, Dr. don Francisco de Guillén, noted that only the pressure from interrogators made Lara change his testimony rather than any likelihood that Matos had any role in the crime.

18. "Testimonio del Quaderno 1ro de la Causa formada sobre el homicidio executado en la Persona del Sr. Dn. Lucas de Gálvez," 1792, AGI, México 3036, no. 118, f. 4.

19. "Memorial ajustado de la causa formada sobre el homicidio del Sr. Don Lucas Galvez—Lista de Reos," 1800, AGN, Criminal 287, f. 1.

20. "Memorial ajustado de la causa formada sobre el homicidio del Sr. Don Lucas Galvez," 1800, AGN, Criminal 287, f. 9.

21. "Testimonio del Cuaderno 1ro de la Causa formada sobre el homicidio evacuado en la persona del Sr. Dn. Lucas de Gálvez," 1792, AGI, México 3036, no. 118, f. 19.

22. "Memorial ajustado de la causa formada sobre el homicidio del Sr. Don Lucas Galvez—Lista de Reos," 1800, AGN, Criminal 287, f. 1.

23. "Testimonio de diligencias relativas a la averiguacion de si Rafael Luna Pardo fue el autor o complize del homicidio executado en la respectable Persona del Sr. Brigadier don Lucas de Gálvez," 1792, AGN, Criminal 299, cuad. 3, f. 302.

24. Ibid., f. 310.

25. Ibid., f. 302.

26. "Testimonio del Quaderno 1ro de la Causa formada sobre el homicidio executado en la Persona del Sr. Dn. Lucas de Gálvez," 1792, AGI, México 3036, no. 118, f. 19.

27. "Testimonio de diligencias relativas a la averiguacion de si Rafael Luna Pardo fue el autor o complize del homicidio executado en la respectable Persona del Sr. Brigadier don Lucas de Gálvez," 1792, AGN, Criminal 299, cuad. 3, ff. 301–4.

28. "Diligencias relativas a la averiguación de si Rafael Luna Pardo fu el autor o complice del homicidio executado en la respetable persona del Sr. Brig^er dn. Lucas de Gálvez," 1792, AGN, Criminal 302, no. 3, ff. 236–37.

29. Ibid., 236v.

30. "Testimonio de diligencias relativas a la averiguacion de si Rafael Luna Pardo fue el autor o complize del homicidio executado en la respectable Persona del Sr. Brigadier don Lucas de Gálvez," 1792, AGN, Criminal 299, cuad. 3, f. 297.

31. Ibid., f. 297. The transcript reads: "Qué vicios son los que le dominan por su fragilidad, si se ha mantenido ocioso por algún tiempo?"

32. Ibid., ff. 77–78.

33. John K. Chance and William B. Taylor classified gilders as "high-status artisans." "Estate and Class in a Colonial City: Oaxaca in 1792," *Comparative Studies in Society and History* 19, no. 4 (October 1977), 467.

34. "Testimonio de diligencias relativas a la averiguacion de si Rafael Luna Pardo fue el autor o complize del homicidio executado en la respectable Persona del Sr. Brigadier don Lucas de Gálvez," 1792, AGN, Criminal 299, cuad. 3, ff. 81v, 117v–18v, 126–27v, 129–30. Juan José Mayor's militia rank is found in "Milicias Blancas de Campeche," 1790, AGS, Secretaría del Despacho de Guerra 7299, no. 5, f. 86v.

35. "Testimonio de diligencias relativas a la averiguacion de si Rafael Luna Pardo fue el autor o complize del homicidio executado en la respectable Persona del Sr. Brigadier don Lucas de Gálvez," 1792, AGN, Criminal 299, cuad. 3, ff. 77–78, 102v.

36. "De la causa formada en averiguación de los agresores," 1794, AGI, México 3036, no. 120, ff. 58–87.

37. Ibid., ff. 58–60. Juan Pinzón identified Matos as his *pariente*, or relative, without specifying the nature of their relationship. Pinzón is listed as a *subteniente*, a

rank below lieutenant and above first sergeant, on a militia roster of 1789 with the Fourth Company of Yucatan's pardo division. "Pardos Tiradores de Yucatán," 1789, AGS, Secretaría del Despacho de Guerra 7299, no. 6, f. 100.

38. "De la causa formada en averiguación de los agresores," 1794, AGI, México 3036, no. 120, ff. 60–62.

39. Ibid., ff. 62–63. Ignacio de Lara served as a blacksmith and a first sergeant in the Second Company of the pardo militia in the 1789 militia roll. "Pardos Tiradores de Yucatán," 1789, AGS, Secretaría del Despacho de Guerra 7299, no. 6, f. 98.

40. A second, younger Juan Pinzón appears as a sixteen-year-old single shoemaker with the rank of a soldier in the Second Company of the pardo militia roster. Ibid., f. 88.

41. "De la causa formada en averiguación de los agresores," 1794, AGI, México 3036, no. 120, ff. 85v–86v.

42. Fictive kinship ties establish "a ceremonially-sanctioned alliance among individuals." Compadrazgo, or co-parenthood, is the most common form of fictive kinship in Latin America. Manuel L. Carlos, "Fictive Kinship and Modernization in Mexico: A Comparative Analysis," *Anthropological Quarterly* 46, no. 2 (April 1973), 76.

43. "De la causa formada en averiguación de los agresores," 1794, AGI, México 3036, no. 120, ff. 86–87.

44. Ibid., f. 87.

45. Restall, *Black Middle*, provides the most comprehensive treatment of Afro-Yucatecans in colonial Yucatan.

46. "Diligencias practicadas por el Sr. Manuel del Castillo Negrete," 1802, AGN, Criminal 329, cuad. 1, ff. 2–4. Such expert tradesmen frequently appeared in criminal cases to determine the place of origin of craft items. To confirm the prohibited English origin of questionable items under investigation in a case involving accusations of contraband in 1791, don Manuel Brito and don Francisco Vallado were called in to verify the foreign origin of several items, including gunpowder, fabric, and aguardiente. "Lucas Vargas y complices—Polvora," 1791, AGI, México 3069, f. 18v.

47. The list itself does not identify the ethnicity of the gremio's (guild) members, but using Maya surnames as an identifier for indigenous blacksmiths and cross-checking the *herreros* who appear on both the free black and white voluntary militia rolls that list professions demonstrate the multiracial nature of Mérida's master blacksmiths. The lists of the militia of the *voluntarios blancos* and *pardos tiradores* of Mérida appear in "Infantería de Voluntarios Blancos. Mérida de Yucatán," 1789, AGS, Secretaría del Despacho de Guerra 7299, no. 3; and "Pardos Tiradores de Yucatán," 1789, AGS, Secretaría del Despacho de Guerra 7299, no. 6. The gremio list appears in "De la causa formada en averiguación de los agresores," 1794, AGI, México 3036, no. 120, ff. 26v–27. Despite the identification of many of the units as *milicias blancos*, many mestizos served in the white militias as well. The 1809 census from the Barrio of San Cristóbal, located in the one quadrant for

which detailed records survive from this year, lists several mestizos who served in the white militia. "Padrón del tercer cuartel de la ciudad de Mérida, formado por el Teniente Dn. Manuel Buendia por orden del gobernador Pérez Valdelomar," 1809, AGEY, Colonial, Censos y Padrones, vol. 1, exp. 1B. A short passage in the *Reglamento para las Milicias de Infantería de la Provincia de Yucatan, y Campeche, aprobado por S. M. y mandado que se oberven todos su Articulos* (Madrid: Imprenta de P. Marín, 1778), in reference to the white militias of Mérida, confirms that many mestizos were among the ranks of the supposedly white militias: "Las quatro Compañías que existen en Mérida; se compondran de la gente de mejor talla, y costumbres que haya en su recinto, y barrios, dependientes de las clases de Españoles, y Mestizos" (2). On occasion, even indios hidalgos, belonging to a category of Maya nobility that will be examined further in chapter 6, served in the nominally white militia units.

48. "De la causa formada en averiguación de los agresores," 1794, AGI, México 3036, no. 120, ff. 26v–27.

49. In *Black Middle*, Restall wrote, "For most of the seventeenth and eighteenth centuries almost all the blacksmiths in Mérida and Campeche were black" (119). Though the majority of blacksmiths in Mérida were of Afro-Yucatecan descent, a significant number of nonblack artisans were also metalworkers. Twenty-seven total militiamen of the white volunteers identified as blacksmiths compared with eighty-seven Afro-Yucatecan blacksmiths, though the ranks of white militiamen included many mestizos as well.

50. "Diligencias practicadas por el Sr. Manuel del Castillo Negrete," 1802, AGN, Criminal 329, cuad. 1, ff. 2–4.

51. "Sobre el homicidio de D. Lucas de Galvez Capitan Gral. de Yucatan," 1793, AGN, Criminal 471, ff. 94v–98v.

52. "Testimonio del Quaderno 2º de las diligencias practicadas en la Causa sobre el homicidio del Sr. Dn. Lucas de Gálvez," 1794, AGI, México 3036, no. 119, ff. 57–59; and "Sobre el homicidio de D. Lucas de Galvez Capitan Gral. de Yucatan," 1793, AGN, Criminal 471, f. 202.

53. For a more thorough treatment of urban Mayas working as artisans, see Mark W. Lentz, "Criados, Caciques y Artesanos: Mayas Urbanos de Yucatán a Finales del Siglo Dieciocho," in *Los indios y las ciudades de Nueva España*, ed. Felipe Castro Gutiérrez (Mexico City: Universidad Autónoma de México/Instituto de Investigaciones Históricas, 2010).

54. "De la causa formada en averiguación de los agresores," 1794, AGI, México 3036, no. 120, f. 27.

55. "Sobre el homicidio de D. Lucas de Galvez Capitan Gral. de Yucatan," 1793, AGN, Criminal 471, f. 107.

56. Although by all accounts Matos had no part whatsoever in the assassination, he had the misfortune of belonging to several social categories associated with criminality in the late eighteenth century. Authorities suspected the artisan class

of having a penchant for delinquent behavior due to their declining wages, the impact of inflation that hit them hard, and increased unemployment. Furthermore, Matos was a pardo. More so than indigenous subjects, mestizos and pardos were seen to have an inclination toward crime. Finally, the painter was young, male, and single—characteristics that drew the attention of law enforcement agents. Authorities sought to both punish crime and impose social order, and Matos was perceived as a threat to this order. He was wrongly implicated in the crime that brought him under scrutiny, but demographic factors and prevailing notions regarding criminality likely contributed to his long stay in prison. See Haslip-Viera, *Crime and Punishment*, 49–62.

57. "Sobre el homicidio de D. Lucas de Galvez Capitan Gral. de Yucatan," 1793, AGN, Criminal 471, ff. 95–101.

58. Ibid., ff. 108–9.

59. Ibid., f. 110.

60. Ibid., f. 111.

61. Ibid., f. 112.

62. "De la causa formada en averiguación de los agresores," 1794, AGI, México 3036, no. 120, ff. 45v–46.

63. Vinson, in *Bearing Arms for his Majesty*, devoted chapter 5, "The *Fuero* Privilege," to the expansion and eventual curtailment of rights for free black militiamen during the early eighteenth century, with special attention to regional variations.

64. "Memorial del Obispo de Mérida de Yucatán, a S. M., solicitando se concedan los derechos de ciudadanos a los militares de la División de Pardos," 1814, AGI, Estado 41, no. 45.

65. Mention of Pérez's militia service is found in "Pardos Tiradores de Yucatán," 1789, AGS, Secretaría del Despacho de Guerra 7299, no. 6, f. 29. Angulo is identified as a mestizo in the 1809 census of the Barrio of San Cristóbal. "Padrón del tercer cuartel de la ciudad de Mérida, formado por el Teniente Dn. Manuel Buendia por orden del gobernador Pérez Valdelomar," 1809, AGEY, Colonial, Censos y Padrones, vol. 1, exp. 1B.

66. "Criminal contra Francisco Canché, por haver robado a Casimiro Chay, una Mula Verdoza mojina, que vendió a Pedro Catilla de Hunucmá en 125," 1802, AGN, Criminal 361, exp. 6, ff. 342–47.

67. Ibid., f. 335.

68. Ibid., ff. 340–44. Canché never explained nor did interrogators ask him how he came up with the name Pedro Castillo.

69. "Juan Rosa Estrella. Procesos," 1797, AGS, Secretaría del Despacho de Guerra 7213, no. 15.

70. "Testimonio de la Denuncia echa por Dn. Esteban de Castro, contra el Agresor del Omicidio perpetrado en la persona del Señor Don Lucas de Gálvez," 1801, AGN, Criminal 484, exp. 2, f. 52v. Although this volume deals with the Gálvez

assassination trial, it includes a brief unrelated section recounting the jailing and release of prisoners for public drunkenness.

71. "Pardos Tiradores de Yucatán" 1789, AGS, Secretaría del Despacho de Guerra 7299, no. 6; and "Infantería de Voluntarios Blancos. Mérida de Yucatán," 1789, AGS, Secretaría del Despacho de Guerra 7299, no. 3. The largest number of Mérida-based white militiamen includes the *granaderos*, or grenadiers, and the first three companies. The first four companies of the pardo militia were based in the provincial capital as well. The smaller total numbers of whites working in the same professions resulted because fewer members of the officers of this militia—as well as some of the rank and file—did not have a profession listed, suggesting that fewer of them needed to perform manual labor to earn a living. Furthermore, the pay scale between the two militia divisions—free black and white—differed significantly. For example, the regularly paid officer corps of the pardo militia included eight captains paid 11 pesos a month, eight lieutenants paid 8 pesos a month, eight subtenientes paid 6 pesos a month, eight sergeants paid 5 pesos a month, and eight drummers paid 3 pesos, 6 reales a month. The monthly pay of the officer corps of the voluntarios blancos was much higher, with eight sergeant majors paid 100 pesos a month, one ayudante mayor paid 50 pesos a month, nine lieutenants paid 30 pesos, 6 reales a month, nine first sergeants paid 18 pesos a month, fourteen second sergeants paid 10 pesos a month, one drummer major paid 18 pesos a month, eighteen drummers paid 6 pesos a month, twenty-one first corporals paid 7 pesos a month, twenty-one second corporals paid 6 pesos a month, and one surgeon paid 30 pesos a month. As a result of this discrepancy in pay, many officers of equal rank in the free black militia had to work to make ends meet. "Infantería de Voluntarios Blancos. Mérida de Yucatán," 1789, AGS, Secretaría del Despacho de Guerra 7299, no. 3, f. 50; and "Pardos Tiradores de Yucatán," 1789, AGS, Secretaría del Despacho de Guerra 7299, no. 6, f. 105.

72. "Padrón del tercer cuartel de la ciudad de Mérida, formado por el Teniente Dn. Manuel Buendia por orden del gobernador Pérez Valdelomar," 1809, AGEY, Colonial, Censos y Padrones, vol. 1, exp. 1B. Censuses were taken for the city center and the three other quarters, but the documents range from being completely to partially destroyed and incomplete, with the exception of the remarkably intact census of the Barrio of San Cristóbal.

73. Ibid.

74. "Parte 4ª del Memorial ajustado de la causa formada sobre el homicidio del Sr. D. Lucas de Galvez," 1800, AGN, Criminal 291, ff. 176–77.

75. "Relación de varios recursos hechos por el Cura Correa," 1800, AGN, Criminal 293, cap. 2, f. 77.

76. "Testimonio de lo contenido en el expediente reservado numº 42," 1795, AGN, Criminal 325, f. 9.

77. For the fullest treatment of the casta category "mestizo," see Joanne M. Rappaport, *The Disappearing Mestizo: Configuring Difference in the Colonial New Kingdom of Granada* (Durham, NC: Duke University Press, 2014).
78. Restall, *Black Middle*, 89, 100–1, 173.
79. The occupational information for the militiamen lodged in Francisco Ek's inn is found in "Infantería de Voluntarios Blancos. Mérida de Yucatán," 1789, AGS, Secretaría del Despacho de Guerra 7299, no. 3, f. 45. In their formal declarations, the lodgers gave their age, name, and militia affiliation—most likely to remind their interrogators of their fueros—but not their professions.
80. "De la causa formada en averiguación de los agresores," 1794, AGI, México 3036, no. 120, ff. 30–35.
81. Rappaport, *Disappearing Mestizo*, 10.
82. "Legitimaciones," vol. 1, 1767–1859, Archivo Histórico del Arzobispado de Yucatán (AHAY), s/f.
83. "Parte 4ª del Memorial ajustado de la causa formada sobre el homicidio del Sr. D. Lucas de Galvez," 1800, AGN, Criminal 291, f. 176.
84. "Diligencias que se practicaron en virtud del homicidio que sufrio el Sr. Brigadier Lucas de Gálvez," 1793, AGN, Criminal 302, exp. 1, ff. 53v–54.
85. "Prosigue la relación de todos las especies e indicios que produce el sumario contra el Tenᵗᵉ Don Toribio del Mazo," 1793, AGN, Criminal 295, f. 56v.
86. "Expediente de la muerte del Gobernador Lucas de Gálvez," 1794, AGI, México 3040, f. 48.
87. "Sobre el homicidio de D. Lucas de Galvez Capitan Gral. de Yucatan," 1793, AGN, Criminal 471, f. 210.
88. In 1794 Mayas made up about 52 percent (14,751) of Mérida's population of 28,392. Census of Mérida, 1794, AGN, Historia 522, exp. 257, reproduced as appendix A in J. Ignacio Rubio Mañé, comp., *Archivo de la historia de Yucatán, Campeche y Tabasco* (Mexico City: Imprenta Aldina, Robredo y Rosell, 1942), 210–34.
89. "De la causa formada en averiguación de los agresores," 1794, AGI, México 3036, no. 120, ff. 31–32.
90. R. Douglas Cope, *The Limits of Racial Domination: Plebeian Society in Colonial Mexico City, 1660–1720* (Madison: University of Wisconsin Press, 1994), 10.
91. Libro de Protocolos, 1791–1792, Archivo Notarial del Estado de Yucatan (ANEY), vol. 29, ff. 18, 24, compact disc 29. The holdings of the ANEY are only available digitally. The collection is now stored in the AGEY. Xix had served in the post of town crier of Mérida since at least 1787, when he announced an auction of confiscated contraband goods. "Lucas Vargas y complices—Polvora," 1791, AGI, México 3069, f. 30. The term *indio ladino* in Yucatan remains a poorly understood descriptor. In another important attempt to understand the role of urban Indians, Pedro Bracamonte y Sosa pinpointed fluency in Castilian and Spanish surnames as the two markers of ladino identity. See "Los solares urbanos de

Mérida y la propiedad territorial indígena en el Yucatán colonial," in *Urbi indi-ano: La larga marcha a la ciudad diversa*, eds. Pablo Yanes, Virginia Molina, and Óscar González (Mexico City: Universidad Autónoma de la Ciudad de México, 2005), 136.

92. Jay Kinsbruner, *The Colonial Spanish-American City: Urban Life in the Age of Atlantic Capitalism* (Austin: University of Texas Press, 2005), 34. The position was often held by nonwhites elsewhere. In the Eastern Andes, blacks often worked as town criers. Lolita Gutiérrez Brockington, *Blacks, Indians, and Spaniards in the Eastern Andes: Reclaiming the Forgotten in Colonial Mizque, 1550–1782* (Lincoln: University of Nebraska Press, 2007), 63, 175.

93. "Demanda puesta por el Sindico del Convento de este Pueblo sobre cantidad de pesos de principal y reditos que Don Juan Lopez está deviendo," 1793, AGEY, Colonial, Judicial, vol. 1, exp. 10, f. 33.

94. "Testimonio de Diligencias que justifican la aprehencion de varias mercaderias executada en el varrio de Sn. Tiago de esta Ciudad," 1768, AGI, México 3053.

95. "Lucas Vargas y complices—Polvora," 1791, AGI, México 3069, exp. 1, f. 48v. Indios ladinos did not monopolize the post, however. A casta or creole named Antonio Chacón served as the pregonero público in the 1780s. "El obispo pide a S. M atender la permuta que los presbíteros, Juan Meneses del curato de Muná y Juan José Gómez del curato de Chichimilá, voluntariamente celebraron de sus respectivos beneficios," 1788, AGI, México 3069, no. 31, f. 19v.

96. "Testimonio del Quaderno 2º de las diligencias practicadas en la Causa sobre el homicidio del Sr. Dn. Lucas de Gálvez," 1794, AGI, México 3036, no. 119, f. 23. Since she identified herself as the widow of don Juan Cantón, this doña María Josefa Pérez was apparently not the same individual as the woman of the same name—María Pérez, wife of José Bermejo.

97. Ibid., f. 20.

98. Mark A. Burkholder and D. S. Chandler, *Biographical Dictionary of Audiencia Ministers in the Americas, 1847–1821* (Westport, CT: Greenwood Press, 1982), 52.

99. "Da qüenta a V. Exa de su llegada a Mérida de Yucatan," 1793, AGI, México 3036, no. 64.

CHAPTER 4

1. Piñeres had begun his term as lieutenant governor in his late twenties. He had barely turned thirty at the time of the assassination. "Gutiérrez de Piñeres y del Arenal Pariente y González de Perdueles, Fernando," 1807, Archivo Histórico Nacional (AHN), Secretaría de las Órdenes Civiles—Orden de Carlos III, exp. 1357.

2. "Lucas Galvez. Procesos," 1792, AGS, Secretaría del Despacho de Guerra 7219, no. 3, f. 109; and "Testimonio del Cuaderno 5º de la Causa formada en averigua-ción de los agresores del homicidio executado en la persona del Sr. Dn. Lucas de

Gálvez," 1792, AGI, México 3036, no. 122, f. 10v. While attacks by unconquered and rebellious Mayas from the uncontrolled interior were rare, they did take place on occasion. For accounts of two eighteenth-century attacks by Mayas on soldiers or their companions, see Mark W. Lentz, "Black Belizeans and Fugitive Mayas: Interracial Encounters on the Edge of Empire, 1750–1803," *The Americas* 70, no. 4 (April 2014): 645–75.

3. "Lucas Galvez. Procesos," 1792, AGS, Secretaría del Despacho de Guerra 7219, no. 3, f. 105.

4. Ibid., f. 105.

5. Ibid., f. 109. According to Bodega's complaint, Troncoso's reluctance to assign him a sizeable escort came from the president's apprehension over sending his son— the officer most likely to receive the assignment—away from Guatemala into dangerous circumstances for a long period of time. Lic. Bodega also indicated that a personal dispute between Troncoso's secretary and Capt. don Salvador Tavalois, another officer whose rank made him a likely candidate to head the armed escort, also hindered his attempts to depart Guatemala with a suitable armed guard. The cost of the expedition may also have led the cash-strapped president to hesitate to expedite the journey. Bodega's travel expenses between Guatemala and Mérida eventually amounted to a sum of 495 pesos. "Testimonio del Cuaderno 5º de la Causa formada en averiguación de los agresores del homicidio executado en la persona del Sr. Dn. Lucas de Gálvez," 1792, AGI, México 3036, no. 122, ff. 4v–5.

6. "Se hace relación deel sumario formado contra el Teniente de Milicias disciplinadas de Blancos de Yucatan Dn.Toribio del Mazo," 1793, AGN, Criminal 295, cap. 3, f. 9.

7. "Testimonio de diligencias preventivas de la Causa Criminal que se ha de seguir contra el Ynfame alevozo, que asesinó al Sr. Don Lucas de Gálvez," 1792, AGN, Criminal 299, cuad. 2, ff. 250–53.

8. "Diligencias que se practicaron en virtud del homicidio que sufrio el Sr. Brigadier Lucas de Galvez," 1793, AGN, Criminal 302, exp. 1, ff. 2–3v.

9. Ibid., ff. 2–3v.

10. "Se hace relación del sumario formado contra el Teniente de Milicias disciplinadas de Blancos de Yucatan Dn.Toribio del Mazo," 1793, AGN, Criminal 295, cap. 3, ff. 3–5. The accounts of this carriage ride given by doña María and her fiancé, don Lorenzo, differ slightly. Don Lorenzo alleged that la Tesorera had invited her along on a secret errand, while his fiancée stated that doña Casiana had simply invited her along for a trip to Hacienda de Miraflores. Doña María Trinidad's version also omitted the confidential conversation between la Tesorera and her carriage driver.

11. Ibid., f. 49. In the letters between doña Casiana and don Toribio seized by Dr. Guillén and contained in "Cartas reservadas pertenecientes a la causa, sobre el homicidio executado en la persona del Sr. don Lucas de Galvez," 1795,

AGN, Criminal 322, parte 2, doña Casiana alternated between addressing don Toribio as "compadre" and "amado dueño de mi corazón" (beloved owner of my heart), depending on her mood. Other testimony confirms don Toribio's ties of compadrazgo to his supposed lover.

12. "Prosigue la relación de todos las especies e indicios que produce el sumario contra el Tente D^n Toribio del Mazo," 1793, AGN, Criminal 295, f. 50. According to Dr. Guillén, Tobi "dio indicantes de que estimava ilicita la amistad de su Ama Dª Casiana con D^n Toribio" (gave indications that he believed the friendship of his mistress, doña Casiana, with don Toribio was sexual in nature) (f. 50).

13. Ibid. ff. 50–51.

14. "Testimonio de diligencias preventivas de la Causa Criminal que se ha de seguir contra el Ynfame alevozo, que asesinó al Sr. Don Lucas de Gálvez," 1792, AGN, Criminal 299, cuad. 2, f. 253.

15. Ibid., f. 253.

16. Ibid., f. 254.

17. Ibid., f. 254.

18. "Prosigue la relación de todos las especies e indicios que produce el sumario contra el Ten^{te} Don Toribio del Mazo," 1793, AGN, Criminal 295, f. 50.

19. Ibid., f. 51.

20. Ibid., f. 51. Muñoz's promotion to the position of dragoon may have resulted from his incriminating testimony regarding the affair and the authorities' desire to protect him from the otherwise inevitable recriminations from the treasurer and his wife.

21. Ibid., f. 51.

22. Ibid., f. 51.

23. Ibid., f. 58.

24. T-LAL/MC, VEMC 50, 1795, exp. 1, ff. 1–3.

25. Ibid., f. 12v.

26. Ibid., f. 13v.

27. Javier Villa-Flores, "'To Lose One's Soul': Blasphemy and Slavery in New Spain, 1596–1669," *Hispanic American Historical Review* 82, no. 3 (August 2002): 435–68.

28. "Prosigue la relación de todos las especies e indicios que produce el sumario contra el Ten^{te} Don Toribio del Mazo," 1793, AGN, Criminal 295, f. 58.

29. Surviving letters from colonial Latin America are quite rare, as Rebecca Earle noted in "Letters and Love in Colonial Spanish America," *The Americas* 62, no. 1 (July 2005): 17–46. Unlike the missives studied by Earle, these letters were of an illicit nature. Even so, they reflected the more personal and passionate tone of romantic partners noted by Earle for the late eighteenth century.

30. "Cartas reservadas pertenecientes a la Causa sobre el homicidio," 1796, AGN, Criminal 322, parte 2, cuad. 23, f. 64.

31. T-LAL/MC, VEMC 50, 1795, exp. 1, ff. 255–56.

32. Libro de Protocolos, 1792–1793, ANEY, vol. 30, ff. 286–87, compact disc 30.

33. "Expediente del Obispo, don Josef Nicolás de Lara, y dn. Josef Phelipe Pastrana," 1783, AGI, México 2599, no. 9, ff. 51–64v.

34. "Se hace relación del resultado sobre Coartada en el plenario," 1794, AGN, Criminal 294, ff. 115–16.

35. "Prosigue la relación de todos las especies e indicios que produce el sumario contra el Ten^te Don Toribio del Mazo," 1793, AGN, Criminal 295, ff. 61–61v.

36. "Testimonio de varias diligencias practicadas en la causa sobre el homicidio que se executó en la persona del Señor don Lucas de Gálvez," 1793, AGN, Criminal 310, cuad. 2, letra B, f. 275.

37. "Aprehensión de cinco negros contraventores de los tratados de paz con Inglaterra," 1793, AGS, Secretaría del Despacho de Guerra 7210, no. 9, exp. 1, ff. 1–3v. The description of their master's words reflects a sense of genuine personal loss, but it is more likely that they fled to one of two maroon communities or even possibly joined a band of Mayas who defied Spanish colonial rule than return to their master. For further discussions on slave flight into uncolonized spaces populated by both runaway slaves and rebel and unconquered Mayas, see Lentz, "Black Belizeans and Fugitive Mayas."

38. See Lentz, "Black Belizeans and Fugitive Mayas."

39. "Papeles exividos por D. José Correa Romero, que se titulan defensa del teniente de milicias Don Toribio del Mazo," 1796, AGN, Criminal 336, f. 448.

40. "Tercera declaración de D^n Esteban de Castro," 1801, AGI, México 3038, nos. 44–46, sub-no. 173.

41. "Testimonio de lo Contenido en el Quaderno Reservado num° 42," 1795, AGI, México 3040, no. 7, f. 143.

42. Ibid., f. 144.

43. "Memorial ajustado de la causa formada sobre el homicidio del Sr. Don Lucas Galvez—Lista de Reos," 1800, AGN, Criminal 287, ff. 1–3. Tomás does not appear on the list of eighty prisoners incarcerated between 1792 and 1800, which includes all of don Toribio's accomplices who faced charges.

44. "Testimonio de diligencias preventivas de la Causa Criminal que se ha de seguir contra el Ynfame alevozo, que asesinó al Sr. Don Lucas de Gálvez," 1792, AGN, Criminal 299, cuad. 2, ff. 258–60.

45. Ibid., ff. 258–60.

46. "Prosigue la relación de todos las especies e indicios que produce el sumario contra el Ten^te Don Toribio del Mazo," 1793, AGN, Criminal 295, f. 52.

47. Ibid., f. 52.

48. The final word in the matter came in the form of an 1809 mandate from the king that ordered don Justo and Lic. don Manuel Palomeque, an ally of Sandoval's, to pay a fine of 200 pesos each for failing to resolve their previous differences. "Expediente sobre exigir la multa al teniente Asesor Ynterino Licenciado Don Justo Serrano," 1809, AGN, Civil 1674, exp. 26.

49. Sandoval's promotion, on 17 March 1796, to the position of auditor de guerra y teniente del gobernador, vacated by don Fernando Gutiérrez de Piñeres in 1795, marked a shift away from the unquestionably favorable political situation for the deceased bishop's rivals and paved the way for retaliatory moves by his partisans. The political battle with Serrano marked one of the instances in which the bishop's former allies struck back at their persecutors—where a low-level official once under investigation now held the upper hand against a rival. Similar but not entirely identical accounts of the dispute are found in "El Defensor de Naturales de Yucatan sobre Privilegios de su empleo," 1797, AGN, Civil 2003, exp. 6; and "Solicitud del Auditor de Yucatan contra el Comisionado Guillén que pasó de órn. del Virrey," 1798, AGI, México 3039, no. 1, s/f.

50. "El Defensor de Naturales de Yucatan sobre Privilegios de su empleo," 1797, AGN, Civil 2003, exp. 6.

51. "Solicitud del Auditor de Yucatan contra el Comisionado Guillén que pasó de órn. del Virrey," 1798, AGI, México 3039, no. 2, s/f.

52. "Solicitud del Auditor de Yucatan contra el Comisionado Guillén que pasó de órn. del Virrey," 1798, AGI, México 3039, no. 3, s/f.

53. Ibid.

54. "The lower classes . . . saw people mainly divided by a 'way of life,'" not by race. Wolfgang Gabbert, "Of Friends and Foes: The Caste War and Ethnicity in Yucatan," *Journal of Latin American Anthropology* 9, no. 1 (Spring 2004): 106.

55. Restall, *Black Middle*, 13; and Ira Berlin, *Many Thousands Gone: The First Two Centuries of Slavery in North America* (Cambridge, MA: Belknap Press of Harvard University Press, 1998), 8.

56. Restricted mobility, which in many cases amounted to confinement in a Spaniard's home, was typical of the slave experience in Yucatan—but not neighboring Belize—under English rule. Just across the vaguely defined border, Belizean black slaves worked in conditions of uncharacteristic freedom and limited supervision. Many did attempt to flee to Yucatan in the hope of gaining their freedom based on a professed desire to convert to Catholicism. See Lentz, "Black Belizeans and Fugitive Mayas." Others, like don Toribio's slaves, Plato and Gaius, were apprehended when they unwittingly strayed into Spanish-claimed territory and were resold to Spanish owners in public auctions. "Aprehensión de cinco negros contraventores de los tratados de paz con Inglaterra," 1793, AGS, Secretaría del Despacho de Guerra 7210, no. 9, exp. 1, ff. 1–3v.

57. Farriss described the level of dependence and integration of criados but not the means by which criados entered Spanish homes in *Maya Society*, 104.

58. The *Diccionario de la lengua española* (http://buscon.rae.es/draeI/) notes the derivation of the word from *criar*. The term *criado*—especially applied to Spaniards—often did not actually refer to one's station in life as much as it served as an insult, much like the derogatory term *paniaguado*, which was used to denigrate one Spaniard as a servile dependent of another.

59. In contrast, in colonial New Mexico and Texas, the two regions of Spanish America where the phenomenon of criados serving in Spanish homes has been well studied, criados were overwhelmingly of indigenous background. See, for example, Alan Gallay, ed., *Indian Slavery in Colonial America* (Lincoln: University of Nebraska Press, 2010); Martina Will de Chaparro, *Death and Dying in New Mexico* (Albuquerque: University of New Mexico Press, 2007); and Ramón A. Gutiérrez, *When Jesus Came, the Corn Mothers Went Away: Marriage, Sexuality, and Power in New Mexico, 1500–1846* (Stanford, CA: Stanford University Press, 1991).

60. "Declaración del Teniente don Toribio del Mazo," 1798, AGI, México 3037, no. 151, sub-no. 3.

61. "Instrucción reservada en que se ponen de manifiesto los varios excesos cometidos por el Liz^do D. Miguel Magdaleno Sandoval Asesor de la Yntendencia de Mérida de Yucatán," 1797, AGI, México 3039, no. 2, sub-no. 64.

62. "Sobre el homicidio de D. Lucas de Galvez Capitan Gral. de Yucatan," 1793, AGN, Criminal 471, f. 46.

63. "Aprehensión de cinco negros contraventores de los tratados de paz con Inglaterra," 1793, AGS, Secretaría del Despacho de Guerra 7210, no. 9, exp. 1, ff. 14–15.

64. Both slaves and criados referred to those whom they served as amos.

65. "Con fha de 15 de Marzo hace presentes los motivos que tuvo para proceder contral el teniente de Granaderos del Batallon de Castilla dn. Juan Josef de Fierros," 1793, AGI, México 3039, no. 82.

66. Ibid.

67. "Sobre el homicidio de D. Lucas de Galvez Capitan Gral. de Yucatan," 1793, AGN, Criminal 471, f. 46.

68. Enslavement of Mayas in the early years of the colony did take place, however. Many of the earliest interpreters were enslaved, and at least one owner of a Maya slave received permission to relocate to Cuba with her slaves in tow. "Solicitud de licencia para sacar esclavos de la isla de Cuba," 1530, AGI, Santo Domingo 1121, lib. 1, f. 49v. At least one Maya slave served as an interpreter. See Joaquín García Icazbalceta, "Itinerario de Grijalva," in *Colección de documentos para la historia de México*, vol. 1 (Mexico City: Librería de J. M. Andrade, 1858).

69. Restall, *Black Middle*, 13–14.

70. Charles Gibson, *The Spanish Tradition in America* (Columbia: University of South Carolina Press, 1968), 205; and Restall, *Black Middle*, 20–24.

71. Two examples of cases in which Yucatecan authorities turned away slaves from Saint-Domingue, either for sale or as refugees, are found in "Desembarco de desterrados negros y mulatos franceses," 1792, AGS, Secretaría del Despacho de Guerra 7237, no. 52; and "El Señor Governador e Yntendente de aquella provincia sobre venta de 15 negros esclavos," 1809, AGN, Civil 2152, exp. 11. For a discussion of the Caribbean situation at the time of Gálvez's assassination, see David Patrick Geggus, "Slavery, War, and Revolution in the Greater Caribbean, 1789–1815," in

A Turbulent Time: The French Revolution and the Greater Caribbean, ed. David Barry Gaspar and David Patrick Geggus (Bloomington: Indiana University Press, 1997).

72. John M. Lipski defined bozales as "slaves born in Africa, who spoke European languages only with difficulty," in his study of bozal Spanish, spoken by African populations and distinct from standard Castilian. The term *bozal* originally meant "savage" or "untamed horse." *A History of Afro-Hispanic Language: Five Centuries, Five Continents* (Cambridge: Cambridge University Press, 2005), 5–6.

73. "Aprehensión de cinco negros contraventores de los tratados de paz con Inglaterra," 1793, AGS, Secretaría del Despacho de Guerra 7210, no. 9, exp. 1, ff. 1–3v.

74. Ibid., f. 5.

75. Ibid., f. 4.

76. For reasons unknown, the slaves also specifically implicated Edward Meigham, another English settler, as a frequent trespasser. A contemporary English traveler, Thomas Jefferys, described English contempt for Spanish efforts to restrict their contraband trade and forbid logging on the Spanish side of the border: "To the north of the first bay the Spaniards have the town of Salamanca de Bacalar, of 120 houses, with a bad fort and a small garrison, designed to hinder the contraband trade, and the excursions of the wood-cutters or bay-men, but which it does not prevent." *The West-India Atlas: or, A Compendious Defcription of the West-Indies. . . .* (London: Printed for Robert Sayer and John Bennett, 1780), 15.

77. "Aprehensión de cinco negros contraventores de los tratados de paz con Inglaterra," 1793, AGS, Secretaría del Despacho de Guerra 7210, no. 9, exp. 1, ff. 10–15.

78. Ibid., ff. 15–17. In this case and in contemporary documents researched for historical context, it appears that fluency in Spanish played the more important role, as many individuals identified as "indios" who had Spanish surnames did not also appear as indios ladinos. Three who did: Xix, the town crier of Izamal; Juan Ek; and Salvador Pech, a Mérida Maya who bought and sold pieces of land in cooperation with Pablo Lira. Ek obviously spoke Spanish because of his position as pregonero and Pech communicated easily in Spanish, judging by the bills of sale he produced that appear in Castilian, opening with "Yo Salbador Pech, Yndio Ladino, vecino de esta muy noble y muy leal ciudad de Mérida." All had Maya surnames. "Demanda puesta por el Sindico del Convento de este Pueblo sobre cantidad de pesos," 1793, AGEY, Colonial, Judicial, vol. 1, exp. 10, f. 33; and Libro de Protocolos, 1791–1792, ANEY, vol. 29, ff. 284–85, compact disc 29.

79. "Aprehensión de cinco negros contraventores de los tratados de paz con Inglaterra," 1793, AGS, Secretaría del Despacho de Guerra 7210, no. 9, exp. 1, ff. 19–21. Xix officiated in an earlier sale of slaves (ibid.), and his name, "Ysidoro Xix Yndio Ladino," appears in the role of town crier and auctioneer in two sales found in Mérida's Notarial Archive as well. Libro de Protocolos, 1791–1792,

ANEY, vol. 29, ff. 18, 24, compact disc 29; and Libro de Protocolos, 1794, ANEY, vol. 31, f. 11, compact disc 31.

80. "Aprehensión de cinco negros contraventores de los tratados de paz con Inglaterra," 1793, AGS, Secretaría del Despacho de Guerra 7210, no. 9, exp. 1, f. 20.

81. Libro de Protocolos, 1791–1792, ANEY, vol. 29, ff. 18, 24, compact disc 29; and Libro de Protocolos, 1794, ANEY, vol. 31, f. 11, compact disc 31.

82. Libro de Protocolos, 1792–1793, ANEY, vol. 30, f. 286, compact disc 30.

83. "Aprehensión de cinco negros contraventores de los tratados de paz con Inglaterra," 1793, AGS, Secretaría del Despacho de Guerra 7210, no. 9, exp. 2, ff. 1–31.

84. "Gobernador de Yucatán sobre de varios esclavos huidos," 1802, AGI, Estado 35, no. 46, letra 5. One slave who escaped before the outbreak of hostilities between England and Spain and three who escaped during warfare were sold off, with the proceeds deposited into the royal treasury, while the small boat used by one of the slaves, named Jack, was returned to the English. Three other Anglophone slaves who escaped after the cessation of warfare were returned to their prewar owner, a Mr. Lori (probably a Spanish rendering of "Laurie" or "Lorry"). For a more detailed examination of the sanctuary policy in Yucatan, which extended the promise of baptism and manumission for slaves fleeing Protestant territories for Catholic territories under Spanish rule, see Restall, "Crossing to Safety?" and Lentz, "Black Belizeans and Fugitive Mayas."

85. Restall, *Black Middle*, 10–13; and Pedro Bracamonte y Sosa and Gabriela Solís Robleda, "Insumisos e idólatras: Los Mayas del Caribe peninsular durante la colonia," in *El Caribe mexicano: Origen y conformación, siglos XVI y XVII*, ed. Carlos Macías Richard (Mexico City: Universidad de Quintana Roo, 2006), 453.

86. Restall, *Black Middle*, 10–13.

87. "Aprehensión de cinco negros contraventores de los tratados de paz con Inglaterra," 1793, AGS, Secretaría del Despacho de Guerra 7210, no. 9, exp. 1, ff. 15v–19.

88. Ibid., ff. 18–23.

89. Restall, *Black Middle*, 336–43, table 2.1; and Dennis N. Valdés, "The Decline of Slavery in Mexico," *The Americas* 44, no. 2 (1987), 171–73. Valdés noted an overall gradual drop in prices for slaves between the ages of eighteen and twenty-five, from a high of 400–500 pesos for male and female slaves in 1585 to an average of 170 pesos or less after the mid-eighteenth century.

90. "Clemente Rodríguez del Trujillo," 1777, AGI, Contratación 5523, no. 2, ramo 150. No Catalan criado matching this description appears on the list of passengers accompanying the bishop en route to Mérida in 1780, though it does include an eighteen-year-old don Toribio. This particular roster only lists three young relatives, a secretary, and the bishop's confessor, but no criados. "Luis Piña y Mazo," 1780, AGI, Contratación 5525, no. 1, ramo 2.

91. "Expediente de información y licencia de pasajero a Indias de Rafael del Castillo y Sucre," 1779, AGI, Contratación 5524, no. 4, ramo 29.

92. Ibid.; "Expediente de información y licencia de pasajero a indias de Antonio Alcalde," 1763, AGI, Contratación 5506, no. 2, ramo 7; "Expediente de información y licencia de pasajero a indias de Francisco de Lara Bonifaz," 1640, AGI, Contratración 5422, no. 29; and "Expediente de información y licencia de pasajero a indias de Juan José Vertiz y Ontañón," 1710, AGI, Contratración 5465, no. 2, ramo 77. See also Restall, *Black Middle*, 310–11.

93. "Expediente de información y licencia de pasajero a indias de Antonio Alcalde," 1763, AGI, Contratación 5506, no. 2, ramo 7, f. 13.

94. Ibid., f. 19.

95. "Ynformación sobre Cristiandad de Juana Canto," 1767–1859, AHAY, Legitimaciones, vol. 1, f. 253.

96. Orlando Patterson explored the concept of "social death" in his work, *Slavery and Social Death: A Comparative Study* (Cambridge, MA: Harvard University Press, 1982). While many subsequent studies have modified the concept of social death as an absolute separation from one's past, the description of this criada's situation implies the accuracy, in this case, of the term *genealogical isolate*, one aspect of Patterson's broader definition. Interestingly, the slaves Plato and Gaius described their places of origin—"Canga" and "Nomabó," respectively, both on the coast of Guinea—in more detail than the criada, who only remembered the first household in which she served, and not her place of birth. "Aprehensión de cinco negros contraventores de los tratados de paz con Inglaterra," 1793, AGS, Secretaría del Despacho de Guerra 7210, no. 9, exp. 1, f. 1.

97. Patterson, *Slavery and Social Death*, 38–51.

98. Muñoz wrote extensively in Maya without the assistance of interpreters. Several examples of formal legal documents sent throughout the province written in his hand in Maya survive in *Legal Documents and Municipal Records from the District of Valladolid, Yucatán, Mexico, 1712–1866*, no. 1604, Edward E. Ayer Collection, Newberry Library. Muñoz may have taken advantage of his role as the highest-ranking government official in his region with regular, unmediated contact with the Maya majority to secure criados, which he then sent on to others to secure political favor.

99. "Ynformación sobre Cristiandad de Juana Canto," 1767–1859, AHAY, Legitimaciones, vol. 1.

100. Ibid.

101. Ibid. A fragmentary reference with no further explanation written in the hand of Juan Andrés de Herrera, *notario mayor* (government notary), appears for the date of 30 May 1801 as follows: "[F]ui el [*sic*] pueblo Negro." The process also includes Muñoz's mention that he did not recall giving anyone a "vecina de color."

102. Libro de Protocolos, 1792–1793, ANEY, vol. 30, f. 118, compact disc 30.

103. Libro de Protocolos, 1791–1792, ANEY, vol. 29, f. 130, compact disc 29.

104. "Instrucción reservada en que se ponen de manifiesto los varios excesos cometidos por el Liz^do D. Miguel Magdaleno Sandoval Asesor de la Yntendencia de Mérida de Yucatán," 1797, AGI, México 3039, no. 2, sub-nos. 69–70.
105. "Parte 4ª del Memorial ajustado de la causa formada sobre el homicidio del Sr. D. Lucas de Galvez," 1800, AGN, Criminal 291, ff. 279–80.
106. "Instrucción reservada en que se ponen de manifiesto los varios excesos cometidos por el Liz^do D. Miguel Magdaleno Sandoval Asesor de la Yntendencia de Mérida de Yucatán," 1797, AGI, México 3039, no. 2, sub-no. 63.
107. "Se refiere otro incidente de la causa del homicidio del Señor Gálvez," 1797, AGN, Criminal 293, cap. 3, f. 255.
108. "Parte 4ª del Memorial ajustado de la causa formada sobre el homicidio del Sr. D. Lucas de Galvez," 1800, AGN, Criminal 291, f. 280.
109. "Testimonio del Quaderno 2° de las diligencias practicadas en la Causa sobre el homicidio del Sr. Dn. Lucas de Gálvez," 1794, AGI, México 3036, no. 119, f. 20.
110. "De la causa formada en averiguación de los agresores," 1794, AGI, México 3036, no. 120, ff. 33, 35–36.
111. "Sobre el homicidio de D. Lucas de Galvez Capitan Gral. de Yucatan," 1793, AGN, Criminal 471, f. 125. This information appeared as part of unsuccessful attempts to link the Quijanos to the murder by establishing a pattern of violence on the part of their slaves and criados on behalf of their powerful patrons.
112. "Testimonio de la Denuncia echa por Dn. Esteban de Castro, contra el Agresor del Omicidio perpetrado en la persona del Señor Don Lucas de Gálvez," 1801, AGN, Criminal 484, exp. 2, f. 52v.
113. "Memorial ajustado de la causa formada sobre el homicidio del Sr. Don Lucas Galvez—Lista de Reos," 1800, AGN, Criminal 287, f. 1.
114. "Yndice de los Quadernos que entregó hoy dia de la fha en esta Secretaria de Cámara del virreinato el D. D. Francisco Guillén," 1802, AGN, Criminal 619, exp. 1, f. 12.
115. "Contiene la Real Orden de 11 de Junio de 96 en cuya virtud se creó la nueva Junta," 1796–1798, AGN, Criminal 337, exp. 1, f. 152.
116. "Reservado," 1802, AGI, México 3038, sub-no. 189, f. 58v; and "Testimonio de las diligencias practicadas por el Excelentisimo Señor Virrey, sobre ratificar las declaraciones dadas en Mérida, ante el Capitan de Fragata Dn. Juan Tabat," 1801, AGN, Criminal 484, f. 114v.
117. The one exception to the identification of slaves as blacks appears in a grant of liberty conceded to María Manuela Gonzáles, identified with the ambiguous label "negra mulata." Apparently, very few mixed-race Yucatecans of African descent—afromestizos—served as slaves. Libro de Protocolos, 1791–1792, ANEY, vol. 29, ff. 292v–93, compact disc 29.
118. "Se hace relación deel sumario formado contra el Teniente de Milicias disciplinadas de Blancos de Yucatan Dn.Toribio del Mazo," 1793, AGN, Criminal 295, cap. 3, ff. 7–9.

CHAPTER 5

1. "El Virrey de N. E. Conde Revilla Gigedo remite testimonio y copias que acreditan las últimas actuaciones hasta el día," 1793, AGI, México 3036, no. 77. O'Neill arrived in Campeche on 15 June 1793 at 1:30 p.m.

2. Intermediaries, treated in more depth for the contact and early colonial era in Latin American scholarship to date, still played a vital role into the late colonial period, even in regions such as Yucatan, where many non-natives acquired the indigenous language. Especially in the legal arena, mediators required expertise with Castilian law and legal concepts and familiarity with both the administrators of Mérida and monolingual Maya speakers in small pueblos. In the homicide investigation under study here, *intermediary* refers to an individual who transmitted information and mediated between agents of the law operating at the level of the intendancy, viceroyalty, or empire, functioning entirely in Castilian, and local individuals whose lives and interactions took place almost entirely in Yucatec Maya. Because of the high profile of the victim, many such go-betweens needed a high level of fluency in Maya and Spanish since their translations would certainly be subject to scrutiny.

3. "Dn. Manuel de la Bodega . . . continua las noticias relativas a la causa de su comisión y propone ciertas providencias que le parecen conducentes," 1793, AGI, México 3036, no. 83.

4. "El Obispo de Yucatan hace presente a V. M. las tribulaciones que sufre. . . . ," 1793, AGI, México 3036, no. 88.

5. "Oficio de este día. . . . ," 1793, AGI, México 3036, no. 89.

6. "Reservada," 1793, AGI, México 3036, no. 66.

7. Ibid., no. 104.

8. "Documentos señalados. . . . ," 1793, AGI, México 3036, no. 105.

9. "Testimonio del Expediente formado sobre recusacion y retiro del Sor Juez Comisionado," 1793, AGI, México 3036, no. 109, ff. 1–4v.

10. "D. Juan Antonio Muxica," 1793, AGI, México 3036, no. 99; "D. Francisco Galera y Leon Medico," 1793, AGI, México 3036, no. 100; "Dn Fernado Guerrero Blanco," 1793, AGI, México 3036, no. 101; and "Documentos señalados. . . . ," 1793, AGI, México 3036, no. 109, f. 5v. For added effect, don Roberto Claverol, a surgeon educated and trained in Barcelona, present in Mérida as a medic aboard a passing ship, concurred with the four resident surgeons of the province.

11. "Dn. Manuel de la Bodega, Alcalde del Crimen de la Real Audiencia de México da cuenta de hallarse relevado de la Comisión," 1794, AGI, México 3039.

12. "El Virrey de Nueva España Conde de Revilla Gigedo da cuenta de los motivos por que ha creido conveniente relevar a D. Manuel de la Bodega," 1793, AGI, México 3036, no. 108. Colin M. MacLachlan's *Criminal Justice in Eighteenth Century Mexico: A Study of the Tribunal of the Acordada* (Berkeley: University of California Press, 1974) describes the court's evolution from a regional ad hoc

judicial innovation reacting to the ineffective response of the Audiencia de México's sala de crimen to rising crime in Querétaro into one of the Bourbon regime's most effective methods for maintaining order beyond Mexico City.

13. Ibid., 36.

14. "El Virrey de Nueva España da cuenta con testimonio de que a representación del Juez de la Acordada, y de Bevidas prohividas, suspendió d estas Asesorias al Liz^do dn. Juan Joseph Barberí y nombró a dn. Francisco Guillén," 1783, AGI, México 1282, no. 238. Dr. Guillén's antecessor in the Acordada, don Juan José de Barberi, was blamed by his superior for the backlog of cases related to the manufacture, transport, and sale of prohibited alcoholic beverages, including mescal and aguardiente.

15. "Carta de Lic. Bodega," 1793, AGI, México 3036, no. 80.

16. Restall, *Maya World*, 53–55.

17. Sergeant Cano was a fascinating figure who later served as the "interpreter," or primary intermediary, for a settlement of former black rebels from Saint Domingue, ex-slaves who had allied with Spain in the turmoil of that island nation's revolution and relocated to San Fernando Aké, a segregated settlement in Yucatan's interior. Jorge Victoria Ojeda and Jorge Canto Alcocer, *San Fernando Aké: Microhistoria de una comunidad afroamericana en Yucatán* (Mérida: Universidad Autónoma de Yucatán, 2006), 47.

18. Three lists of prisoners survive from the proceedings related to Gálvez's assassination. One is found in "Memorial ajustado de la causa formada sobre el homicidio del Sr. Don Lucas Galvez—Lista de Reos," 1800, AGN, Criminal 287, ff. 1–3, and contains the names, alleged crimes, terms of prison, and place(s) of incarceration of all of the major prisoners held in Mérida. The other two—an original in Maya and its translation in Spanish by Eugenio Cano—are from Tihosuco and contain a list of the prisoners jailed by the local Maya authorities; they are found in "Cuenta de los Yndios presos," 1795, AGN, Criminal 392, exp. 2, ff. 457–59; and "Cuentail Uincob h mascab nalob," 1795, AGN, Criminal 392, exp. 2, ff. 423–28v.

19. "Cuenta de los Yndios presos," 1795, AGN, Criminal 392, exp. 2, ff. 457–59.

20. "Criminal contra Francisco Canche, por haver rovado a Casimiro Chay una Mula," 1802, AGN, Criminal 361, exp. 6, f. 345.

21. "Memorial ajustado de la causa formada sobre el homicidio del Sr. Don Lucas Galvez—Lista de Reos," 1800, AGN, Criminal 287, f. 1. During the entirety of his incarceration, Lara was never suspected of any complicity, however remote, in the actual assassination.

22. "Expediente Reservado, que comprehende ciertos procedimientos observados en el Padre Cura del Pueblo de Chiquinsonot," 1796, AGN, Criminal 335, exp. 2, cuad. 56, f. 199v.

23. Ibid., ff. 159–60.

24. Ibid., f. 158v.

25. Ibid., f. 208. The definition of fiscal de doctrina is found in Woodrow Wilson Borah, *Justice by Insurance: The General Indian Court of Colonial Mexico and the Legal Aides of the Half-Real* (Berkeley: University of California Press, 1983), 166.

26. "Nueva información hecha en el pueblo de Chikindzonot a pedimiento del reo," 1795, AGN, Criminal 332, cuad. 50, ff. 87v–88, 96v, 122, 126v.

27. Ibid., f. 82. Yama signed most of the Maya-language documentation as "escribano," but Yupit also signed his testimony as "escribano." Ibid., f. 57v.

28. "Cuenta de los Yndios presos," 1794, AGN, Criminal 392, exp. 2, ff. 457–59. Although at first glance Cano's translations appear to be impeccable, he seems to have confused the gender of the unidentified black prisoner.

29. The major act leading to the restructuring of rule in New Spain was the *Real ordenanza para el establecimiento é instruccion de intendentes de exército y provincia en el reino de la Nueva España* of 1786.

30. Unlike elsewhere in the Spanish Empire, Yucatan had no corregidores, though similar figures were appointed as local administrators, including *capitanes a guerra, tenientes a guerra*, and cabos de justicia. Pedro Sánchez de Aguilar wrote, "No ai Corregidores en Yucatã, por q son muy perjudiciales y por cedulas está prohibido, q no los aya, como cõsta por las cedulas q tiene la villa de Valladolid, mi patria," in Pedro Sánchez de Aguilar, *Informe contra idolorum cultores del obispado de Yucatán* (Madrid, 1639), 19v. Many of the reforms contained in the *Real Ordenanza de Intendentes* had their roots in earlier recommendations made by don Lucas's distant relation, don José de Gálvez, who had recommended the removal of alcaldes mayores as early as 1768. Josefina Zoraida Vázquez, "El siglo XVIII mexicano de la modernización al descontento," in Vázquez, *Interpretaciones del siglo XVIII mexicano*, 18.

31. In the habit of challenging as many bureaucratic appointments made by don Lucas as possible, fray Luis did indeed contest the appointment of at least one of the subdelegados. The language of the ordinance of intendants was clear: as intendant, Gálvez did have final authority over the appointments of these new administrators.

32. Laura Machuca Gallegos, *Los hacendados de Yucatán, 1785–1847* (Mexico City: CIESAS, 2011), 108–9.

33. In Yucatan, the capitanes a guerra had tended to be encomenderos; the subdelegados were not. Ibid., 104.

34. Pietschmann, *Las reformas borbónicas*, 249.

35. Vinson, *Bearing Arms for His Majesty*, 39–50, describes the impact of eighteenth-century militia reforms on the free colored militias. A classic but still highly useful work, Lyle N. McAlister's *The "Fuero Militar" in New Spain, 1746–1800* (Gainesville: University of Florida Press, 1957), also addresses the changes to the military in the Americas imposed by the Bourbon regime.

36. The Decree of Intendants of 1786 was much more than military and political reform. Much of the text also deals with the minutiae of economic management and taxation.

37. "Infantería de Voluntarios Blancos. Mérida de Yucatán," 1789, AGS, Secretaría del Despacho de Guerra 7299, no. 3, ff. 41, 49; and "Estado de las Milicias Urbanas de Tizimín y Chancenote", 1790, AGS, Secretaría del Despacho de Guerra 7207, no. 41, f. 220.

38. "Diligencias para averiguar el Agresor y Complizes de la alevosa muerte executada en la respetable persona del Sor. Brig. Don Lucas de Galvez," 1792, AGN, Criminal 302, no. 6, f. 252v; and "Infantería de Voluntarios Blancos. Mérida de Yucatán," 1789, AGS, Secretaría del Despacho de Guerra 7299, no. 3, f. 50.

39. "Diligencias para averiguar el Agresor y Complizes de la alevosa muerte executada en la respetable persona del Sor. Brig. Don Lucas de Galvez," 1792, AGN, Criminal 302, no. 6, ff. 254–55; and "Infantería de Voluntarios Blancos. Mérida de Yucatán," 1789, AGS, Secretaría del Despacho de Guerra 7299, no. 3, f. 48v.

40. "Diligencias para averiguar el Agresor y Complizes de la alevosa muerte executada en la respetable persona del Sor. Brig. Don Lucas de Galvez," 1792, AGN, Criminal 302, no. 6, f. 195; and "Demanda del Cacique de Motul contra el Cabo de Justicia de dicho pueblo, por tenerlo privado de su libertad," 1790, AGEY, Colonial, Judicial, vol. 1, exp. 1. Ramírez signed as juez español, while the cacique of Motul identified him as the cabo de justicia.

41. Machuca Gallegos, *Los hacendados de Yucatán*, explores the ongoing profiteering and abuse of power of subdelegados in the era of the intendancies in more detail.

42. Though Yucatan had no corregidores, repartimientos were often imposed by either the governor or lower-ranking officials who worked in an administrative capacity similar to corregidores. In one of the most notorious instances, several leading caciques challenged the enactment of Governor don Rodrigo Flores de Aldaña's widespread scheme to enforce the repartimiento. "Residencia de Rodrigo Flores de Aldana, Governador e la provincia de Yucatán por Frutos Delgado, oidor de la audiencia de México," 1670, AGI, Escribanía de Cámara 316B, pieza 70.

43. "Expediente formado a consequencia del fallecimiento de D. Pedro Gutiérrez, Capitan de Milicias Urbanas de Chiquinsonot, y Juez Español que fue de dho Pueblo," 1794, AGN, Criminal 316, cuad. 48, ff. 3–4, includes a list of confiscated documents containing receipts from the deceased juez español's store and his sales of aguardiente.

44. The language of the Decree of Intendants was unequivocal regarding the authority of the intendant over such appointments: "Su nombramiento ha de hacerlo con Título formal, y sin derechos, el Intendente de la Provincia por si solo, y por el tiempo de su voluntad." *Real ordenanza para el establecimiento é instruccion de intendentes de exército y provincia en el reino de la Nueva España* (Madrid, 1786), 19.

45. "Reservado. Sobre el actual gobierno en Yucatan," 1791, AGN, Civil 1454, exp. 6. As late as 1788, Antolín was still identified as capitán a guerra. "Plano y perspectiva de la Casa de Capitanía, Quarteles, Casa Real Audiencia y Carzel del Pueblo de Yzamal, fabricadas por el capitán a Guerra D. Manuel Antolín," 1788, AGI, Mapas y Planos-Mexico 765.

46. Apparently, the bishop felt that the Decree of Intendants should have only formalized and regulated the status quo and not have altered the existing political arrangement—a matter over which he had no authority.

47. "Manuel Antolín. Empleos," 1793, AGS, Secretaría del Despacho de Guerra 7210, no. 18, f. 55. With Gálvez out of the way, many leading Mérida families monopolized the posts after 1792. See Machuca Gallegos, *Los hacendados de Yucatán.*

48. "Expediente Reservado, que comprehende ciertos procedimientos observados en el Padre Cura del Pueblo de Chiquinsonot," 1796, AGN, Criminal 335, exp. 2, cuad. 56, f. 161.

49. "Acaecimientos posteriores al homicidio en Chiquinsonot," 1800, AGN, Criminal 295, f. 189v; and "Expediente Reservado, que comprehende ciertos procedimientos observados en el Padre Cura del Pueblo de Chiquinsonot," 1796, AGN, Criminal 335, exp. 2, cuad. 56, f. 39. In his last days, the dying and deposed juez español requested to have money sent from Chikindzonot to avoid the confiscation of his possessions. Don Gabriel Correa, father of the priest, had the money in his possession, giving credibility to Captain Cárdenas's denunciation of the juez español's status as a dependent of the priest. "Expediente formado a consequencia del fallecimiento de D. Pedro Gutiérrez, Capitan de Milicias Urbanas de Chiquinsonot, y Juez Español que fue de dho Pueblo," 1794, AGN, Criminal 316, cuad. 48, ff. 1–2.

50. "Se hace relación deel sumario formado contra el Teniente de Milicias disciplinadas de Blancos de Yucatan Dn.Toribio del Mazo," 1800, Criminal 295, cap. 3, ff. 7–9.

51. "Ratificaciones," 1795, AGN, Criminal 317, exp. 1, f. 214v.

52. Ibid., ff. 198–202, 211v–12, 214–15.

53. "Expediente Reservado, que comprehende ciertos procedimientos observados en el Padre Cura del Pueblo de Chiquinsonot," 1796, AGN, Criminal 335, exp. 2, cuad. 56, ff. 214–15.

54. Ibid., ff. 234–37v. Cárdenas's service records are included in a petition for promotion supported by Brigadier O'Neill in the Archivo General de las Simancas. "Mateo Cárdenas, Recomendaciones," 1796, AGS, Secretaría del Despacho de Guerra 7211, no. 47.

55. "Expediente Reservado, que comprehende ciertos procedimientos observados en el Padre Cura del Pueblo de Chiquinsonot," 1796, AGN, Criminal 335, exp. 2, cuad. 56, f. 235v.

56. *Topil*, a term of Maya origin, apparently predated the Spanish reformulation of Maya municipal government. Along with batabs, the office survived the conquest

and was amalgamated to the Spanish-mandated cabildos. See Thompson, *Tekanto*, 344–49.

57. Fortunately for the two alguaciles and two topiles, priests were prohibited from administering their own jails or cells. In 1574, in response to the egregious abuses inflicted on Mayas by fray Diego de Landa during his extirpation campaign, Philip II forbid the practice of imprisoning Mayas in monasteries. "Provisión de la Real Audiencia de México inserta una cedula, para que los Religiosos no tengan cepos, ni cárceles," in Sánchez de Aguilar, *Informe contra idolorum cultores*, 8v–11v.

58. "Expediente Reservado, que comprehende ciertos procedimientos observados en el Padre Cura del Pueblo de Chiquinsonot," 1796, AGN, Criminal 335, exp. 2, cuad. 56, ff. 168–75.

59. Ibid., ff. 199v, 207, 210.

60. "Petición de las autoridades y vecinos para que suspende la fabrica de la iglesia por su mucha pobreza y necesidad que tienen de dedicarse a sus labranzas," Baca, 1790, AGEY, Colonial, Ayuntamientos, vol. 1, exp. 3, ff. 1–6. Puc, Juan Chable, Pedro Chable, Antonio Ek, Andrés Uc, and Tomás Uc wrote the first letter. A later note of receipt written in Spanish identified these non-cabildo members as "Yndios Magnates." Baca's cabildo, which wrote the second letter, was composed of Juan Noh, cacique or batab; Clemente Cox and Bentura Ytza as alcaldes; Nicolás Hoil, Juan de la Cruz Chim, Nicolás Ytza, and Nicolás Poot as regidors; and Simón Canche as escribano. The petitions, written on 12 July and 24 July 1790, respectively, were both written in Maya.

61. Ibid., ff. 1–9.

62. "Religiosos," 1793, AGEY, Colonial, Reales Cédulas, vol. 1, exp. 28, no. 5. The Franciscans' resentment of Quintana may have stemmed in part from his earlier adjudication in an idolatry case involving a Maya man, Gaspar Moo. Traditionally, idolatry cases had fallen under the purview of friars. "Contiene el oficio del Juez Español del Pueblo de Akil en que participa lo acaecido con el Yndio Gaspar Moó; su remicion al Sõr Governador, y la providencia acesorada de su SSᵃ para que el subdelegado de la Sierra procediese a la averigacion de los que se expresa," 1791, AGN, Civil 1454, no. 4.

63. "Religiosos," 1793, AGEY, Colonial, Reales Cédulas, vol. 1, exp. 28, no. 5.

64. "Demanda del Cacique de Motul contra el Cabo de Justicia de dicho puebo, por tenerlo privado de su libertad," 1790, AGEY, Colonial, Judicial, vol. 1, exp. 1, ff. 1, 3.

65. Ibid., f. 3.

66. Ibid.

67. By at least 1531, royal policy required two interpreters to translate and record the testimony of all Indians in New Spain in order to avoid fraud and mistranslation. By doing so, authorities would compare their translations to verify that the two translations, taken separately, coincided. Vasco de Puga, comp., *Prouisio[n]es cedulas instruciones de su Magestad: ordena[n]ças d[e] difu[n]tos y audie[n]cia,*

p[ar]a la buena expedicio[n] de los negocios, y administracio[n] d[e] justicia: y gouernacio[n] d[e]sta Nueua España: y p[ar]a el bue[n] tratamie[n]to y [con] servacio[n] d[e] los yndios, dende [sic] el año 1525. hasta este presente de. 63 (Madrid, 1563), 41, in the John Carter Brown Library, Providence, RI. Without citing the specific law, don Toribio complained that Eugenio Cano gathered testimony in Sotuta and elsewhere without another interpreter present. He believed that Cano, unchecked by the presence of additional unbiased bilingual individuals, had influenced the witnesses to deliver statements that incriminated don Toribio. The bishop's nephew also objected to Cano's turn as an interpreter because he had served as a guard during don Toribio's imprisonment and had also given incriminating testimony against him. "Comprensivo de las nuebas providencias," 1795, AGN, Criminal 392, cuad. 23, f. 411.

68. "Expediente Reservado, que comprehende ciertos procedimientos observados en el Padre Cura del Pueblo de Chiquinsonot," 1796, AGN, Criminal 335, exp. 2, cuad. 56, f. 197. Borah noted that the long-standing tradition of Mayas traveling to Mérida with their complaints went against the intended design set out in the 1591 real cédula. However, possibly due to precontact traditions, Mayas continued to travel to Mérida to have their grievances redressed. *Justice by Insurance*, 362.

69. See Beatriz Rojas, ed., *Cuerpo político y pluralidad de derechos: Los privilegios de las corporaciones novohispanas* (Mexico City: Centro de Investigación y Docencia Económicas, Instituto de Investigaciones Dr. José María Luis Mora, 2007), for several chapters covering the persistence of jurisdictional pluralism in the late eighteenth century.

70. "Resumen Concisco del Extracto General," 1803, AGI, México 3040, f. 60.

71. Puga, *Prouisio[n]es cedulas instruciones*, 41.

72. "Cúmulo de Bandos Promulgados," 1792, AGN, Criminal 302, no. 8, ff. 247–49.

73. "Infantería de Voluntarios Blancos. Mérida de Yucatán," 1799, AGS, Secretaría del Despacho de Guerra 7299, no. 3.

74. Ibid.

75. "Diligencias para averiguar el Agresor, y complices de la alevosa muerte executada en la respectable persona del Sr. Intendente don Lucas de Galvez," 1792, AGN, Criminal 302, no. 5, ff. 237–46; "Expediente formado a consequencia del fallecimiento de D. Pedro Gutiérrez, Capitan de Milicias Urbanas de Chiquinsonot, y Juez Español que fue de dho Pueblo," 1794, AGN, Criminal 316, cuad. 48, ff. 18–20, 70; and "Infantería de Voluntarios Blancos. Mérida de Yucatán," 1789, AGS, Secretaría del Despacho de Guerra 7299, no. 3, f. 49v.

76. "Ratificación de Remigio Ucan," 1795, AGN, Criminal 317, exp. 1, f. 187.

77. "Expediente Reservado, que comprehende ciertos procedimientos observados en el Padre Cura del Pueblo de Chiquinsonot," 1796, AGN, Criminal 335, exp. 2, cuad. 56, ff. 157, 164–79, 201.

78. Ibid., ff. 34–36.

79. The two both translated and signed as "interprete general" during the 1792 inter-rogations of Luis Lara. "De la causa formada en averiguación de los agresores," 1794, AGI, México 3036, no. 120, f. 71; and "Petición de las autoridades y vecinos para que suspende la fabrica de la iglesia por su mucha pobreza y necesidad que tienen de dedicarse a sus labranzas," AGEY, f. 1.

80. Machuca Gallegos, *Los hacendados de Yucatán*, 119.

81. "Extracto de las Actuaciones de revalidación y ampliaciones," 1801, AGI, México 3038, no. 11, sub-no. 173. Without citing his source, Molina Font stated that the interpreter and the intendant had a close relationship. Molina Font, *Gesta de los Mayas*, 195.

82. "Recaudo del nombramiento de ynterprete grāl este dicho dn. Diego de Vargas," 8 March 1578, AGI, México 102, ramo 3.

83. "Revalidación de las diligencias," 1802, AGN, Criminal 329, exp. 1, f. 116v.

84. Machuca Gallegos, *Los hacendados de Yucatán*, 119. Further evidence of Torres's substantial financial holdings, greater than those of most of his counterparts, are found in "Tributos," 1809, AGN, Indiferente Virreinal, caja 1942, exp. 20; and "Cuatrocientos pesos devueltos por don Blas Torres," 1818, AGN, Bienes Nacionales, vol. 16, exp. 5.

85. "Nueva información hecha en el pueblo de Chikindzonot a pedimiento del reo," 1795, AGN, Criminal 332, cuad. 50; "Expediente formado a consequencia del fallecimiento de D. Pedro Gutiérrez, Capitan de Milicias Urbanas de Chiquinsonot, y Juez Español que fue de dho Pueblo," 1794, AGN, Criminal 316, cuad. 48; and "Diligencias para averiguar el Agresor y Complizes de la alevosa muerte executada en la respetable persona del Sor. Brig. Don Lucas de Galvez," 1792, AGN, Criminal 302, no. 6, ff. 6–7.

86. *Real ordenanza para el establecimiento é instruccion de intendentes de exército y provincia en el reino de la Nueva España*, 19.

87. See Machuca Gallegos, *Los hacendados de Yucatán*, for a discussion of the growth of haciendas in Yucatan in the late eighteenth and early nineteenth centuries. Patch, *Maya and Spaniard* also provides a macro discussion of the trend.

88. *Reglamento para las Milicias de Infantería de la Provincia de Yucatan*, tit. 13.

89. Jorge Victoria Ojeda, "Piratería y estrategía defensiva en Yucatán durante el siglo XVIII," *Revista Complutense de Historia de América* 20 (1994): 136.

90. "Del Fuero, y Gozes de los Cuerpos de Milicias," in *Reglamento para las Milicias de Infantería de la Provincia de Yucatan*, tit. 5.

91. "Ejercito de Yucatán. Estados," 1799, AGS, Secretaría del Despacho de Guerra 7299, no. 10. A short passage in the *Reglamento para las Milicias* confirms what scholars have long suspected—that many mestizos were among the ranks of the supposedly white militias: "Las quatro Compañías que existen en Mérida; se compondran de la gente de mejor talla, y costumbres que haya en su recinto, y barrios, dependientes de las clases de Españoles, y Mestizos," in reference to the white militias of Mérida (2). Moreover, though large sections of the 1809 census

of Mérida are illegible due to decay, several of Mérida's mestizos were listed as "soldado" without any further description. Pardos had separate units and a few of the milicias urbanas still were composed of indios hidalgos, but mestizos and Spaniards served together in the so-called milicias blancas.

92. "Batallón de Milicias Blancas de Mérida," in *Reglamento para las Milicias de Infantería de la Provincia de Yucatan*, tit. 1.

93. Machuca Gallegos, *Los hacendados de Yucatán*, 111.

94. "Estado de las Milicias Urbanas de Tizimín y Chancenote," 1790, AGS, Secretaría del Despacho de Guerra 7207, no. 41; and "Revista de Inspección de las Milicias Urbanas del Partido de la Sierra," 1790, AGS, Secretaría del Despacho de Guerra, no. 27.

95. "Testimonio no 4°," 1793, AGI, México 3036.

96. Even though early prosecutors scrutinized Ferrera's alibi and later investigators rigorously questioned Muñoz since he had detailed knowledge of the treasurer's financial and personal dealings, neither appears with a racial label. The racial-taxonomic impulse—specifically, the tendency to retroactively assign racial categories to holders of specific posts when in doubt—overstates the correlation of certain jobs to individuals from set racial or ethnic groups. A more likely explanation is that that upper-strata Afro-Yucatecans occupied posts similar to creoles of middling status and that the socioeconomic distance between middle-class mestizos and non-elite criollos was minimal, especially in an occupational context. As a result, despite including one's name, age, and profession when describing these mayordomos, race did not matter as much to contemporaries in certain contexts as it did to contemporary Anglo scholars. See, for example, Patch, *Maya and Spaniard*, 195, which concludes that since two mayordomos of the eighteenth century were not addressed as "don," they must have been "mestizos" or "mulattoes." For an example of the rather permeable division between mestizos and Spaniards, see Restall, *Black Middle*, 89, in which the mestizo population of Izamal became known as Spaniards in the first decade of the nineteenth century. Moreover, racial identity rested heavily on race. As Machuca Gallegos noted in *Los hacendados de Yucatán*, many mayordomos managed to move up from hacienda manager to hacendado at the turn of the nineteenth century, which likely led to many of them being accepted as Spaniards regardless of ancestry.

97. Patch, *Maya and Spaniard*, 140–45.

98. See Nichols, "Solares in Tekax," for a study of the impact of sugar on one pueblo. In *Los hacendados de Yucatán*, Machuca Gallegos examines the involvement of subdelegados in the rise of sugar planting, often through illegal exploitation of Indian towns under their jurisdiction.

99. "Expediente formado a consequencia del fallecimiento de D. Pedro Gutiérrez, Capitan de Milicias Urbanas de Chiquinsonot, y Juez Español que fue de dho Pueblo," 1794, AGN, Criminal 316, cuad. 48, f. 5.

100. "Tercera declaración de Dn Esteban de Castro," 1801, AGI, México 3038, nos. 44–46, sub-no. 173

101. Kitchin, *Present State of the West-Indies*, 39–40.

102. José Antonio Calderón Quijano, *Historia de las fortificaciones en Nueva España*, 2nd ed. (Madrid: Consejo Superior de Investigaciones Científicas, 1984), 387–96.

103. "Testimonio del Quaderno 2° de las diligencias practicadas en la causa sobre el hom° del Sōr Dn Lucas de Galvez," 1793, AGI, México 3036, no. 119, f. 63.

104. "Nueva información hecha en el pueblo de Chikindzonot a pedimiento del reo," 1795, AGN, Criminal 332, cuad. 50, f. 161.

105. "Se hace relación del incidente relativa a Lucas Vargas y José Pavía," 1800, AGN, Criminal 295, f. 411.

106. "Lucas Vargas y complices—Polvora," 1791, AGI, México 3069, exp. 1.

107. Ibid.

108. "Comprensivo de las nuebas providencias," 1794, AGN, Criminal 392, cuad. 27, f. 278v.

109. "Se hace relación del incidente relativa a Lucas Vargas y José Pavía," 1800, AGN, Criminal 295, f. 411.

110. Ibid., f. 420.

111. See Nichols, "Solares in Tekax," and Laura Machuca Gallegos, "Hacienda y movilidad social en Yucatán en la primera mitad del siglo XIX," *Letras Históricas* 5 (Autumn 2011–Winter 2012): 81–100, for descriptions of the upward mobility of rural elites after 1800.

112. Farriss, *Maya Society*, 355.

113. Restall, *Black Middle*, remains the most comprehensive treatment of Afro-Yucatecan upward mobility across the colonial era.

114. "Pardos Tiradores de Yucatán," 1789, AGS, Secretaría del Despacho de Guerra 7299, no. 6, f. 105; "Pardos Tiradores de Campeche. Yucatán," 1790, AGS, Secretaría del Despacho de Guerra 7299, no. 8, f. 120; and "Ejército de Yucatán. Estados," 1790, AGS, Secretaría del Despacho de Guerra 7299, no. 10, f. 134.

115. "Revistas de inspección," 1790, AGS, Secretaría del Despacho de Guerra 7207, no. 27, f. 151.

116. "Estado de las Milicias Urbanas de Tizimín y Chancenote," 1790, AGS, Secretaría del Despacho de Guerra 7207, no. 41, f. 240.

117. Nancy P. Appelbaum, Anne S. Macpherson, and Karin Alejandra Rosemblatt, eds. "Introduction: Racial Nations," in *Race and Nation in Modern Latin America* (Chapel Hill: University of North Carolina Press, 2003), 9. The introduction does not discuss Yucatan but rather the social status of mulattos as an "intermediary category" more broadly.

118. "Expediente Reservado, que comprehende ciertos procedimientos observados en el Padre Cura del Pueblo de Chiquinsonot," 1796, AGN, Criminal 335, exp. 2, cuad. 56, f. 195.

119. In Yucatan and elsewhere, "Larger racial categories, such as 'Indian' . . . and 'black' were meaningless at the local community level, where self-identity tended to be rooted." Matthew Restall, ed., "Introduction: Black Slaves, Red Paint," in *Beyond Black and Red: African-Native Relations in Colonial Latin America* (Albuquerque: University of New Mexico Press), 5.

120. "Nueba informacion echa en el Pueblo de Chiquinsonot a pedimento del reo," 1795, AGN, Criminal 332, cuad. 50, ff. 32–33, 102–3. The casta men are distinguished from the Mayas not only by their surnames but by their identification as vecinos.

121. One of the men who signed his name and spoke Spanish actually went by two names—Pablo Flota and Fabián Flota. He stated that he went by Pablo Flota for the sake of his Maya neighbors, who found it easier to pronounce "Pab" rather than "Fab," since the sound "f" does not exist in Maya. "Nueva información hecha en el pueblo de Chikindzonot a pedimiento del reo," 1795, AGN, Criminal 332, cuad. 50, f. 143. In a second round of questioning he appears as "Fabian Flota (alias Pablo)." "Se hace relación del resultado sobre Coartada en el plenario," 1794, AGN, Criminal 294, f. 230v.

122. "Nueva información hecha en el pueblo de Chikindzonot a pedimiento del reo," 1795, AGN, Criminal 332, cuad. 50, ff. 3–33, 102–3.

123. Ibid., ff. 226–95. Doña María Agueda Osorio identified herself as the widow of Fernando Navarrette and Tomasa Santos was the widow of don Pedro Gutiérrez, the deceased juez español.

124. Ibid., ff. 226–95.

125. During the last decade of the eighteenth century, male slaves outnumbered female slaves by more than 2 to 1. O. Nigel Bolland, *The Formation of a Colonial Society: Belize, from Conquest to Crown Colony* (Baltimore: Johns Hopkins University Press, 1977), 51.

126. "Nueva información hecha en el pueblo de Chikindzonot a pedimiento del reo," 1795, AGN, Criminal 332, cuad. 50, ff. 6, 10, 32–33.

127. "Acaecimientos posteriores al homicidio en Chiquinsonot," 1800, AGN, Criminal 295, ff. 198–200.

128. Ibid., f. 211.

129. Douglas Butterworth and John K. Chance, *Latin American Urbanization* (Cambridge: Cambridge University Press, 1981), 22–23.

130. "Autos promovidos por el pardo Francisco Medina, por disenso de María Luisa Herrera, al matrimonio," 1791, AGEY, Colonial, Judicial, vol. 1, exp. 6.

131. "Expediente Reservado, que comprehende ciertos procedimientos observados en el Padre Cura del Pueblo de Chiquinsonot," 1796, AGN, Criminal 335, exp. 2, cuad. 56. While the curate and subdelegado of Izamal did not agree that Manuela Tolosa was a Spaniard, they did recognize her mother's right to have the final say in the matter and forbade Francisco from marrying her. For a detailed account on royal policy regarding parental consent and marriage, see Patricia Seed, *To*

Love, Honor, and Obey in Colonial Mexico: Conflicts over Marriage Choice, 1574–1821. 1st ed. (Stanford, CA: Stanford University Press, 1988).

CHAPTER 6

1. Exhaustive research by scholars such as Matthew Restall, Philip C. Thompson, and Arturo Güémez Pineda has created a comprehensive picture of cabildo structure and authority. See Restall, *Maya World*, 51–83; Philip C. Thompson, "The Structure of the Civil Hierarchy in Tekanto, Yucatan: 1785–1820," *Estudios de Cultura Maya* 16 (1985): 183–205; and Arturo Güémez Pineda, "El poder de los cabildos mayas y la venta de propiedades privadas a través del Tribunal de los Indios. Yucatán (1750–1821)," *Historia Mexicana* 54, no. 3 (January–March 2005): 697–760.

2. Restall, *Maya World*, 16–17, 88–94, gives a detailed exploration of the similar but not exactly synonymous *almehen* and *indio hidalgo*.

3. Thompson, "Structure of the Civil Hierarchy," 185, and Restall, *Maya World*, 63.

4. Matthew Restall, *Maya Conquistador* (Boston: Beacon Press, 1999), 45. See also John F. Chuchiak IV, "'Anhelo de un escudo de armas': La falta de concesiones de escudos de armas indígenas mayas y la iconografía apócrifa de la heráldica colonial en Yucatán," in *Los escudos de armas indígenas. De la colonia al México independiente*, ed. María Castañeda de la Paz and Hans Roskamp (Mexico City: Universidad Nacional Autónoma de México, 2013).

5. See also Thompson, *Tekanto*, for an alternative perspective on indios hidalgos.

6. For the origins of the Mesoamerican allies in the conquest of Yucatan, see John F. Chuchiak IV, "Forgotten Allies: The Origins and Roles of Native Mesoamerican Auxiliaries and Indios Conquistadores in the Conquest of Yucatan, 1526–1550," in *Indian Conquistadors: Indigenous Allies in the Conquest of Mesoamerica*, ed. Laura E. Matthew and Michel R. Oudijk (Norman: University of Oklahoma Press, 2007), 175–226.

7. "Revistas de Inspección," 1790, AGS, Secretaría del Despacho de Guerra 7207, no. 27, f. 151. Oxkutzcab's hidalgo militia was headed by don Pedro Nic as captain, don Marcelo Nic as first lieutenant, don José Antonio Catzin as second lieutenant, and don José Nic as sublieutenant. In Tekax, don Felipe Santiago Pech headed the unit as captain, followed by don Pedro Catzin as first lieutenant, don Juan José Pech as second lieutenant, and Juan Ypolito Pech as sublieutenant. Capt. don Santiago Dias headed the Ticul company, followed by don Juan de la Cruz Tun as first lieutenant, don Leonardo Ci as second lieutenant, and don Carlos Mis as sublieutenant. Muna's hidalgo militia officer corps consisted of Capt. don Teodoro Cen, don Pascual Orozco as first lieutenant, don Tiburcio Cen as second lieutenant, and don Mariano Canul as sublieutenant.

8. "Estado de las Milicias Urbanas de Tizimín y Chancenote," 1790, AGS, Secretaría del Despacho de Guerra 7207, no. 41, f. 240.

9. "Nueva información hecha en el pueblo de Chikindzonot a pedimiento del reo," 1795, AGN, Criminal 332, cuad. 50, ff. 15–27.

10. A firsthand description of the province in 1766 noted that a growing number of indios hidalgos exempt from tribute coincided with the growing population of tribute-paying natives. F. X. de C., *Extracto de la descripción política y geográfica de las provincias de Campeche y Yucatan hecha en el año de 1766 por D. F. X. de C. por orden del Sor. D. Josef de Galvez* (Mexico City, 1766), 502.

11. "Autos promovidos Roque Pech, indio hidalgo de Motul," 1791, AGEY, Colonial, Judicial, exp. 8, vol. 1.

12. Sergio Quezada and Tsubasa Okoshi Harada, *Papeles de los Xiu de Yaxá, Yucatán* (Mexico City: Universidad Nacional Autónoma de México, 2001), 147–65.

13. "Intestado de Pablo Pacab vecino que fue de Mérida," 1784, AGEY, Colonial, Sucesiones Intestadas, vol. 1, exp. 1, f. 19.

14. "Quaderno numero 32 formado en virtud de lo mandado en Auto de 15 de Abril," 1794, AGN, Criminal 322, parte 1, exp. 1,f. 22v. The record of the suit appears on the list of papers sequestered from the deposed subdelegado of Tihosuco, don Pedro Rafael Pastrana. The confiscated papers do not appear, only a reference to them: "Ytt: N° 31 con un pedimento de María Yutan Yndia Ydalga de Chunhuhub contra Miguel Burgos de Maní, demanda de esponsales, y un despacho diligenciado para solicitarlo."

15. "Comprensivo de las nuebas providencias," 1795, AGN, Criminal 392, cuad. 23, f. 411.

16. "Declaraciones de Remigio Ucan, Pedro Pot y Lorenzo Yama," 1795, AGN, Criminal 317, exp. 1, ff. 179–82.

17. "Criminal contra Francisco Canché, por haver robado a Casimiro Chay, una Mula Verdoza mojina, que vendió a Pedro Castilla de Hunucmá," 1802, AGN, Criminal 361, exp. 6, ff. 352–55.

18. "Lucas Vargas y complices—Polvora," 1791, AGI, México 3069, f. 3v. Functionaries involved in the Vargas case also bypassed an interpreter in resolving the matter of property confiscated from Vargas that he had not paid for that belonged to a Maya muleteer. Baltasar Peraza, identified only as "conversant in the Yucatecan and Castilian languages," produced a copy in Spanish for official record keeping. He was not identified as an interpreter, nor does he appear elsewhere as a translator.

19. "Expediente Reservado, que comprehende ciertos procedimientos observados en el Padre Cura del Pueblo de Chiquinsonot," 1796, AGN, Criminal 335, exp. 2, cuad. 56, f. 195.

20. "Testimonio de la Sumaria que sobre los recelos que mostró el Capitán D. Juan José de Fierros, le formó el Sõr D. Jose Savido de Vargas," 1795, AGI, México 3039, no. 2, ff. 15–17. According to a 1790 militia roster, Briseño would have served as a soldier for over five years by 1795 and would have been forty-two years old. "Batallón de Castilla de Campeche, Yucatán," 1790, AGS, Secretaría del Despacho de Guerra 7299, no. 2, f. 4v.

21. "Nueva información hecha en el pueblo de Chikindzonot a pedimiento del reo," 1795, AGN, Criminal 332, cuad. 50, f. 237.

22. "Testimonio de Diligencias preventativas de la causa criminal que se ha de seguir contra el Ynfame alevozo, que asesinó al Señor Don Lucas de Galvez. . . . ," 1792, AGN, Criminal 299, cuad. 3, ff. 202–10v. The definition of *mayorcol* is found in Terry Rugeley, *Yucatán's Maya Peasantry and the Origins of the Caste War* (Austin: University of Texas Press, 1996), 74.

23. "Cúmulo de Bandos Promulgados," 1793, AGN, Criminal 302, no. 8, ff. 327–33.

24. Ibid., ff. 332v.

25. Ibid., f. 150.

26. "Expediente formado a consequencia del fallecimiento de D. Pedro Gutiérrez, Capitan de Milicias Urbanas de Chiquinsonot, y Juez Español que fue de dho Pueblo," 1794, AGN, Criminal 316, cuad. 48, f. 3v.

27. "Nueva información hecha en el pueblo de Chikindzonot a pedimiento del reo," 1795, AGN, Criminal 332, cuad. 50, f. 237.

28. "Quaderno numero 32 formado en virtud de lo mandado en Auto de 15 de Abril," 1794, AGN, Criminal 322, parte 1, exp. 1, ff. 22–28. Only one of these Maya-language documents found its way into the volume of correspondence related to the case. The subdelegado, who valued Maya documents much less than a modern historian, turned over the certification page of the Mayas of Sacalaca and used it to write a personal letter of his own. Ibid., 49v.

29. *Legal Documents and Municipal Records from the District of Valladolid, Yucatán, Mexico, 1712–1866*, Newberry Library, Edward E. Ayer Collection, no. 1604, ff. 71–84, consists entirely of documents written by Muñoz between 1785 and 1789. Additional documents appear to be written in Muñoz's hand as well, but the severe damage to the original documents reproduced in the photostats renders these documents unintelligible.

30. In describing an analogous situation in colonial Guatemala, one scholar described the retention of Caqchikel writing during the colonial period as a "major medium of resistance to both Spanish rule and Spanish culture." Robert M. Hill II, *Colonial Cakchiquels: Highland Maya Adaptation to Spanish Rule, 1600–1700* (Fort Worth: Harcourt Brace Jovanovich, 1992), 127.

31. María Margarita Rospide, "La real cédula del 10 de Mayo de 1770 y la enseñanza del castellano: Observaciones sobre su aplicación en el territorio altoperuano," in *Memoria del X Congreso del Instituto Internacional de Historia del Derecho Indiano* (Mexico City: Escuela Libre de Derecho/Universidad Nacional Autónoma de México, 1995).

32. The notion that the secularization of parishes—a transition from Franciscan oversight to secular clergymen as heads of pueblo churches—correlated with a decline in fluency and literacy in Yucatec Maya on the part of curates seems to be mistaken. In his request for priests from Yucatan to man the understaffed parishes of Petén, the presidio commander, don José de Gálvez (not a known relation of either don Lucas or his more famous namesake) wrote of the

desirability of clergymen from Yucatan, who were all fluent in Yucatec Maya according to his petition. "El Padre Cura de aquel Presidio sre que de cuenta de la Real Hazienda se expense un sacerdote mas, para los fines que expresa," 1800, Archivo General de Centro América (AGCA), A1.11.7, leg. 186, exp. 3813, ff. 26v–29v. Jesuits spent less time among the Maya but learned the language all the same, to the point that some served as unofficial interpreters and others aided in the creation of late colonial grammars and dictionaries. See Mark W. Lentz, "'The Mission' That Wasn't: Yucatan's Jesuits, the Mayas, and El Petén, 1703–1767," *World History Connected* 10, no. 3 (October 2013).

33. Rugeley, *Yucatán's Maya Peasantry*, 23, examines the prominence of priests in pueblo politics in the late eighteenth and early nineteenth centuries.

34. "Ratificación de José Guadalupe Uc," 1795, AGN, Criminal 317, f. 192v.

35. Ibid., ff. 192v–94, 199v.

36. "Expediente del Governador de Yucatán, dn. Christoval de Zayas, sobre el Oficio que pasó con el Obispo de aquella Diocesis, para que removiese del Curato del Pueblo de Becar al Bachiller dn. Bernardo Echevarría," 1767, AGI, México 3053.

37. "Expediente Reservado, que comprehende ciertos procedimientos observados en el Padre Cura del Pueblo de Chiquinsonot," 1796, AGN, Criminal 335, exp. 2, cuad. 56, f. 222–29v.

38. "Reservada," 1794, AGN, Criminal 335, exp. 2, cuad. 59, ff. 254–54v.

39. Another example of the concept of the church building as a structure outside royal jurisdiction took place when don Manuel Torralba arrived in Chikindzonot, refused to show his passport, and took refuge in the church to avoid arrest. "Expediente Reservado, que comprehende ciertos procedimientos observados en el Padre Cura del Pueblo de Chiquinsonot," 1796, AGN, Criminal 335, exp. 2, cuad. 56, ff. 193–99.

40. "Ratificación de Gregorio Yama," 1795, AGN, Criminal 317, f. 198.

41. "Acaecimientos posteriores al homicidio en Chiquinsonot," 1800, AGN, Criminal 295, ff. 198–201v.

42. For a discussion of how jurisdictional lines were drawn under Philip II, see Jorge E. Traslosheros, "Los indios, la Inquisición y los tribunales eclesiásticos ordinarios en Nueva España: Definición jurisdiccional y justo proceso, 1571–c. 1750," in *Los indios ante los foros de justicia religiosa en la Hispanoámerica virreinal*, ed. Jorge E. Traslosheros and Ana de Zaballa Beascoechea (Mexico City: Universidad Nacional Autónoma de México, 2010).

43. "Se hace relación de otras diligencias relativas a coartada y distancia de Mérida a Chiquinsonot," 1800, AGN, Criminal 295, cap. 3, f. 207v.

44. "Expediente Reservado, que comprehende ciertos procedimientos observados en el Padre Cura del Pueblo de Chiquinsonot," 1796, AGN, Criminal 335, exp. 2, cuad. 56, ff. 158, 161.

45. As local-level judges of the Provisorato de Indios, priests claimed the right to first instance trials—to hear cases for the first time (i.e., not an appellate court)—of a wide variety of crimes perceived as "sins" that fell under the church's jurisdiction such as bigamy, adultery, and drunkenness. John F. Chuchiak IV, "The Indian Inquisition and the Extirpation of Idolatry: The Process of Punishment in the *Provisorato de Indios* of the Diocese of Yucatan, 1563-1812," (PhD diss., Tulane University, 2000), 10, 14-17.

46. "Resumen Conciso del Extracto General," 29 June 1794, AGI, México 3040, f. 61. In an attempt to limit the influence of outsiders on the testimony of the residents of Chikindzonot, Subdelegado Cárdenas published an order that no Maya could leave without permission from the cacique, don Gregorio, and no vecino could leave without permission from Juez Español Ancona.

47. "Expediente Reservado, que comprehende ciertos procedimientos observados en el Padre Cura del Pueblo de Chiquinsonot," 1796, AGN, Criminal 335, exp. 2, cuad. 56, f. 200. Not surprisingly, the priest don Domingo de Cárdenas disobeyed these orders and sent one of his Maya mayores of the convent, Leonardo Pat, to Mérida without notifying either Maya or Spanish authorities. Pat appears as one of the "mayoles" [*sic*] on an extensive list of the forty-five assistants of the priest in Ibid., ff. 208.

48. "Papeles exividos por D. José Correa Romero, que se titulan defensa del teniente de milicias Don Toribio del Mazo," 1796, AGN, Criminal 336, f. 285.

49. Ibid., ff. 285, 467-69.

50. Torres apparently never rose above the rank of soldier, likely due to his unfortunate role, however small, in covering up for don Toribio. "Revista de Comisario," 1801, AGEY, Colonial, Militar, vol. 1, exp. 18.

CHAPTER 7

1. Brigadier O'Neill's letter informing the crown of Cárdenas's death described a long sickness that left him paralyzed and without movement in his right arm. "Mateo Cárdenas, Fallecimiento," 22 October 1797, AGS, Secretaría del Despacho de Guerra 7212, no. 51, f. 435.

2. For a discussion of the battle's role in the formation of the national myth and a critique of its role in subsequent Belizean historiography from a gendered and ethnic perspective, see Anne S. MacPherson, *From Colony to Nation: Women Activists and the Gendering of Politics in Belize, 1912-1982* (Lincoln: University of Nebraska Press, 2007).

3. For an extensive, thoroughly researched discussion of how rumor and public reputation influenced one's standing in a court of law, see Tamar Herzog, *Upholding Justice: Society, State, and the Penal System in Quito (1650-1750)* (Ann Arbor: University of Michigan Press, 2004).

4. For discussions of the rise of the hacendados, see Patch, *Maya and Spaniard*, 190–200, and Machuca Gallegos, *Los hacendados de Yucatán*.

5. For a discussion of the construction and development of the city center of Mérida, see Mark Childress Lindsay, "Spanish Mérida: Overlaying the Maya City," (PhD diss., University of Florida, 1999), 40–48. Restall, *Maya World*, 32, has a map of colonial central Mérida.

6. J. Ignacio Rubio Mañé, *La casa de Montejo en Mérida de Yucatán* (Mexico City: Imprenta Universitaria, 1941), 101–2.

7. Rare among Yucatecans, the Solís descendants of don Cristóval Alonso de Solís, regidor and adelantado of Yucatan, had noble origins in Spain and laid claim to significant landholdings in Castile in a seventeenth-century succession dispute. In part due to distance, the Yucatecan Solíses lost their appeal against a rival claimant, don Gabriel de Solís. Joseph Fernández de Retes, "Consulta Iuridica sobre el pleito que esta pendiente antes los señores Presidente, y Oydores de la Real Chancillería de Valladolid; entre D. Gabriel de Solís, y el Colegio de la Aprobacion de la Ciudad de Salamanca, y D. Christoval Alonso de Solis, Adelantado de Yucatan, vezino, y Regidor de la dicha Ciudad," 1670, Biblioteca Nacional de España Manuscript Collection, Porcones, 706–6.

8. Rubio Mañé, *La casa de Montejo*, 97–98.

9. More detail on the layout of the city center and the residents of the central homes is unfortunately lacking, in part due to the severe deterioration of the records of an 1809 census that recorded the owners and residents of homes for the city center.

10. Heredía traveled from Spain in Gálvez's company in 1787 and remained one of his closest allies until his death. "Expediente de información y licencia de pasajero a indias del capitán de navío Lucas de Gálvez," 1787, AGI, Contratación 5531, no. 4, ramo 20.

11. Piñeres defended the lack of progress in prosecuting the case in a 1792 letter, complaining of his recent arrival and blaming the delay on the fact that he knew little of the province or its inhabitants. "Segundo Quaderno," 1792, AGI, México 3036, no. 116, f. 20. Having well-placed relatives elsewhere in Spain's empire was often of little use in Yucatan. Piñeres's uncle don Juan Gutiérrez de Piñeres served as an oidor of the Casa de la Contratación, a connection of little use in Mérida. "Provistos," 1776, AGI, Contratación 5786, lib. 3, ff. 36v–40.

12. "Relación de los testigos que sospecharon que D^n. Toribio del Mazo fue el homicida del Sr. Galvez," 1800, AGN, Criminal 295, cap. 2, ff. 55v–56.

13. "Expediente formado a representacion del Yllustrisimo Señor Don Fray Suis de Piña y Mazo Obispo de Yucatan," 1782, AGN, Civil 1679, exp. 12, describes the 1782 incident. In this case, the bishop confronted the authority of the cabildo—specifically that of the alcalde, don Ignacio Rendón—who intended to punish Solís for cohabitation with a woman to whom he was not married. Beyond the obvious challenge to the church's legal privileges entailed by the cabildo's

prosecution of a church notary, cohabitation itself was an infraction that leading churchmen believed to be under their purview.

14. "Se hace relación de la confesión de D. Toribio del Mazo," 1794, AGN, Criminal 294, f. 118v.

15. "Testimonio de lo contenido en el expediente reservado numº 42," 1795, AGN, Criminal 325, ff. 1–10, describes the confrontation between the bishop and his dependents, such as don Antonio Poveda, and witnesses against his nephew, such as don Luis Durán, don Pedro Rivas Rocafull, and don José Rivas.

16. "Testimonio de varias diligencias practicadas en la causa sobre el homicidio que se executó en la persona del Señor don Lucas de Gálvez," 1793, AGN, Criminal 310, cuad. 2, letra B, f. 271.

17. Martínez Ortega, *Estructura y configuración*, 36–48.

18. Ibid., 51–57.

19. There were exceptions to this rule, in Campeche at least. In 1708 the notary stood accused of being of Indian and "mulatto" ancestry. Likewise, at least one member of the Afro-Yucatecan family Duque de Estrada—don Alejandro José Duque de Estrada—served on Campeche's cabildo. Don Miguel Duque de Estrada, who suffered the ignominy of rejection from representing Yucatan at the Cádiz Cortes, overcame this brief setback and served on Campeche's cabildo in the final years of the colonial period. Martínez Ortega, *Estructura y configuración*, 56, and Melchor Campos García, "Ciudadanía doceañista y reputación sin objeciones: El caso Duque de Estrada," in *Encrucijadas de la ciudadanía y la democracia: Yucatán, 1812–2004*, ed. Sergio Quezada (Mérida: Universidad Autónoma de Yucatán, 2005), 44.

20. Martínez Ortega, *Estructura y configuración*, appendix 1, 252.

21. Ibid., 43.

22. Tertulias in areas that were hotbeds of early independence movements have received more coverage in recent historical work due to their role in the creation of separatist sentiment. See, for example, Evelyn Cherpak, "The Participation of Women in the Independence Movement in Gran Colombia, 1780–1830," in *Latin American Women: Historical Perspectives*, ed. Asunción Lavrin (Westport, CT: Greenwood Press, 1978). In Yucatan, the cradle of autonomist sentiment was not the condesa viuda's home, it was the sacristy of the Church of San Juan Bautista in Mérida, which led to the identification of its major figures as *sanjuanistas*. J. Ignacio Rubio Mañé, "Los Sanjuanistas de Yucatán. I. Manuel Jiménez Solís, el padre Justis," *Boletín del Archivo General de la Nación* 8, 2nd series, nos. 3–4 (July–December 1967): 731–57.

23. A census from the time lists only one person of titled nobility. "Estado General de la población de la jurisdicción de Mérida. . . . ," AGN, Historia 522, exp. 257, in Rubio Mañé, *Archivo de la historia de Yucatán*, 210–12.

24. T-LAL/MC, VEMC 50, 1795, exp. 1, ff. 1–2.

25. Ibid., f. 2.

26. Ibid., ff. 24, 29, 30v, in the testimony of Trujillo and don Enrique de los Reyes and Pedro Rivas Rocafull.

27. Susan Migden Socolow, in *The Women of Colonial Latin America* (Cambridge: Cambridge University Press, 2000), observed that some of the seemingly innocent neighborly favors the condesa viuda did for Piñeres—including washing his clothes, cooking for him, and visiting at odd hours—were indeed considered evidence for a "mala amistad" (73).

28. T-LAL/MC, VEMC 50, 1795, exp. 2, ff. 3–20.

29. T-LAL/MC, VEMC 50, 1795, exp. 1, ff. 2v–3.

30. Ibid., ff. 10–14v.

31. T-LAL/MC, VEMC 50, 1795, exp. 2, f. 4.

32. Ibid., ff. 22, 25.

33. T-LAL/MC, VEMC 50, 1795, exp. 1, f. 4v.

34. Ibid., f. 12v.

35. Ibid., f. 12v.

36. Ibid., f. 19.

37. Ibid., f. 11.

38. T-LAL/MC, VEMC 50, 1795, exp. 2, f. 106.

39. "Nombramiento de fiscal de Manila a Gutiérrez de Piñeres," 1796, AGI, Filipinas 346, lib. 17, ff. 17r–20v.

40. T-LAL/MC, VEMC 50, 1795, exp. 2, f. 104v–7.

41. T-LAL/MC, VEMC 50, 1795, exp. 1, f. 18.

42. Carrillo y Ancona, *El obispado de Yucatán*, 2:952.

43. "Copia del Dictamen," 1798, AGI, México 3037, no. 136, f. 1. In his apt epigraph that opened one of his lengthy but direct summaries of the evidence against don Toribio, Guillén wrote, "Calumny takes up little paper; the satisfaction requires more." "La calumnia ocupa poco papel; La satisfaccion requiere mas" is a quotation from the Golden Age poet Francisco de Quevedo. The quotation, from a lesser-known work, is found in Antonio Valladares de Sotomayor, *Semanario erudito, que comprehende varias obras ineditas, criticas, morales, instructivas, politicas, historicas, satiricas, y jocosas, de nuestros mejores autores antiguos, y modernos* (Madrid: Imprenta y librería de Alfonso Lopez, 1787), 213.

44. "Ynstrucción Reservada, en que se pone de manifiesto los varios excesos cometidos por el Licenciado D. Miguel Magdaleno Sandoval Asesor de la Yntendencia de Mérida de Yucatan a efecto de impedir la Administracion de Justicia en la causa formada contra el alevoso homicida del Señor D. Lucas de Gálvez," 1798, AGI, México 3037, no. 137, f. 2.

45. "Reservada," 1798, AGI, México 3039, no. 31, f. 2.

46. "El Virrey de Nueva España da cuenta con testimonio de que a representación del Juez de la Acordada, y de Bevidas prohividas, suspendió d estas Asesorias al Liz^do dn. Juan Joseph Barberí y nombró a dn. Francisco Guillén," 1783, AGI, México 1282, no. 238.

47. Eric Beerman, "Arturo O'Neill: First Governor of West Florida during the Second Spanish Period," *Florida Historical Quarterly* 60, no. 1 (July 1981): 29–41.

48. Ibid., 31.

49. W. S. Murphy, "The Irish Brigade of Spain at the Capture of Pensacola, 1781," *Florida Historical Quarterly* 38, no. 3 (January 1960): 216–25.

50. "Oficio y Contestación," 1797, AGI, México 3039, no. 3. See Laura Machuca Gallegos, "Los Quijano de Yucatán: Entre la tradición y la modernidad," *Caravelle* 101 (December 2013) for a discussion of the friendship between Brigadier O'Neill and the Quijano family. O'Neill and several of the Quijanos were also regular attendees of the tertulias hosted by the condesa viuda de Miraflores.

51. The best description of the Quijanos, their origins and influence at the municipal level, and their rivalries is found in Machuca Gallegos, "Los Quijano de Yucatán." See also Patch, *Maya and Spaniard*, 191–92.

52. "Quinto Estado de la Causa de Homicidio," 1801, AGI, México 3037, no. 167, sub-no. 3.

53. See Machuca Gallegos, *Los hacendados de Yucatán*, for the ascent of the Quijanos as important figures within the rising hacendado class.

54. "Negación del uso de bastón a Juan Esteban Quijano, escribano de Gobierno y Guerra," 1792, AGS, Secretaría del Despacho de Guerra 7209, no. 17, f. 79, and Martínez Ortega, *Estructura y configuración*, appendix 1, 260.

55. "Expediente de información y licencia de pasajero a indias de José Miguel Quijano," 1786, AGI, Contratación 5530, no. 2, ramo 17.

56. "Quinto Estado de la Causa de Homicidio," 1801, AGI, México 3037, no. 167, sub-nos. 3–4.

57. Ibid., no. 167, sub-no. 4.

58. "Concesión de licencia de matrimonio," 1788, AGS, Secretaría del Despacho de Guerra 7222, no. 20, f. 126; and "Testimonio del Quaderno 1ro de la Causa formada sobre el homicidio executado en la Persona del Sr. Dn. Lucas de Gálvez," 1792, AGI, México 3036, no. 118, f. 44.

59. "Quinto Estado de la Causa de Homicidio," 1801, AGI, México 3037, no. 167, sub-no. 4; and "Extracto de las Diligencias practicadas en Yucatan por el Capitán de Fragata D. Juan Tabat," 1801, AGI, México 3038, no. 142, sub-no. 173.

60. "Ignacio Quijano, Grados," 1789, AGS, Secretaría del Despacho de Guerra 7206, no. 46, f. 309.

61. "Copia de Carta," 1793, AGI, México 3036, ff. 76v–92. Gálvez accused Captain Quijano of mismanagement of funds without outright allegations of fraud, though he clearly insinuated that he suspected Quijano was using the funds for equipping his militia for personal use.

62. "Quinto Estado de la Causa de Homicidio," 1801, AGI, México 3037, no. 167, sub-no. 4. Although Capt. don Ignacio Quijano outranked Captain Poblaciones in the militia hierarchy, he had the trust of Bourbon administrators and had recently been named a knight in the Order of Santiago ("Expedientillos," 1789,

AHN, Consejo de Órdenes, no. 9400) and had overseen the residencia (review of service of Gálvez's predecessor in the post of governor). "Residencia tomada al Gobernador Don José Merino," 1789, AGI, México 3041.

63. "Quinto Estado de la Causa de Homicidio," 1801, AGI, México 3037, no. 167, sub-no. 4.

64. Unlike Gálvez, who alienated a number of powerful Yucatecans of all backgrounds, his successor, don Arturo O'Neill, seems to have gained the favor of many of the leading lights of the city, especially the Quijanos. Noting the financial assistance the paterfamilias, don Juan Esteban Quijano, made to the war effort against the British settlement in Belize—over 90,000 pesos—O'Neill promoted don José Miguel Quijano to the post of commander of the militia unit in Hunucmá. One of the intendant's final official acts in Mérida was to recommend Lt. Col. don Ignacio Quijano for a governorship upon the vacation of such a post in 1801. "Recomendación a favor de Ignacio Quijano, capitán de la Compañía de Dragones de Mérida," 1800, AGS, Secretaría del Despacho de Guerra 7213, no. 35, ff. 319–21; and "Solicitud de un informe sobre la propuesta de establecer un comandante de Milicias en la subdelegación de Hunucmá, solicitada por José Miguel de Quijano, capitán de Milicias de Mérida," 1799, AGS, Secretaría del Despacho de Guerra 7213, no. 36.

65. See Seed, *To Love, Honor, and Obey*, 205–25, for a detailed discussion of the reaffirmation of parental authority over marriage choices with the promulgation of the Royal Pragmatic of 1776.

66. "Noveno estado de la Causa de homicidio cometido en la persona de D. Lucas de Galvez," 1802, AGI, México 3040, no. 174, cuad. 2.

67. Rubio Mañé, "Los Sanjuanistas de Yucatán," 213, 222.

68. "Ynstrucción Reservada, en que se pone de manifiesto los varios excesos cometidos por el Licenciado D. Miguel Magdaleno Sandoval Asesor de la Yntendencia de Mérida de Yucatan a efecto de impedir la Administracion de Justicia en la causa formada contra el alevoso homicida del Señor D. Lucas de Gálvez," 1798, AGI, México 3037, no. 137.

69. Ibid.

70. "Minuta de Oficio al Secretario de Gracia y Justicia," 1800, AGI, Estado 40, no. 77.

71. "Miguel Magno Sandoval al Embajador de Francia," 1807, AGI, Estado 42, no. 18.

72. T-LAL/MC, VEMC 50, 1795, exp. 2, f. 82.

73. "Yndice de los Quadernos que entregó hoy dia de la fha en esta Secretaria de Cámara del virreinato el D. D. Francisco Guillén," 1802, AGN, Criminal 619, exp. 1, f. 4.

74. "Testimonio de varias diligencias practicadas en la causa sobreel homicidio que se executó en la persona del Señor don Lucas de Gálvez," 1793, AGN, Criminal 310, cuad. 2, letra B, f. 258v.

75. Herzog, *Upholding Justice*, 208–9.

76. Copies of two of the poems, each of which was followed by a sonnet as part of a single composition, are found in "Carta reservada," AGI, México 3036, no. 118, ff. 73v–76; two others are in "Lucas Galvez. Procesos," 1792, AGS, Secretaría del Despacho de Guerra 7219, no. 3, ff. 93, 95.

77. Ibid., f. 94.

78. Ibid., f. 94.

79. Though never mentioned in the proceedings, likely due to the impolitic nature of casting aspersions on a counselor so close to the court, fray Luis's brother Dr. don Pedro de Piña y Mazo served as a fiscal of the Council of the Indies. Maximiliano Castrillo Martínez, *Opúsculo sobre la historia de la villa de Astudillo* (Burgos: Imprenta de la viuda de Villanueva, 1877), 147.

80. "Lucas Galvez. Procesos," 1792, AGS, Secretaría del Despacho de Guerra 7219, no. 3, f. 95.

81. "Testimonio del Quaderno 1ro de la Causa formada sobre el homicidio executado en la Persona del Sr. Dn. Lucas de Gálvez," 1792, AGI, México 3036, no. 118, ff. 73v.–75.

82. Ibid., ff. 75v.–76.

83. "Diligencias instruidas en averiguación de ciertos versos," 1793, AGN, Criminal 302, cuad. 10, f. 8.

84. The line in one of the poems, "De España vino la causa," seemed to refer to the outside prosecutor; Piñeres took offense at the poems, interpreting them as an insult to his effectiveness in bringing the assassin to justice. Ibid., ff. 1–5v.

85. Ibid., f. 6.

86. "Sobre el homicidio de D. Lucas de Galvez Capitan Gral. de Yucatan," 1793, AGN, Criminal 471, f. 47.

87. "Diligencia para el conocimiento de ciertos versos," 1794, AGI, México 3036, no. 119, f. 43. The details of the rivalry between Lara and the bishop are found in "Expediente del Obispo, don Josef Nicolás de Lara, y dn. Josef Phelipe Pastrana," 1782–1790, AGI, México 2599; and "Expediente sobre los incidents suscitados entre el Obispo de Yucatán, don Fray Luis de Piña y Mazo, y el cura de la iglesia del Sagrario de la cathedral, don Jose Nicolás de Lara, apoyado por el alcalde de Mérida, don José Felipe de Pastrana, por diveros asuntos," 1785–1790, AGI, México 2600.

88. "Relación de varios recursos hechos por el Cura Correa," 1800, AGN, Criminal 293, cap. 2, f. 87.

89. "Diligencias instruidas en averiguación de ciertos versos," 1793, AGN, Criminal 302, cuad. 10, f. 7.

90. Ibid., ff. 3–9.

91. Ibid., f. 3v.

92. T-LAL/MC, VEMC 50, 1795, exp. 2, f. 52v.

93. "Relación de los testigos que sospecharon que Dn. Toribio fue el homicida del Sr. Galvez," 1800, AGN, Criminal 295, cap. 2, ff. 55v–57v.

94. "Expediente de información y licencia de pasajero a indias del capitán de navío Lucas de Gálvez," 1787, AGI, Contratación 5531, no. 4, ramo 20. Like don Francisco de Heredía, don José Morán remained a steadfast ally of the intendant's faction and an opponent of the bishop after Gálvez's death.
95. "Relación de los testigos que sospecharon que D^n. Toribio fue el homicida del Sr. Galvez," 1800, AGN, Criminal 295, cap. 2, ff. 57v–60v.
96. The involvement of the individuals in the conspiracy of gossips is found in "Papeles exividos por D. José Correa Romero, que se titulan defensa del teniente de milicias Don Toribio del Mazo," 1796, AGN, Criminal 336, f. 14; and "Instrucción reservada en que se ponen de manifiesto los varios excesos cometidos por el Liz^{do} D. Miguel Magdaleno Sandoval Asesor de la Yntendencia de Mérida de Yucatán," 1797, AGI, México 3039, no. 2, sub-nos. 62–63.
97. "Testimonio del Expediente formado a consecuencia de Rl. Cédula de S. M. de 20 de Agosto ultimo," 1796, AGI, México 3037, no. 131.
98. "Parte 4ª del Memorial ajustado de la causa formada sobre el homicidio del Sr. D. Lucas de Galvez," 1800, AGN, Criminal 291, f. 180.
99. "Instrucción reservada en que se ponen de manifiesto los varios excesos cometidos por el Liz^{do} D. Miguel Magdaleno Sandoval Asesor de la Yntendencia de Mérida de Yucatán," 1797, AGI, México 3039, no. 2, sub-no. 67.
100. Ibid., no. 2, sub-no. 69.
101. Ibid., no. 2, sub-nos. 66, 70.
102. "Memorial ajustado de la causa formada sobre el homicidio del Sr. Don Lucas Galvez—Lista de Reos," 1800, AGN, Criminal 287, f. 2v.
103. Tamar Herzog, *La administración como un fenómeno social: La justicia penal de la ciudad de Quito (1650–1750)* (Madrid: Centro de Estudios Constitucionales, 1995), 274–79.
104. "Se hace relación del resultado sobre Coartada en el plenario," 1794, AGN, Criminal 294, ff. 115–16.
105. "Expediente del Obispo, don Josef Nicolás de Lara, y dn. Josef Phelipe Pastrana," 1782–1790, AGI, México 2599, ff. 51–64v. Peón was the sole peninsular on the cabildo.
106. "Relación de lo que resulta instruido acerca del genio, conducta, y circunstancias del Ten^{te} D^n Toribio del Mazo," 1800, AGN, Criminal 295, cap. 3, f. 61.
107. Ibid., ff. 61–61v.
108. Ibid., f. 61v.
109. Ibid., f. 62.
110. Ibid., ff. 62–64.
111. "Solicitud del Auditor de Yucatan contra el Comisionado Guillén que pasó de órn. del Virrey," 1798, AGI, México 3039, no. 3, ff. 5–8.
112. Ibid., cap. 1, ff. 49–51.
113. "Cartas reservadas pertenecientes a la Causa sobre el homicidio," 1796, AGN, Criminal 322, parte 2, cuad. 23, ff. 211, 213v.

114. "Autos acerca de la calidad de la amistad del Teniente Mazo con Dª. Casiana," 1800, AGN, Criminal 295, cap. 1, ff. 51v–52.

115. Ibid., ff. 52v–53.

116. "Varios papeles que se encontraron al Teniente Dn. Toribio del Mazo, y se mandaron separar delos demás por lo que puedan conducir a la averiguación de que se trata en al causa sobre el homicidio executado en la Persona del Sr. Dn. Lucas de Gálvez," 1796, AGN, Criminal 472, cuad. 15, ff. 104–18.

117. "Testimonio de lo Contenido en el Quaderno Reservado numº 42," 1795, AGI, México 3040, no. 7, ff. 36, 58.

118. "Declaración del D. Luis Durán," AGI, México 3040, no. 7, ff. 64–65.

119. Ibid., ff. 64–65; and "Extracto de las diligencias practicadas en Yucatan por el Capitán de Fragata don Juan Tabat," 1801, AGI, México 3038, no. 11, sub-no. 173.

120. "Testimonio de lo Contenido en el Quaderno Reservado numº 42," 1795, AGI, México 3040, no. 7, f. 128.

121. One witness, don Luis Durán, criticized the bishop for his frequent use of charges of sexual misconduct while ignoring the indiscretions of his own allies. Ibid., f. 64.

122. "Testimonio de varias diligencias practicadas en la causa sobreel homicidio que se executó en la persona del Señor don Lucas de Gálvez," 1793, AGN, Criminal 310, cuad. 2, letra B, f. 257v–58.

123. "Sobre el homicidio de D. Lucas de Galvez Capitan Gral. de Yucatan," 1793, AGN, Criminal 471, ff. 46, 68, 108, 110.

124. "Tribunal del Capitán General. Diligencias reservadas a pedimento de don José Julián Peón y Cárdenas, contra doña Felipa Maldonado, su esposa, y don José Carreño," 1806, AGEY, Colonial, Judicial, vol. 1, exp. 14.

125. "Testimonio de lo Contenido en el Quaderno Reservado numº 42," 1795, AGI, México 3040, no. 7, f. 58.

126. Ibid., ff. 43, 53.

127. Ibid., ff. 67–69.

128. Ibid., f. 53.

129. Under Spanish law, subjects reached legal majority at the age of twenty-five. See Socolow, *Women of Colonial Latin America*, 10. Escudero herself seems to have weathered the controversy without damage to her reputation. She later served as the hostess of tertulias for the conservative faction in the Constitutional Crisis of 1812–1814. Melchor Campos García, *Sociabilidades políticas en Yucatán: Un studio sobre los espacios públicos, 1780–1834* (Mérida: Universidad Autónoma de Yucatán, 2003), 45.

130. "Disposiciones para que cesen las relaciones ilícitas entre Francisco Heredia y Vergara, secretario de la Capitanía general, y María Josefa Escudero," 1799, AGS, Secretaría del Despacho de Guerra 7212, no. 35, f. 356.

131. Ibid., f. 356.

132. "Expediente de información y licencia de pasajero a indias del capitán de navío Lucas de Gálvez," 1787, AGI, Contratación 5531, no. 4, ramo 20.

133. "Disposiciones para que cesen las relaciones ilícitas entre Francisco Heredia y Vergara, secretario de la Capitanía general, y María Josefa Escudero," 1799, AGS, Secretaría del Despacho de Guerra 7212, no. 35, f. 363.

134. T-LAL/MC, VEMC 50, 1795, exp. 2, ff. 101–4. Piñeres's attorney, don Anselmo Rodríguez Balda, called the bishop's personal attack on the alleged lovers a "destruction of their honor, reputation, and good standing," including both Piñeres and the condesa viuda (f. 101).

135. "Reservada no. 2," 1798, AGI, México 3039, no. 27, f. 3.

136. T-LAL/MC, VEMC 50, 1795, exp. 2, f. 36v.

137. Jorge Ignacio Rubio Mañé, *El virreinato: Expansión y defensa* (Mexico City: Universidad Nacional Autónoma de México, 1961), 160.

138. "Extranjeros en Mérida y Campeche en 1796," 1796, AGN, Civil 1335, reprinted in *Diario de Yucatán*, 15 February 1938, 3, 6.

139. "Branciforte sobre los franceses existentes en aquel reino," 1796, AGI, Estado 24, no. 19, sub-no. 9, 1j. Most of the twenty-one French nationals residing in Yucatan were permitted to stay in Yucatan after a cursory examination of their permanence, economic activity, familial status, lifestyle, and political outlook. The two expelled bachelors were not suspected of any subversive activity. Instead, they seem to have been targeted for lack of steady work as part of the late Bourbon emphasis on criminalizing vagrancy. See Jorge I. Castillo Canché, "El contramodelo de la ciudadanía liberal: La vagancia en Yucatán, 1812–1842," in Quezada, *Encrucijadas de la ciudadanía*, 61–82.

140. "Estado General de la población de la jurisdicción de Mérida. . . . ," in Rubio Mañé, *Archivo de la historia de Yucatán*, 210–12.

141. Rugeley, *Yucatán's Maya Peasantry*, 92.

142. "Intestado de Pablo Bacab, Vecino que fue de Mérida," 1784, AGEY, Colonial, Sucesiones Intestadas, vol. 1, exp. 1. This dispute over native property, a sitio much larger than the solares (residential plots of land in or near cities) most urban Mayas possessed, shows that a small landed urban native elite still existed in Mérida, although the eighteenth century saw their landholdings diminish greatly. See also Bracamonte y Sosa, "Los solares urbanos de Mérida," 129–42.

143. A more typical almehen, Santiago Ucan, was not addressed as don and sold only a small amount of land, a solar. Libro de Protocolos, 1790–1792, ANEY, vol. 28, cuad. 2, f. 301, compact disc 28.

144. In Chile, Juan Valiente rose from black slave to encomendero in the post-conquest era. After the conquest period, when the permeability of social boundaries gave a few black conquistadors the chance to make the transition from slave to encomendero, individuals of African descent found their way to such rapid advancement blocked for the most part. Matthew Restall, "Black Conquistadors: Armed Africans in Early Spanish America," *The Americas* 57, no. 2 (October 2000), 174.

145. Restall, *Black Middle*, 195–96; and Campos García, "Ciudadanía doceañista y reputación sin objeciones," 30–37.
146. Patch, *Maya and Spaniard*, 192.
147. Terry Rugeley, *Rebellion Now and Forever: Mayas, Hispanics, and Caste War Violence in Yucatán, 1800–1880* (Stanford, CA: Stanford University Press, 2009), 26, 65, 83.
148. Patch, *Maya and Spaniard*, 192.
149. "Testimonio de lo contenido en el expediente reservado numº 42," 1795, AGN, Criminal 325, f. 12.
150. "Testimonio de varias diligencias practicadas en la causa sobre el homicidio que se executó en la persona del Señor don Lucas de Gálvez," 1793, AGN, Criminal 310, cuad. 2, letra B, ff. 255v–56v.
151. "Careo y confrontación del Reo con Dn. Miguel Quixano," 1795, AGN, Criminal 317, exp. 1, ff. 431–32.
152. "Testimonio del Quaderno 2º de las diligencias practicadas en la Causa sobre el homicidio del Sr. Dn. Lucas de Gálvez," 1794, AGI, México 3036, no. 119, f. 50.
153. See Seed, *To Love, Honor, and Obey*, 205–25. The Real Pragmatica, enacted by Carlos III, likely aimed to eliminate ecclesiastics as intermediaries who acted against parental wishes rather than strengthening patriarchal authority, its more significant impact. It also reversed an earlier policy that had emerged during the Council of Trent that granted free will in marriage choices to two consenting suitors who had reached majority, in spite of their parents' wishes.
154. "Sobre matrimonio de Dª. Mariana Echeverría con un hombre desigual vecino de Mérida de Yucatán," 1792, AGN, Civil 1567, exp. 10.
155. "Juzgado de la Costa. Diligencias promovidas por Dionicio Ricalde para impedir el matrimonio de Julio Puerto con Urbana Palma, Vecinos de Motul," Motul, 1803, AGEY, Colonial, Judicial, vol. 1 exp. 13.
156. Silvio Zavala, *La encomienda indiana* (Mexico City: Editorial Porrúa, 1992), 723. Baldos also oversaw a major transition of property to the church to assure the continuation of education in Mérida after the expulsion of the Jesuits. "Papeles varios sobre México y Yucatán, referente a la ocupación de temporalidades de jesuitas expulsos," 1771–1787, Biblioteca Nacional, Madrid, f. 342v.

CHAPTER 8

1. "Expediente promovido por don Bernardo Rejón sobre asistencias de los fondos de esta Real Carcel," 1803, AGN, Criminal 329, exp. 3, f. 358. Rejón was a first lieutenant with the Ninth Company of the milicias urbanas of Mérida.
2. "Papel curioso sobre el asesinato del Sr. Gálvez," 1807, AGI, México 3040, no. 178, cuad. 2.
3. "Extracto de las Diligencias practicadas en Yucatan por el Capitán de Fragata D. Juan Tabat," 1801, AGI, México 3038, no. 44, sub-no. 173.

4. "Testimonio de las últimas ocurrencias acaecidas en la causa," 1801, AGI, México 3037, no. 169, f. 8.

5. "Memorial ajustado de la causa formada sobre el homicidio del Sr. Don Lucas Galvez—Lista de Reos," 1800, AGN, Criminal 287, f. 3.

6. Andrés Cavo and Carlos María de Bustamante, *Suplemento a la historia de los tres siglos de México, durante el gobierno español*, vol. 3 (Mexico City: Imprenta de la testamentaria de D. Alejandro Valdes, 1836), 109. Contemporaries credited Bustamante's success in securing don Toribio's freedom as the event that launched his notable career. Hubert Howe Bancroft, *The Works of Hubert Howe Bancroft: History of Mexico* (San Francisco: History Company, 1887), 5:803.

7. Cavo and Bustamante, *Suplemento a la historia*, 110.

8. "Memorial ajustado de la causa formada sobre el homicidio del Sr. Don Lucas Galvez—Lista de Reos," 1800, AGN, Criminal 287, f. 2.

9. Ibid., f. 2.

10. Cavo and Bustamante, *Suplemento a la historia*, 108. Oddly, Molina Font credited Bustamante with an able defense—not of don Toribio but of Castro. *Gesta de los mayas*, 210.

11. "Extracto de las Diligencias practicadas en Yucatan por el Capitán de Fragata D. Juan Tabat," 1801, AGI, México 3038, no. 142, sub-no. 173.

12. "Testimonio del Memorial ajustado que formó el Sr. D. Manuel del Castillo Negrete," 1801, AGI, México 3038, no. 180, sub-no. 1.

13. "Lucas de Galvez Diligencias en la investigación del crimen del citado," 1802, AGN, Archivo Histórico de Hacienda 808, exp. 11, s/f.

14. "Diligencias practicadas por el Sr. Don Manuel del Castillo Negrete del consejo de S. M. su Alcalde de Corte y Juez de Provincia de esta N. E. y por el Sr. Dr. Don Jose María Bucheli, Juez Provisor y Vicario Capitular de este Arzobispado," 1802, AGN, Criminal 329, exp. 1, f. 102.

15. "Declaración del Ten^te de Granaderos Dn Juan José Fierros," 1793, AGI, México 3036, f. 42; and "Testimonio no 2⁰," 1793, AGI, México 3036, f. 50.

16. Ibid., f. 14.

17. "Extracto de las Diligencias practicadas en Yucatan por el Capitán de Fragata D. Juan Tabat," 1801, AGI, México 3038, no. 25, sub-no. 173.

18. Ibid., no. 89, sub-no. 173.

19. Ibid., no. 97, sub-no. 173.

20. "Testimonio de las últimas ocurrencias acaecidas en la causa," 1801, AGI, México 3037, no. 169, f. 15. López wrote a clandestine note to Rejón, pressuring him to testify that Gálvez and Padre Armas had fought and the Franciscan joined the conspiracy out of fear of exile, though this likely had no basis in fact. "Testimonio de las Diligencias practicadas por Örn del Excelentisimo Señor Virrey," 1802, AGN, Criminal 484, ff. 9–10.

21. "Diligencias practicadas por el Sr. Don Manuel del Castillo Negrete del consejo

de S. M. su Alcalde de Corte y Juez de Provincia de esta N. E. y por el Sr. Dr. Don
Jose María Bucheli, Juez Provisor y Vicario Capitular de este Arzobispado," 1802,
AGN, Criminal 329, exp. 1, f. 62.

22. "Lucas de Galvez Diligencias en la investigación del crimen del citado," 1802,
AGN, Archivo Histórico de Hacienda 808, exp. 11, s/f .

23. "Diligencias practicadas por el Sr. Don Manuel del Castillo Negrete del consejo
de S. M. su Alcalde de Corte y Juez de Provincia de esta N. E. y por el Sr. Dr. Don
Jose María Bucheli, Juez Provisor y Vicario Capitular de este Arzobispado," 1802,
AGN, Criminal 329, exp. 1, ff. 11–12.

24. Ibid., ff. 73–74.

25. Ibid., f. 17.

26. "Diligencias practicadas por el Sr. Don Manuel del Castillo Negrete del consejo
de S. M. su Alcalde de Corte y Juez de Provincia de esta N. E. y por el Sr. Dr. Don
Jose María Bucheli, Juez Provisor y Vicario Capitular de este Arzobispado," 1802,
AGN, Criminal 329, exp. 1, f. 12.

27. "Papel curioso sobre el asesinato del Sr. Gálvez," 1807, AGI, México 3040, no. 178,
cuad. 2.

28. "Diligencias practicadas por el Sr. Don Manuel del Castillo Negrete del consejo
de S. M. su Alcalde de Corte y Juez de Provincia de esta N. E. y por el Sr. Dr. Don
Jose María Bucheli, Juez Provisor y Vicario Capitular de este Arzobispado," 1802,
AGN, Criminal 329, exp. 1, ff. 15–18.

29. Ibid., f. 62.

30. Ibid., ff. 18–19.

31. Ibid., ff. 18–19.

32. "Extracto de las Actuaciones de revalidación, y ampliaciones. . . . ," 1802, AGI,
México 3038, no. 11, sub-no. 192.

33. "El Virrey avisa aver recibido el Real Despacho," 1800, AGI, México 3040, no. 178,
sub-no. 6.

34. "Extracto de las Diligencias practicadas en Yucatan por el Capitán de Fragata D.
Juan Tabat," 1801, AGI, México 3038, nos. 180–94, sub-no. 173.

35. Ibid., nos. 193–95, sub-no. 173.

36. Ibid., no. 187, sub-no. 173.

37. Ibid., nos. 187–88, sub-no. 173. In the end, Castro only paid her for the first two
months, a total of 16 pesos. "Diligencias practicadas por el Sr. Don Manuel del
Castillo Negrete del consejo de S. M. su Alcalde de Corte y Juez de Provincia de
esta N. E. y por el Sr. Dr. Don Jose María Bucheli, Juez Provisor y Vicario
Capitular de este Arzobispado," 1802, AGN, Criminal 329, exp. 1, f. 77v.

38. Ibid., f. 75v.

39. Ibid., ff. 64–65; and "Quaderno en que constan extractadas las diligencias practicadas por el Capitán de Fragata don Juan Tabat," 1803, AGN, Criminal 726, exp. 1,
f. 27.

40. Though Farriss stated that there were no links of compadrazgo between Mayas and Spaniards after the early colonial period, López's fictive kinship with his Maya confidant demonstrates that there were exceptions. *Maya Society*, 106.

41. "Diligencias practicadas por el Sr. Don Manuel del Castillo Negrete del consejo de S. M. su Alcalde de Corte y Juez de Provincia de esta N. E. y por el Sr. Dr. Don Jose María Bucheli, Juez Provisor y Vicario Capitular de este Arzobispado," 1802, AGN, Criminal 329, exp. 1, f. 62v.

42. "Extracto de las Diligencias practicadas en Yucatan por el Capitán de Fragata D. Juan Tabat," 1801, AGI, México 3038, no. 117, sub-no. 173.

43. Ibid.

44. "Diligencias practicadas por el Sr. Don Manuel del Castillo Negrete del consejo de S. M. su Alcalde de Corte y Juez de Provincia de esta N. E. y por el Sr. Dr. Don Jose María Bucheli, Juez Provisor y Vicario Capitular de este Arzobispado," 1802, AGN, Criminal 329, exp. 1, ff. 101–4.

45. "Extracto de las Actuaciones de revalidación, y ampliaciones. . . . ," 1802, AGI, México 3038, no. 6, sub-no. 192.

46. "Testimonio de las últimas ocurrencias acaecidas en la causa," 1801, AGI, México 3037, no. 169, f. 15v.

47. Ibid., f. 15v.

48. Ibid., f. 24.

49. "Consejo de 1º de Diciembre de 1801," 1801, AGI, México 3040, no. 178.

50. Burkholder and Chandler, *Biographical Dictionary*, 62.

51. "Carta Reservada no. 34," 1802, AGI, México 3040, no. 6.

52. "Extracto de las Actuaciones de revalidación, y ampliaciones. . . . ," 1802, AGI, México 3038, no. 6, sub-no. 192; "Correspondencia del Gobernador de Luisiana," 1793, AGI, Cuba 134A, 134B; and "Correspondencia a los intendentes de Luisiana," 1799, AGI, Cuba 602A, 602B.

53. Tabat outlived his predecessor, Dr. Guillén, which provided him the opportunity to prove his loyalty to the crown on repeated occasions, rising through the ranks of the military hierarchy at a time of insurgency. In 1820, when Spain saw its colonies breaking away in the wars of independence in Latin America, Tabat served as the secretary of war. "Oficio de Juan Tabat al Secretario de Estado," 1820, AGI, Estado 89, no. 97.

54. "Diligencias practicadas por el Sr. Don Manuel del Castillo Negrete del consejo de S. M. su Alcalde de Corte y Juez de Provincia de esta N. E. y por el Sr. Dr. Don Jose María Bucheli, Juez Provisor y Vicario Capitular de este Arzobispado," 1802, AGN, Criminal 329, exp. 1, f. 6v.

55. "Extracto de las Actuaciones de revalidación, y ampliaciones. . . . ," 1802, AGI, México 3038, no. 11, sub-no. 192.

56. "Testimonio de las últimas ocurrencias acaecidas en la causa," 1801, AGI, México 3037, no. 169, ff. 30–32.

57. "Diligencias practicadas por el Sr. Don Manuel del Castillo Negrete del consejo de S. M. su Alcalde de Corte y Juez de Provincia de esta N. E. y por el Sr. Dr. Don Jose María Bucheli, Juez Provisor y Vicario Capitular de este Arzobispado," 1802, AGN, Criminal 329, exp. 1, f. 2.

58. "Quinto Estado de la Causa de Homicidio," 1801, AGI, México 3037, no. 167, sub-no. 2.

59. Ibid.; and "Extracto de las Actuaciones de revalidación, y ampliaciones. . . . ," 1802, AGI, México 3038, no. 6, sub-no. 192.

60. "Testimonio de las últimas ocurrencias acaecidas en la causa," 1801, AGI, México 3037, no. 169, f. 21v.

61. "Diligencias practicadas por el Sr. Don Manuel del Castillo Negrete del consejo de S. M. su Alcalde de Corte y Juez de Provincia de esta N. E. y por el Sr. Dr. Don Jose María Bucheli, Juez Provisor y Vicario Capitular de este Arzobispado," 1802, AGN, Criminal 329, exp. 1, ff. 73–74.

62. Ibid., 62.

63. Cavo and Bustamante, *Suplemento a la historia*, 108.

64. "Extracto de las Actuaciones de revalidación, y ampliaciones. . . . ," 1801, AGI, México 3038, no. 63, sub-no. 173.

65. "Lucas de Galvez Diligencias en la investigación del crimen del citado," 1802, AGN, Archivo Histórico de Hacienda 808, exp. 1, ff. 4–5.

66. "Yndice de los Quadernos que entregó hoy dia de la fha en esta Secretaria de Cámara del virreinato el D. D. Francisco Guillén," 1802, AGN, Criminal 619, exp. 1, f. 12.

67. "Extracto de las Actuaciones de revalidación y ampliaciones," 1801, AGI, México 3038, no. 11, sub-no. 173.

68. "Diligencias practicadas por el Sr. Don Manuel del Castillo Negrete del consejo de S. M. su Alcalde de Corte y Juez de Provincia de esta N. E. y por el Sr. Dr. Don Jose María Bucheli, Juez Provisor y Vicario Capitular de este Arzobispado," 1802, AGN, Criminal 329, exp. 1, f. 136.

69. "Extracto de las Actuaciones de revalidación, y ampliaciones. . . . ," 1802, AGI, México 3038, no. 11, sub-no. 192.

70. "Quinto Estado de la Causa de Homicidio," 1801, AGI, México 3037, no. 167, sub-no. 1.

71. "Testimonio del Memorial ajustado que formó el Sr. D. Manuel del Castillo Negrete," 1801, AGI, México 3038, no. 180.

72. Ibid.

73. "Diligencias practicadas por el Sr. Don Manuel del Castillo Negrete del consejo de S. M. su Alcalde de Corte y Juez de Provincia de esta N. E. y por el Sr. Dr. Don Jose María Bucheli, Juez Provisor y Vicario Capitular de este Arzobispado," 1802, AGN, Criminal 329, exp. 1, ff. 111v, 117v.

74. "Extracto de las Diligencias practicadas en Yucatan por el Capitán de Fragata D. Juan Tabat," 1801, AGI, México 3038, no. 117, sub-no. 173.

75. "Extracto de las Actuaciones de revalidación, y ampliaciones. . . . ," 1802, AGI, México 3038, no. 11, sub-no. 192.

76. "Testimonio del Memorial ajustado que formó el Sr. D. Manuel del Castillo Negrete," 1801, AGI, México 3038, no. 180.

77. Ibid.

78. Ibid.

79. "Extracto de las Actuaciones de revalidación, y ampliaciones. . . . ," 1802, AGI, México 3038, no. 11, sub-no. 192.

80. "Diligencias practicadas por el Sr. Don Manuel del Castillo Negrete del consejo de S. M. su Alcalde de Corte y Juez de Provincia de esta N. E. y por el Sr. Dr. Don Jose María Bucheli, Juez Provisor y Vicario Capitular de este Arzobispado," 1802, AGN, Criminal 329, exp. 1, f. 116.

81. "Quinto Estado de la Causa de Homicidio," 1801, AGI, no. 167, sub-no. 4.

82. "Diligencias practicadas por el Sr. Don Manuel del Castillo Negrete del consejo de S. M. su Alcalde de Corte y Juez de Provincia de esta N. E. y por el Sr. Dr. Don Jose María Bucheli, Juez Provisor y Vicario Capitular de este Arzobispado," 1802, AGN, Criminal 329, exp. 1, f. 116v.

83. Machuca Gallegos, "Los Quijano de Yucatán," citing 1786, AGEY, Archivo Notarial del Estado de Yucatán, vol. 22, f. 348.

84. "Diligencias practicadas por el Sr. Don Manuel del Castillo Negrete del consejo de S. M. su Alcalde de Corte y Juez de Provincia de esta N. E. y por el Sr. Dr. Don Jose María Bucheli, Juez Provisor y Vicario Capitular de este Arzobispado," 1802, AGN, Criminal 329, exp. 1, ff. 111–13.

85. Ibid., ff. 48–62.

86. Ibid., ff. 79–81.

87. Ibid., ff. 97.

88. "Extracto de las Diligencias practicadas en Yucatan por el Capitán de Fragata D. Juan Tabat," 1801, AGI, México 3038, no. 117, sub-no. 173.

89. Ibid.

90. "Extracto de las Actuaciones de revalidación, y ampliaciones. . . . ," 1802, AGI, México 3038, no. 11, sub-no. 192.

91. Ibid.

92. Ibid.

93. "Extracto de las Diligencias practicadas en Yucatan por el Capitán de Fragata D. Juan Tabat," 1801, AGI, México 3038, no. 117, sub-no. 173.

94. The early twentieth-century Yucatecan poet and genealogist José María Valdes Acosta also omitted the term *don* for Esteban de Castro, though he continued to use the honorific in his descriptions of most creole Yucatecan families he discussed, including the Quijanos. *A través de las centurías: Historia genealógica de las familias yucatecas*, vol. 2 (Mérida: Talleres Pluma y Lapíz, 1926), 437.

95. "Extracto de las Actuaciones de revalidación y ampliaciones," 1801, AGI, México 3038, no. 11, sub-no. 173.

96. "Papel curioso sobre el asesinato del Sr. Galvez Gob^{or} de Yucatan," 1807, AGI, México 3040, No. 178, s/f.

97. "Testimonio del Voto Consultivo de la Real Sala del Crimen," 1802, AGI, México 3038, no. 183, f. 22.

98. "Lucas de Galvez Diligencias en la investigación del crimen del citado," 1802, AGN, Archivo Histórico de Hacienda 808, exp. 11, s/f.

99. "Testimonio del Voto Consultivo de la Real Sala del Crimen," 1802, AGI, México 3038, no. 183, ff. 15–17, 20.

100. "Subdelegaciones militares," 1807, AGN, Reales Cédulas Originales, exp. 38, f. 1.

101. "Lucas de Galvez Diligencias en la investigación del crimen del citado," 1802, AGN, Archivo Histórico de Hacienda 808, exp. 3.

102. Ibid., no. 10.

103. Ibid., no. 16 , ff. 1–16.

104. Ibid., no. 16, ff. 4–8.

105. "Testimonio del Voto Consultivo de la Real Sala del Crimen," 1802, AGI, México 3038, no. 183, f. 36v.

106. "Noveno Estado de la Causa," 1802, AGI, México 3040, no. 211, s/f.

107. "Diligencias practicadas por el Sr. Don Manuel del Castillo Negrete del consejo de S. M. su Alcalde de Corte y Juez de Provincia de esta N. E. y por el Sr. Dr. Don Jose María Bucheli, Juez Provisor y Vicario Capitular de este Arzobispado," 1802, AGN, Criminal 329, exp. 1, f. 122v.

108. Ibid., ff. 131–36.

109. "Noveno Estado de la Causa," 1802, AGI, México 3040, no. 211, s/f.

110. "La Sala del Crimen de Mexico. . . . ," 1811, AGI, México 3037, no. 150, sub-no. 2.

111. "Lucas de Galvez Diligencias en la investigación del crimen del citado," 1802, AGN, Archivo Histórico de Hacienda 808, exp. 18, f. 2.

112. Ibid., ff. 12–12v.

113. "Superior Despacho de los Sres Presidente, Regente, y Oydores de la Rl. Sala de Crimen," 1807, AGN, Criminal 726, ff. 184–87.

114. Ibid., ff. 212–16.

115. "La Sala del Crimen de Mexico. . . . ," 1811, AGI, México 3037, no. 150, sub-no. 2.

116. "Superior Despacho de los Sres Presidente, Regente, y Oydores de la Rl. Sala de Crimen," 1807, AGN, Criminal 726, ff. 180–82. Don Carlos María de Bustamante, don Toribio's able defender, had taken up Castro's cause in 1806 as the interpreter's "defensor nombrado," a marked reversal of his earlier efforts to exonerate don Toribio and secure Castro's conviction.

117. "Superior Despacho de los Sres Presidente, Regente, y Oyodres de la Rl. Sala de Crimen," 1812, AGN, Criminal 726, ff. 267–69.

118. "Superior Despacho de los Sres Presidente, Regente, y Oyodres de la Rl. Sala de Crimen," 1813, AGN, Criminal 726, ff. 281–85.

119. "Copia del punto, auto, y diligencia de tormento,"1807, AGI, México 3040, no. 139.

120. Cavo and Bustamante, *Suplemento a la historia*, 110.

121. "Superior Despacho de los Sres Presidente, Regente, y Oydores de la Rl. Sala de Crimen," 1821, AGN, Criminal 726, f. 281.

122. "Demanda promovida por Dña Josefa Quijano y Zetina contra su hermano el coronel Dn. Ygnacio, que como albacea del Pbro. José Tadeo Quijano y Zetina, se niega a entregarle la quinta Miraflores que por donación del último le pertenece," 1812, AGEY, Colonial, Tierras, vol. 1, exp. 13, f. 2.

123. "Litigio entre los Indios de Seye y Tahmek, representados por Raimundo Pérez, Cura de Hoctún, y José Felipe Baldos Quijano, proprietario de la Estancia Holactún. Con una real Cédula ganada a favor de los Indios," 1817, AGEY, Colonial, Tierras, vol. 1, exp. 17, f. 2.

124. Rubio Mañé, "Los Sanjuanistas de Yucatán," 44.

125. *Colección de leyes, decretos y órdenes o acuerdos de tendencia general del poder legislativo del estado libre y soberano de Yucatán: 1841–1845* (Mérida, Yucatán: Imprenta de Rafael Pedrera, 1850), 28.

126. For the most recent scholarship on the impact of henequen, Yucatan, and North American agriculture, see Juliette Levy, *The Making of a Market: Credit, Henequen, and Notaries in Yucatán, 1850–1900* (University Park: Penn State University Press, 2012), and Sterling Evans, *Bound in Twine: The History and Ecology of the Henequen-Wheat Complex for Mexico and the American and Canadian Plains, 1880–1950* (College Station: Texas A&M University Press, 2013).

127. Jorge Flores D., "La vida rural en Yucatán en 1914," *Historia Mexicana* 10, no. 3 (1961), 477, quoted in Allan Meyers, *Outside the Hacienda Walls: The Archaeology of Plantation Peonage in Nineteenth-Century Yucatán* (Tucson: University of Arizona Press, 2012), 56.

128. Allan Meyers's well-researched archaeological study of Tabi provides some of the most gruesome depictions of these hardships, drawing from archaeological evidence, archival research, and oral histories. Ibid. Heather McCrea described the plight of henequen hacienda workers in graphic detail, concluding that "[t]he broad base of Yucatecan affluence was campesino misery." *Diseased Relations: Epidemics, Public Health, and State-Building in Yucatán, Mexico, 1847–1924* (Albuquerque: University of New Mexico Press, 2010), 127.

CONCLUSION

1. Hubert Howe Bancroft, *The Works of Hubert Howe Bancroft: History of Mexico.* Vol. 5: *1824–1861* (San Francisco, History Company, 1887), 803.

2. "Resumen Concisco del Extracto General," 1803, AGI, México 3040.

3. His uncle, Juan Francisco Gutiérrez de Piñeres, ended his career as a *ministro togado* of the Council of the Indies. Burkholder and Chandler, *Biographical Dictionary*, 155.

4. Ibid., 154.

5. Ibid., 52.

6. *Instrucciones que los Virreyes de Nueva España dejaron a sus sucesores: Añádense algunas que los mismos trajeron de la Corte y otros documentos semejantes a las instrucciones* (Mexico City: Ignacio Escalante, 1873), 152.

7. Burkholder and Chandler, *Biographical Dictionary*, 52.

8. *Instrucciones que los Virreyes*, 152.

9. Mariano José de Zúñiga y Ontiveros, *Calendario manual y guía de forasteros en México, para el año de 1800* (Mexico City, 1799), 107.

10. "Teniente don Toribio del Mazo demanda cantidad de pesos a los bienas del difunto don Francisco Guillen y al Escribano Fernando Sandoval," 1802, AGN, Indiferente Virreinal, Civil, caja 6417, exp. 76, f. 1.

11. Burkholder and Chandler, *Biographical Dictionary*, 80.

12. Carrillo y Ancona, *El obispado de Yucatán*, 2:907.

13. Eligio Ancona, *Historia de Yucatán, desde la época más remota hasta nuestros días*, vol. 2 (Mérida: Imprenta de M. Heredia Argüelles, 1878), 487, 491.

14. *Gaceta de Madrid*, vol. 2 (Madrid: Imprenta Real por Antonio Bizarrón, 1807), 918.

15. Pérez Galaz, *El asesinato*, 7. Now part of the urban zone of Mérida, the main building functions as Centro Cultural Wallis, where, in echoes of don Toribio's festivities, guitar and dance lessons are taught.

16. "Licencia por dos años para pasar a España a Jose Toribio del Mazo," 28 December 1803, AGN, Reales Cedulas Originales, vol. 188, exp. 294, f. 1.

17. "Nombramiento de don Toribio del Mazo y Villazan capitán graduado del ejercito y teniente veterano del Batallón de milicias de Yucatán, como subdelegado del partido de Tehuantepec en Oaxaca," 1807, AGN, Indiferente Virreinal, Indiferente de Guerra, caja 2898, exp. 5, f. 1.

18. According to Molina Font, Gálvez also refused to allow him to sit in a high-backed chair that served to mark Quijano's authority. *Gesta de los Mayas*, 196.

19. "Oficio y Contestación," 1797, AGI, México 3039, no. 3.

20. Machuca Gallegos, "Los Quijano de Yucatán."

21. "Demanda promovida por doña Josefa Quijano y Zetina contra su hermano el coronel Dn. Ygnacio," 1812, AGEY, Colonial, Tierras, vol. 1, exp. 13.

22. Machuca Gallegos, "Los Quijano de Yucatán."

23. "Demanda promovida por doña Josefa Quijano y Zetina contra su hermano el coronel Dn. Ygnacio," 1812, AGEY, Colonial, Tierras, vol. 1, exp. 13.

24. "La Sala del Crimen de Mexico. . . . ," 1811, AGI, México 3037, no. 150, sub-no. 2.

25. Ángel Gutiérrez Romero, "La última obra del arte virreinal," *Diario de Yucatán*, 7 July 2015.

26. "Testimonio de lo contenido en el Quad° reservado num° 42," 1795, AGI, México 3040, no. 7, f. 3.

Bibliography

PRIMARY ARCHIVAL SOURCES

Archivo General de Centro América (AGCA), Guatemala City, Guatemala
Archivo General de las Indias (AGI), Seville, Spain
  Ramos
    Audiencia de Cuba
    Audiencia de México
    Audiencia de Santo Domingo
    Contratación
    Estado
    Filipinas
Archivo General de la Nación (AGN), Mexico City, Mexico
  Ramos
    Archivo Histórico de Hacienda
    Bienes Nacionales
    Civil
    Clero Regular y Secular
    Criminal
    Indiferente de Guerra
    Indiferente Virreinal
    Indios
    Justicia
    Obispos y Arzobispos
    Reales Cedulas Originales
Archivo General de las Simancas (AGS), Simancas, Spain
  Ramo
    Secretaría del Despacho de Guerra
Archivo Histórico de la Nación (AHN), Madrid, Spain
  Ramos

Consejo de Órdenes
Secretaría de las Órdenes Civiles—Orden de Carlos III
Archivo Histórico del Arzobispado de Yucatán (AHAY), Mérida, Yucatan, Mexico
Ramos
Asuntos terminados
Legitimaciones
Archivo General del Estado de Yucatán (AGEY), Mérida, Yucatan, Mexico
Fondo Colonial
Ramos
Ayuntamientos
Criminal
Judicial
Reales Cedulas
Sucesiones Intestadas
Tierras
Varios
Archivo Notarial del Estado de Yucatán
Ramo
Colonial
Tulane Latin American Library Manuscript Collection
Collections
William Gates Collection of Yucatecan Letters, 1778–1863
Viceregal and Ecclesiastical Mexican Collection
Yucatán Collection
Newberry Library, Chicago
Edward E. Ayer Collection

PRIMARY PRINTED AND PUBLISHED SOURCES

An eye draft of Logger-head Cay near to Cape Catoche in 21 de: 20 mi: N: L: (ca. 1760), John Carter Brown Map Collection, Brown University, Providence, RI, cabinet Ef760 /1 Ms.

Bustamante, Carlos María de, Manuel Calvillo, and Rina Ortiz. *Diario histórico de México.* Mexico City: SEP, Instituto Nacional de Antropología e Historia, 1980.

Cavo, Andrés, and Carlos María de Bustamante. *Los tres siglos de Méjico durante el gobierno español hasta la entrada del ejército trigarante.* Mexico City: Imprenta de J. R. Navarro, 1852.

———. *Suplemento a la historia de los tres siglos de Mexico, durante el gobierno español.* Imprenta de la testamentaria de D. Alejandro Váldes, 1836.

Ciudad Real, Antonio de. "Relación de las cosas que sucedieron al R. P. Comisario General Fray Alonso Ponce. . . ." 1588. In *Colección de documentos inéditos para la historia de España.* Vols. 57 and 58. Madrid: Imprenta de la Viuda de Calero, 1872.

Colección de leyes, decretos y órdenes o acuerdos de tendencia general del poder legislativo del estado libre y soberano de Yucatán: 1841–1845. Mérida: Imprenta de Rafael Pedrera, 1850.

De C., C. F. X. *Extracto de la descripción politica y geográfica de las provincias de Campeche y Yucatan hecha en el año de 1766 por C. F. X. de C. por orden del Sor. D. Josef de Galvez*. Mexico City, 1766.

Gaceta de Madrid. Vol. 2. Madrid: Imprenta Real por Antonio Bizarrón, 1807.

García Icazbalceta, Joaquín. *Colección de documentos para la historia de México*. Vol. 1. Mexico City: Librería de J. M. Andrade, 1858.

Instrucciones que los Virreyes de Nueva España dejaron a sus sucesores: Añádense algunas que los mismos trajeron de la Corte y otros documentos semejantes a las instrucciones. Mexico City: Ignacio Escalante, 1873.

Jefferys, Thomas. *The West-India Atlas or, A Compendious Defcription of the West-Indies: Illustrated with Forty Correct Charts and Maps . . . Together with an Hiftorical Account of the Several Countries and Islands Which Compose That Part of the World*. London: Printed for Robert Sayer and John Bennett, 1780.

Kitchin, Thomas. *The Present State of the West-Indies: Containing an Accurate Description of What Parts Are Possessed by the Several Powers in Europe*. London, 1778.

Puga, Vasco de., comp. *Prouisio[n]es cedulas instruciones de su Magestad: ordena[n]ças d[e] difu[n]tos y audie[n]cia, p[ar]a la buena expedicio[n] de los negocios, y administracio[n] d[e] justicia: y gouernacio[n] d[e]sta Nueua España: y p[ar]a el bue[n] tratamie[n]to y [con]servacio[n] d[e] los yndios, dende [sic] el año 1525. hasta este presente de. 63* (Madrid, 1563).

Reglamento para las Milicias de Infantería de la Provincia de Yucatan, y Campeche, aprobado por S. M. y mandado que se oberven todos su Articulos (Madrid: Imprenta de P. Marín, 1778).

Sánchez de Aguilar, Pedro. *Informe contra idolorum cultores del obispado de Yucatán*. Madrid, 1639.

Zúñiga y Ontiveros, Mariano José de. *Calendario manual y guía de forasteros en México, para el año de 1800*. Mexico City, 1799.

SECONDARY SOURCES

Adelman, Jeremy. *Sovereignty and Revolution in the Iberian Atlantic*. Princeton, NJ: Princeton University Press, 2006.

Aguirre Beltrán, Gonzalo. *La Población Negra de México: Estudio Etnohistórico*. 2nd ed. Mexico City: Fondo de Cultura Económica, 1972.

Alban, Juan Pedro Viqueira, and Sonya Lipsett-Rivera. *Propriety and Permissiveness in Bourbon Mexico*. Wilmington: Scholarly Resources, 2004.

Ancona, Eligio. *Historia de Yucatán, desde la época más remota hasta nuestros días*. Vol. 2. Mérida: Imprenta de M. Heredia Argüelles, 1878.

——. *Memorias de un alférez: Novela histórica*. Mérida: El Peninsular, 1904.

Anna, Timothy E. *The Fall of the Royal Government in Mexico City*. Lincoln: University of Nebraska Press, 1978.

Antochiw, Michel. *Artillería y fortificaciones en la península de Yucatán siglo XVIII*. Campeche: Gobierno del Estado de Campeche, 2004.

——. *Historia cartográfica de la península de Yucatán*. Campeche: Gobierno del Estado de Campeche, 1994.

——. *Milicia de Yucatán (siglos XVI y XVII): La unión de armas de 1712*. Mexico City: Instituto Nacional de Antropología e Historia/CONACULTA, 2006.

Appelbaum, Nancy P., Anne S. Macpherson, and Karin Alejandra Rosemblatt, eds. *Race and Nation in Modern Latin America*. Chapel Hill: University of North Carolina Press, 2003.

Archer, Christon I., ed. *The Birth of Modern Mexico, 1780–1824*. Wilmington: Scholarly Resources, 2003.

Bancroft, Hubert Howe. *History of Mexico: Being a Popular History of the Mexican People from the Earliest Primitive Civilization to the Present Time*. New York: Bancroft, 1914.

——. *The Works of Hubert Howe Bancroft: History of Mexico*. Vol. 5: *1824–1861*. San Francisco: History Company, 1887.

Baquiero, Serapio. *Reseña geográfica, histórica y estadística del estado de Yucatán desde los primitivos tiempos de la península*. Mexico City: Imprenta de Francisco Díaz de León, 1881.

Barrera Vásquez, Alfredo. *Estudios lingüísticos: Obras completas*. 2 vols. Mérida: Fondo Editorial de Yucatán, 1980.

Baskes, Jeremy. *Indians, Merchants, and Markets: A Reinterpretation of the Repartimiento and Spanish-Indian Economic Relations in Colonial Oaxaca, 1750–1821*. Stanford, CA: Stanford University Press, 2000.

Beerman, Eric. "Arturo O'Neill: First Governor of West Florida during the Second Spanish Period." *Florida Historical Quarterly* 60, no. 1 (July 1981): 29–41.

Bennett, Herman L. *Africans in Colonial Mexico: Absolutism, Christianity, and Afro-Creole Consciousness, 1570–1640*. Bloomington: Indiana University Press, 2005.

Berlin, Ira. *Many Thousands Gone: The First Two Centuries of Slavery in North America*. Cambridge, MA: Belknap Press of Harvard University Press, 1998.

Bertrand, Michel. *Grandeza y miseria del oficio: Los oficiales reales de la Real Hacienda de la Nueva España, siglos XVII y XVIII*. Trans. Mario Zamudio. Mexico City: Fondo de Cultura Económica, 2013.

Bolland, O. Nigel. *The Formation of a Colonial Society: Belize, from Conquest to Crown Colony*. Baltimore: Johns Hopkins University Press, 1977.

Borah, Woodrow Wilson. *Justice by Insurance: The General Indian Court of Colonial Mexico and the Legal Aides of the Half-Real*. Berkeley: University of California Press, 1983.

Bracamonte y Sosa, Pedro. *Amos y sirvientes: Las haciendas de Yucatán, 1789–1860*. Mérida: Universidad Autónoma de Yucatán, 1993.

———. *Espacios mayas de autonomía: El pacto colonial en Yucatán*. Mérida: Universidad Autónoma de Yucatán, 1996.

———. *La encarnación de la profecía Canek en Cisteil*. Mexico City: CIESAS, 2004.

———. *La memoria enclaustrada: Historia indígena de Yucatán, 1750–1915*. Mexico City: CIESAS, 1994.

———. *Los mayas y la tierra: La propiedad indígena en el Yucatán Colonial*. Mérida: Instituto de Cultura de Yucatán, 2003.

Brading, D. A. *The First America: The Spanish Monarchy, Creole Patriots and the Liberal State, 1492–1867*. Cambridge: Cambridge University Press, 1991.

Bricker, Victoria Reifler. *The Indian Christ, the Indian King: The Historical Substrate of Maya Myth and Ritual*. Austin: University of Texas Press, 1981.

Brown, Christopher Leslie, and Philip D. Morgan, eds. *Arming Slaves: From Classical Times to the Modern Age*. New Haven: Yale University Press, 2006.

Burkholder, Mark A., and D. S. Chandler. *Biographical Dictionary of Audiencia Ministers in the Americas, 1687–1821*. Westport, CT: Greenwood Press, 1982.

Butterworth, Douglas, and John K. Chance. *Latin American Urbanization*. Cambridge: Cambridge University Press, 1981.

Calderón Quijano, José Antonio. *Historia de las fortificaciones en Nueva España*. 2nd ed. Madrid: Consejo Superior de Investigaciones Científicas, 1984.

Campos García, Melchor. *Castas, feligresía y ciudadanía en Yucatán: Los afromestizos bajo el régimen constitucional español, 1750–1822*. Mérida: Universidad Autónoma de Yucatán, 2005.

———. *De provincia a estado de la república Mexicana: La península de Yucatán, 1786–1835*. Mérida: Universidad Autónoma de Yucatán/CONACYT, 2004.

———. *Sociabilidades políticas en Yucatán: Un estudio sobre los espacios públicos, 1780–1834*. Mérida: Universidad Autónoma de Yucatán, 2003.

Carlos, Manuel L. "Fictive Kinship and Modernization in Mexico: A Comparative Analysis." *Anthropological Quarterly* 46, no. 2 (April 1973): 75–91.

Carrillo y Ancona, Crescencio. *El obispado de Yucatán: Historia de su fundación y de sus obispos desde el siglo XVI hasta el XIX, seguida de las constituciones sinodales de la diócesis y otros documentos relativos*. Mérida: Imprenta y Lit. de Ricardo B. Caballero, 1895.

Castañeda de la Paz, María, and Hans Roskamp, eds. *Los escudos de armas indígenas: De la colonia al México independiente*. Mexico City: Universidad Nacional Autónoma de México, 2013.

Castrillo Martínez, Maximiliano. *Opúsculo sobre la historia de la villa de Astudillo*. Burgos: Imprenta de la viuda de Villanueva, 1877.

Castro Gutiérrez, Felipe. *La extinción de la artesanía gremial*. Mexico City: Universidad Nacional Autónoma de México, Instituto de Investigaciones Históricas, 1986.

——. ed. *Los indios y las ciudades de Nueva España*. Mexico City: Universidad Autónoma de México/Instituto de Investigaciones Históricas, 2010.

——. *Nueva ley y nuevo rey: Reformas borbónicas y rebelión popular en Nueva España*. Zamora: Colegio de Michoacán, 1996.

Cevallos-Candau, Francisco Javier, Jeffrey A. Cole, Nina M. Scott, and Nicomedes Suárez-Araúz, eds. *Coded Encounters: Writing, Gender, and Ethnicity in Colonial Latin America*. Amherst: University of Massachusetts Press, 1994.

Chamberlain, Robert Stoner. *The Conquest and Colonization of Yucatan, 1517–1550*. Washington, DC: Carnegie Institution of Washington, 1948.

Chance, John K. *Conquest of the Sierra: Spaniards and Indians in Colonial Oaxaca*. Norman: University of Oklahoma Press, 2001.

——. *Race and Class in Colonial Oaxaca*. Stanford, CA: Stanford University Press, 1978.

——, and William B. Taylor. "Estate and Class in a Colonial City: Oaxaca in 1792." *Comparative Studies in Society and History* 19, no. 4 (October 1977): 454–87.

Chasteen, John Charles. *Americanos: Latin America's Struggle for Independence*. Oxford: Oxford University Press, 2008.

Chuchiak, John F., IV. "'The Indian Inquisition and the Extirpation of Idolatry: The Process of Punishment in the *Provisorato de Indios* of the Diocese of Yucatan, 1563–1812." PhD diss., Tulane University, 2000.

Clendinnen, Inga. *Ambivalent Conquests: Maya and Spaniard in Yucatan, 1517–1570*. 2nd ed. Cambridge: Cambridge University Press, 2003.

Commons de la Rosa, Aurea. *Las intendencias de la Nueva España*. Mexico City: Universidad Nacional Autónoma de México, 1993.

Cook, Noble David, and Alexandra Parma Cook. *Good Faith and Truthful Ignorance: A Case of Transatlantic Bigamy*. Durham, NC: Duke University Press, 1991.

Cope, R. Douglas. *The Limits of Racial Domination: Plebeian Society in Colonial Mexico City, 1660–1720*. Madison: University of Wisconsin Press, 1994.

Coronel, Juan. *Arte en lengua de maya y otros escritos*. Mexico City: Universidad Nacional Autónoma de México, 1998.

Davis, Natalie Zemon. *The Return of Martin Guerre*. Cambridge, MA: Harvard University Press, 1983.

DeNoble, Augustine. *Benedictines in Mexico: Monks and Bishops*. St. Benedict, OR: Mount Angel Abbey, 1996.

De Vos, Jan. *La Paz de Dios y del rey: La conquista de la selva lacandona (1525–1821)*. Mexico City: Fondo de Cultura Económica, 1988.

Diego-Fernández Sotelo, Rafael, María Pilar Gutiérrez Lorenzo, and Luis Alberto Arrioja Díaz Viruell, eds. *De reinos y subdelegaciones: Nuevos escenarios para un nuevo orden en la América borbónica*. Zamora: El Colegio de Michoacán, 2014.

Ducey, Michael T. *A Nation of Villages: Riot and Rebellion in the Mexican Huasteca, 1750–1850*. Tucson: University of Arizona Press, 2004.

Dumond, Don E. *The Machete and the Cross: Campesino Rebellion in Yucatan*. Lincoln: University of Nebraska Press, 1997.

Earle, Rebecca. "Letters and Love in Colonial Spanish America." *The Americas* 62, no. 1 (July 2005): 17–46.

Edmonson, Munro S. *Heaven Born Mérida and Its Destiny: The Book of Chilam Balam of Chumayel*. Austin: University of Texas, 1986.

Evans, Sterling. *Bound in Twine: The History and Ecology of the Henequen-Wheat Complex for Mexico and the American and Canadian Plains, 1880–1950*. College Station: Texas A&M University Press, 2013.

Fallon, Michael J. "The Secular Clergy in the Diocese of Yucatan, 1750–1800." PhD diss., Catholic University of America, 1979.

Farriss, Nancy M. *Crown and Clergy in Colonial Mexico, 1759–1821: The Crisis of Ecclesiastical Privilege*. London: Athlone, 1968.

———. *Maya Society under Colonial Rule: The Collective Enterprise of Survival*. 2nd ed. Princeton, NJ: Princeton University Press, 1992.

———. "Remembering the Future, Anticipating the Past: History, Time, and Cosmology among the Maya of Yucatan." *Comparative Studies in Society and History* 29, no. 3 (July 1987): 566–93.

Few, Martha. *Women Who Live Evil Lives: Gender, Religion, and the Politics of Power in Colonial Guatemala, 1650–1750*. Austin: University of Texas Press, 2002.

Fisher, Lillian Estelle. *The Intendant System in Spanish America*. Berkeley: University of California Press, 1929.

———. *Viceregal Administration in the Spanish-American Colonies*. Berkeley: University of California Press, 1926.

Florescano, Enrique, and Isabel Gil. *Descripciones económicas regionales de Nueva España: Provincias del centro, sureste y sur, 1766–1827*. Mexico City: Secretaría de Educación Pública/Instituto Nacional de Antropología e Historia, 1976.

Gabbert, Wolfgang. *Becoming Maya: Ethnicity and Social Inequality in Yucatán since 1500*. Tucson: University of Arizona Press, 2004.

———. "Of Friends and Foes: The Caste War and Ethnicity in Yucatan." *Journal of Latin American Anthropology* 9, no. 1 (Spring 2004): 90–118.

Gallay, Alan, ed. *Indian Slavery in Colonial America*. Lincoln: University of Nebraska Press, 2010.

García Ayluardo, Clara, ed. *Las reformas borbónicas, 1750–1808*. Mexico City: Fondo de Cultura Económica, 2010.

García Bernal, Manuela Cristina. *Desarrollo agrario en el Yucatán colonial: Repercusiones económicas y sociales*. Mérida: Universidad Autónoma de Yucatán, 2006.

———. *Economía, política y sociedad en el Yucatán colonial*. Mérida: Ediciones de la Universidad Autónoma de Yucatán, 2005.

———. *La sociedad de Yucatán, 1700–1750*. Seville: Escuela de Estudios Hispano-Americanos de Sevilla, 1972.

———. *Población y encomienda en Yucatán bajo los Austrias.* Seville: Escuela de Estudios Hispano-Americanos, 1978.

Gaspar, David Barry, and David Patrick Geggus. *A Turbulent Time: The French Revolution and the Greater Caribbean.* Bloomington: Indiana University Press, 1997.

Gerhard, Peter. *The Southeast Frontier of New Spain.* Norman: University of Oklahoma Press, 1993.

Gibson, Charles. *The Aztecs under Spanish Rule: A History of the Indians of the Valley of Mexico, 1519–1810.* Stanford, CA: Stanford University Press, 1964.

———. *The Spanish Tradition in America.* Columbia: University of South Carolina Press, 1968.

Ginzburg, Carlo. *The Cheese and the Worms: The Cosmos of a Sixteenth-Century Miller.* Baltimore: Johns Hopkins University Press, 1992.

Gómez, José Humberto Fuentes. *Espacios, actores, prácticas e imaginarios urbanos en Mérida, Yucatán. México.* Mérida: Universidad Autónoma de Yucatán, 2005.

González Muñoz, Victoria. *Cabildos y grupos de poder en Yucatán (siglo XVII).* Seville: Diputación Provincial de Sevilla, 1994.

Gosner, Kevin. *Soldiers of the Virgin: The Moral Economy of a Colonial Maya Rebellion.* Tucson: University of Arizona Press, 1992.

Grab, Alexander. *Napoleon and the Transformation of Europe.* New York: Palgrave Macmillan, 2003.

Greenleaf, Richard E. *The Mexican Inquisition of the Sixteenth Century.* Albuquerque: University of New Mexico Press, 1969.

Güémez Pineda, Arturo. "El poder de los cabildos mayas y la venta de propiedades privadas a través del Tribunal de Indios. Yucatán (1750–1821)." *Historia Mexicana* 54, no. 3 (January–March 2005): 697–760.

Gutiérrez, Ramón A. *When Jesus Came, the Corn Mothers Went Away: Marriage, Sexuality, and Power in New Mexico, 1500–1846.* Stanford, CA: Stanford University Press, 1991.

Gutiérrez Brockington, Lolita. *Blacks, Indians, and Spaniards in the Eastern Andes: Reclaiming the Forgotten in Colonial Mizque, 1550–1782.* Lincoln: University of Nebraska Press, 2007.

Gutiérrez Romero, Ángel. "La última obra del arte virreinal." *Diario de Yucatán,* 7 July 2015.

Harrington, Raymond Patrick. "The Secular Clergy in the Diocese of Mérida de Yucatán, 1780–1850: Their Origins, Careers, Wealth and Activities." PhD diss., Catholic University of America, 1983.

Haskett, Robert Stephen. *Indigenous Rulers: An Ethnohistory of Town Government in Colonial Cuernavaca.* Albuquerque: University of New Mexico Press, 1991.

Haslip-Viera, Gabriel. *Crime and Punishment in Late Colonial Mexico City, 1692–1810.* Albuquerque: University of New Mexico Press, 1999.

Herzog, Tamar. *La administración como un fenómeno social: La justicia penal de la ciudad de Quito (1650–1750)*. Madrid: Centro de Estudios Constitucionales, 1995.

———. *Upholding Justice: Society, State, and the Penal System in Quito (1650–1750)*. Ann Arbor: University of Michigan Press, 2004.

Hill, Robert M., II. *Colonial Cakchiquels: Highland Maya Adaptations to Spanish Rule, 1600–1700*. Fort Worth: Harcourt Brace Jovanovich, 1992.

Hunt, Marta Espejo-Ponce. "Colonial Yucatan: Town and Region in the Seventeenth Century." PhD diss., University of California, Los Angeles, 1974.

Jones, Grant D., ed. *Anthropology and History in Yucatán*. Austin: University of Texas Press, 1977.

———. *The Conquest of the Last Maya Kingdom*. Stanford, CA: Stanford University Press, 1998.

———. *Maya Resistance to Spanish Rule: Time and History on a Colonial Frontier*. Albuquerque: University of New Mexico Press, 1989.

Joseph, Gilbert M. *Rediscovering the Past at Mexico's Periphery: Essays on the History of Modern Yucatán*. Tuscaloosa: University of Alabama Press, 1986.

———. *Revolution from Without: Yucatán, Mexico, and the United States, 1880–1924*. Cambridge: Cambridge University Press, 1982.

———, and Daniel Nugent, eds. *Everyday Forms of State Formation: Revolution and the Negotiation of Rule in Modern Mexico*. Durham, NC: Duke University Press, 1994.

Kinsbruner, Jay. *The Colonial Spanish-American City: Urban Life in the Age of Atlantic Capitalism*. Austin: University of Texas Press, 2005.

———. *Independence in Spanish America: Civil Wars, Revolutions, and Underdevelopment*. Albuquerque: University of New Mexico Press, 2000.

Kuethe, Allan J., and Kenneth J. Andrien. *The Spanish Atlantic World in the Eighteenth Century: War and the Bourbon Reforms*. Cambridge: Cambridge University Press, 2014.

Lane, Kris. *Quito 1599: City and Colony in Transition*. Albuquerque: University of New Mexico Press, 2002.

Lanz, Manuel A. *Compendio de historia de Campeche*. Campeche: Tip "El Fénix" de P. L. Marcín, 1905.

Lavrin, Asunción, ed. *Latin American Women: Historical Perspectives*. Westport, CT: Greenwood Press, 1978.

Lentz, Mark W. "Black Belizeans and Fugitive Mayas: Interracial Encounters on the Edge of Empire, 1750–1803." *The Americas* 70, no. 4 (April 2014): 645–75.

———. "Castas, Creoles, and the Rise of an Indigenous Lingua Franca in 18th-Century Yucatan." *Hispanic American Historical Review* 97, no. 1 (February 2017): 29–61.

———. "Criados, Caciques y Artesanos: Mayas Urbanos de Yucatán a Finales del Siglo Dieciocho," in *Los indios y las ciudades de Nueva España*, ed. Felipe Castro Gutiérrez. Mexico City: Universidad Autónoma de México/Instituto de Investigaciones Históricas, 2010.

——. "'The Mission' That Wasn't: Yucatan's Jesuits, the Mayas, and El Petén, 1703–1767." *World History Connected* 10, no. 3 (October 2013).

Levy, Juliette. *The Making of a Market: Credit, Henequen, and Notaries in Yucatán, 1850–1900.* University Park: Penn State University Press, 2012.

Lindsay, Mark Childress. "Spanish Mérida: Overlaying the Maya City." PhD diss., University of Florida, 1999.

Lipski, John M. *A History of Afro-Hispanic Language: Five Centuries, Five Continents.* Cambridge: Cambridge University Press, 2005.

Lockhart, James. *The Nahuas after the Conquest: A Social and Cultural History of the Indians of Mexico, Sixteenth through Eighteenth Centuries.* Stanford, CA: Stanford University Press, 1992.

——. "The Social History of Colonial Spanish America: Evolution and Potential." *Latin American Research Review* 7, no. 1 (1972): 6–45.

——, and Stuart B. Schwartz. *Early Latin America: A History of Colonial Spanish America and Brazil.* Cambridge: Cambridge University Press, 1983.

Macías Richard, Carlos, ed. *El Caribe mexicano: Origen y conformación, siglos XVI y XVII.* Mexico City: Universidad de Quintana Roo, 2006.

Machuca Gallegos, Laura. "Hacienda y movilidad social en Yucatán en la primera mitad del siglo XIX." *Letras Históricas* 5 (Autumn 2011–Winter 2012): 81–100.

——. *Los hacendados de Yucatán, 1785–1847.* Mexico City: CIESAS, 2011.

——. "Los Quijano de Yucatán: Entre la tradición y la modernidad." *Caravelle* 101 (December 2013).

MacLachlan, Colin M. *Anarchism and the Mexican Revolution: The Political Trials of Ricardo Flores Magón in the United States.* Berkeley: University of California Press, 1974.

——. *Criminal Justice in Eighteenth Century Mexico: A Study of the Tribunal of the Acordada.* Berkeley: University of California Press, 1974.

——. *Spain's Empire in the New World: The Role of Ideas in Institutional and Social Change.* Berkeley: University of California Press, 1992.

MacPherson, Anne S. *From Colony to Nation: Women Activists and the Gendering of Politics in Belize, 1912–1982.* Lincoln: University of Nebraska Press, 2007.

Mantilla Trolle, Marina, Rafael Diego-Fernández Sotelo, and Agustín Moreno Torres, eds. *Real Ordenanza para el establecimiento é instrucción de intendentes de exército y provincia en el reino de la Nueva España:* Guadalajara: Universidad de Guadalajara, 2008.

Martínez Ortega, Ana Isabel. *Estructura y configuración socioeconómica de los cabildos de Yucatán en el siglo XVIII.* Seville: Diputación Provincial de Sevilla, 1993.

Matthew, Laura E., and Michel R. Oudijk, eds. *Indian Conquistadors: Indigenous Allies in the Conquest of Mesoamerica.* Norman: University of Oklahoma Press, 2007.

McAlister, Lyle N. *The "Fuero Militar" in New Spain, 1764–1800.* Gainesville: University of Florida Press, 1957.

McCrea, Heather. *Diseased Relations: Epidemics, Public Health, and State-Building in Yucatán, Mexico, 1847–1924*. Albuquerque: University of New Mexico Press, 2010.

McFarlane, Anthony. "The 'Rebellion of the Barrios': Urban Insurrection in Bourbon Quito." *Hispanic American Historical Review* 69, no. 2 (May 1989): 283–330.

Memoria del X Congreso del Instituto Internacional de Historia del Derecho Indiano. Mexico City: Escuela Libre de Derecho/Universidad Nacional Autónoma de México, 1995.

Menegus, Margarita, comp. *El repartimiento forzoso de mercancías en México, Perú y Filipinas*. Mexico City: Instituto de Investigaciones Dr. José María Luis Mora, 2000.

Menéndez, Carlos R. *Visiones de Mérida*. Mérida, 1942.

Meyers, Allan. *Outside the Hacienda Walls: The Archaeology of Plantation Peonage in Nineteenth-Century Yucatán*. Tucson: University of Arizona Press, 2012.

Miller, Robert Ryal, and William J. Orr, eds. *Daily Life in Colonial Mexico: The Journey of Friar Ilarione da Bergamo, 1761–1768*. Norman: University of Oklahoma Press, 2011.

Minchom, Martin. *The People of Quito, 1690–1810*. Boulder, CO: Westview Press, 1994.

Molina Font, Gustavo. *Gesta de los Mayas: Y otros relatos del Viejo Yucatán*. Mexico City: Imprenta M. León Sánchez, 1965.

Molina Solís, Juan Francisco. *Historia de Yucatán durante la dominación española*. Mérida: Imprenta. de la Lotería del Estado, 1904.

Murphy, W. S. "The Irish Brigade of Spain at the Capture of Pensacola, 1781." *Florida Historical Quarterly* 38, no. 3 (January 1960): 216–25.

Navarro García, Luis. *Las reformas borbónicas en América: El plan de intendencias y su aplicación*. Seville: Universidad de Sevilla, 1995.

Nichols, Christopher M. "Solares in Tekax: The Impact of the Sugar Industry on a Nineteenth-Century Yucatecan Town." *Ethnohistory* 50, no. 1 (Winter 2001): 161–89.

O'Gorman, Edmundo, ed. "Incorporación de encomiendas en la provincial de Yucatán y Tabasco." *Boletín del Archivo de la Nación* 9, no. 4 (1938): 597–609.

Okoshi Harada, Tsubasa. "Los canules: Análisis etnohistórico del Códice de Calkiní." PhD diss., Universidad Nacional Autónoma de México, 1992.

Palmer, Colin A. *Slaves of the White God: Blacks in Mexico, 1570–1650*. Cambridge, MA: Harvard University Press, 1976.

Patch, Robert W. "Agrarian Change in Eighteenth-Century Yucatán." *Hispanic American Historical Review* 65, no. 1 (February 1985): 21–45.

———. *Maya and Spaniard in Yucatan, 1648–1812*. Stanford, CA: Stanford University Press, 1993.

———. *Maya Revolt and Revolution in the Eighteenth Century*. Armonk, NY: M. E. Sharpe, 2002.

———. "Sacraments and Disease in Mérida, Yucatán, Mexico, 1648–1727." *The Historian* 58, no. 4 (Summer 1996): 731–43.

Patterson, Orlando. *Slavery and Social Death: A Comparative Study.* Cambridge, MA: Harvard University Press, 1982.

Pearce, Adrian J. *The Origins of Bourbon Reform in Spanish South America, 1700–1763.* New York: Palgrave Macmillan, 2014.

Peón, José Julián. *Crónica sucinta de Yucatán.* 2nd ed. Mérida: Imprenta Nueva de C. Leal, 1901.

Pérez Galaz, Juan de Dios. *El asesinato de dn. Lucas de Gálvez (Un pasaje de la historia de Yucatán).* Campeche: Talleres Linotipográficos del Gobierno del Estado de Campeche, 1942.

Pérez-Mallaína Bueno, Pablo Emilio. *Comercio y autonomía en la intendencia de Yucatán (1797–1814).* Seville: Escuela de Estudios Hispano-Americanos de Sevilla/ Consejo Superior de Investigaciones Científicas, 1978.

Phelan, John Leddy. *The People and the King: The Comunero Revolution in Colombia, 1781.* Madison: University of Wisconsin Press, 1978.

Piccato, Pablo. *City of Suspects: Crime in Mexico City, 1900–1931.* Durham, NC: Duke University Press, 2001.

Pietschmann, Horst. *Las reformas borbónicas y el sistema de intendencias de Nueva España.* Trans. Rolf Roland Meyer Misteli. Mexico City: Fondo de Cultura Económica, 1996.

Plasencia, Adela Pinet, and Archivo General de la Nación (Mexico). *La Península de Yucatán en el Archivo General de la Nación.* Mexico City: Universidad Nacional Autónoma de México, 1998.

Quezada, Sergio, ed. *Encrucijadas de la ciudadanía y la democracia: Yucatán, 1812–2004.* Mérida: Universidad Autónoma de Yucatán, 2005.

———. *Historia de los pueblos indígenas de México: Los pies de la república. Los indios peninsulares, 1550–1750.* Mexico City: CIESAS/INI, 1997.

———, and Elda Moreno Acevedo. "Del déficit a la insolvencia. Finanzas y real hacienda en Yucatán, 1760 –1816." *Mexican Studies/Estudios Mexicanos* 21, no. 2 (Summer 2005): 307–31.

———, and Tsubasa Okoshi Harada, eds. and trans. *Papeles de los Xiu de Yaxá, Yucatán.* Mexico City: Universidad Nacional Autónoma de México, 2001.

Ramos y Duarte, Féliz. *Diccionario de curiosidades históricas, geográficas, hierográficas, cronológicas, etc., de la República Mexicana.* Mexico City: Imprenta de Eduardo Dublán, 1899.

Rappaport, Joanne M. *The Disappearing Mestizo: Configuring Difference in the Colonial New Kingdom of Granada.* Durham, NC: Duke University Press, 2014.

Reed, Nelson. *The Caste War of Yucatan.* Rev. ed. Stanford, CA: Stanford University Press, 2002.

Restall, Matthew, ed. *Beyond Black and Red: African-Native Relations in Colonial Latin America.* Albuquerque: University of New Mexico Press, 2005.

———. "Black Conquistadors: Armed Africans in Early Spanish America." *The Americas* 57, no. 2 (October 2000): 171–205.

——. *The Black Middle: Africans, Mayas, and Spaniards in Colonial Yucatan.* Stanford, CA: Stanford University Press, 2009.

——. "Crossing to Safety? Frontier Flight in Eighteenth-Century Belize and Yucatan." *Hispanic American Historical Review* 94, no. 3 (August 2014): 381–419.

——. "Heirs to the Hieroglyphs: Indigenous Writing in Colonial Mesoamerica." *The Americas* 54, no. 2 (October 1997): 239–67.

——. "A History of the New Philology and the New Philology in History." *Latin American Research Review* 38, no. 1 (2003): 113–34.

——. *Life and Death in a Maya Community: The Ixil Testaments of the 1760s.* Lancaster, CA: Labyrinthos, 1995.

——. *Maya Conquistador.* Boston: Beacon Press, 1999.

——. "Maya Ethnogenesis." *Journal of Latin American Anthropology* 9, no. 1 (2004): 64–89.

——. *The Maya World: Yucatec Culture and Society, 1550–1850.* Stanford, CA: Stanford University Press, 1997.

Robins, Nicholas A. *Genocide and Millennialism in Upper Peru: The Great Rebellion of 1780–1782.* Westport, CT: Greenwood Press, 2002.

——. *Native Insurgencies and the Genocidal Impulse in the Americas.* Bloomington: University of Indiana Press, 2005.

Rojas, Beatriz, ed. *Cuerpo político y pluralidad de derechos: Los privilegios de las corporaciones novohispanas.* Mexico City: Centro de Investigación y Docencia Económicas/Instituto de Investigaciones Dr. José María Luis Mora, 2007.

Roniger, Luis, and Tamar Herzog, eds. *The Collective and the Public in Latin America: Cultural Identities and Political Order.* Brighton: Sussex Academic Press, 2001.

Roper, Lyndal. *The Holy Household: Women and Morals in Reformation Augsburg.* Oxford: Oxford University Press, 1989.

Roys, Ralph Loveland. *The Indian Background of Colonial Yucatan.* Norman: University of Oklahoma Press, 1972.

——. *The Political Geography of the Yucatan Maya.* Washington, DC: Carnegie Institution of Washington, 1957.

——. *The Titles of Ebtun.* Washington, DC: Carnegie Institution of Washington, 1939.

Rubio-Argüelles, Angeles. *Asesinato en Yucatán: Verídica historia del alevoso asesinato cometido en la ciudad de Mérida el año 1792, en la persona de don Lucas de Gálvez, Gobernador, Capitán General e Intendente de la Provincia de Yucatán.* Mexico City, Ediciones A. R-A., 1956.

Rubio Mañé, J. Ignacio. *Archivo de la historia de Yucatán, Campeche y Tabasco.* Mexico City: Imprenta Aldina, Robredo y Rosell, 1942.

——. *El virreinato: Expansión y defensa.* Mexico City: Universidad Nacional Autónoma de México, 1961.

——. *La casa de Montejo en Mérida de Yucatán.* Mérida: Imprenta Universitaria, 1941.

———. "Los Sanjuanistas de Yucatán. I. Manuel Jiménez Solís, el padre Justis." *Boletín del Archivo General de la Nación Segunda* 8, 2nd series, nos. 3–4 (July–December 1967): 731–57.

Rugeley, Terry. "The Maya Elites of Nineteenth-Century Yucatán." *Ethnohistory* 42, no. 3 (Summer 1995): 447–93.

———. *Of Wonders and Wise Men: Religion and Popular Cultures in Southeast Mexico, 1800–1876.* Austin: University of Texas Press, 2001.

———. *Rebellion Now and Forever: Mayas, Hispanics, and Caste War Violence in Yucatán, 1800–1880.* Stanford, CA: Stanford University Press, 2009.

———. *Yucatán's Maya Peasantry and the Origins of the Caste War.* Austin: University of Texas Press, 1996.

Ruz Menéndez, Rodolfo. *Por los viejos caminos del Mayab: Ensayos históricos y literarios.* Mérida: Universidad Autónoma de Yucatán, 1973.

Salvatore, Ricardo D., Carlos Aguirre, and Gilbert M. Joseph, eds. *Crime and Punishment in Latin America: Law and Society since Late Colonial Times.* Durham, NC: Duke University Press, 2001.

Schroeder, Susan. *Native Resistance and the Pax Colonial in New Spain.* Lincoln: University of Nebraska Press, 1998.

Scott, James C. *Domination and the Arts of Resistance: Hidden Transcripts.* New Haven: Yale University Press, 1990.

Seed, Patricia. "Social Dimensions of Race: Mexico City, 1753." *Hispanic American Historical Review* 62, no. 4 (November 1982): 569–606.

———. *To Love, Honor, and Obey in Colonial Mexico: Conflicts over Marriage Choice, 1574–1821.* 1st ed. Stanford, CA: Stanford University Press, 1988.

Sharer, Robert, and Loa Traxler. *The Ancient Maya.* 6th ed. Stanford, CA: Stanford University Press, 2005.

Socolow, Susan Migden. *The Women of Colonial Latin America.* Cambridge: Cambridge University Press, 2000.

Solís Robleda, Gabriela, and Paola Peniche. *Idolatría y sublevación: Documentos para la historia indígena de Yucatán.* Vol. 1. Mérida: Universidad Autónoma de Yucatán, 1996.

Stein, Stanley J. "Bureaucracy and Business in the Spanish Empire, 1759–1804: Failure of a Bourbon Reform in Mexico and Peru." *Hispanic American Historical Review* 61, no. 1 (February 1981): 2–28.

———, and Barbara H. Stein. *Apogee of Empire: Spain and New Spain in the Age of Charles III, 1759–1789.* Baltimore: Johns Hopkins University Press, 2003.

Sullivan, Paul. *Xuxub Must Die: The Lost Histories of a Murder on the Yucatan.* Pittsburgh: University of Pittsburgh Press, 2006.

Taylor, William B. *Drinking, Homicide, and Rebellion in Colonial Mexican Villages.* Stanford, CA: Stanford University Press, 1979.

———. *Landlord and Peasant in Colonial Oaxaca.* Stanford, CA: Stanford University Press, 1972.

————. *Magistrates of the Sacred: Priests and Parishioners in Eighteenth-Century Mexico*. Stanford, CA: Stanford University Press, 1996.

Terraciano, Kevin. *Ñudzahui History: Sixteenth through Eighteenth Centuries*. Stanford, CA: Stanford University Press, 2001.

Thompson, J. Eric. *Maya History and Religion*. Norman: University of Oklahoma Press, 1990.

Thompson, Philip C. "The Structure of the Civil Hierarchy in Tekanto, Yucatan: 1785–1820." *Estudios de Cultura Maya* 16 (1985): 183–205.

————. *Tekanto, a Maya Town in Colonial Yucatan*. New Orleans: Middle American Research Institute, Tulane University, 1999.

Thomson, Sinclair. *We Alone Will Rule: Native Andean Politics in the Age of Insurgency*. Madison: University of Wisconsin Press, 2002.

Toledo, Sonia Pérez. *Los hijos del trabajo: Los artesanos de la ciudad de México, 1780–1853*. Mexico City: Universidad Autónoma Metropolitana Iztapalapa, 1996.

Toussaint, Manuel. *Paseos coloniales*. Mexico City: Editorial Porrúa, 1983.

Traslosheros, Jorge E., and Ana de Zaballa Beascoechea, eds. *Los indios ante los foros de justicia religiosa en la Hispanoámerica virreinal*. Mexico City: Universidad Nacional Autónoma de México, 2010.

Twinam, Ann. *Public Lives, Private Secrets: Gender, Honor, Sexuality, and Illegitimacy in Colonial Spanish America*. Stanford, CA: Stanford University Press, 1999.

Valdés, Dennis N. "The Decline of Slavery in Mexico." *The Americas* 44, no. 2 (October 1987): 167–94.

Valdes Acosta, José María. *A través de las centurías: Historia genealógica de las familias yucatecas*. Vol. 2. Mérida: Talleres Pluma y Lapíz, 1926.

Van Young, Eric. *The Other Rebellion: Popular Violence, Ideology, and the Mexican Struggle*. Stanford, CA: Stanford University Press, 2001.

Victoria Ojeda, Jorge. *Mérida de Yucatán de las Indias: Piratería y estrategia defensiva*. Mérida: Ayuntamiento de Mérida, 1995.

————, and Jorge Canto Alcocer. *San Fernando Aké: Microhistoria de una comunidad afroamericana en Yucatán*. Mérida: Ediciones de la Universidad Autónoma de Yucatán, 2006.

Villa-Flores, Javier. "'To Lose One's Soul': Blasphemy and Slavery in New Spain, 1596–1669." *Hispanic American Historical Review* 82, no. 3 (August 2002): 435–68.

Vinson, Ben, III. *Bearing Arms for His Majesty: The Free-Colored Militia in Colonial Mexico*. Stanford, CA: Stanford University Press, 2001.

Walker, Charles F. *Shaky Colonialism: The 1746 Earthquake-Tsunami in Lima, Peru, and Its Long Aftermath*. Durham, NC: Duke University Press, 2008.

————. *Smoldering Ashes: Cuzco and the Creation of Republican Peru, 1780–1840*. Durham, NC: Duke University Press, 1999.

————. *The Tupac Amaru Rebellion*. Cambridge, MA: Harvard University Press, 2014.

Wells, Allen, and Gilbert M. Joseph. *Summer of Discontent, Seasons of Upheaval: Elite Politics and Rural Insurgency in Yucatán, 1876–1915.* Stanford, CA: Stanford University Press, 1996.

Wightman, Ann M. *Indigenous Migration and Social Change: The Forasteros of Cuzco, 1570–1720.* Durham, NC: Duke University Press, 1990.

Will de Chaparro, Martina. *Death and Dying in New Mexico.* Albuquerque: University of New Mexico Press, 2007.

Yanes, Pablo, Virginia Molina, Óscar González, eds. *Urbi indiano: La larga marcha a la ciudad diversa.* Mexico City: Universidad Autónoma de la Ciudad de México, 2005.

Yannakakis, Yanna. *The Art of Being In-between: Native Intermediaries, Indian Identity, and Local Rule in Colonial Oaxaca.* Durham, NC: Duke University Press, 2008.

Zavala, Silvio Arturo. *La encomienda indiana.* Mexico City: Editorial Porrúa, 1992.

Zeitlin, Judith Francis. *Cultural Politics in Colonial Tehuantepec: Community and State among the Isthmus Zapotec, 1500–1750.* Stanford, CA: Stanford University Press, 2005.

Zoraida Vázquez, Josefina, ed. *Interpretaciones del siglo XVIII mexicano: El impacto de las reformas borbónicas.* Mexico City: Nueva Imagen, 1991.

Index

absolutism, 31, 90, 104, 149

accusations, diversionary, 2, 54, 57, 68

adultery, 42, 63–68, 110, 143, 160, 161, 171–76, 180, 202, 214–15

Afro-Yucatecans, 8, 9, 36, 43, 46, 221n4; and courts, 37–38, 42–52; intermarriage with Mayas, 125–27; and land ownership, 43; and lay religiosity, 45; in Maya pueblos, 103, 123–27; as Maya speakers, 124–25, 135; in Mérida, 178; of Belizean origin, 124, 127; and upward mobility, 178

aguardiente, 106, 120, 139, 194, 196

Alcalá, don Manuel, 105, 109, 111, 133

alcaldemascabob. See alcaldes de la cárcel

alcaldes de la cárcel, 100

alcaldes mayores, 104

alcaldes ordinarios, 52, 114

alguaciles, 101–2

almehen, 130, 178

Álvarez, don Domingo, 48–49

amancebado, 175

amo/ama, 59, 80

Ancona, Mariano, 105, 109–11, 122, 133, 143, 175, 214

Angulo, Juan Lino, 51

Antolín, don Manuel, 79, 174–75, 183; career trajectory of, 106–7; death of,

194–95; exoneration of, 201; as suspect, 186–88, 197, 199

Argais, Juan Antonio, 48–50, 214–15

Armas, fray Manuel Antonio, 186–87, 194, 198, 199, 201

artisans, 38, 41, 46–50, 90; Afro-Yucatecan, 44–46; mestizo, 55; multiethnic, 46–49

asiento, 81

Atlantic Revolutions, Age of, 81

Audiencia de Mexico, 25, 146

Ávila, don Vicente de, 116

ayuntamiento. See Cabildo of Mérida

Bacalar, 64

Baldos Murciano, don Tomás, 182, 188, 196

bandos, 35–36, 40

Barrio de Santiago, 44, 48, 59, 133

Barrio of San Cristóbal, 53–54, 133

batabs, 8, 101, 109, 130; of Mérida, 178. See also caciques

Belize, 4, 18, 82; border disputes with, 82; as place of origin for Afro-Yucatecans, 124–26; slave flights to, 127; as source of contraband, 25, 117, 120; as source of slaves, 81–83;

Bermejo, José, 39, 55, 57, 88, 168–69

Betancur, José Antonio, xi, 63, 79

posadas, 58
Poveda, don Antonio de, 26, 57, 91, 150,
173
pregonero público, 58–59
pregones, 84
principales, 9
probanza de hidalguía, 130
procurador de los indios, 51
promotor fiscal, 83
public intoxication, 50, 52, 90, 141, 143
punishment, Bourbon modes of, 1, 10
puta de noche (poison), 183

Qui, don Miguel, 113
Quijano family, 60, 90, 158, 180–82, 186–
90, 212–13; domination of the cabildo,
159–62, 196; doña Josefa, 160, 181–82,
187, 188, 192, 196–98, 201–4, 212–13;
doña Tomasa, 160, 161, 180; don Joa-
quin, 159, 162; in the early nineteenth
century, 203, 212–13; Ignacio, 24, 159–
60, 162, 197; and illegitimacy, 179; José
Miguel, 24, 116, 156, 159; José Tadeo,
24, 91, 159, 192–93, 195–97, 200, 212–13;
Juan Esteban (father), 24, 159–61; Juan
Esteban (son), 24, 159; and marriage
partners, 180, 196; and suspicions
over murder, 180, 186
Quintana, don Gregorio, 112

Ramos, Juan. *See* Tío Juan
Real Ordenanza de Intendentes, 8, 31,
104. *See also* Decree of Intendants
Rejón, Lt. don Bernardo Lino, 183, 187–
91, 192–93, 198–200, 203, 213
repartimiento, 8, 104, 106; prohibition of,
24
república de españoles, 9
república de indios, 9, 37. *See also* Maya
pueblo
reputation, 26, 41, 169–76, 200–201
Restall, Matthew, 224n34, 227n53

Rivas Betancourt, Roberto de, 27–28
Robins, Nicholas A., 226n36
Rodríguez, fray Francisco, 44
Rodríguez de Trujillo, Clemente, xi, 57,
60, 64, 83–84, 201; as murder suspect,
65
Royal Pragmatic of 1776, 181, 196
Rubio, don Eugenio, 52
Rubio, Father Jacinto, 101, 103, 108, 110–
11, 140–43
rumors as evidence, 35, 39, 41, 57, 60, 68,
146, 169

Sabido de Vargas, don José, xii, 25, 27–28,
32, 54, 95; conflict with Bodega, 95–96
Salazar, José Yanuario, 52, 183, 186–91,
192–93, 198, 200, 203; return to career,
213
Sandoval, Miguel Magdaleno, 76–77, 83,
149, 153–54, 163, 193
San José de los Negros, 73
scapegoating, 54; of urban plebe, 33
sculptors, 46
second conquest, 14, 30, 122
Serrano, Justo don, 76–77, 83, 91, 149, 167
servants, domestic, 63; Christian status
of, 70; escapes of, 72–73, 92, 126; gendered roles, 80; household tasks, 78;
as informants, 68; legal status, 73, 89;
loyalty of, 73–74; origins, 80; and
paternalism, 73, 76, 92; relocation of,
70; and reputations of owners, 72; testimonies of, 63, 67, 70
servicio personal, 14, 24, 117, 199, 232n25
shoemakers, 58
slaves, 63–67, 92; African origin, 80; and
bonds of paternalism, 74–77; Christian status of, 81; compared to *criados*, 77–80; legal status, 69–70, 90–92;
origins, 80; protection of, 38; and
racial hierarchies, 77; as refugees, 81;
sale of, 71